*Revolutions, Rebellions, and Resistance*

By Devon Bowers

Foreword by Andrew Gavin Marshall

Table of Contents

*This page left intentionally blank*

I first became acquainted with Devon Douglas-Bowers in the summer of 2011 when I was working as a research associate with the Centre for Research on Globalization (CRG) in Montreal, Canada. At the time, I was 23-years old and had been doing research and writing for the CRG's main media site, Global Research, for roughly two years. Devon was just 19 at the time and had begun submitting his own articles to Global Research when he reached out to me to conduct email interviews on subjects ranging from social engineering to NATO's war on Libya.

Being a youngster in the field myself, I was immediately impressed with the even younger Devon's depth of knowledge, his critical eye, and a desire to understand and articulate painful truths about important topics that are governing and changing the world around us. At the time, I felt I had found a comrade in quills, a fellow warrior of words with whom I have common cause in the quest for truth and justice in a world so lacking in both. In the ensuing five years I have known Devon, not only do I continue to feel that way, but I have also made a true friend.

Though we have yet to meet in person (as of this writing) – Devon resides in the United States, and I in Canada – and though we come from seemingly different worlds and backgrounds, our journeys seemed to have run at long-distance parallels. Over the years since we first corresponded, Devon and I continued to exchange emails, he continued to feature me in more interviews, and I invited him to join the External Advisory Board of the People's Book Project, an independent writing project I began several years ago, after I left the Centre for Research on Globalization.

We both continued to do our research and writing, working – as writers often do – individually and on our own. But our interests, subjects and ideas would often overlap. Our more frequent contact, and increasingly less formal exchanges, served to remind me that though such a journey is often experienced on one's own, one is still never quite alone. For when I am able to freely and easily express some of my many personality abnormalities (to which most writers can relate), and feel no judgment, no condescension or condemnation, I know I have found a friend. And these are just some of the qualities that Devon brings to his writing, that guide his research and imprint upon his understandings.

Shortly after I joined the Hampton Institute in 2013, "a working-class think tank" based in the United States, Devon joined the group as Chair of the Politics & Government Department. It was through these wider interactions with more like-minded individuals, intellectuals, activists, researchers and writers that Devon would excel in a most inspiring burst of energy and effort that would include establishing and hosting a Hampton Institute podcast show ("A Different Lens") in which he would continue to discuss important topics and interview a wide range of individuals and experts.

Over the years, Devon has been published with Global Research, Occupy, Foreign Policy Journal, 4th Media, American Herald Tribune, Global Policy Forum, Activist Post, Common Dreams, Nation of Change, the Hampton Institute, and has even had an article published in an academic journal (QED: A Journal in GLBTQ Worldmaking) in which he discussed the gay community's rejection of transgender issues, notably in the shameful reactions to the famous Wikileaks whistleblower, Chelsea Manning.

This trajectory of a young researcher and writer is what I find to most enjoyable and interesting about this anthology of Devon's work, *Revolutions, Rebellions, and Resistance*. Starting with articles he wrote in 2011, he guides us through not only a wide range of challenging and important global topics, but also through his own personal and professional evolution as a researcher and writer. Always a diligent researcher, as the years go on and the articles progress, one can read in the text the growing confidence and clarity of thought as Devon increasingly finds his own voice.

While all the material is heavily researched and cited, as the compendium continues, Devon does not shy away from including more of his own unique commentary and diverges into new and challenging topics both for him and the reader. In this anthology, he takes on the brutal realities of imperialism, the institutions and effects of the global economic order and the poverty it produces, issues of race, gender and sexuality, to movements and methods of resistance and revolution. He has extended a clear, critical, and empathic mind and voice to bring light to our deeply muddied, myopic, and often dehumanizing world order.

The themes of power and resistance run throughout the text: Who and what has the power? How is it used and abused? To what end is it exercised? How is power challenged, and by whom, for what purpose? What are the alternatives? What is being done? What can be done? These are important questions, and imperative ones in our troubling times. Devon, like everyone before and after him, does not have all the answers. But the questions pour through the pages as one follows him on his own journey of discovering the world around us.

The book begins by describing the global balance of power as one of a "master-slave relationship" that was a hallmark of the formal colonial era. He guides the reader through the constructs of the American Empire, its military and economic components, its manifestations in foreign policy in the Middle East and elsewhere, the rise of China, the Arab Spring, the role of non-governmental organizations (NGOs) as the "missionaries of empire," and the continuing conflict in Syria.

Devon also takes the reader to lesser known conflicts in Africa, such as those in Mali, the Central African Republic, and the Congo.

While these conflicts largely fail to make headlines in the Western world, he delves deep into their histories, analyzing the evolution of the "master-slave relationship" between rich and powerful Western nations and their former colonies, as well as the complex ethnic and tribal variations and conflicts.

As is so often lacking in commentaries about war and conflict, Devon does not simplify an argument or understanding to a superficial level. Instead, he extends his research capabilities to multiple spheres and like an intellectual spider web, he attempts to catch as much information as possible in order to come to a more coherent and ultimately more concise conclusion, to nourish the reader with the most important and relevant details and concepts. Accounting for complexity is sadly rare in the field, but he shows wisdom well beyond his years in his research methodology and in the way he elucidates the intricacies of the world in an intelligible and coherent way for the reader to access and digest.

Devon then guides the reader through his anthology, discussing the 'Great Recession' and the pivotal (and nefarious) role of Credit Rating Agencies. He delves into the history of convict leasing and judicially imposed racism in the United States and debt slavery. He even takes on the oldest and most secretive international economic institution in the world, the Bank for International Settlements (BIS), and provides the reader with intriguing insights into the more recent so-called "free trade agreements" that are designed to re-shape the global trading order in the 21st-century. These include the Trans Pacific Partnership (TPP), the Transatlantic Trade and Investment Partnership (TTIP), and the Trade in Services Agreement (TiSA), all of which will have profound consequences on the countries involved, and the quality of life for the people within them.

The anthology also includes 20 separate interviews that Devon has conducted with various researchers, writers, activists and others (including a couple with myself), ranging widely in topics, from anarchism and activism to journalism, the Israel-Palestine conflict, sexuality and art. Not only do these interviews serve as examples of his own breadth of knowledge and interests, but they also reflect his consistent objective to give a platform to others, in which they are able to express themselves freely and honestly.

Perhaps most interesting, and certainly most hopeful, is Devon's work on social and resistance movements to the world's many power structures, institutions and ideologies of repression and segregation. Here, he guides the reader through anarchist theory, the role of independent journalism and media, Occupy Wall Street, the Arab Spring, Indigenous resistance, the 'Cowboy-Indian Alliance' that developed in response to the Keystone XL pipeline project, black-Palestinian solidarity, and the Black Lives Matter movement which sprung out of such events as the revolts in Ferguson.

Though the global political and economic system is designed to benefit those who built it, and those who run it, there have always been and continues to be continuing and emergent forms and movements of resistance out of which springs new hope for a different kind of world. In the article entitled Why We Must Fight, Devon reminds the reader that in spite of the seemingly never-ending list of problems and challenges facing humanity and the growing power of state and corporate institutions, the bubbling bursts of resistance around the world are evidence that change is, in fact, possible and necessary. People are realizing their own power, which "is – and always has been – inside of them." If the world is to change for the better, he suggests, "we must fight and not just for our own sake, but for the sake of those who have yet to be born."

In a time when powerful institutions like the World Economic Forum, the International Monetary Fund, and major global banks and corporations refer to the educated, over-indebted and underemployed youth of the world as "the lost generation," Devon Douglas-Bowers is establishing himself as a voice of and for that generation; to help the lost find their way and change the world for the better. This anthology speaks to that truth, and the truths he seeks throughout.

# Foreign Policy

The power balance in the world is still clearly the master-slave relationship that was seen in the heyday of colonialism in the 19th century.

The US-NATO-Israel triangle is attempting to gain large amounts of influence over the nations of the Middle East. Simultaneously, the US is engaged in the Asia Pacific region, along with its South Korean ally, in attempting to coerce North Korea into ending its nuclear weapons program and to maintain the ceasefire with South Korea.

In terms of China, the US is attempting to surround them with an Asian version of NATO made up of US allies to contain what is viewed as a threat to US hegemony.

In the past, the imperial powers were those of Europe and many of them advocated direct imperialism, sending in soldiers and administrators to directly run and colonize a country. Other nations have used an indirect form of colonialism by controlling a country through groups or individuals that would obey the colonial power. National independence movements took place in Africa, Latin America and Asia in the 1950s and 60s, and it seemed like colonial domination was over, yet it wasn't. Even today, imperialism still rears its ugly head; however, unlike in previous times, people are actually able to resist the imperial power that is the United States and its allies.

Firstly, we must establish a definition of what imperialism is. According to the Merriam- Webster dictionary, imperialism is defined as, "The policy, practice, or advocacy of extending the power and dominion of a nation especially by direct territorial acquisitions or by gaining indirect control over the political or economic life of other areas." [1]

The main goal of imperialism today is to ensure that the former imperial states still maintain economic dominance over their former colonies. This is accomplished in the form of neo-colonialism. When neo-colonialism first took hold, political scientists were unable to formulate a concise definition. After independence, many assumed that the newly liberated nations would begin to "to develop very rapidly, politically and economically." [2] However, when that did not come to fruition, political scientists looked again at the dependency theory and added a second part. This new addition acknowledged that underdevelopment in the newly liberated countries continued due to highly developed countries dominating underdeveloped economies "by paying low prices for agricultural products and flooding those economies with cheap manufactured goods." [3] Because of this, the post-colonial countries would be unable to industrialize their economies, and thus would remain at the mercy of their former colonizers.

Also, the colonial powers used debt to keep their former colonies in check. One example is odious debt, which is defined as "unjust debt that is incurred as rich countries loaned dictators or other corrupt leaders when it was known that the money would be wasted." [4] In loaning out this money, it served the colonial powers in two ways. One, they could use the debt to keep the nation(s) under their control, and two; they made money off the high interest rates.

When it comes to loaning money there has been complete hypocrisy between developed and developing nations. One example is after WWII, when the US loaned the U.K. at low interest rates, and the Allies cancelled most of Germany's debt. In both cases, it was intended to enable the developed nations to rebuild in the wake of World War II. Yet, when in it comes to third-world nations, double standards prevail. Many sub-Saharan African countries are being forced to pay back debt at rates "three to five times the level that Britain or Germany paid after World War II." [5]

In addition to insuring dependency of the former colonized nations on their old masters, the colonial powers also encouraged their companies to move in and take full control of the economy of developing countries. This was presented to the public as "economic liberalization." In this process, the International Monetary Fund (IMF) was the tool used.

One tragic case of IMF intervention is Jamaica. After the island nation's economy crashed in the early 1970s, the Prime Minister of Jamaica, Michael Manley, giving into pressure from the IMF and the conservative People's National Party, came up with an initiative that "included many elements of democratic socialism as it called for disengagement from international capitalism, socializing the means of production and exchange, increasing Jamaica's self-reliance, and diversification of foreign economic relations." [6] The conservative People's National Party was not pleased with this idea of "democratic socialism," and thus went to the IMF for aid. This was disastrous for Jamaica. They were lent the money in 1977, but had to agree to "pension and wage [cuts and] the removal of price controls" [7] and by 1980, "the economy in Jamaica was in worse condition than before the IMF loan. Thirty percent of the island's workforce was unemployed and the foreign exchange deficit was significantly higher than in 1977." [8] The freeze on pensions and wages were beneficial to the foreign corporations, who later moved in as they were now able to fully exploit the Jamaican people without having to worry about any minimum wage or labor laws.

We can see that the IMF being used by the European Central Bank to protect the interests of the economic elite in the situation of Ireland's debt crisis. This is also evident in Greece, where the banks are being bailed out at the expense of the working class, sending them into of crushing austerity measures. However, the populations of Ireland and Greece, realizing what is at stake, are determined to resist. They will not take this oppression lying down.

Instead, they actively protest the acts of their government and demand that they not be held responsible for the incompetence of the powerful economic elite.

Even though the United States and its allies constitute a power force, a resistance movement is in the making. In the future, we may see developing nations wielding influence over their own domestic affairs; and neo-colonialism, much like the direct colonialism that preceded it, could become a thing of the past.

**Endnotes**

1: Merriam-Webster Dictionary, Imperialism, http://www.merriam-webster.com/dictionary/imperialism

2: Science Encyclopedia, *Neocolonialism-Bibliography*, http://science.jrank.org/pages/7920/Neocolonialism.html

3: Ibid

4: Anup Shah, Third World Debt Undermines Development, Global Issues, http://www.globalissues.org/issue/28/third-world-debt-undermines-development (June 3, 2007)

5: Ibid

6: http://science.jrank.org/pages/7920/Neocolonialism.html

7: Ibid

8: Ibid

**Introduction**

The American Empire came into full being after its main rival, the Soviet Union, collapsed. The US then found itself as the world's sole military and economic superpower. With this new found position in the world, America could have used its power to help those in need and aid in global security. However, the events of 9/11 changed all of this and the US went from a once proud, powerful, law-abiding nation, to what it is today: a declining empire that is virtually bankrupt and has moved from using diplomacy to a "might makes right" mindset (as can be shown from its current engagement in multiple wars across the world in order to maintain its global empire), as well as trying to make sure that new powers, such as China, do not threaten its dominance.

This series is an examination of how this downfall took place, how the US strayed from its original military, economic, and foreign policy plans to become an empire in decline, from the 1990s to the present day, ending with an analysis what may lay in the future for the Empire.

**Military**

During the Cold War, the US had had troops stationed all over the world, from Europe to Asia. Its military doctrine consisted of a policy of containing the Soviets and battling the 'Communist threat' where ever it was. Battling the 'Communist threat' meant (either directly or indirectly) overthrowing leftist governments in Latin America, Asia, and Europe or supporting right-wing death squads, as was seen in Latin America (some of these coups led to the massacre of innocent civilians). Despite this, it seemed that after the Soviet Union fell, the US was going to change its military doctrine.

Even though the US was now the world's unrivaled superpower, it still planned to "devote the necessary resources to military, diplomatic, intelligence and other efforts" [1] to maintain its global leadership position and also wanted to "shape the international environment through a variety of means, including diplomacy, economic cooperation, international assistance, arms control and nonproliferation, and health initiatives" [2] to establish and keep the new status quo.

In shaping this new world, American planned for diplomacy to play a major role. The thinking was that diplomacy was "essential" to ensuring that US interests were met, sustaining alliances, averting global crises/solving regional conflicts, and ensuring global economic stability. "Preventive" diplomacy would play a major role in helping to solve potential conflicts before they blew up. The military would only be put into play as a last resort. Military force would only be used if it would "advance U.S. interests," was "likely to accomplish [its] objectives," "the costs and risks of their employment [were] commensurate with the interests at stake," and "other non-military means [were] incapable of achieving [US] objectives." [3]

Thus, with the collapse of the Soviets, the US plan was to shape a new world order in which they would lead, yet diplomacy would take the lead in shaping this new order instead of military might. The reason for this was two-fold. The US had already spent $13 trillion on defense spending during the entirety of the Cold War [4] and using diplomacy on a regional and international level would allow it to cut back on defense expenditures. Also by using diplomacy, it would give nations the illusion that they were on equal footing with the US, when in reality, if the diplomacy failed, the US may decide that the conditions had been met for them to use military force in order to "advance U.S. interests." It was, in a way, following Theodore Roosevelt's advice of speaking softly, but carrying a big stick.

America was also changing its nuclear defense policy. America had "reduced [its] nuclear stockpile, through both the START [Strategic Arms Reduction Treaty] I cuts and reciprocal unilateral initiatives" [5] as well as did the following under the 1991 Presidential Nuclear Initiative:

• [Eliminated its] entire inventory of ground-launched non-strategic nuclear weapons (nuclear artillery and LANCE surface-to-surface missiles);

• [Removed] all non-strategic nuclear weapons on a day-to-day basis from surface ships, attack submarines, and land-based naval aircraft bases;

• [Removed its]strategic bombers from alert;

• [Stood] down the Minuteman II ICBMs scheduled for deactivation under START I;

• [Terminated] the mobile Peacekeeper and mobile Small ICBM programs; and

• [Terminated] the SRAM-II nuclear short-range attack missile. [6]

In addition to this, the US took further steps in 1992. Due to the second Presidential Nuclear Initiative, the US was "limiting B-2 production to 20 bombers; canceling the entire Small ICBM program; ceasing production of W-88 Trident SLBM warheads; halting purchases of advanced cruise missiles; and stopping new production of Peacekeeper missiles." [7] Due to decreasing the number of nuclear weapons and nuclear weapon transporters, the US government saved a large amount of money and still ensured that it would have nuclear first-strike capability for quite some time.

Overall, the United States was lowering its guard not only due to the collapse of its main rival, but also due to financial concerns and its plans to reshape the world.

**Economics**

Near the turn of the century, new economic thought was being brought up, namely globalization. Globalization was only but another step in the transformation of capitalism that would allow corporations to move capital and people on a global scale and therefore cut costs and increase profits. By pushing this new economic thought, governments were able to push the thinking that a more inter-connected society was good not only for corporations, but for people as well, while ignoring the problems globalization would bring.

Globalization is defined as "the process of moving toward a world in which we produce, distribute, sell, finance, and invest without regard to national boundaries." [8] By disregarding national boundaries, it would allow for corporations to "also gain access to new sources of raw materials and intermediate inputs, and to lower-cost locations for assembly operations that use unskilled labor." [9] This would allow for US companies to move in and have their way in the third-world without the CIA or the US military having to engage in regime change (either covertly or overtly). US corporations would also have more stability as a corporation that "operates in many countries will find that recessions and booms in the many markets in which it operates are likely to be out of sync," [10] thus they will be able to move people and capital to the locations which are doing well.

However, while this shifting of people and capital across the world would create benefits for corporations, it would bring about problems for workers. "As with the relocation of manufacturing in the U.S., globalization generates some of its gains by allowing — or sometimes forcing — relocation of production. Not everyone benefits. Just as relocation of manufacturing from Pennsylvania to South Carolina generates losers as well as winners, so does globalization." [11]

Even when globalization was first being discussed, it was acknowledged that it "contributed to the decline in real wages of those with few skills and little education." [12] What this meant for the US was that it would experience the death of the working class as jobs would be shipped overseas. When this subject was bought up, proponents of globalization would argue that "In the process of shifting resources, **some production facilities are abandoned and some workers suffer unemployment. They do not share the gains, at least not immediately**." [13] (emphasis added). As we now know, those who are unemployed due to offshoring/outsourcing rarely, if ever, "share in the gains" of globalization. It was not meant to benefit the working class, but rather corporate greed.

Another factor that was ignored by proponents of globalization is that foreign economic shocks have more of an effect on the US economy. As Edward G. Boehne, President of the Federal Reserve Bank of Philadelphia, said to the World Affairs Council of Greater Valley Forge:

The US economy and the global economy at large, would be put more at risk due to there being greater interconnectedness. However, despite these risks, globalization was endorsed by the US and the effects have been seen in the form of the decimation of the American economy and also the global economy at large was put more at risk, all for the sake of corporate profits. [14]

## NATO Alliance

After the Cold War, it seemed that the NATO alliance had lost its reason for existing. Western Europe was no longer under the threat of Communist takeover, thus NATO's mission had been a success. However, NATO, instead of disbanding or keeping a stable membership, decided to go on an era of expansion which continues to this day.

After the Soviet Union collapsed, there was some debate for a short while as to what NATO would do, now that it no longer had an enemy, yet in 1990 NATO "began its adaptation from a Cold War institution to a modern instrument of North Atlantic and European security, revising strategy and restructuring force posture to reflect the changed European security environment and the disappearance of the Soviet threat." [15] This force restructure consisted of maintaining "an adequate military capability and clear preparedness to act collectively in the common defense remain central to the Alliance's security objectives." [16]

NATO also integrated even deeper into Europe. The alliance's 1999 Strategic Concept stated:

The European Allies have taken decisions to enable them to assume greater responsibilities in the security and defense field in order to enhance the peace and stability of the Euro-Atlantic area and thus the security of all Allies. On the basis of decisions taken by the Alliance, in Berlin in 1996 and subsequently, the European Security and Defense Identity will continue to be developed within NATO. This process will require close cooperation between NATO, the WEU and, if and when appropriate, the European Union. [17]

This further integration with Europe would greatly serve US interests in the future as it would aid the US in dominating all of Europe and the Mediterranean (currently a nation that wants to join the EU, must first join NATO). [18] Also, by having the European Security and Defense Identity continue its development within NATO; it would allow the US to make sure that European defense arrangements were subordinate to US interests.

When NATO expansion was bought up, there was a battle between the White House and the Pentagon as then-President Bill Clinton was interested in expanding NATO yet the Pentagon was against it, and with good reason as there were several problems with NATO expansion. Clinton was quite interested in NATO serving US interests. In a letter to Senator Kay Bailey Hutchinson, he stated that "Europe has changed dramatically over the past decade and NATO must also adapt if it is to continue to serve our interests in the future as well as it has done in the past." [19] In an question and answer session with the Senate, Bill Clinton argued for NATO expansion by making Russia into a bogeyman, saying that expansion would "make NATO more effective in meeting its core mission: countering aggression against its member states," "help guard against non-traditional security threats from outside Europe that threaten NATO members, such as the spread of weapons of mass destruction and long-range delivery systems," and that NATO "must be prepared for other contingencies, including the possibility that Russia could abandon democracy and return to the threatening behavior of the Soviet period." [20] Many of the arguments were aimed at Russia, to keep alive the idea of Russian aggression. However, Russia being a threat was near impossible as they were going through was going through the IMF's "shock therapy" and the entire nation was hurting.

By pushing for the expansion of NATO, the Clinton Administration was also pushing for US-NATO involvement in the religious, ethnic, and other conflicts of central Europe. When questioned on this, President Clinton responded that NATO "will make such disputes less likely and increase the chances that they will be peacefully resolved" [21] as states would have to resolve their disputes before they could join the alliance and that "There is nothing in the historical record to suggest that current Central and East European disputes are more deep-rooted or violent than, say, past disputes between France and Germany." [22] However, there was a major difference as the conflicts in central Europe were based on "border, ethnic, nationalist, and religious disputes," where the populace of states were fractured and stayed within their own groups. The disputes between France and Germany, on the other hand, were between two states whose people were homogeneous in the sense that they all saw themselves as being French or German.

There were also economic concerns that were bought up. The Administration reported to Congress in February 1997, that the "United States would pay only 15 percent of the direct enlargement costs, with the new members paying 35 percent of the bill, and the current (non- U.S.) members paying 50 percent." [23] When the Senate asked if new or current members would pay that amount and would this cost-sharing plan be part of negotiations, Clinton responded that each country would pay the upkeep of its own military, yet enhancements would be 40% nationally-funded and 60% NATO-funded (or "common-funded"). Of the NATO-funded costs "the United States would pay its 24 percent share of the common-funded enhancements (about 15 percent of the total direct enlargement bill, or approximately $1.5-2.0 billion over the 2000-2009 timeframe), averaging between $150 and $200 million per year." [24] However, these costs estimates were not accurate, as they varied quite widely. A 1996 RAND Corporation study predicted costs of $17-$82 billion, the US Congressional Budget Office predicted $21 to $125 billion, and the British Defense Ministry predicted $18-20 billion. With costs fluctuating all over the place, there was no way to get an accurate cost assessment for expansion.

The Senate also bought up the question of economic competition, stating that "By conferring NATO membership on a few nations now, those nations will have a distinct advantage over their neighbors in the competition to attract new business and foreign investment. This type of economic competition and imbalance could well breed friction and instability in Central Europe." [25] In his response, Clinton said:

While the role of the EU is critical, there is no reason to insist on a choice between EU enlargement and NATO enlargement. Both are important. Both make independent contributions to European prosperity and security. EU enlargement alone, however, is not sufficient to secure our nation's security interests in post-Cold War Europe. Unlike NATO, the EU lacks a military capability. Military capability remains the heart of NATO's strength and continues to be needed to preserve European security. [26]

The fact that Clinton said that EU enlargement alone was "not sufficient" to ensure America's security interests in Europe suggests that he may have thought that the EU and NATO were two sides of the same coin. The EU would provide the economic stability while NATO would provide the military protection.

A final problem with expansion of NATO is that many European countries did not want it, regarding it as a US initiative. They had "stated privately for months that they are not going to raise taxes or cut social programs to pay for Washington's pet scheme. (Indeed, one leader, French president Jacques Chirac, stated publicly that France would not pay a single franc for NATO expansion.)" [27]

Besides the aforementioned problems, the Pentagon did not back the expansion as they no longer wanted to be a part of a larger, more costly NATO. They preferred to go the route of the "Partnership for Peace, which allowed East European nations to join in NATO military exercises but not be full members." [28] However, the White House kept pressing the issue and in 1994 senior Defense officials ended up having a shouting match with Assistant Secretary of State Richard Holbrooke. Holbrooke was stated to have yelled "The President has made the decision, and you're being insubordinate!" [29]

Eventually the Pentagon fell in line.

**Middle East Foreign Policy**

     With the collapse of the Soviet Union, the United States found itself the region's most powerful and influential outside player. America's main goal was to keep the oil flowing by any means as could be seen by the establishment of the Carter Doctrine which stated the US intended to keep Mideast oil flowing, even if it meant military intervention and created Central Command, which covered the entire Middle East.

     Due to the Middle East being of vital importance to the US, America sought to contain certain "governments or political forces that use violence as a matter of policy to advance a hostile agenda" and to "expand the depth and breadth of [US] partnerships with friendly governments in the region to promote peace, stability, and prosperity." [30] In addition to this, the Americans also "sought to encourage states in the region that have developed the bad habit of acting outside of international norms to change [their] ways that would permit reintegration into the international community." [31] This diplomatic language disguises the true nature of US Middle East policy. What the US means to do is to make sure that pro-US regimes are propped up and to isolate any and every nation that threatens US interests.

     The US had major plans for Iraq and Iran. Since US policy had failed in that the Iranian revolution took place and the US went to war with Iraq in 1991, the US decided to contain both nations since they "judged that both regional powers, while war–weary and economically weakened, were still militarily ambitious and clearly hostile to the United States and our interests in the region." [32] The US wanted to keep tabs on Saddam Hussein and make sure that Iran wasn't acquiring or developing WMDs. With regards to Iran, however, just as today, the American government had no proof whatsoever that Iran was trying to acquire such weapons.

     While the US aimed to contain both Iraq and Iran, there were different strategies for both nations. With Iraq, the US decided that Iraq could no longer "be rehabilitated or reintegrated into the community of nations" and would "work with forces inside and outside Iraq, as well as Iraq's neighbors, to change the regime in Iraq and help its new government rejoin the community of nations." [33] This last part may hints at US interest in regime change. The US kept UN sanctions on Iraq as to permanently damage its military and economically decimate the country. It should also be noted when it came to regime change, the US was willing to support anyone as long as they were anti-Saddam, as well as wanted to destabilize Iraq. The US saw the support of Iraqi exiles as "indispensable" and argued that the "internal Iraqi resistance [needed] a voice, through the Iraqi Opposition living in freedom, to make clear to all Iraqis and to the world its aims." [34]

     The US also gave $8 million in Economic Support Funds to Iraq and used the funds to "strengthen the political unity of the opposition, to support the Iraq war crimes initiative, to support humanitarian programs and the development of civil society, and for activities inside Iraq." [35] By supporting internal dissidents, the US made sure that if there was an overthrow (successful or not) of the Saddam regime, that it would seem as if the entire struggle was internal and that it represented the will of the Iraqi people, when in reality, the overthrow would have been backed (and probably planned and financed) by the US and the new Iraqi regime would be nothing but a puppet government that followed its orders from Washington.

     In regards to Iran, the US strategy was much different. Besides sanctions, there was a large amount of economic warfare against Iran. The US opposed "bilateral debt rescheduling, Paris Club debt treatment for Iran, and the extension of favorable credit terms by Iran's principal foreign creditors" [36] as well as international monetary agencies such as the IMF and the World Bank loaning Iran money. Also the US government continued to argue that Iran was trying to create WMDs. "Clandestine efforts to procure nuclear, chemical, and biological weapons continue despite Iran's adherence to relevant international nonproliferation conventions." [37] In terms of nuclear weapons, the US had no proof that Iran was trying to develop them.

The issue of energy security was also bought up in the formulation of US Middle East policy. The US saw the Middle East as its new main source of energy since "at the end of 1997, U.S. crude reserves had declined to 29.8 billion barrels" and since the 1970s, the US had "become even more dependent on [oil] imports and thus theoretically [was] more vulnerable to crude oil supply distributions" [38] than ever before. Seeing the Middle East as unstable, America wanted to have most of its crude come from Western sources, however, there were still shortfalls even when the Strategic Petroleum Reserve was factored in. This, coupled with the fact that it was predicted by 2015 that US oil production would have declined to 5-7 million barrels daily and that "baring development of huge new reserves in the western hemisphere, the US [would] become increasingly dependent on the more unstable sources of crude oil, such as from the Middle East," [39] it was in US interests to make sure that the regimes of Arab nations with large amounts of oil were under the control of Washington and that the status quo of American regional dominance was maintained in order to keep the oil flowing.

**The Chinese Threat**

In its plan to create a new global status quo where the US was in charge, the US government had to make sure that there would be no current threats to its dominance in the future. While it may seem that today the US is viewing China as a major threat, this manner of thinking goes back to the 1990s.

In terms of defense issues, the US thought China's "defense modernization programs and foreign policy objectives could realistically pose a challenge to US interests and security," [40] specifically noting China's "nuclear weapons modernization program and her related arms control policies could pose some possibly severe implications to world peace" and "China's sale of nuclear technology." [41] By acquiring modern weaponry China was ensuring that it would be better able to protect its nation, but from the American perspective it was a threat because it threatened US military technological dominance. By selling nuclear technology, China was threatening US nuclear dominance as more countries would potentially be able to acquire nuclear weapons and therefore were less likely to be intimidated by America and less likely to concede to US demands. In order to combat China's nuclear program, the US planned to "make a concerted effort to involve China in any future talks concerning nuclear proliferation," [42] however, these talks would involve China decreasing its amount of nuclear weapons while America's nuclear weapons stockpile went untouched.

Economically, the US wanted to have a "stable and prosperous China," but for its own reasons. Bill Clinton stated

> A stable, open, prosperous, and strong China is important to the US and to our friends and allies in the region. A stable and open China is more likely to work cooperatively with others and to contribute positively to peace in the region and to respect the rights and interests of its people. **A prosperous China will provide an expanding market for American goods and services. We have a profound stake in helping to ensure that China pursues its modernization in ways that contribute to the overall security and prosperity of the Asia Pacific region.** (emphasis added) [43]

While it may seem by Clinton's statement that he wants to best for China, what he is actually doing is passively attacking the Chinese government and promoting US corporate interests. By saying that "A stable and open China is more likely to work cooperatively with others and to contribute positively to peace in the region and to respect the rights and interests of its people," Clinton is implying that certain actions of China (such as modernizing its military and encouraging economic growth) weren't in the interests of its people. How is modernizing one's military and nuclear program not in the interests of the Chinese people? Also, by saying that "A prosperous China will provide an expanding market for American goods and services," Clinton is backing economic globalization.

In order to get China to bend to its will, America planned on using "the positive applications of the instruments of power (political/diplomatic, economic, information, and military) rather than their coercive use." [44] By using diplomacy, the US would give China the illusion that both nations were on par with one another, when in reality they weren't.

Another reason engagement was chosen was due to speculation that the containment of China would not work as "it would be hard to obtain a domestic consensus to subordinate other policy goals (including trade and investment) to dealing with a Chinese threat that is as yet, to say the least, far from manifest" [45] and that containment "would require, to be effective, the whole-hearted cooperation of regional allies and most of the other advanced industrial countries of the world." [46]

There was also speculation as to China's defense situation by 2015. It was predicted that by 2015, China could emerge "as a formidable power, one that might be labeled a *multidimensional regional competitor.*" (emphasis is the author's) [47] It was speculated that as such, China could potentially "exercise sea denial with respect to the seas contiguous to China," "contest aerospace superiority in a sustained way in areas contiguous to China's borders," "threaten US operating locations in East Asia with a variety of long-range nuclear assets," challenge US information dominance," and "pose a strategic nuclear threat to the United States." [48] In order to make sure that these predictions did not come true, as well as get markets for US corporations and attempt to curb China's rise, the US may have decided to engage China.

**Rise of the Neoconservatives**

The group that played a major role in American defense and foreign policy in the 21st century was the neoconservatives. They were a new breed of conservatives that favored laissez faire economics and a strong, robust military. Several neoconservatives came together to form the Project for the New American Century (PNAC). This think tank was to become extremely influential in the Bush Administration.

PNAC and other neoconservatives shared a disdain for and criticized average Republicans, saying:

Conservatives have criticized the incoherent policies of the Clinton Administration. They have also resisted isolationist impulses from within their own ranks. But conservatives have not confidently advanced a strategic vision of America's role in the world. They have not set forth guiding principles for American foreign policy. They have allowed differences over tactics to obscure potential agreement on strategic objectives. And they have not fought for a defense budget that would maintain American security and advance American interests in the new century. [49]

It initially seemed that this new group was not that dangerous as the goal of neoconservatives was to promote and sustain American global leadership. They wanted "a military that is strong and ready to meet both present and future challenges; a foreign policy that boldly and purposefully promotes American principles abroad; and national leadership that accepts the United States' global responsibilities." [50] They were extremely dedicated to the idea of America leading the world and were near-fanatical in pushing for the US to have global dominance, saying that America "cannot safely avoid the responsibilities of global leadership or the costs that are associated with its exercise" and that "America has a vital role in maintaining peace and security in Europe, Asia, and the Middle East." [51] This was not the language of people who want to just stick to the plans that were already outlined, it sounded more like the language of people who want to take the already laid-out plans to their extremes and in many cases change them entirely.

In PNAC's document Rebuilding America's Defenses: Strategy, Forces and Resources for a New Century, PNAC outlines its main goal which is to see the entire world dominated by American global military might. The document outline four main goals for the US military which were to "defend the American homeland; fight and decisively win multiple, simultaneous major theater wars; perform the 'constabulary' duties associated with shaping the security environment in critical regions; [and to] transform U.S. forces to exploit the 'revolution in military affairs.'" [52] It can be seen here that PNAC was already planning for there to be a major shift in America's foreign affairs and that they had a war-mongering agenda.

This militaristic agenda was going to be felt throughout the world. Besides the fact that they wanted the US military to "fight and decisively win multiple, simultaneous major theater wars," PNAC also pushed for having America's nuclear deterrent based "upon a global, nuclear net assessment that weighs the full range of current and emerging threats, not merely the U.S.- Russia balance" and for the US to "develop and deploy global missile defenses to defend the American homeland and American allies, and to provide a secure basis for U.S. power projection around the world." [53] The phrase "current and emerging threats" in reality means any nation that is currently or in the future will threaten US global dominance, such as China and Russia. This notion is further proven by the fact that PNAC wanted the US to reposition US "permanently-based forces to Southeast Europe and Southeast Asia" and to change "naval deployment patterns to reflect growing U.S. strategic concerns in East Asia." [54] Doing this would ensure that America would always be able to keep an eye on its rivals and quickly counter any military moves that they made.

In addition to wanting to assure American dominance on Earth, PNAC also wanted to move the American military into space. The group advocated for American "control [of] the new 'international commons' of space and 'cyberspace'" and for America to "pave the way for the creation of a new military service – U.S. Space Forces – with the mission of space control." [55] In advocating for US control of space, PNAC was also arguing for the destruction of the long- term tradition that space was meant to be used for peaceful purposes, as can be shown in the Resolution Preventing Arms Race in Outer Space which was passed by the UN General Assembly in 2007 which itself reaffirmed the 1967 Outer Space Treaty, which stated that space should remain demilitarized.

It was this group of militaristic, war-mongering Americans that would lead America to try and dominant the world in the 21st century by taking the original plans and twisting them to facilitate a foreign policy based on a "might makes right" mentality, which would lead America to becomes the world's first truly global empire.


## Endnotes

1: Federation of American Scientists, A National Security Strategy for a New Century, http://fas.org/man/docs/nssr-1299.pdf (December 1999)

2: Ibid

3: Ibid

4: Center for Defense Information, US Military Spending, 1945-1996, https://web.archive.org/web/19961031144620/http://www.cdi.org/issues/milspend.html

5: US Congress, House, Senate Armed Services Committee, Strategic Forces Subcommittee, Statement of the Honorable Edward L. Warner, III, Assistant Secretary of Defense, https://web.archive.org/web/20120910183612/http://www.armed-services.senate.gov/statemnt/980331ew.htm (March 31, 1998)

6: Ibid

7: Ibid

8: Edward G. Boehne, *Globalization and Its Effects on the US Economy*, Federal Reserve Bank of Philadelphia, https://www.philadelphiafed.org/publications/speeches/boehne/1998/03-20- 98_world-affairs-council (March 20, 1998)

9-14: Ibid

15: Federation of American Scientists, *Fact Sheet- NATO Adaptation/Enlargement*, http://www.fas.org/man/nato/offdocs/us_97/dos970212.htm (February 12, 1997)

16: North Atlantic Treaty Organization, *The Alliance's Strategic Concept*, http://www.nato.int/cps/en/natolive/official_texts_27433.htm (April 24, 1999)

17: Ibid

18: Rick Rozoff, "US To Dominate All Europe, Mediterranean Through NATO," *Global Research*, March 5, 2011 (http://www.globalresearch.ca/index.php?context=va&aid=23525)

19: Berlin Information Center For Trans-Atlantic Security, *President Clinton's Response To Senators' Questions On NATO Enlargement*, http://www.bits.de/NRANEU/docs/ClintonNATOEnlargement.htm (September 12, 1997)

20-26: Ibid

27: Ted Galen Carpenter, *NATO Expansion As Empty Symbolism*, CATO Institute, http://www.cato.org/pub_display.php?pub_id=6034 (December 5, 1997)

28: Douglas Waller, "How Clinton Decided On NATO Expansion," *Time*, July 14, 1997 (http://content.time.com/time/magazine/article/0,9171,986677,00.html)

29: Ibid

30: Martin S. Indyk, *United States Policy Toward The Middle East*, Defense Institute of Security Assistance Management, http://www.disam.dsca.mil/pubs/v.21_4/Indyk_ME_Policy.pdf (1999)

31-37: Ibid

38: Perry Management, *Energy Security Challenges-National Security*, http://perrymanagement.com/energy-policy/energy-security-challenges-national-security/ (November 15, 1998)

39: Ibid

40: Major Brian A. Simpson, *China's Future Intent: Responsible World Power or International Rogue State*, Federation of American Scientists, http://www.fas.org/nuke/guide/china/doctrine/97-0198.pdf (March 1997)

41-44: Ibid

45: Daniel L.Byman, Zalmay M. Khalilzad, David T. Orletsky, David Shalpak, Abram M. Shulsky, Ashley J. Tellis, *The United States and a Rising China: Strategic and Military Implications*, RAND Corporation, http://www.rand.org/content/dam/rand/pubs/monograph_reports/2007/MR1082.pdf (1999)

46-50: Ibid

51: Project for the New American Century, *Statement of Principles*, https://web.archive.org/web/20020407145529/http://www.newamericancentury.org/statementofp rinciples.htm (June 3, 1997)

52: Ibid

53: Ibid

54: Project for a New American Century, *Rebuilding America's Defenses: Strategy, Forces, and Resources For A New Century*, https://web.archive.org/web/20130817122719/http://www.newamericancentury.org/RebuildingA mericasDefenses.pdf (September 2000)

55: Ibid

The official narrative is that 9/11 was planned by Al Qaeda leader and mastermind Osama bin Laden. However, what the government will not mention is its ties to Bin Laden, starting out in the 1980s, during the Soviet invasion of Afghanistan.

In 1979, bin Laden left Saudi Arabia in order to join Afghan mujaheddin fighters in fighting the Soviet Union. By 1984, he "was running a front organization known as Maktab al- Khidamar – the MAK – which funneled money, arms and fighters from the outside world into the Afghan war." [1] The MAK had ties to the CIA as it was run by the Pakistani Inter-Services Intelligence agency, which the CIA used to arm the Islamic fighters.

After the Soviets left Afghanistan, bin Laden returned to Saudi Arabia and started up Al Qaeda, including some of the more extremist members of the MAK. [2] Due to US training, Al Qaeda and other Islamic extremist groups that sprang up after the Soviets left Afghanistan had "the arms, money – and most importantly – the knowledge of how to run a war of attrition violent and well-organized enough to humble a superpower." [3] On September 11, 2001, this decision to back known Islamic extremists simply came home to roost for the US government.

**Aftermath of 9/11**

Soon after 9/11, President Bush in an address to Congress and the nation in which he declared the War on Terror, saying that America would "direct every resource at our command — every means of diplomacy, every tool of intelligence, every instrument of law enforcement, every financial influence, and every necessary weapon of war — to the destruction and to the defeat of the global terror network." [4]

He made it clear to the American people and the world that the War on Terror was going to be quite long, saying "Our war on terror begins with al Qaeda, but it does not end there. It will not end until every terrorist group of global reach has been found, stopped and defeated" and that "Americans should not expect one battle, but a lengthy campaign unlike any other we have ever seen." [5] He also made an appeal to the world for aid to fight terrorism, saying that the War on Terror is not "just America's fight" that it was "civilization's fight" and "the fight of all who believe in progress and pluralism, tolerance and freedom." [6]

This was an attempt to make the War on Terror seem as if it were truly a just cause, however invading Afghanistan was in the plans of the Project for the New American Century; the same day that President Bush gave that speech (September 20, 2001), PNAC sent a letter to him with recommendations as to what the first opening moves of the War on Terror should be. In regards to Osama bin Laden, PNAC said that the US should **support the necessary military action in Afghanistan** and the provision of substantial financial and military assistance to the anti-Taliban forces in that country." (emphasis added) [7]

In providing "substantial financial and military assistance" to anti-Taliban forces in Afghanistan, it was meant that the US would back the Northern Alliance, which was a mixture of Uzbeks, Tajiks, Hazaras, and Pashtuns, among others, who were anti-Taliban. While the US media made it seem that the Northern Alliance were the 'good guys,' in reality, they were just as bad as the Taliban. One of the alliance members, General Rashid Dostum, was accused of having massacred between 250 and 3,000 (the number depends on one's source) Taliban members in the Dasht-i-Leili desert. In addition to this, there were large amounts of in fighting with in the Northern Alliance, as the Afghan tribes settled disputes between one another.

The letter also mentions Iraq, saying that Iraq may have "provided assistance in some form to the recent attack on the United States." However, the letter goes further, arguing for an invasion of Iraq.

**But even if evidence does not link Iraq directly to the attack, any strategy aiming at the eradication of terrorism and its sponsors must include a determined effort to remove Saddam Hussein from power in Iraq.** Failure to undertake such an effort will constitute an early and perhaps decisive surrender in the war on international terrorism. **The United States must therefore provide full military and financial support to the Iraqi opposition. American military force should be used to provide a "safe zone" in Iraq from which the opposition can operate.** And American forces must be prepared to back up our commitment to the Iraqi opposition by all necessary means. (emphasis added) [8]

This was, without a doubt, a clear admission that the neoconservatives wanted to invade Iraq by any means necessary; PNAC was blatantly encouraging the President to engage in destabilizing the Iraqi government and then sending in US troops to overthrow Saddam.

Unfortunately due to the neoconservative elements in the Bush Administration these plans would come to fruition.

### 9/11 Commission Report

In 2004, the US government released the 9/11 Commission Report, which told how 9/11 had been perpetrated. The report bought up evidence that the US government may have known that 9/11 was going to occur beforehand.

According to the report, in early 2001 counter-terrorism officials began "receiving frequent but fragmented reports" concerning "possible threats almost everywhere the United States had interests-including at home." [9] During the entire year of 2001, CIA Director George Tenet "was briefed regularly regarding threats and other operational information regarding Osama bin Laden" [10] and this information was passed, via Tenet himself, to President Bush on a daily basis. Thus, President Bush had to have some information that terrorists were planning to attack the US, especially in the spring of 2001 when "the level of reporting on terrorist threats and planned attacks increased dramatically to its highest level." [11] In May of 2001 as well as in later months, it was reported that bin Laden's plans were advancing, however the US government still did not take any major action.

The report also advocated making serious changes to the US intelligence structure. The report advocated that the Director of Central Intelligence be replaced "by a National Intelligence Director with two main areas of responsibility: (1) to oversee national intelligence centers on specific subjects of interest across the US government and (2) to manage the national intelligence program and oversee the agencies that contribute to it." [12] However, this could have potentially been problematic as the powers of this National Intelligence Director were never clearly defined and the creation of such a position would move in on the turf of already established homeland, foreign, and defense intelligence agencies, thus the newly created Department of Homeland Security, CIA, and the Defense Intelligence Agency might have ended up having a serious turf war with the National Intelligence Director and his/her team.

Yet, what is most interesting about the 9/11 Commission Report is that President Bush originally did not want it to occur. In 2004, it was reported by the Australian Broadcasting Corporation in an interview between Rafael Epstein and Eleanor Hall that "it was George W. Bush who initially didn't want this commission to take place. He fought with them about adequate funding, and whether or not he should give them access to documents, and whether or not he and his staff should talk to them." [13] It is quite interesting that a man, who seemed to care so much about the events of 9/11, even going so far as to declare a War on Terror, would fight said event being investigated.

### Patriot Act

On October 26, 2001, President Bush signed into law the Patriot Act, which at the time was hailed as a major part of fighting terrorism at home and keeping Americans safe. What was not known at the time were the destructive policies of the Patriot Act which allowed for the government to begin eroding the civil liberties of American citizens.

The Patriot Act expanded the definition of domestic terrorism to be

> an act "dangerous to human life" that is a violation of the criminal laws of a state or the United States, if the act appears to be intended to: (i) intimidate or coerce a civilian population; (ii) influence the policy of a government by intimidation or coercion; or (iii) to affect the conduct of a government by mass destruction, assassination or kidnapping. [14]

This definition of terrorism was so broad as to "encompass the activities of several prominent activist campaigns and organizations" such as "Greenpeace, Operation Rescue, Vieques Island and WTO protesters and the Environmental Liberation Front." [15] This broad definition was (and still is) quite dangerous as it allows the government to target groups that protests its agenda and imprison them indefinitely.

There was already resistance to the Patriot Act soon after it was signed into law. It was reported that several civil libertarians argued that "the surveillance powers give law enforcement too much leeway to collect private information on people on the periphery of investigations" as the Patriot Act included "the expansion of Internet eavesdropping technology," [16] in addition to the illegal wiretapping of phones.

However, this resistance wasn't large enough, and the erosion of citizen's civil liberties would continue.


**War in Afghanistan**

Leading up to the invasion of Afghanistan, the US government told Americans and the world that they were going into Afghanistan to hunt down Al Qaeda and establish a democracy in Afghanistan; however, this was nothing but the typical deceit of the American government. In reality, the US had been planning to go into Afghanistan before 9/11 and not to kill bin Laden, but rather to establish an oil pipeline.

It was a fact that America had been planning to invade Afghanistan before 9/11. A BBC News article released just days after 9/11 stated that "Niaz Naik, a former Pakistani Foreign Secretary, was told by senior American officials in mid-July that military action against Afghanistan would go ahead by the middle of October." [17] It may have seemed that 9/11 was just an excuse to invade Afghanistan, however, Naik also stated that "it was doubtful that Washington would drop its plan" even if the Taliban had given up bin Laden.

In addition to this, President Bush "was expected to sign detailed plans for a worldwide war against al-Qaida two days before Sept. 11 but did not have the chance before the terrorist attacks in New York and Washington." [18] Thus, even if the 9/11 attacks had not occurred, the US still would have launched an invasion of Afghanistan.

However, in reality, the US didn't care about getting Osama bin Laden or Al Qaeda; rather they were interested in the greater Central Asian region because it didn't want any Central Asian nation to come within the Chinese or Russian sphere of influence, thus closing out US and general Western access to the oil and gas wealth of that region. So far at that point, the "sales of Central Asia's states' large energy holdings [were] restricted to Russia."[19] To overcome this, the US tried to create other pipelines such as the Baku-Tbilisi-Ceyhan pipeline and the Turkmenistan-Afghanistan-Pakistan pipeline so that Western oil companies would be able to get at the oil and gas reserves

The creation of new pipelines would serve two major US interests in the region besides accessing oil. America would "isolate Iran from Central Asian energy by urging states to build pipelines that bypass Iran and enforcing sanctions upon those states and firms who are trading with Iran" and it would disrupt the creation of a "Russian pipeline or overall [Russian-led] energy monopoly from forming in the oil market." [20] By disrupting the formation of a Russian led "oil cartel" and attempting to create a US pipeline, America was also protecting its European allies as "the degree to which Central Asian energy markets are open or closed is an issue of great and increasing importance to European states' energy security." [21] The US knew that Europe was importing large amounts of gas from Russia and to make sure that the Russians didn't use this as a political weapon, America planned on making sure that their European allies were able to access the gas of Central Asia.

Thus the American government wasn't as truly interested in avenging the deaths of the 9/11 victims as they so professed, they also wanted to expand the empire.

**Venezuelan Coup**

In early 2002, the US government attempted to overthrow democratically-elected leader Hugo Chavez in an attempted coup, due to the fact that he wouldn't subjugate himself to Western economic interests. Chavez "was elected on a radical program of opposition to the austerity measures of the outgoing regime" and as soon as he entered office, Chavez began "to take measures against the economic and political establishment" [22] through actions such as building roads, schools, and hospitals, increasing taxes on the wealthy, and purging sections of former state apparatus. His actions and attitude had far reaching changes as could be seen in the insurrectionary events which took place in Ecuador at the beginning of 2002. There, a movement spearheaded by the organizations of indigenous peoples, who make up 40% of the population, overthrew the government and established a National Salvation Assembly. Looking to Venezuela the new leadership proclaimed their "Chavismo" after Chavez. [23]

In addition to this, Chavez nationalized the oil company PDVSA, "encouraged lowering oil production to raise prices," and "changed a 60 year-old agreement with oil companies that raised royalties for Venezuela." [24] This, along with his other moves to turn Venezuela socialist, did not please the US and thus they began to hatch a plan for a coup.

The coup began to be created when in June 2001, "American military attaches had been in touch with members of the Venezuelan military to examine the possibility of a coup." [25] On April 11, 2002, there was a "killing of 17 anti-Chavez protesters by snipers" (the surrounding events of which are still murky) which the Venezuelan military used as an excuse to overthrow Chavez.

Once the shootings took place, TV announcements that had been produced by the CIA argued that "Chavez 'provoked' the crisis by ordering his supporters to fire on peaceful protesters in Caracas." [26] After the military had overthrown Chavez and sent him to an island prison, they installed "Pedro Carmona, a wealthy businessman and former business associate of George Bush Sr., into office." His first move as president was to "'dissolve the Constitution, national legislature, Supreme Court, attorney general's office, and comptroller's office,'" [27] thus taking dictatorial control of Venezuela. It is quite reminiscent of the coups the CIA perpetrated in Latin America during the Cold War.

Thankfully, however, Chavez was bought back into power due to "a huge anti-coup civil protest involving hundreds of thousands of people" and because of this "within two days Carmona stepped down and Chavez returned to power" [28] and thus was bought back to his rightful place as president of Venezuela.

Even though the coup did not go as planned, that did not stop the US from continuing to portray Chavez as an evil doer, which continues to this day.

**War in Iraq**

Just as with the war in Afghanistan, the war in Iraq was filled with lies and deceit, however only more so. There were lies that Saddam had connections to and supported Al Qaeda and that he had WMDs, all of this now we know as untrue, however, even if PNAC had not recommended attacking Iraq, the US was already planning it.

The administration "began planning to use U.S. troops to invade Iraq within days after the former Texas governor entered the White House." [29] The Bush Administration was planning even on 9/11 as "barely five hours after American Airlines Flight 77 plowed into the Pentagon, Defense Secretary Donald H. Rumsfeld was telling his aides to come up with plans for striking Iraq." [30] Rumsfeld's notes are quoted as saying that he wanted '"best info fast. Judge whether good enough hit S.H.' – meaning Saddam Hussein – 'at same time. Not only UBL' – the initials used to identify Osama bin Laden." [31]

US military doctrine changed greatly for the invasion of Iraq. Instead of using overwhelming force, the US military used a new doctrine called "rapid dominance."

Rapid Dominance "rests in the ability to affect the will, perception, and understanding of the adversary through imposing sufficient Shock and Awe to achieve the necessary political, strategic, and operational goals of the conflict or crisis that led to the use of force." [31]The purpose of rapid dominance was to effect the enemy's will to fight by denying him of information and creating perceptions, specifically overpowering the enemy "through the adversary's perception and fear of his vulnerability and [America's] own invincibility." [32] Rapid Dominance was also very different in that it was very time-oriented, focusing on the fact that taking action in a timely and decisive manner "multiplies substantially the chances of ultimate success" and that action needed "to be taken precisely when it will have greatest impact." [33] The entire point of Rapid Dominance was to achieve military supremacy in a short amount of time, using low amounts of troops and high levels of technology.

The Iraq war did well in lining the pockets of defense contractors and oil companies; however, it had deeply negative effects on the Iraqi population from education to economics to the destruction of Iraq's cultural heritage. In November 2010, it was reported that since the invasion of Iraq, "more than 700 primary schools have been bombed, 200 have been burnt and over 3,000 looted" and that the number of teachers in Baghdad have fallen by 80%. [34] In addition to this "Between March 2003 and October 2008, 31,598 violent attacks against educational institutions were reported in Iraq, according to the Ministry of Education." [35] Iraq's middle class was destroyed because since the educated class had "been subject to a systematic and ongoing campaign of intimidation, abduction, extortion, random killings and targeted assassinations."[36] Thus, they fled Iraq, with only a few coming back in 2010. Iraq's culture was destroyed as "attacks on national archives and monuments that represent the historical identity of the Iraqi people." [37]

However, this destruction of the Iraqi state didn't matter to the US and its allies as they aided Western economic interests in the form of introducing new economic laws that "instituted low taxes, 100% foreign investor ownership of Iraqi assets, the right to expropriate all profits, unrestricted imports, and long-term 30-40 year deals and leases." [38]

With Afghanistan and Iraq subdued, it was time for the Empire to focus on its main regional enemy: Iran.

**Iran**

In 2002, the US government began propagating the myth that Iran was attempting to create nuclear weapons, with President Bush labeling Iran part of an "axis of evil" in the world and that they "aggressively pursue" nuclear weapons.

In later years the Bush administration would get more serious about trying to find evidence that Iran was making nuclear weapons, even going to far as to send unmanned aerial vehicles over Iran in 2005. [39] However, in that same year, it was acknowledged in a US intelligence review that Iran was "about a decade away from manufacturing the key ingredient for a nuclear weapon, roughly doubling the previous estimate of five years." [40] Due to this review, the question must be bought up of why the US was pushing so hard on the issue, when Iran was supposedly a decade away from gaining nuclear weapons. The answer is because the US was using the Iranian nuclear fabrication as a pretext to invade Iran. The very next year it was reported as fact that "some senior officials have already made up their minds: They want to hit Iran." [41] This was without a doubt true, as in 2007 it was noted that America had plans attack Iran, as did Israel. However, what was not mentioned was the fact that the US and Israel had had plans to attack Iran for quite some time, with the US, Israel, and Britain working to create an unstable Iran which would in turn create a pretext for invasion. [42]

The US media and the Western media more generally toed the line that Iran was attempting to make nuclear weapons, however, even with all the screaming and yelling, the US and its allies have yet to lay down any real evidence proving that Iran is trying to attain nuclear weapons.

## Color Revolutions

In the years 2004 and 2005 new governments came about in Georgia, Ukraine, and Kyrgyzstan. In the West, these were hailed as democratically elected governments, however, in reality the elections were controlled by the United States in a bid to make sure that those states didn't stray from the American sphere of influence.

### *Georgia*

In November 2003, Georgian leader Edouard Shevardnadze was swept aside in the aftermath of the Rose Revolution to make room for Mikheil Saakashvili. This came about due to US and Western NGOs (non governmental organizations) creating "an atmosphere of popular protest against the existing regime" as Shevardnadze was "no longer useful to Washington when he began to make a deal with Moscow over energy pipelines and privatizations." [43]

The plan involved having the NGOs led by US ambassador to Georgia, Richard Miles, and using George Soros' Open Society Georgia Foundation, the Washington-based Freedom House, the US-funded National Endowment for Democracy, and the Georgia Liberty Institute in such a manner as to create a movement of that was anti-Russian, pro-Western, and would back Saakashvili in the elections preceding the parliamentary election fiasco, in which it was revealed that the voting system was rigged and there were calls for new elections among the US-backed protesters.

Once in power Saakashvili "led a policy of large-scale arrests, imprisonment, torture and deepened corruption" and created a "de facto one-party state, with a dummy opposition occupying a tiny portion of seats in the parliament." [44]

Even though the people of Georgia suffered under a vicious dictator and had their hopes of a true democracy crushed, this was entirely fine with the US as it coincided with their interests in Georgia. The Rose Revolution aided the US in attaining oil from the Caucus region as Georgia was "crucial in the wider project of building an East-West transportation corridor" for oil and gas and important to the creation of "a [railroad] transit route connecting Europe to Central Asia, China, and India via the Black Sea, Georgia, Azerbaijan, and the Caspian Sea" [45] which would have allowed the West to ship goods inexpensively across Asia. This creation of an oil pipeline fit in perfectly with America's goal for Central Asia which was to deny the creation of a Russian-led energy cartel.

*Ukraine*

The Orange Revolution in Ukraine took place from November 2004 to January 2005. The entire thing was "an American creation, a sophisticated and brilliantly conceived exercise in western branding and mass marketing" [46] where the US organized and funded the installation of another puppet regime. The same formula that established a US puppet in Georgia was followed here. It included the same players as well, with a few new ones such as the National Democratic Institute and International Republican Institute which are NGOs used by both the Democratic and Republican parties, respectively, to push a pro-American agenda around the world. There was the usual youth protest movement, Otpor (meaning resistance), but also the Americans "ordered opposition parties to unite behind the dour, elderly trade unionist, Vladimir Goncharik, because he appealed to much of the Lukashenko constituency." [47]

With the protest movement in place, the opposition parties united, and the aid of having "thousands of local election monitors trained and paid by western groups," [48] the US threw its weight behind Viktor Yushchenko. Even though there was a massive protest after the original run-off votes which caused the Ukrainian Supreme Court to declare a re-vote on December 26, 2004, Yushchenko still succeeded in attaining the presidency.

Once in power, the Yushchenko regime "turned out to be just as incompetent and rife with cronyism as his corrupt and venal predecessors, if not more so" as large amounts of Western aid was siphoned off into the personal coffers of the elite. Overall, Ukraine "disintegrated, not only economically but socially as centrifugal forces of culture, language, and the weight of history were brought to bear on the unity of the country, and things began to come apart." [49]

Once again, Washington came out on top as the Yushchenko regime wanted "closer ties with the European Union, NATO, and the United States, with the goal of eventual NATO and EU membership." [50] The new US puppet regime would also hurt Russia due to its plans to get its oil from other sources. The Ukrainian government was "studying how to move forward with a plan to extend into Poland an oil pipeline that currently runs from an oil terminal at the port of Odesa to the town of Brody" which would be used to transport Caspian Sea oil into Western Europe, "thereby reducing [European] dependence on Russian oil, and reducing Russia's control of regional pipelines." [51] By reducing European dependence on Russian oil, the US was once again making sure that Russia would be unable to use their oil wealth as a political weapon and by creating a new puppet state; the US was ensuring that it would be able to keep an eye on Russia and quickly counter any moves they made.

*Kyrgyzstan*

During early 2005, the US engineered its last takeover in Central Asia where Kyrgyz President Askar Akayev was ousted due to his efforts to increase economic and political ties with Russia and China. On March 24, 2005, rioters forced Akayev to flee the country which allowed "a loose coalition of opposition forces under the leadership of Kurmanbek Bakiyev seized power." [52] This occurred after parliamentary run-off elections on March 13th which were widely seen as fraudulent and in response to this; the opposition movement began holding protests. This opposition movement was "largely the product of US intervention in the country, owing its existence to the financial and logistical resources provided either directly from Washington or through US-funded non-governmental organizations" [53] such as Freedom House, which published opposition newspapers in an effort to stir up popular discontent.

The events seemed to be going according to plan; however the Americans were surprised on March 13, 2005 "when Akayev was still in power, the opposition leadership began backing off its initial calls for the president's resignation and instead demanded negotiations with the ruling authorities," [54] and protests became violent. By next week America was calling "for an end to the violence, urging 'all parties in Kyrgyzstan to engage in dialogue and resolve differences peacefully and according to the rule of law'" [55] and had US Ambassador Stephen Young attempt to work with opposition forces and Akayev to find a solution. A solution was found: A new parliament was formed and Akayev resigned from the presidency. This allowed US front-man, Kurmanbek Saliyevich Bakiyev, to be elected President.

America's main interests in Kyrgyzstan was that "the country is of great geopolitical significance due to its proximity to oil-producing countries" and that the "US military base near Bishkek is also critical to American efforts in Afghanistan." [56]

Overall, Washington succeed in fulfilling its main interests of expanding oil routes and limiting Russian influence on its neighbors. However, the US also gained a foothold that would more easily allow for an attack or invasion of Iran or potentially a staging ground to do covert operations in Russia.

**Africom**

In October 2007, the US established Africa Command (Africom). Its stated goal was to aid the African people in military operations and promote US foreign policy; however, there was also the other goal of combating China as they were making moves into the continent to get at the continent's oil resources. With the creation of Africom, the US would become the first nation in history to have military commands that covered literally the entire planet.

America was concerned about the Chinese making moves to access African oil due to the fact that "African oil supplies [would] account for 25% of its [America's] energy demands by 2015." [57] In addition to this the US viewed Africa "as a backdrop" to take out terrorists.

Even before Africom was created, African leaders put up such a strong resistance "that commanders abandoned initial ambitions to install a headquarters on the continent." [58] In general most Africans didn't trust Africom as they didn't even "trust their own militaries, which in places like [the] Congo [where militaries] have turned weapons on their own people." Also, since Africom was itself a military force, many Africans were worried that the Americans wanted to make African states "proxies" and would use Africom to look out for American interests.

While dealing with this policy of imperial domination of the globe, the Empire's homeland was economically about to crumble.

**Financial Crisis**

In late 2007, a massive financial crisis that originated in the US hit the world and its effects are being felt to this day. It began with the housing market having an upward spiral as people began snapping up houses due to easy credit, predatory lending by realtor companies, and massive government deregulation. This deadly mixture would lead to the global economy being put on the brink of collapse.

After the 9/11 attacks, the Federal Reserve "lowered the Federal funds rate 11 times – from 6.5% in May 2000 to 1.75% in December 2001 – creating a flood of liquidity in the economy." [59] This access to easy credit (as well as predatory lending and Americans being able to purchase houses via Freddie Mac and Fannie Mae in many cases) led people to buy houses that they were unable to afford. With houses being snapped up quickly, it "made investments in higher yielding subprime mortgages look like a new rush for gold." [60] Thus, companies began putting their money into these subprime mortgages. This only increased when the Federal Reserve lowered interest rates to 1% in June 2003. Financial companies then created a secondary market for subprime mortgages by repackaging them into collateralized debt obligations, which, while they were quite risky, if successful, would pay off handsomely.

The risk increased in October 2004 when the Security Exchange Commission relaxed the net capital requirement for Goldman Sachs, Merrill Lynch, Lehman Brothers, Bear Stearns, and Morgan Stanley. This allowed the banks to "leverage up to 30-times or even 40-times their initial investment." [61] This was essentially a green light from the feds for financial companies to take more risks with their investments.

Things began to go sour when "U.S. homeownership had peaked at 70%" in 2004 and "during the last quarter of 2005, home prices started to fall, which led to a 40% decline in the U.S. Home Construction Index during 2006." [62] This was already bad as the job boom in the construction sector would end, but also many people began defaulting on their loans, which in turn made banks wary of lending people money.

The effects of this mass mortgage defaulting would come home in 2007 as the financial companies couldn't solve the problem on their own and the crisis began spreading around the world. Even though the Federal Reserve began to slash discount and fund rates, the situation continued to worsen as corporations like Lehman Brothers and Merril Lynch collapsed. In an attempt to solve this, in 2008 the US government bailed out the financial companies to the tune of $700 billion. While this saved the financial corporations, it did nothing for those that had lost retirement or pension funds in the crisis. Many of those who were directly involved in creating the crisis got multi-million dollar bonuses, while average Americans suffered in the form of skyrocketing unemployment and loss of investments.

While this financial disaster led to the near collapse of the global economy, there was also a moral collapse of America. Due to the unjustified war in Iraq, the torturing of prisoners, the illegal wiretapping, and the American government's general disregard for both national and international law, the United States lost its moral standing with the world. No longer was it the nation that was the beacon of freedom, democracy, and liberty. Now the US was in an onset of imperial decline, something from which it would never come back from.

**Endnotes**

1: Michael Moran, "Bin Laden Comes Home To Roost," *MSNBC*, August 24, 1998 (http://www.msnbc.msn.com/id/3340101/t/bin-laden-comes-home-roost/)

2: Ibid

3: Ibid

4: CNN, *Transcript of President Bush's Address*, http://www.cnn.com/2001/US/09/20/gen.bush.transcript/index.html?_s=PM:US (September 20, 2001)

5: Ibid

6: Ibid

7: Project for the New American Century, *Letter to President Bush*, https://web.archive.org/web/20020203082701/http://newamericancentury.org/Bushletter.htm (September 20, 2001)

8: Ibid

9: National Commission on Terrorist Attacks upon the United States, *9/11 Commission Report*, http://www.9-11commission.gov/report/911Report.pdf (July 22, 2004)

10-12: Ibid

13: Rafael Epstein, "Commission Finds Missed Opportunities to Avert 9/11," *Australian Broadcasting Corporation*, July 23, 2004 (http://www.abc.net.au/worldtoday/content/2004/s1160522.htm)

14: American Civil Liberties Union, *How The USA Patriot Act Redefines 'Domestic Terrorism,'* http://www.aclu.org/national-security/how-usa-patriot-act-redefines-domestic-terrorism

15: Ibid

16: Stefanie Olsen, "Patriot Act Draws Privacy Concerns," *CNET*, August 30, 2002 (http://news.cnet.com/2100-1023-275026.html)

17: George Arney, "US 'Planned Attack on Taliban," *BBC*, September 18, 2001 (http://news.bbc.co.uk/2/hi/south_asia/1550366.stm)

18: Alex Johnson, Jim Miklaszewski, "US Planned for Attack on Al Qaida," *MSNBC*, May 16, 2002 (http://www.msnbc.msn.com/id/4587368/)

19: Stephen J. Blank, Strategic Studies Institute, US Army War College, *US Interests in Central Asia and the Challenges to Them*, http://www.strategicstudiesinstitute.army.mil/pubs/download.cfm?q=758 (March 2007)

20: Ibid

21: Ibid

22: Frontline, *Latin America*, http://www.redflag.org.uk/articles/issix/is6samer.html

23: Ibid

24: Project Censored, *Bush Administration Behind Failed Military Coup in Venezuela*, http://www.projectcensored.org/top-stories/articles/12-bush-administration-behind-failed- military-coup-in-venezuela/ (April 29, 2010)

25-28: Ibid

29: CNN, *O'Neill: Bush Planned Iraq Invasion Before 9/11*, http://www.cnn.com/2004/ALLPOLITICS/01/10/oneill.bush/ (January 14, 2004)

30: Joel Roberts, "Plans For Iraq Attack Began on 9/11," *CBS News*, September 4, 2002 (http://www.cbsnews.com/stories/2002/09/04/september11/main520830.shtml)

31: Harlan K. Ullman, James P. Wade, *Shock and Awe: Achieving Rapid Dominance*, International Command and Control Institute, http://www.dodccrp.org/files/Ullman_Shock.pdf (October 1996)

32: Ibid

33: Ibid

34: Dirk Adriaensens, "'Ending States that Sponsor Terrorism:' Dismantling the Iraqi State, Destroying an Entire Country," *Global Research*, November 5, 2010 (http://www.globalresearch.ca/ending-states-that-sponsor-terrorism-dismantling-the-iraqi-state- destroying-an-entire-country/21781)

35-38: Ibid

39: Dafna Linzer, "US Uses Drones to Probe Iran For Arms," *Washington Post*, February 13, 2005 (http://www.washingtonpost.com/wp-dyn/articles/A19820-2005Feb12.html)

40: Dafna Linzer, "Iran Is Judged 10 Years From Nuclear Bomb," *Washington Post*, August 2, 2005 (http://www.washingtonpost.com/wp- dyn/content/article/2005/08/01/AR2005080101453.html)

41: Joseph Cirincione, "Fool Me Twice," *Foreign Policy*, March 27, 2006 (http://www.foreignpolicy.com/articles/2006/03/26/fool_me_twice)

42: Michel Chossudovsky, "Planned US-Israeli Attack On Iran," *Global Research*, May 1, 2005 (http://globalresearch.ca/index.php?context=va&aid=66)

43: F. William Engdahl, *The Puppet Masters Behind Georgia President Saakashvili, Geopolitics-Geoeconomics*, http://www.engdahl.oilgeopolitics.net/Geopolitics___Eurasia/Saakashvili/saakashvili.html (August 12, 2008)

44: Ibid

45: Svante E. Cornell, Strategic Studies Institute, US Army War College, *Georgia After The Rose Revolution: Geopolitical Predicament and Implications for US Policy*, http://www.strategicstudiesinstitute.army.mil/pdffiles/pub757.pdf (February 2007)

46: Ian Traynor, "US Campaign Behind The Turmoil in Kiev," *The Guardian*, November 25, 2004 (http://www.guardian.co.uk/world/2004/nov/26/ukraine.usa)

47: Ibid

48: Ibid

49: Justin Raimondo, "The Orange Revolution, Peeled," *Antiwar*, February 8, 2010 (http://original.antiwar.com/justin/2010/02/07/the-orange-revolution-peeled/)

50: Steven Woehrel, Ukraine's Orange Revolution and US Policy, *Washington Headquarters Services*, http://www.whs.mil/library/crs/crs%2007.20.05.5.pdf (July 1, 2005)

51: Ibid

52: Andrea Peters, "Kyrgyz President Forced to Flee as Opposition Seizes Power," *World Socialist Website*, March 28, 2005 (http://www.wsws.org/articles/2005/mar2005/kyrg- m28.shtml)

53-56: Ibid

57: Salim Faraji, Jahi Issa, *Revisiting and Reconsidering AFRICOM*, GhanaWeb, http://www.ghanaweb.com/GhanaHomePage/features/artikel.php?ID=165121 (July 12, 2009)

58: Fox News, *Africans Fear Hidden US Agenda in New Approach to AFRICOM*, http://www.foxnews.com/story/0,2933,430564,00.html (September 30, 2008)

59: Manoj Singh, *The 2007-08 Financial Crisis In Review*, Investopedia, http://www.investopedia.com/articles/economics/09/financial-crisis- review.asp#axzz1RH3yoU3h (October 28, 2008)

60-62: Ibid

**Overview**

The America: an Empire in Decline series examines the rise and decline of the American Empire. In Part 1, *Dawn of a New Century*, I analyzed America's original plans for the 21$^{st}$ century, immediately after the end of the Cold War, which imagined a world where the US would be the sole superpower and preventive diplomacy would be used to ensure no flare-ups occurred.

However, with the rise of the neoconservatives, first with the Project for the New American Century think tank and then later in the form of Donald Rumsfeld, Dick Cheney, Paul Wolfowitz, and Condoleeza Rice as Cabinet members in the Bush administration, a vision that saw the fall of the Soviet Union as an opportunity for the United States to become a full-fledged empire became deeply rooted in the American political and military psyche. They envisioned a world in which America would be the dominant economic, political, and military power and whose enemies and potential rivals would be kept in check. All they needed was an incident to make this possible and the devastating attacks on 9/11 provided an excuse for the US to God the globe.

In *Onset of Imperial Decline*, I examined America's actions both at home and abroad. Domestically, the rights of citizens were being curbed in the name of the War on Terror due to the Patriot Act which allowed for the government to illegally spy on its citizens without a warrant. Abroad, America used 9/11 as a casus belli to launch an attack on Afghanistan, even though it was later revealed that the US had already been planning to invade Afghanistan prior to the attacks. It was also revealed that on 9/11, once notified of the attacks, Donald Rumsfeld ordered his aides to find a link between the attacks and Saddam Hussein as to create a pretext to invade Iraq. Soon after the invasion of Afghanistan, the US failed in an attempt to covertly overthrow Hugo Chavez of Venezuela, started its campaign of lies and deceit about Iran's nuclear facilities, and engineered several pseudo-democratic uprising in Eastern Europe and Central Asia to ensure a pro-Western encirclement was kept around Russia. The US then turned its attention to the continent of Africa, establishing a continental wide command there as to combat the influence of rival nations such as China. However, at home, due to the incompetence of Washington and the greed of Wall Street bankers, the US experienced a massive recession which led to ripple effects around the world.

In this final installment of the series, an examination of America's recent foreign policy and military adventures will take place, concluding with a prediction of what may lay in the future for the Empire.

**Escalation in Afghanistan, False Drawdown In Iraq**

Soon after being elected into office on the idea of hope and change, President Obama truly showed how much change he wanted when he stated at West Point that it was in America's "vital national interest to send an additional 30,000 U.S. troops to Afghanistan." [1] He also announced "a strategy recognizing the fundamental connection between our war effort in Afghanistan and the extremist safe havens in Pakistan." [2] While Pakistan did allow for Afghan Taliban and Al Qaeda members safe haven near the Pakistan-Afghanistan border, by including Pakistan in the strategy to succeed in Afghanistan, Obama effectively made the mission even more difficult since now the US would have to deal with the Afghan and Pakistani Talibans, as well as with the corruption and general incompetence of the Pakistani government, as they would often make deals with the militants instead of crushing them as Washington wanted.

Escalating the war in Afghanistan brings out the irony of President Obama having received the Nobel Peace Prize. How is a man who controls the most powerful military force in history, increases military spending to historic levels, and escalates a then-eight year old war, a man of peace? This can only occur when, as Michel Chossudovsky said, "war becomes peace," "a global military agenda is heralded as a humanitarian endeavor," and most importantly, "when [a] lie becomes the truth." [3]

In addition to escalating the war in Afghanistan, Obama oversaw a false drawdown in Iraq. While it was true that all combat forces had left, it was reported "that as many as 50,000 Marines and soldiers would remain until the end of 2011" and that the "pace of the drawdown [would] be left to commanders and determined by events on the ground as well as politics in Washington." [4] Officially, the remaining 50,000 troops "would remain in Iraq after Aug. 31, 2010, to train, equip and advise Iraqi forces, help protect withdrawing forces and work on counter-terrorism." [5] However, these soldiers were not entirely trainers, as in September alone US troops "waged a gun battle with a suicide squad in Baghdad, dropped bombs on armed militants in Baquba and assisted Iraqi soldiers in a raid in Fallujah." [6] US troops are still fighting in Iraq, although now it is under the guise of training Iraqi forces. US forces may very well stay permanently in Iraq as it has been reported that the US government has worked out a deal with Iraq to allow US troops to stay until 2012, yet the Iraqi government denies it. [7]

**Drone Strikes**

The US has been doing drone strikes for quite some time, yet in recent years they have been escalated and the number of targets increased. In addition to targeting terrorists in Pakistan, the strikes were expanded to Yemen and Somalia as well as several other countries.

In 2011, it was reported that the CIA was preparing to initiate a secret program to kill Al Qaeda militants in Yemen. The plan "would give the U.S. greater latitude than the current military campaign [against AQ militants]" and is a shift from previous tactics as "Now, the spy agency will carry out aggressive drone strikes itself alongside the military campaign." [8] While the Americans may think that this is a good idea, it may cause even more instability in Yemen and push a new government away from the US.

Major revelations about America's campaign against drone strikes have come to light due to the UK-based Bureau of Investigative Journalism study on drone strikes which resulted in a "fundamental reassessment of the covert US campaign [and] involved a complete re-examination of all that is known about each US drone strike." [9] The study revealed that "many more CIA attacks on alleged militant targets [have taken place] than previously reported. At least 291 US drone strikes are now known to have taken place since 2004" [10] and that 1,100 people had been injured in drone strikes. This study has worried the establishment to the point where the CIA is "attempting to link the Bureau's 'suspect' work to unsubstantiated allegations that one of its many sources is a Pakistani spy" and "directly challenging the data itself." [11]

However, these drone strikes can end up creating more enemies for America. One such example being in Somalia, where Dr. Omar Ahmed, an academic and Somali politician argues that US helicopter and drone attacks only help Al Shabaab:

> "There is no reason for the western countries to use airstrikes against al-Shabaab. **It will only increase the generations supporting al-Shabaab," he said. "For example, when the Americans killed Aden Eyrow, the capability of al-Shabaab was very low. From that day forward, the militia increased in size day-after-day.** They recruited many youths, persuading them that infidels attacked their country and want to capture it." [12] (emphasis added)

Even though the US strategy is not working, the Americans still continue it due to the political and military elite having fooled themselves to such a point where they think that the drone strikes do work, when in reality they increase anti-American sentiment and actually help the very people America is trying to defeat.

## Assassinations

While things were already dismal on the domestic front due to the Patriot Act and the horrid economic crisis, things were to get worse as President Obama was given the power to assassinate American citizens.

Last year, the Obama Administration authorized the assassination of "the radical Muslim cleric Anwar al-Awlaki, who is believed to have shifted from encouraging attacks on the United States to directly participating in them." [13] Awlaki was an American citizen who was born in New Mexico and had been an imam in the United States, before going to Yemen. American officials stated that he had joined Al Qaeda and became a recruiter.

While this may seem like a new precedent, in reality it isn't as after 9/11 "Bush gave the CIA, and later the military, authority to kill U.S. citizens abroad if strong evidence existed that an American was involved in organizing or carrying out terrorist actions against the United States or U.S. interests." [14] (emphasis added) Thus, the entire illegal act of assassinating US citizens had been on the board since 2001 and therefore was nothing but Obama continuing the draconian practices of the previous administration.

The entire idea of assassinating US citizens is not only wrong, but illegal under US law. Executive Order 12333, put into place by Ronald Reagan, states that "No person employed by or acting on behalf of the United States Government shall engage in, or conspire to engage in, assassination." [15] However, it goes even further for all US intelligence agencies, stating that no one in the intelligence apparatus should participate in any activities that are forbidden under Order 12333, which includes assassinations.

The continued policy of assassinating US citizens only shows the continued moral decline of the Empire and the continued concentration of power in the Executive Branch.

## Cyber Command

While the US was waging war in Iraq, Afghanistan, Yemen, and other locations, the Americans turned their attention to cyberspace and with the creation of Cyber Command (CyCom), effectively turned cyberspace into a battle zone.

In 2010, the US created CyCom whose mission, among other things, was to "conduct full-spectrum military cyberspace operations in order to enable actions in all domains, ensure US/Allied freedom of action in cyberspace and deny the same to our adversaries." [16] By stating that the US would ensure its "freedom of action in cyberspace," the Americans clearly implied that they may attack other nations via the internet.

The US went even further with turning CyCom into a weapon of war when the Pentagon announced "that computer sabotage coming from another country can constitute an act of war, a finding that for the first time opens the door for the U.S. to respond using traditional military force," with a US military official stating "'**If you shut down our power grid, maybe we will put a missile down one of your smokestacks.**'" [17] (emphasis added) Thus, without a doubt, the US was planning to use cyberspace as a way to increase its military might.

## Iranian Green Movement

In June 2009, there began mass protests in Iran due to suspicions of election fraud, with reports of the government blocking communications and alleged vote rigging. While the protest movement was no doubt organic, there may very well have been US involvement as they had been launching covert operations within recent years.

In 2007, the CIA received a "secret presidential approval to mount a covert 'black' operation to destabilize the Iranian government." [18] The operation itself was designed to pressure Iran to end its nuclear enrichment program. It was also reported that the US was "secretly funding militant ethnic separatist groups in Iran in an attempt to pile pressure on the Islamic regime to give up its nuclear program." [19] CIA officials were working with known terrorists, such as the Mujahedeen-e Khalq, to overthrow the Iranian government. The Americans may have been hopeful that something might occur which would allow them to militarily intervene, seeing as how they positioned a second aircraft carrier near Iran's coastal waters and "also moved six heavy bombers from a British base on the Pacific island of Diego Garcia to the Al Udeid Air Base in Qatar." [20]

In 2008, things went even further when it was reported that the US government had decided "to fund a major escalation of covert operations against Iran" which were "designed to destabilize the country's religious leadership." [21] If Ayatollah Khomeini, the country's highest ranking political and religious figure, was overthrown or assassinated, it would cause massive political turmoil in Iran, which would turn provide the Americans with an excuse to intervene in Iran or allow for US puppets to take control of the nation.

It is interesting to note that at this time the US ramped up its rhetoric against Iran, reviving charges that the Iranian leadership had been involved in the killing of American soldiers in Iraq: both directly, by dispatching commando units into Iraq, and indirectly, by supplying materials used for roadside bombs and other lethal goods. [22]

This occurred around the time when "a National Intelligence Estimate, [which had been] released in December, [concluded] that Iran had halted its work on nuclear weapons in 2003." [23]

Aiding terrorist attacks in Iran may very well have helped to create an atmosphere where ordinary Iranians felt that the current regime was not protecting them and thus had to challenge the regime, though not knowing they were being used as a way to fulfill American interests.

Not soon after the Iranian elections had died down, the US turned its attention to North Korea and China.

**Cheonan Incident**

In March of 2010, it was reported that South Korea's ship, the Cheonan, had sunk in waters near the border with North Korea. The ship went down due to an unexplained explosion. Initially, South Korea "suspected the North Korean hand in the mishap but without convincing proof, it did not charge North Korea of this act." [24] Thus a Joint Civilian-Military Investigation Group (JIG) was established to investigate the incident.

Preliminary investigations established the fact that the explosion was external and the JIG speculated that "the Cheonan was hit by a torpedo or a floating mine and that the blast impact originated from outside the vessel." [25] After collaborating several reports from sailors aboard the Cheonan and simulations, the JIG "collected propulsion parts, including propulsion motor with propellers and a steering section from the site of the sinking to corroborate with the fact that it was a torpedo attack" [26] and found that the markings on one propulsion section were consistent with the marking of a North Korean torpedo that had been obtained prior to the Cheonan incident. This convinced the JIG that "the recovered parts were made in North Korea and therefore established Pyongyang's complicity. **The JIP, therefore, eliminated other plausible factors such as grounding, fatigue failure, mines, collision and internal explosion.**" [27] (emphasis added)

In addition to the South Korean JIG, there was also an international investigatory committee known was the Multinational Combined Intelligence Task force, which was made up of five states, "including the US, Australia, Canada and the UK" [28] (emphasis added) and the findings of this group also pointed the finger at North Korea.

This is quite serious as not only did South Korea ignore other plausible factors that may have led to the sinking of the Cheonan, but they also trusted a group that was overwhelmingly under the influence of Western nations who are known to be hostile to North Korea. It is possible that South Korea was looking to blame the North, seeing as how they stopped immediately after they could even plausibly establish a link to North Korea.

In response to the attacks, the US and South Korea held joint war games in which the United States sent its supercarrier, the USS George Washington. The war games were to be held in the Yellow Sea, which is in China's exclusive economic zone. Once news that the war games were going to be held in the Yellow Sea came out, China stated that it "opposes any military acts in its exclusive economic zone without permission." [29] The Americans and South Koreans had to have done this on purpose, seeing as how launching war games would not ease tensions, but rather escalate them. One must also factor in the notion that the US had been considering China a potential threat to its dominance of the Asia-Pacific region since the 1990s.

Not only were the South Korean war games a threat to China, but also no sooner after the US had concluded those war games, did "the U.S. [begin] a week-long exercise with Japan off the second nation's islands near the South Korean coast." [30] The entire point of these war games with both South Korea and Japan was to send a message to China, saying that the US was still in control of the Asia-Pacific region.

In the midst of this, an organization that was and continues to change the world was going to blow the lid on the Empire, showing their true foreign policy.

**Wikileaks**

In 2010, a then fairly unknown organization called Wikileaks released a video now known as Collateral Murder which shows an Apache helicopter firing on reporters from *Reuters* and blatantly murdering Iraqi civilians. This had the US government so worried that they conducted a counterintelligence investigation into Wikileaks, saying that the organization "represents a potential force protection, counterintelligence, operational security (OPSEC), and information security (INFOSEC) threat to the US Army." [31]

In its extreme worry, the investigatory committee may have become slightly paranoid as they did not rule out the possibility that "current employees or moles within DoD or elsewhere in the US government are providing sensitive or classified information to Wikileaks.org" and that "former US government employees [leaking] sensitive and classified information is highly suspect." [32] However, the chance that former US government employees would leak classified information is slim, seeing as how most are loyal to the government.

However, the Wikileaks situation would get extremely serious later when they released 250,000 documents detailing America's true foreign policy. The documents revealed that America had been "running a secret intelligence campaign targeted at the leadership of the United Nations, including the secretary general, Ban Ki-moon and the permanent Security Council representatives from China, Russia, France and the UK." [33] In July 2009, US Secretary of State Hillary Clinton ordered US diplomats to gather "forensic technical details about the communications systems used by top UN officials, including passwords and personal encryption keys used in private and commercial networks for official communications" as well as "credit card numbers, email addresses, phone, fax and pager numbers and even frequent-flyer account numbers for UN figures and 'biographic and biometric information on UN Security Council permanent representatives.'"[34] The entire operation seems to be involved in aiding the CIA and the National Security Agency for the purposes of building biographical profiles, data mining, and surveillance operations.

Due to the massive dump, some became so enraged that they called for Julian Assange's head. Jeffrey T. Kuhner, a columnist in the Washington Times, stated that Julian Assange poses a clear and present danger to American national security. The Wikileaks founder is more than a reckless provocateur. **He is aiding and abetting terrorists in their war against America. The administration must take care of the problem – effectively and permanently.** [35] (emphasis added)

However, what Kuhner and other people who wanted Assange dead were truly enraged about was that US foreign policy was exposed for what it truly is: the US government working hard to fulfill its interests by any means necessary, with complete and total disregard for the sovereignty of other nations, as can be shown by the fact that the US government intimidated Spanish Prime Minister Zapatero into ending his criticism of the Iraq war.

The US media as well as others jumped on the story when Julian Assange was accused of rape and began spreading it everywhere. Yet, they were quite incorrect as Assange was accused of violating a Swedish law against sex without a condom. It was reported that Sweden's Public Prosecutor's Office "leaked to the media that it was seeking to arrest Assange for rape, then on the same day withdrew the arrest warrant because in its own words there was 'no evidence.'" [36] Even though the media did their best to smear Assange's name, Wikileaks was going play a role in lighting a spark that would take the Arab world by storm.

**Arab Spring**

In 2011, the United States had its dominance of the Middle East seriously threatened due to massive peaceful protests that were sweeping the Arab world. No longer were people going to put up with corrupt and oppressive regimes that were backed by Washington. No longer would they put up with horrid dictatorships in which the only freedom they had was to obey. In 2011 protests in Tunisia began what would become known as the Arab Spring.

*Tunisia*

The spark that launched the Arab Spring began on December 17, 2010. Mohammed Bouazizi was selling fruit without a license and when the authorities confiscated his scale, he became enraged, confronted the police, and was slapped in the face. This led him to plead his case in the town's government office, but when it was rebuffed, he went outside and lit himself aflame. This small act became noticed by the populace at large and the anger "spread to other towns in the interior of the country, where unemployment among university graduates was approaching 50 percent." [37] Mass protests soon began with calls to end dictator Ben Ali's rule and democratic elections, however, Ali turned to the police and the slaughtering of protesters began in earnest.

The organization Wikileaks also played a role in starting up the protests, as files were released just days before Bouazizi lit himself aflame, which confirmed suspicions that many Tunisians already had: that Ben Ali was a corrupt dictator, that his family was extremely corrupt, and that life was incredibly difficult for the Tunisian poor and unemployed.

When this occurred, the US was deeply worried as Tunisia had significant military ties to the US. Tunisia cooperated "in NATO's Operation Active Endeavor, which provides counter- terrorism surveillance in the Mediterranean," participated in NATO's Mediterranean Dialogue, "and [allowed] NATO ships to make port calls at Tunis." [38] Every now and then the US would criticize Tunisia for its record on political rights and freedom of expression, yet "In parallel with these expressions of concern, the United States continued to provide military and economic assistance to the Tunisian government." [39] Thus, the US began to play both sides. About two weeks after Ben Ali had fled the nation, America sent their top Middle East envoy to Tunisia and tried "to press its advantage to push for democratic reforms in the country and further afield." [40] While it may have appeared that the US was quickly trying to position itself on Tunisia's good side, they may have had a hand in Ali's ousting as "According to some rumors in Tunis, the country's army chief consulted with Washington before withdrawing his support from Ben Ali — a move which sealed the ousted president's fate." [41]

Almost as soon as the US was finished in Tunisia, they had even bigger problems on their hands with the protests in Egypt.


*Egypt*

Due to being inspired by the success of the Tunisian protests, the Egyptian people launched their own protest movement, calling for the overthrow of US puppet Hosni Mubarak. However, the US was busy co-opting the protest movement.

The US used the National Endowment for Democracy (NED) as a cover to help co-opt the protest movement. Ironically, the NED is not used for the spreading of democracy; rather it was established by the Reagan administration to aid in the overthrow of foreign governments, after the CIA's covert operations were revealed. The NED was supported "As a bipartisan endowment, with participation from the two major parties, as well as the AFL-CIO and US Chamber of Commerce, the NED took over the financing of foreign overthrow movements, but overtly and under the rubric of 'democracy promotion.'" [42] Thus, the US supported both Mubarak and the protesters in a bid to make sure that no matter what occurred America would still get its way.

Washington already had influence in Egyptian pro-democracy circles as in May 2009 many Egyptian activists that would eventually organize protests calling for the end of the dictator Mubarak's reign

**spent a week in Washington receiving training in advocacy and getting an inside look at the way U.S. democracy works.** After their training, the fellows were matched with civil society organizations throughout the country where they shared experiences with U.S. counterparts. The activists [wrapped] up their program this week by visiting U.S. government officials, members of Congress, media outlets and think tanks. [43] (emphasis added)

Thus, due to the US aiding the activists, the Americans ensured that the protesters owed them a debt and that US interests would be secure even if Mubarak was ousted.

The Egyptian military also played a role in US plans. While they originally had protected protesters and refused to fire upon them, the Egyptian military showed just how supportive they were of a democratic Egypt when they began arresting and trying them before military courts, dissolved parliament, and suspended the constitution. In reality, the military junta that now controls Egypt is no different than the Mubarak regime when it controlled Egypt.

While the Egyptian military is currently in control until elections, no matter what occurs, America will still have its way.

*Bahrain*

Protests also began taking place in Bahrain. The people were tired of a government which "failed to abide by their own constitution, refused to investigate the crimes of torture and continued to expropriate more than half of the land of the country." [44] The Bahraini government was controlled by the Al Khalifa family, which has ruled Bahrain for over 300 years and has created an economy where there is a powerful and wealthy Sunni minority while the Shiite majority constantly faces discrimination in jobs and education, has little political representation, and are barred from many government and military positions.

The US was deeply troubled because of the protests as the Al Khalifa regime allowed for the Americans to station their Fifth Fleet in the country, which allows the US to patrol "the Persian Gulf, the Red Sea, the Arabian Sea, and the east coast of Africa," "keep an eye on – and, if necessary, rattle sabers – close to oil shipping lanes, Iran, and the increasing activity of pirates," and " [provide] basing and overflight clearances for US aircraft engaged in Afghanistan and [help] cut off money supplies to suspected Islamic terrorists." [45] Thus, the Bahraini regime was of major importance to US regional interests.

The US showed that it would do anything to make sure that its puppet stayed in power when they backed the Saudi military intervention in Bahrain. The Saudis intervened on the behalf of the Bahraini government and began shooting into crowds of Bahraini protesters. [46] However, even though the protesters were being gunned down, they still were determined to fight for their rights against America's puppets.

*Libya*

The Arab Spring movement also reached all the way to Libya, however, things were quite different as instead of having peaceful protests, opposition forces were picking up arms and fighting the Libyan military. Due to the then-leader of Libya, Col. Mummar Gaddafi, having never truly been a Western puppet, America launched a propaganda war to allow the US-NATO war machine to intervene in Libya on the grounds of "humanitarian intervention."

The question that must be first asked is why the West even wanted to intervene in Libya. The answer is because Libya has Africa's largest oil reserves and Western oil companies wanted access to them. However, there are also larger economic reasons. Months prior to the intervention, Gaddafi had called upon African and Muslim nations to adopt a single currency: the gold dinar. This would have excluded the dollar as the gold dinar would have been used to purchase goods, thus threatening the economies of Western nations. However, the creation of a gold dinar may have also empowered the people of Africa, something black activists say the US wants to avoid at all costs.

"The US [has] denied self-determination to Africans inside the US, so we are not surprised by anything the US would do to hinder the self-determination of Africans on the continent," says Cynthia Ann McKinney, a former US Congresswoman. [47]

There was also geopolitics at work as during the war, Gaddafi "vowed to expel Western energy companies from the country and replace them with oil firms from China, India, and Russia." [48] This would have effectively excluded the West from ever getting at Libya's oil. By ousting Gaddafi, the West would be able to have a puppet regime to counter Chinese and Russian moves in North Africa as well as access to Libyan oil.

What many of the media never asked until the conflict was nearing its end was who exactly were the rebels. In the Iraq war, most of the foreign fighters came from Libya. Specifically, **almost all of them came from eastern Libya, the center of the anti-Gaddafi rebellion.**" [49] (emphasis added) A Libyan rebel commander even admitted that some of his soldiers had links to Al Qaeda:

In an interview with the Italian newspaper Il Sole 24 Ore, Mr. al-Hasidi admitted that he had recruited "around 25″ men from the Derna area in eastern Libya to fight against coalition troops in Iraq. Some of them, he said, are "today are on the front lines in Adjabiya".

Mr. al-Hasidi insisted his fighters "are patriots and good Muslims, not terrorists, "but added that the **"members of al-Qaeda are also good Muslims and are fighting against the invader."** [50] (emphasis added)

Thus, the US and NATO were backing terrorists, yet they may have known seeing as how a 2007 West Point Study revealed that the Benghazi-Darnah-Tobruk area was a world leader in Al Qaeda suicide bomber recruitment. [51]

Due to the US and its NATO allies not wanting to look like the imperialists they truly were, Obama pressured the UN to pass a resolution allowing for the establishment of a no fly zone over Libya and an arms embargo on the nation. However, both were broken quite soon. The UN resolution clearly allowed all member states "acting nationally or through regional organizations or arrangements, to take all necessary measures to protect civilians under threat of attack in the country, including Benghazi, while excluding a foreign occupation force of any form on any part of Libyan territory." [52] However, the imperialists admitted that they wanted to overthrow Gaddafi in an op-ed piece, when Cameron, Sarkozy, and Obama stated: "Our duty and our mandate under U.N. Security Council Resolution 1973 is to protect civilians, and we are doing that. **It is not to remove [Gaddafi] by force. But it is impossible to imagine a future for Libya with [Gaddafi] in power**." [53] (emphasis added) The US and NATO clearly stated that their main goal was to overthrow Gaddafi.

The hypocrisy of the West ran deep as they found an excuse to intervene in Libya, but not in Egypt, Bahrain, Palestine, or any other location where people were being oppressed by local regimes. However, Western hypocrisy was shown near the outset of the conflict when it was reported that Egypt's military had begun to ship arms to the rebels with Washington's knowledge. [54] This clearly shows that supposed arms embargo on Libya was in reality, an embargo on Gaddafi's forces.

To whip up support for their "intervention," a massive media propaganda campaign was conducted against Gaddafi. The mainstream media were reporting things such as Gaddafi gave his troops Viagra to rape women, bombed civilians, and that Libyan troops gunned down civilians. Despite these claims being false, the mainstream media still reported it. However, what many people ignored was the fact of rebel and NATO war crimes. In mid-August, "a NATO bombing campaign near the Libyan city of Zlitan earlier this month reportedly killed almost 100 civilians — more than half of them women and children." [55] However, NATO denied all claims arguing that they had struck legitimate targets. This is just one example of many NATO war crimes in Libya, ranging from killing civilians to bombing the rebels themselves.

There were also reports that Libyan rebels were targeting and killing black Africans. All across eastern Libya the rebels "and their supporters [were] detaining, intimidating and frequently beating African immigrants and black Libyans, accusing them of fighting as mercenaries on behalf of [Gaddafi]," in some cases "executed suspected mercenaries captured in battle, according to Human Rights Watch and local Libyans," and "arbitrarily killed some mercenaries and in others cases failed to distinguish between them and non-combatants." [56] Yet, despite these and other numerous reports, the Libyan rebels excused their war crimes, saying that they didn't have the structures in place to deal with matters such as these.

What was also somewhat ignored was the fact that the rebels were extremely fractured; only united in their goal to overthrow Gaddafi. This was clearly seen after the assassination of General Al-Younes and two top military commanders' aides. Their deaths "resulted in internal fighting within the Transitional Council" with "Factional divisions [developing] within rebel forces." [57] This factional divide may soon play itself out in the creation of a new Libyan government.

Finally, there was the fact that Western special forces were on the ground. The initial appearance of Western special forces was when British SAS troops were captured near Benghazi in March. However, US CIA agents were in Libya [58] and there may have been French and US special forces in Libya aiding the rebels. In a March interview on The O'Reilly Show, retired Colonel David Hunt of the US Army and Lt. Col. Tony Shaffer, a former Army intelligence officer were interviewed about the situation in Libya. Hunt stated the following when asked about special forces being in Libya:

**Yes, absolutely. You've got British service been in there about three weeks ago and actually got captured and released. The French GIGN have been in there and our special forces and our U.S. intelligence operatives and their assets. We do not conduct operations like this, large scale air operations, without people on the ground.** They have been very successful, very good, not a lot of contact with the rebels because you don't know who to talk to. But, yes, we have got intel gathering and rescue guys and special operations guys on the ground, have had them for about 12 days. [59] (emphasis added)

Shaffer agreed, saying:

**Yes, I have heard from my sources — I got a call from one of my key sources on Monday and that's exactly what's going on**. Let's be really clear here. You have got to have these individuals doing what Dave just said, especially when you are talking about trying to protect, and the stated goal here, Bill, is humanitarian support. **So you don't want to have weapons hitting the wrong targets. So, Dave is very good on the fact that we have special operations guys sitting there with laser designators.** Bill, you saw... [60] (emphasis added)

The Americans constantly denied that they had boots on the ground, yet, as usual, they were lying.

The imperialists already had plans for a post-Gaddafi Libya, which consisted of "proposals for a 10,000-15,000 strong 'Tripoli task force', resourced and supported by the United Arab Emirates, to take over the Libyan capital, secure key sites and arrest high-level Gaddafi supporters." [61] However, the plan may be problematic as it is "highly reliant on the defection of parts of the Gaddafi security apparatus to the rebels after his overthrow." [62] There were far reaching economic consequences as it was reported that the new government would favor Western oil companies at the expense of Russian, Chinese, and Brazilian firms. [63]

Due to the imperialists succeeding in Libya, many are worried that the US-NATO war machine may set its sights on a new target: Syria.

*Syria*

Protests in Syria began in earnest in May 2011 and have not let up since then. While there are calls for intervention into Syria, there is much at stake for America in terms of Syria's relationship with Iran.

The Americans are quite interested in the link between Iran and Syria, noting that there have been several joint ventures between the two nations in the financial and manufacturing sectors, as it was noted that "there have been several reports of increased Iranian investment and trade with Syria," "Iran has stated its intention to establish a joint Iranian-Syrian bank, possibly involving Bank Saderat and the Commercial Bank of Syria," and "the Iran Khodro Industrial Group has established a car assembly plant in Syria through a joint venture known as the Syrian- Iranian Motor Company." [64] There are also military links as Iran supplies weapons to Syria which, from the US perspective, pose a threat to its ally Israel. "In June 2010, Iran reportedly sent Syria an air defense radar system designed to detect Israeli aircraft or possibly increase the accuracy of Syrian and Hezbollah missile strikes against Israel in the event of a regional war." [65] Thus, the US was deeply worried about the link between two anti-American nations and the growing friendship between them.

Due to these worries, the US became involved in Syria's protest movement, using methods that are similar to the ones the Americans used in the Egyptian revolution and in the Libya conflict.

**For the past five to six years, the US policy toward Syria has used what could be called a two-pronged strategy to push for regime change.** The US has supported "civil society" activists or external opposition organizations. It has also worked to delegitimize, destabilize and isolate the country through the application of sanctions and various other measures, which could be applied to exploit vulnerabilities. [66] (emphasis added)

One "civil society" organization that is being used by the US is the Movement for Justice and Development (MJD), which is "closely affiliated with the London-based satellite channel Barada TV, which started broadcasting in April 2009 but 'ramped up operations to cover the mass protests in Syria.'" [67] The Americans may have wanted to work with MJD due to the fact that they are a moderate Islamic group which wants to end the Assad regime via democratic reforms. Their plans may very well play right into America's hands as if the US does intervene in Syria, they can back the MJD and argue that they are the same as Libya's rebels: people who want to end their oppressive regime and replace it with a democracy.

The US is using organizations such as "Freedom House, American Bar Association, American University, Internews and work done by MEPI with the Aspen Strategic Initiative Institute, Democracy Council of California, Regents of the University of New Mexico and the International Republican Institute" [68] to aid in fomenting regime change in Syria by working with and funding Syrian "civil society" groups.

There have been many reports of the Syrian regime attacking unarmed protesters; however, one should be quite skeptical of these reports. The US media has reported that there are violent Syrian protesters [69], which should make one question the official narrative that the protesters are peaceful. One must also include the fact that there are absolutely no outside media sources in Syria whatsoever. Journalists have contacts whom they can get information from, but who says that these sources are being objective, much less telling the truth? All the reports that are being shown in the mainstream media may very well be half-truths, if not outright fabrications.

The US may very well plan to attack Syria if manipulating civil societies does not work.

The Arab Spring, while an overall movement to overthrow oppressive regimes, has too many times been co-opted by foreign powers who seek only their personal gain. Due to this, the Arab people may never experience true freedom.

**Debt Ceiling and Credit Downgrade**

Once again, while the Empire was busy abroad attempting to impose its will on other nations, it was having major fiscal problems at home. In July 2011 the debt ceiling debate began as the Republicans decided to make what should have been a non-issue into a major problem and almost let the nation default in the process.

The debt ceiling would have been passed as usual, yet the Tea Partiers in the House decided to refuse to increase the debt ceiling, citing the fact that the US was already $14 trillion in debt and something needed to be done to solve the debt crisis before it became a major problem. Their remedy for the massive debt was to implement massive austerity measures. The Republicans specifically wanted to target Social Security, Medicare, and Medicaid for large cuts. The Democrats barely put up a fight to defend their constituents, and the debt ceiling agreement ended up being compromised solely of spending cuts, with a 'Super Congress' (officially known as the United States Congress Joint Select Committee on Deficit Reduction) of 6 Democrats and six Republicans to come together and decide which group they were going to hurt the most.

While the media ate up the entire story, they didn't ask any serious questions such as how did the US ended up with such a massive debt in the first place. The answer is because of the Wall Street bailouts, the quest for global military domination, tax cuts for the super-rich, and the increasing costs of healthcare, mainly due to medical insurance companies jacking up prices. However, the corporate media, which is in the hands of the ruling elite, has created a perception that the reason for this debt crisis is due to social programs even though this is completely false. [70] In the debt ceiling debacle, this perception would win out and would bring about America's credit downgrade.

Standard & Poor's downgraded the US debt rating to AA+ due to its loss of confidence in the US government and the stock market plunged as people viewed the downgrade as an indication that the US may very well be in decline. However, there were already signals prior to the S&P downgrade that America's economic situation was not well. In July, the IMF effectively pronounced the US bankrupt. [71] That same month, Dagong, a Chinese credit-rating agency, pointed out the problems with increasing the debt ceiling, stating that "Raising the [debt] limit is just a legislative measure to allow the government to borrow more money, but it does not change the fact that the US lacks momentum for economic growth" and that "The fundamental problem is that the US' ability to generate wealth is far from compensating its increasing debt." [72] (emphasis added) The month before that, German rating agency Feri downgraded US bonds from AAA to AA on the grounds that "The U.S. government has fought the effects of the financial market crisis primarily by an increase in government debt" and they do "not see that there is sufficient attention being paid to other measures" [73] of how to combat the financial crisis.

However, this brings up the larger picture of the role of credit rating agencies. Usually, they can be used as an indicator of the creditworthiness of a nation, but now it seems that they have undue influence in the economic and political realms of a nation. In essence, they can hold an entire country hostage by threatening to downgrade the nation's credit rating if the agency's demands aren't fulfilled.

**The Future of the American Empire**

The American Empire has is now obviously in decline due to its waging of wars, tax cuts for the super wealthy, and massive debt. Thus this brings up the question that is on the minds of many Americans: What will happen to America in the future?

Economically, the US may not fare well as even after the bailout of Wall Street and $700 billion meant to stimulate the economy, the "insolvency of the global financial system, and of the Western financial system in the first place, returns again to the front of the stage" [74] in the form of the US credit downgrade. US government debt may take a major hit as "US banks are starting to reduce their use of US Treasury Bonds to guarantee their transactions for fear of the increasing risks weighing on US government debt" and even US allies such as Saudi Arabia are worried about US debt. [75] The dollar is most likely going to decline to "something of a first among equals in a basket of currencies" which very well "may force the US into difficult tradeoffs between achieving ambitious foreign policy goals and the high domestic costs of supporting those objectives," [76] such as constant military adventures every decade and massive aid to client states.

With the rise of new powers such as China, US military superiority, while safe on conventional grounds, may be shaky in the realm of cyberspace and the US may have its rule challenged, not only in the Asia-Pacific region by China, but also in Latin America by Brazil and eastern Europe by Russia. This could potentially create situation where the Empire will have to choose between fighting against these new adversaries or work with them. If the Empire's attitude today is any indication, they will fight rather than work with the new powers to create a multipolar international order.

While the American Empire is currently in decline, this could potentially lead to what has been called "a blossoming of the republic" in which the United States returns to its democratic and moral roots. No longer will the US support dictators and third-world governments, disregard international and domestic law, and prevent the self-determination of all peoples. Rather, the new America will respect the rule of law, support organic democratic uprisings, and reject its past history of militarism and unilateralism. This is the vision of America that I and many others around the world wish to see come to fruition.


**Endnotes**

1: The White House, *Remarks by the President in Address to the Nation on the Way Forward in Afghanistan and Pakistan*, http://www.whitehouse.gov/the-press-office/remarks-president- address-nation-way-forward-afghanistan-and-pakistan (December 1, 2009)

2: Ibid

3: Michel Chossoudovsky, "Obama and the Nobel Prize: When War becomes Peace, When the Lie becomes the Truth," *Global Research*, October 11, 2009, (http://www.globalresearch.ca/index.php?context=va&aid=15622)

4: Steven Thomma, "Obama to extend Iraq withdrawal timetable: 50,000 troops to stay," *McClatchy DC*, February 27, 2009, (http://www.mcclatchydc.com/news/nation- world/world/middle-east/article24527323.html)

5: Ibid

6: Capitol Hill Blue, *American Soldiers Still Fighting In Iraq*, http://www.capitolhillblue.com/node/33255 (September 24, 2010)

7: Reid J. Epstein, "Panetta: US to Stay In Iraq into 2012," *Politico*, August 19, 2011, (http://www.politico.com/news/stories/0811/61731.html)

8: Adam Entous, Siobahn Gorman, "CIA Plans Yemen Drone Strikes," *Wall Street Journal*, June 14, 2011, (http://www.wsj.com/articles/SB10001424052702303848104576384051572679110)

9: Chris Woods, "Drone War Exposed- The Complete Picture of CIA Strikes in Pakistan," *The Bureau of Investigative Journalism*, August 10, 2011 (http://www.thebureauinvestigates.com/2011/08/10/most-complete-picture-yet-of-cia-drone- strikes/)

10: Ibid

11: Chris Woods, "Attacking The Messenger: How the CIA Tried to Undermine Drone Study," *The Bureau of Investigative Journalism*, August 12, 2011 (http://www.thebureauinvestigates.com/2011/08/12/attacking-the-messenger-how-the-cia-tried- to-undermine-drone-study/)

12: Aweys Cadde, "Airstrikes Hit Lower Juba... Again," *Somalia Report*, July 6, 2011 (http://www.somaliareport.com/index.php/post/1105/Airstrikes_Hit_Lower_JubaAgain)

13: Scott Shane, "US Approves Targeted Killing of American Cleric," *New York Times*, April 6, 2010 (http://www.nytimes.com/2010/04/07/world/middleeast/07yemen.html)

14: Dana Priest, "US Military Teams, Intelligence Deeply Involved in Aiding Yemen on Strikes," *Washington Post*, January 27, 2010 (http://www.washingtonpost.com/wp-dyn/content/article/2010/01/26/AR2010012604239.html?hpid=topnews&sid=ST2010012700394 )

15: Granite Island Group, *Executive Order 12333*, http://www.tscm.com/EO12333.html (December 4, 1981)

16: United States Strategic Command, *US Cyber Command*, https://web.archive.org/web/20110216120928/http://www.stratcom.mil/factsheets/Cyber_Comm and/ (October 2010)

17: Julian E. Barnes, Siobah Gorman, "Cyber Combat: Act of War," *Wall Street Journal*, May 31, 2011 (http://www.wsj.com/articles/SB10001424052702304563104576355623135782718)

18: Richard Esposito, Brian Ross, "Bush Authorizes New Covert Action Against Iran," *ABC News*, May 24, 2007 (http://blogs.abcnews.com/theblotter/2007/05/bush_authorizes.html)

19: Colin Freeman, William Lowther, "US Funds Terror Groups to Sow Chaos in Iran," *Telegraph*, February 25, 2007 (http://www.telegraph.co.uk/news/worldnews/1543798/US-funds- terror-groups-to-sow-chaos-in-Iran.html#)

20: Ibid

21: Seymour M. Hersh, "Preparing The Battlefield," *New Yorker*, July 7, 2008 (http://www.newyorker.com/magazine/2008/07/07/preparing-the-battlefield)

22: Ibid

23: Ibid

24: Rajaram Panda, "Cheonan Sinking: Implications for Peace in Northeast Asia," *Mainstream Weekly*, June 1, 2010 (http://www.mainstreamweekly.net/article2094.html)

25-28:Ibid

29: Xinhua News, *China Opposes Any Military Acts in Exclusive Economic Zone Without Permission*, http://news.xinhuanet.com/english2010/china/2010-11/26/c_13624036.htm (November 26, 2010)

30: Rick Rozoff, "North Korea As A Pretext: US Builds Military Alliance Against China and Russia," *Global Research*, December 3, 2010 (http://www.globalresearch.ca/index.php?context=va&aid=22248)

31: Wikileaks, *US Intelligence Planned to Destroy Wikileaks*, http://web.archive.org/web/20100821150751/http://mirror.wikileaks.info/leak/us-intel- wikileaks.pdf (March 15, 2010)

32: Ibid

33: Robert Booth, Julian Borger, "US Diplomats Spied on UN Leadership," *The Guardian*, November 28, 2010 (http://www.guardian.co.uk/world/2010/nov/28/us-embassy-cables-spying- un)

34: Jeffery T. Kuhner, "Kuhner: Assassinate Assange?" *Washington Times*, December 2, 2010 (http://www.washingtontimes.com/news/2010/dec/2/assassinate-assange/)

35: Ibid

36: James D. Catlin, "When it comes to Assange rape case, the Swedes are making it up as they go along," *Crikey*, December 2, 2010 (http://www.crikey.com.au/2010/12/02/when-it-comes-to- assange-r-pe-case-the-swedes-are-making-it-up-as-they-go-along/)

37: Bob Simon, "How A Slap Sparked Tunisia's Revolution," *CBS News*, February 22, 2011 (http://www.cbsnews.com/news/how-a-slap-sparked-tunisias-revolution-22-02-2011/)

38: Carol Migdalovitz, *Tunisia: Current Issues*, Federation of American Scientists, https://web.archive.org/web/20090804011900/http://www.fas.org/sgp/crs/row/RS21666.pdf (June 29, 2009)

39: Ibid

40: Christopher Schmidt, "US Helping Shape Outcome of Tunisian Uprising," *Associated Foreign Press*, January 27, 2011 (http://web.archive.org/web/20110129042635/http://www.google.com/hostednews/afp/article/A LeqM5hDbfg1WFaPPd7sbU5Ghogi4YHQ2w?docId=CNG.148a6c382024ebbebe64021de441da c9.b91)

41: Ibid

42: Stephen Gowans, *The NED, Tibet, North Korea, and Zimbabwe*, What's Left http://gowans.wordpress.com/2010/03/22/the-ned-tibet-north-korea-and-zimbabwe/ (March 22, 2010)

43: Freedom House, *Egyptian Activists Stress Democracy, Human Rights in talks with Secretary of State*, https://freedomhouse.org/article/egyptian-activists-stress-democracy-human-rights- talks-us-secretary-state?page=70&release=989 (May 28, 2009)

44: Islamic Human Rights Commission, *Bahrain's Revolution Underway as Day of Rage Announced*, http://www.ihrc.org.uk/activities/press-releases/9568-bahrains-revolution-underway- as-the-day-of-rage-announced (February 3, 2011)

45: Brad Knickerbocker, "US Faces Difficult Situation in Bahrain, home to US Fifth Fleet," *Christian Science Monitor*, February 9, 2011 (http://www.csmonitor.com/USA/Foreign- Policy/2011/0219/US-faces-difficult-situation-in-Bahrain-home-to-US-Fifth-Fleet)

46: Yiink, "Bahrain Uprising Police Shoot Unarmed Protester," https://www.youtube.com/watch?v=CWeakKzY1E8 (March 15, 2011)

47: Russia Today, *Saving The World Economy From Gaddafi*, http://rt.com/news/economy-oil- gold-libya/ (May 5, 2011)

48: Newsmax, *Gadhafi to Kick Out Western Oil Firms, Turning to Russia and China*, http://www.newsmax.com/Newsfront/gadhafi-west-oilcompanies-conflict/2011/03/17/id/389809 (March 17, 2011)

49: David Wood, "Anti-American Extremists Among Libyan Rebels US Has Vowed To Protect," *Huffington Post*, March 19, 2011 (http://www.huffingtonpost.com/2011/03/19/extremists-among-libya-rebels_n_837894.html)

50: Duncan Gardham, Nick Squires, Praven Swami, "Libyan Rebel Commander Admits His Fighters Have Al-Qaeda Links," *Telegraph*, March 25, 2011 (http://www.telegraph.co.uk/news/worldnews/africaandindianocean/libya/8407047/Libyan-rebel-commander-admits-his-fighters-have-al-Qaeda-links.html)

51: Webster G. Tarpley, "The CIA's Libya Rebels: The Same Terrorists Who Killed US, NATO Troops in Iraq," *Global Research*, March 24, 2011 (http://www.globalresearch.ca/index.php?context=va&aid=23949)

52: UN Security Council, *Security Council Approves 'No-Fly Zone' over Libya, Authorizing 'All Necessary Measures' to Protect Civilians, by Vote of 10 in Favor with 5 Abstentions*, http://www.un.org/News/Press/docs/2011/sc10200.doc.htm#Resolution (March 17, 2011)

53: David Cameron, Barack Obama, Nicolas Sarkozy, "Libya's Pathway to Peace," *New York Times*, April 15, 2011 (http://www.nytimes.com/2011/04/15/opinion/15iht-edlibya15.html)

54: Charles Levinson, Matthew Rosenberg, "Egypt Said to Arm Libya Rebels," *Wall Street Journal*, March 17, 2011 (http://online.wsj.com/article/SB10001424052748704360404576206992835270906.html)

55: Alex Newman, "NATO Rebels Accused of Committing War Crimes in Libya," *The New American*, August 18, 2011 (http://www.thenewamerican.com/world-mainmenu-26/africa- mainmenu-27/8651-nato-rebels-accused-of-war-crimes-in-libya)

56: David Zucchino, "Libyan Rebels Accused of Targeting Blacks," *Los Angeles Times*, March 4, 2011 (http://articles.latimes.com/2011/mar/04/world/la-fg-libya-mercenaries-20110305)

57: Michel Chossudovsky, Mahdi Darius Nazemroaya, "The War on Libya: Divisions within The Transitional Council and Rebel Forces," *Global Research*, July 29, 2011 (http://www.globalresearch.ca/index.php?context=va&aid=25827)

58: Mark Mazzetti, Eric Schmitt, "CIA Agents in Libya Aid Airstrikes and Meet Rebels," *New York Times*, March 31, 2011 (http://www.nytimes.com/2011/03/31/world/africa/31intel.html?_r=1)

59: Fox News, *Are US Troops Already on the Ground in Libya*, https://web.archive.org/web/20110327145818/http://www.foxnews.com/on- air/oreilly/transcript/are-us-troops-already-ground-libya (March 24, 2011)

60: Ibid

61: The Australian, *Iraq Haunts Plan for Post-Gaddafi Libya*, http://www.theaustralian.com.au/news/world/iraq-haunts-plans-for-post-gaddafi-libya/story- e6frg6so-1226111211251 (August 9, 2011)

62: Ibid

63: Euro News, *Libya Endgame Pulls Down Oil Prices*, http://www.euronews.net/2011/08/22/libya-end-game-pulls-down-oil-prices/ (August 22, 2011)

64: Jeremy M. Sharp, *Syria: Issues for the 112th Congress and Background on US Sanctions*, Federation of American Scientists, http://web.archive.org/web/20110504225926/http://www.fas.org/sgp/crs/mideast/RL33487.pdf (March 28, 2011)

65: Ibid

66: Kevin Gosztola, "Wikileaks Cables Show US Strategy for Regime Change in Syria As Protesters Are Massacred," *Shadowproof*, August 5, 2011 (https://shadowproof.com/2011/08/05/wikileaks-cables-the-us-strategy-to-push-for-regime- change-in-syria/)

67: Ibid

68: Ibid

69: CBS News, *Syria's Once Peaceful Protesters Turn To Guns*, http://www.cbsnews.com/stories/2011/05/30/501364/main20067379.shtml (May 30, 2011)

70: Ismael Hossein-Zadeh, "Escalating Military Spending and the Debt Ceiling: Lots of Posturing, No Solution," *Global Research*, July 30, 2011 (http://www.globalresearch.ca/index.php?context=va&aid=25838)

71: Laurence Kotlikoff, "US Is Bankrupt and We Don't Even Know It," *Bloomberg*, August 11, 2010 (http://www.bloomberg.com/news/2010-08-11/u-s-is-bankrupt-and-we-don-t-even-know- commentary-by-laurence-kotlikoff.html)

72: Wei Tian, "Dagong is likely to downgrade US rating," *China Daily*, July 13, 2011 (http://www.chinadaily.com.cn/cndy/2011-07/13/content_12889286.htm)

73: Zero Hedge, *German Rating Agency Feri Downgrades US Government Bonds AAA to AA*, http://www.zerohedge.com/article/german-rating-agency-feri-downgrades-us-government- bonds-aaa-aa (June 10, 2011)

74: Global Europe Anticipation Bulletin, *Europe and America: Global Debt Crisis*, June 21, 2011, Global Research, (http://www.globalresearch.ca/index.php?context=va&aid=25354)

75: Ibid

76: Office of the Director of National Intelligence, *Global Trends 2025: A Transformed World*, http://web.archive.org/web/20081122005637/http://www.dni.gov/nic/PDF_2025/2025_Global_T rends_Final_Report.pdf (November 2008)

Non-governmental organizations (NGOs) are an increasingly important part of the 21st century international landscape performing a variety of humanitarian tasks pertaining to issues of poverty, the environment, and civil liberties to name a few. However, there is a dark side to NGOs. They have been and are currently being used as tools of foreign policy, specifically with the United States. Instead of using purely military force, the US has now moved to using NGOs as tools in its foreign policy implementation, specifically the National Endowment for Democracy, Freedom House, and Amnesty International.

**National Endowment for Democracy**

According to its website, the National Endowment for Democracy (NED) is "a private, nonprofit foundation dedicated to the growth and strengthening of democratic institutions around the world," [1] however this is sweet sounding description is actually quite far from the truth.

The history of the NED begins immediately after the Reagan administration. Due to the massive revelations concerning the CIA in the 1970s, specifically that they were involved in attempted assassinations of heads of state, the destabilization of foreign governments, and were illegally spying on the US citizens, this tarnished the image of the CIA and of the US government as a whole. While there were many committees that were created during this time to investigate the CIA, the Church Committee (led by Frank Church, a Democrat from Idaho) was of critical importance as its findings "demonstrated the need for perpetual surveillance of the intelligence community and resulted in the creation of the permanent Select Committee on Intelligence." [2] The Select Committee on Intelligence's purpose was to oversee federal intelligence activities and while oversight and stability came in, it seemed to signal that the CIA's 'party' of assassination plots and coups were over. Yet, this was to continue, but in a new way: under the guise of a harmful NGO whose purpose was to promote democracy around the world- the National Endowment for Democracy.

The NED was meant to be a tool of US foreign policy from its outset. It was the brainchild of Allen Weinstein who, before creating the Endowment, was a professor at Brown and Georgetown Universities, had served on the *Washington Post*'s editorial staff, and was the Executive Editor of The Washington Quarterly, Georgetown's Center for Strategic and International Studies, a right-wing neoconservative think tank which would in the future have ties to imperial strategists such as Henry Kissinger and Zbigniew Brzezinski. [3] He stated in a 1991 interview that "A lot of what we do today was done covertly 25 years ago by the CIA." [4]

The first director of the Endowment, Carl Gershman, outright admitted that the Endowment was a front for the CIA. In 1986 he stated:

> **We should not have to do this kind of work covertly. It would be terrible for democratic groups around the world to be seen as subsidized by the CIA**. We saw that in the '60s, and that's why it has been discontinued. We have not had the capability of doing this, and that's why the endowment was created. [5] (emphasis added)

It can be further observed that the Endowment is a tool of the US government as ever since its founding in 1983, it "has received an annual appropriation approved by the United States Congress as part of the United States Information Agency budget." [6]

No sooner than the Endowment was founded did it begin funding groups that would support US interests. From 1983 to 1984, the Endowment was active in France and "supported a 'trade union-like organization that for professors and students' to counter 'left-wing organizations of professors,'" [7] through the funding of seminars, posters, books, and pamphlets that encouraged opposition to leftist thought. In the mid and late 1990s, the NED continued its fight against organized labor by giving in excess of $2.5 million to the American Institute of Free Labor Development which was a CIA front used to undermine progressive labor unions.

Later on, the Endowment became involved in interfering with elections in Venezuela and Haiti in order to undermine leftwing movements there. The NED is and continues to be a source of instability in nations across the globe that don't kneel before US imperial might. Yet the Endowment funds another pseudo-NGO: Freedom House.

**Freedom House**

Freedom House was originally founded in 1941 as a pro-democracy and pro-human rights organization. While this may have been true in the past, in the present day, Freedom House is quite involved in pushing US interests in global politics and its leaders have connections to rather unsavory organizations, such as current Executive Director David Kramer being a Senior Fellow to the Project for the New American Century, many of whose members are responsible for the current warmongering status of the US. [8]

During the Bush administration, the President used Freedom House to support the so-called War on Terror. In a March 29, 2006 speech, President Bush stated that Freedom House "declared the year 2005 was one of the most successful years for freedom since the Freedom House began measuring world freedom more than 30 years ago" and that the US should not rest "until the promise of liberty reaches every people and every nation" because "In this new century, the advance of freedom is a vital element of our strategy to protect the American people, and to secure the peace for generations to come." [9]

Later, it was revealed that Freedom House became more and more supportive of the Bush administration's policies because of the funding it was getting from the US government. According to its own internal report in 2007, the US government was providing some 66% of funding for the organization. [10] This funding mainly came from the US Agency for International Development (USAID), the US State Department, and the National Endowment for Democracy. Thus, we see not only the political connection of Freedom House to US government, but major financial connections as well.

It should be noted, however, that Freedom House was not alone in supporting the government. Under the Bush administration, the US government forced NGOs to become more compliant to their demands. In 2003, USAID Administrator Andrew Natsios stated in a speech given at a conference of NGOs that in Afghanistan the relationship between NGOs and USAID does affect the survival of the Karzai regime and that Afghans "believe [their life] is improving through mechanisms that have nothing to do with the U.S. government and nothing to do with the central government. That is a very serious problem." [11] On the situation in Iraq, Natsios stated that when it comes to NGO work in the country "proving results counts, but showing a connection between those results and U.S. policy counts as well." [12] (emphasis added) NGOs were essentially told that they were tools of the US government and were being made part of the imperial apparatus.

Most recently, Freedom House was active in the Arab Spring, where they aided in the training and financing of civil society groups and individuals "including the April 6 Youth Movement in Egypt, the Bahrain Center for Human Rights and grass-roots activists like Entsar Qadhi, a youth leader in Yemen." [13]

While the Endowment and Freedom House are being used as tools of US foreign policy that does not mean that the US government isn't looking for new tools, namely Amnesty International.

**Amnesty International**

The human rights organization Amnesty International is the newest tool in the imperial toolbox of the American Empire. In January 2012, Suzanne Nossel was appointed the new Executive Director of Amnesty International by the group itself. Before coming to Amnesty, Nossel already had deep connections to the US government as she had "served as Deputy Assistant Secretary for International Organizations at the U.S. Department of State." [14]

Nossel is known for coining the term 'smart power' which she defined as knowing that "US interests are furthered by enlisting others on behalf of U.S. goals, through alliances, international institutions, careful diplomacy, and the power of ideals." [15] While this definition may seem harmless, 'smart power' seems to be an enhanced version of Joseph Nye's 'soft power,' which itself is defined as "the ability to obtain the outcomes one wants through attraction rather than using the carrots and sticks of payment or coercion." [15] A possible example of this 'smart power' is the war in Libya, where the US used the UN as a means to get permission to engage in 'humanitarian intervention.'

Yet, even before Nossel was appointed to Amnesty, the group was unwittingly aiding in the media war against Syria. In a September 1, 2011 Democracy Now interview, Neil Sammonds, the researcher and one of the author's for Amnesty's report Deadly Detention: Deaths in Custody Amid Popular Protest in Syria, spoke about the manner in which the research was done for the report. He stated:

**I've not been into Syria. Amnesty International has not been allowed into the country during these events, although we have requested it. So the research for this report was done mostly from London, but also from some work in neighboring countries and through communications with a large network of contacts and relatives of the families**, and, you know, other sources. [16] (emphasis added)

How can one write a report with any amount of authority if their only sources are through second-hand sources that may or may not have a bias or an agenda to push? How can you write a report using sources whose information has no way of being verified? It is reminiscent of the media war against Gaddafi, where it was reported in the mainstream media that he was bombing his own people and had given Viagra to his soldiers as so they could rape women, but absolutely none of this was verified.

While NGOs can have a positive influence on society at large, one must be aware of their background, who's in charge of them, and from whom they are getting funding from because the nature of the NGO is changing, it is being more and more integrated into the imperial apparatus of domination and exploitation. NGOs are fast becoming the missionaries of empire.

## Endnotes

1: National Endowment for Democracy, *About The National Endowment For Democracy*, http://www.ned.org/about

2: United States Senate, *Church Committee Created*, http://www.senate.gov/artandhistory/history/minute/Church_Committee_Created.htm

3: Right Web, *Center for Strategic and International Studies*, http://www.rightweb.irc-online.org/articles/display/Center_for_Strategic_and_International_Studies#P3782_823232 (January 8, 1989)

4: William Blum, *Rogue State: A Guide to the World's Only Superpower*, 3rd ed. (Monroe, ME: Common Courage Press, 2005) pg 239

5: Ibid, pg 239

6: Justia US Law, *Organization for the National Endowment for Democracy Title 22 Foreign Relations*, http://law.justia.com/cfr/title22/22-1.0.1.7.42.html

7: Blum, pg 240

8: Freedom House, *Staff Member Information David J. Kramer*, http://web.archive.org/web/20110630143054/http://freedomhouse.org/template.cfm?page=92&st aff=450

9: CNN, *President Bush Addresses Freedom House in Washington*, http://transcripts.cnn.com/TRANSCRIPTS/0603/29/se.01.html (March 29, 2006)

10: Freedom House, *2007 Annual Report*, http://web.archive.org/web/20100331104836/http://www.freedomhouse.org/uploads/special_rep ort/71.pdf

11: USAID, *Remarks by Andrew S. Natsios, Administrator*, USAID, https://web.archive.org/web/20110303144732/http://www.usaid.gov/press/speeches/2003/sp0305 21.html (May 21, 2003)

12: Ibid

13: Ron Nixon, "US Groups Helped Nurture Arab Spring," *New York Times*, April 15, 2011 (http://www.nytimes.com/2011/04/15/world/15aid.html?pagewanted=all)

14: Suzanne Posel, *Smart Power*, Democracy Arsenal, http://www.democracyarsenal.org/SmartPowerFA.pdf

15: Joseph Nye, "Barack Obama and Soft Power," *Huffington Post*, June 20, 2008 (http://www.huffingtonpost.com/joseph-nye/barack-obama-and-soft-pow_b_106717.html)

16: Democracy Now, *Amnesty International Decries Assad Regime's "Brutal" Crackdown on Syrian Protesters*, http://www.democracynow.org/2011/9/1/amnesty_international_decries_assad_regimes_brutal (September 1, 2011)

It has been revealed in May 2012 that the US and Turkey are in fact aiding the Syrian rebels and that the push for intervention is growing. It is important to realize the affects of this not only in Syria, but also for that of Iran and Russia, two of the most prominent and vocal backers of the Assad regime.

The *Washington Post* stated on May 15, 2012 that the Syrian rebels "have begun receiving significantly more and better weapons in recent weeks, an effort paid for by Persian Gulf nations and coordinated in part by the United States, according to opposition activists and U.S. and foreign officials" (emphasis added). [1] It was also noted by *The Telegraph* that Turkey is arming the Syrian rebels. Michael Weiss wrote:

> **Rebel sources in Hatay told me last night that not only is Turkey supplying light arms to select battalion commanders, it is also training Syrians in Istanbul. Men from the unit I was embedded with were vetted and called up by Turkish intelligence in the last few days and large consignments of AK-47s are being delivered by the Turkish military to the Syrian-Turkish border**. No one knows where the guns came from originally, but no one much cares. [2] (emphasis added)

There is also help from the Muslim Brotherhood in Egypt which has "opened its own supply channel to the rebels, using resources from wealthy private individuals and money from Gulf States."

This influx of weapons is having a positive effect on the fighting as the Post noted that a clash that occurred on May 14, 2012 near the city of Rastan, with the rebels overrunning a Syrian army outpost, killing a total of 23 Syrian troops according to the Syrian Observatory of Human Rights. Yet, it could potentially boost the Assad regime as now the Syrian government's claims [3] that the violence is being caused by outside interference are verifiable.

It is quite important to factor in the role of the Russian government, one of the staunchest supporters of the Assad regime. Russia has been one of the few countries involved in Syria that seems to be legitimately interested in peace. The *New York Times* reported in February that two senior Russian officials, Foreign Minister Sergei Lavrov and Mikhail Fradkov, the director of Foreign Intelligence, had gone to Damascus to discuss "dialogue with the opposition, offering a referendum on a new constitution, and the Arab League resuming its 'stabilizing' mission."[4]

But they too, have their own interests namely military and commercial. Militarily, the Kremlin is concerned with ensuring that they are able to maintain their naval facilities at the port of Tartus, the only naval access Russia has into the Mediterranean, whereas commercially, Russia has made a considerable amount of money by selling arms to the Assad regime such as $500 million in weapons contracts.[5] Thus, if the Assad regime falls, the Russians will have to deal with a serious economic loss and have to confront the fact that they may be ejected from the Mediterranean, leaving them not only with a loss of power projection, but also being left out of the massive amount of oil and gas found there [6] and the economic and geopolitical power that comes with controlling such natural resources.

Iran, another major backer of the Assad regime, must also be kept in mind. It has been noted that Iran is aiding Assad financially by sending them money which is "funneled in through banks in Lebanon" and is assisting in other ways "[including] small arms and assistance in helping the Syrian government use computer monitoring to root out opposition using social media and other Internet tools."[7] Iran is aiding Syria due to the fact that Syria is Iran's only ally in the greater Middle East region. If Syria falls, Iran will be completely isolated and that, when coupled with the push to go to war in both the US and Israel, may very well result in an attack or invasion of Iran.

The increase in violence plays into the hands of the West, especially the United States. Weiss wrote that "Turkey wouldn't take such a course of action without express American consent or encouragement" and that Senator Joseph Lieberman wouldn't "indicate that the administration was inching toward a military response to the humanitarian crisis [...] unless he was fairly sure it was indeed doing so." Thus, the violence is being fomented by the US and its allies in an order to make way for 'humanitarian' intervention which will only result in regime change. This may be coming closer than we think as CNN reported that:

> **While troops from 19 countries, including the United States, have converged in Jordan for the Eager Lion military exercise, U.S. and Jordanian elite forces are doing additional training to prepare for potential fallout should Syria's government collapse.**
>
> **U.S. Army Green Berets are training Jordanian special forces in a number of so called "worst-case scenarios" including Syria's chemical and biological weapons** falling out of the control of government forces, U.S. sources tell CNN. [8] (emphasis added)

One must question as to why the US and Jordanian military would be preparing to go into Syria if it doesn't seem as if the current regime is going to go under anytime soon. It may be because the US and its allies are currently in the process of creating a situation as to where they will be able to send boots on the ground to secure Syria's chemical and biological weapons as well as have soldiers there to train and aid the Syrian rebels.

The road to war continues.

**Endnotes**

1: Karen DeYoung and Liz Sly, "Syrian rebels get influx of arms with gulf neighbors' money, U.S. coordination," *Washington Post*, May 15, 2012 (http://www.washingtonpost.com/world/national-security/syrian-rebels-get-influx-of-arms-with- gulf-neighbors-money-us-coordination/2012/05/15/gIQAds2TSU_story.html?wprss=rss_world)

2: Michael Weiss, "Syrian rebels say Turkey is arming and training them," *The Telegraph*, May 22, 2012 (http://blogs.telegraph.co.uk/news/michaelweiss/100159613/syrian-rebels-say-turkey- is-arming-and-training-them/)

3: Associated Press, *Syrian leader Assad says terrorists are behind unrest*, http://www.foxnews.com/world/2012/05/17/syrian-leader-says-terrorists-are-behind- unrest/ (May 17, 2012)

4: Dmitri Trenin, "Why Russia Supports Assad," *New York Times*, February 9, 2012 (http://www.nytimes.com/2012/02/10/opinion/why-russia-supports-assad.html?_r=1)

5: Fred Weir, "Russia closes deal on $550 million worth of warplanes for Syria," *Christian Science Monitor*, January 23, 2012 (http://www.csmonitor.com/World/Global- News/2012/0123/Russia-closes-deal-on-550-million-worth-of-warplanes-for-Syria)

6: F. William Engdahl, "New Mediterranean oil and gas bonanza," *Russia Today*, February 26, 2012 (http://www.rt.com/news/reserves-offshore-middle-east-engdahl-855/)

7: Barbara Starr, "Iran propping up Syria's dwindling cash reserves," *CNN*, May 21, 2012 (http://security.blogs.cnn.com/2012/05/21/iran-propping-up-syrias-dwindling-cash-reserves/)

8: *CNN*, May 21, 2012

Currently, the crisis in Syria is chaotic and ever-changing with the situation consistently on uneven ground. The ongoing fighting between Western-backed rebel forces and the Syrian regime have plunged the country into a civil war and many government figures, such as US Senators John McCain and Joe Lieberman, as well as Vice Israeli Prime Minister Shaul Mofaz, have argued for armed intervention against the Syrian regime.

It must be realized that tensions are quite high, as can be seen by the current debacle over a Turkish plane being downed on June 22, 2012. There are competing claims as to whose airspace it was in when the plane was shot down with the Turks, while admitting violating Syrian airspace, claimed that the plane was shot down in international waters while the Syria claims that it was taken down in their airspace.

The wreckage was found in Syrian territorial waters. This tense situation has resulted in the Turks threatening military action if there is "any future violation of its border by Syrian military elements." [1]While the situation is still murky, military intervention has not been taken off the table. A view of what is at stake for major players, how an intervention would go about, and what its effects on the region could potentially be is thus needed.

**Who Cares About Syria?**

There are several major players in the Syrian crisis on both the regional and international scene, each with its own interests and objectives concerning Syria in the geo-political, military, and economic realms. While many of these actors are allied with one another, be it by military pact or an alliance of convenience, it does not mean that their interests are the same, and as such one must examine the interests of each actor on an individual level.

**The United States**

The United States has its concerns with Syria that are primarily linked to Iran and terrorist organizations. In April 2010, the US government acknowledged that Syria "[continued] to support Hamas and Hezbollah" and had financial relations with Iran as Iranian companies "invested in concrete production, power generation, and urban transportation."[2]

At that time, such involvement with Iran was viewed as a problem for US interests due to their being the possibility of an Israeli strike on Iran. [3] The Syrian-Iranian alliance would potentially prove a problem for the US and Israel if a strike had occurred as it could have allowed the Iranians to wage an effective retaliation on Israel, thus harming America's interests by damaging a main regional ally. Today, the unease concerning the Syria-Iran alliance remains.

Concerning the recent civil war in Syria, the US seems to be hoping for the ousting of the Assad regime, stating that were the rebels to be found victorious in the civil war, "a more democratic Syria may seek to broaden its relationships with Western democracies and could choose to reduce its dependence on its current alliance with Iran." [4] Yet, while the US may want a rebel victory, they are worried about infiltration of the Syrian opposition by terrorist groups, namely Al Qaeda.

The Americans have been worried about the Syrian opposition being infiltrated for quite some time, with US officials stating in 2012 that "the violence and disorder paralyzing Syria appears to be creating opportunities for Al Qaeda operatives or other violent Islamist extremists to infiltrate the country and conduct or plan attacks" and that "Sunni extremists have infiltrated Syrian opposition groups, which may be unaware of the infiltration." [5]

Yet, this infiltration of Sunni extremists becomes rather interesting when one acknowledges that the US knows Al Qaeda is in the Syrian opposition and that the US is supporting the opposition. Al Qaeda's presence in the Syrian rebel groups was acknowledged in February by Director of Intelligence James R. Clapper when he said that "Members of al-Qaeda have infiltrated Syrian opposition groups, and likely executed recent bombings in the nation's capital and largest city." [6]

In June 2012 it was reported that the CIA was giving arms to the Syrian rebels. [7] Thus, not only is the US aiding to arm elements of Al Qaeda, but also the US and Al Qaeda are (however indirectly) working together to dismantle the Assad regime. What peculiar bedfellows this situation is making!

The final interest that the US has in the Syrian crisis is taking out a major Iranian ally. As was stated earlier, a Syrian-Iranian alliance deeply troubles the US and taking Syria out of the picture would aid America in its quest to isolate Iran on a regional level.

If the Assad regime were to fall, it would "cut off Iran's access to its proxies (Hezbollah in Lebanon and Hamas in Gaza) and visibly dent its domestic and international prestige, possibly forcing a hemorrhaging regime in Tehran to suspend its nuclear policies." [8]

Furthermore, with the Assads gone, it would result in Iran having no Middle East ally and being fully isolated, which would make it easier to invade or attack, seeing as how regime change in Iran is not off the table either.

**Israel**

Regarding the Assad situation, Israel is in a rather unenviable situation of essentially having to choose between an enemy it does know or siding with an unknown group that may be even more hostile to Israel.

Israel may choose to deal with the Assad regime, but not due to any fondness for it. It should be acknowledged that "Syria fought Israel directly in October 1973 and via proxy in Lebanon between 1982 and 2000. Since 2000, Syria has continued to support Hezbollah in Lebanon and Hamas in Gaza." [9]

Yet, while Israel is no fan of the current government, they do realize that "the Assad regime will not attempt to repossess the Golan Heights by military force and will meet with Israeli leaders to negotiate for peace, which occurred in 1991, 1995-1996, 1999-2001, and 2008." [10] Thus, while Assad may not be the friendliest neighbor, they are better than the alternative.

In addition to this, if a new regime is established that has more popular support than the current government (last checked, Assad had the support of 55% of the population [11]), it would allow for the Syrian government to position its military resources to external threats, namely the Jewish state. Thus, from an Israeli security standpoint it is better for the Syrian government to be tied up in suppressing rebels rather than potentially threatening Israel.

Just like the Americans, the situation regarding Iran is also at the front of the minds of the Israeli government, however it may not be for the reasons that one would assume. While governments and the media have been stating for years now that Iran is attempting to get nuclear weapons, in reality, Israeli (along with American and European) intelligence has acknowledged that **"Tehran does not have a bomb, has not decided to build one, and is probably years away from having a deliverable nuclear warhead."** [12] (emphasis added)

Thus, if Iran is "years away from having a deliverable nuclear warhead," much less building a nuclear weapon, this leads one to wonder what the real reason is that Israel is so worried about Iran possibly attaining nuclear weapons? The real reason is that Israel is worried about losing its nuclear monopoly in the region and security risks that come with it.

**Israel's real fear — losing its nuclear monopoly and therefore the ability to use its conventional forces at will throughout the Middle East — is the unacknowledged factor driving its decision-making toward the Islamic Republic. For Israeli leaders, the real threat from a nuclear-armed Iran is not the prospect of an insane Iranian leader** launching an unprovoked nuclear attack on Israel that would lead to the annihilation of both countries.

It's the fact that Iran doesn't even need to test a nuclear weapon to undermine Israeli military leverage in Lebanon and Syria. Just reaching the nuclear threshold could embolden Iranian leaders to call on their proxy in Lebanon, Hezbollah, to attack Israel, knowing that their adversary would have to think hard before striking back. (emphasis added) [13]

Thus, Israel does see Iran as a threat but much more to its regional military hegemony than rather a threat to its very existence.

Finally, both the current Assad regime and Iran come into play with Israel's final regional interest, Hezbollah. Israel is worried that they may gain non-conventional weapons if the Assad regime fell. Most likely, Israel is concerned about Hezbollah coming into chemical and biological weapons as they are already rehearsing drills for if such a situation were to occur. [14]

Such an occurrence would empower the terrorist group and by extension its financier, Iran, as well as become a potential security concern. The Israeli government realizes that "The outcome of the internal conflict in Syria will have a decisive impact on Hezbollah's strength and behavior, as well as on the political and security situation in Lebanon generally, and on Israel's relationship with Lebanon," [15] and thus are keeping a close eye on the situation in Lebanon and how what occurs in Syria could affect their northern neighbor.

## Russia

Russia's concerns about Syria stem from its military and commercial interests in Syria as well as its worries about the radical Islamist elements in the Syrian opposition and protecting its own borders.

Putin is pushing against military intervention due to the fact that the Kremlin thinks that "allowing the United States to use force at will and without any external constraints might lead to foreign interventions close to Russian borders, or even within those borders—namely, in the North Caucasus." [16]

This possibility of intervention near Russia's borders alarms the government as NATO has already been busy allying itself with many of the satellite states of the former Soviet Union in addition to the creation and implementation of the European missile shield. Russia may view such a possibility as an attempt to isolate and intimidate Russia.

Two other concerns of Russia are its commercial and military interests. In Syria, Russia maintains control of its naval base in Tartus, its only access to the Mediterranean Sea.

However, If Russia were to lose this base, it would hurt doubly as not only would Russia lose Middle East projection power, but also access to much of the natural gas and oil that is in the Mediterranean [17] and the power that comes with controlling such resources.

There are also commercial interests at stake as "Russia has long been Syria's primary military supplier and currently has about $4 billion worth of contracts for future arms deliveries to Damascus." Having a client for military weaponry is important but beyond that, Russian companies have made a number of investments in Syria.

These projects are worth roughly $20 billion and include some from Russia's powerful energy sector, such as a natural gas production facility and pipeline. [18] Thus, the loss of the Assad regime would not only hurt the defense sector, but would also harm the massive investments made in the Syrian energy sector.

Finally, Russia is deeply concerned with the extreme Islamist elements in the Syrian opposition. Russia backs Assad as they realize that "if the regime in Damascus falls, the whole 'terrorist international' that is now fighting against Bashar al-Assad will begin to fight elsewhere. It is quite possible that the fighting could spread to the Caucasus or Central Asia." [19]

Such a possibility worries the Kremlin as the rebels in the Chechnya region have many Islamic links, including having Al Qaeda fight alongside them. [20] In the mind of the Kremlin the Islamist threat is quite serious as it potentially threatens not only their rule but also the stability of the country.

**Turkey**

Turkey, a close neighbor of Syria, also has many vested interests in seeing the fall of the Assad regime. The Turks view the situation through the lens of their economic and foreign policy interests as well as their domestic interests in relation to the Kurdish situation.

Turkey has viewed Syria quite some time as a stepping stone on its way to "[becoming] a political, economic and self-described 'moral' leader in the Middle East." Economically, the Syrian crisis concerns Turkey, who has made major economic gains because of trade between the two nations. The Turkish government is concerned about

> **creating an environment that is conducive to the flowering of Turkish trade and the expansion of the Turkish economy. In that sense, one of Ankara's main interests vis-à-vis Syria is to use the country as an outlet for Turkish exporters**, particularly from the highly entrepreneurial regions bordering Syria, such as Gaziantep and Hatay. The statistics from the last few years demonstrate the success of this policy: Turkish exports to Syria skyrocketed from $266 million in 2002 to $1.6 billion in 2010. (emphasis added) [21]

On a regional scale, there is a battle between Iran and Turkey over influence in Syria. Turkey and Iran are both attempting to influence the Syrian regime for their own purposes.

To Turkey, Syria would be "the proving ground for Turkey's moderating effects on its neighbors and the place to showcase Turkey's role as a kind of regional reform whisperer. Ties to Syria were seen as the cornerstone of a new regional order, one based on more open borders and the free flow of goods and people." [22] Turkey needs to keep Syria in its sphere of influence if it is to establish a new regional order in which Turkey is the leader.

The Kurdish question also plays into Turkey's concern about the situation in Syria. The Turkish leadership looks forward to the fall of the Assad regime as it would allow for "Kurdish rights [to] be recognized within 'the unity of the Syrian state.' Thus, Syria's Kurds would be prevented from gaining any form of autonomy, the PKK's branch in Syria – the Democratic Union Party (PYD) – would be undermined, and Turkey's own Kurdish separatist movement would not be further inflamed." [23]

Keeping the Kurds in line and pacification them is quite important to the Turkish government as the Kurds have demands that range from recognition of cultural rights to the creation of a Kurdish state that includes majority Kurd areas in Turkey. Thus, Turkey must attempt to play all sides in order to ensure that it comes out on top.

**Iran**

Iran is a steadfast ally of Assad and a longtime ally of Syria. Yet even close allies have their own reasons for supporting the current regime. While economic and military interests play a role, a unique factor in this relationship is that the leadership of both regimes are of the Shiite sect of Islam in a region that is filled with those of the Sunni sect.

Just like Russia, Iran has major economic ties to Syria as can be seen by the fact that Syria gives Iran a place to invest money and a trading partner. "Iran has high-profile assets like auto factories, a cement plant, and an oil refinery in Syria, all of which rely on the stability of the Assad regime. Leaders in the two nations also share theological ties, as Shiite Muslims, and a mutual distaste for the West." [24] This economic alliance is made all the more important with the international trade sanctions that have afflicted Iran's economy for years.

Iran is also concerned about its aid to Hezbollah as such a blow would affect Iran itself. Syria has allowed Iran to "transform Hezbollah into a force that the Israeli military cannot defeat." If the Assad government falls, Iran will find itself without a way to back Hezbollah and result in a "[decrease in] Iran's ability to deter Israel from attacking its nuclear facilities." [25] Thus, Iran needs Syria as part of a larger strategy to deter Israeli aggression.

## China

While far away in Asia, the Chinese government has extremely large investments in Syria and is backing the Assad government as a way to ensure the needed stability- and cash flow- continues unabated.

China has made major investments into Syria. In 2007 it was reported that the real figure of Chinese exports to Syria is around $1.2 billion and that Syrian officials predicted it would double by 2011 [26], meaning that the Chinese government has about $2.4 billion in investments that are currently at stake as of 2012.

It also needs to be addressed that the majority of China's imports from Syria are oil and crude oil imports. Oil is something that China greatly needs if it is to continue fueling its massive economic growth and growing military power.

While the US has the governments of most of the major oil producing nations under its influence, China has been looking outward, from Africa to Middle Eastern enemies of the West, in order to attain natural resources. While it may not seem like it, China, without a doubt, wants to ensure that its investments as well as the transfer of oil are protected whether regime change occurs or not.

## The Possibility of Military Intervention?

While there is still a question of whether or not there will be a military intervention in Syria on behalf of the rebels, the option has not been taken off the table. There have been many calls for intervention from many prominent figures such as Senators John McCain and Joe Lieberman in the US [27] and Vice Prime Minister Shaul Mofaz in Israel. [28] There is still the possibility that a military intervention would occur and as such, it is needed that the military capabilities of all the potential players involved, including the Syrian military itself, be examined.

## The United States

While the intervention would without a doubt include European NATO members and potentially Western allies in the Middle East, it is quite likely that the US will have its regional military assets actively involved in the military intervention.

The Middle East region is covered by the US military command Central Command (CentCom). While CentCom has no fighting units that are directly subordinate to it, the command does have naval, ground, marine, air, and special forces components. If an intervention occurs, the US could activate its nearby Fifth Fleet in Bahrain which consists of "20-plus ships, with about 1,000 people ashore and 15,000 afloat, consists of a Carrier Battle Group, Amphibious Ready Group, combat aircraft, and other support units and ships." [29]

In the region the US has the aircraft carrier the USS Enterprise and several air force bases including Incirlik and Izmir in Turkey, as well as Camp Udairi in Kuwait which serves as a base for Middle Eastern Theater reserve soldiers. [30] Such air bases as well as the Enterprise would be useful for the US to do such things as launch airstrikes, deploy special forces to aid and train the rebels, bomb Syrian military forces, and give supplies to the rebels.

An intervention in Syria could play into a changing in US military doctrine, at least for the US Third Army which is connected to CentCom. Third Army plans on (or is already) adopting a new strategy known as the campaign plan which is defined as "a series of major operations and efforts across the joint, interagency and multinational spectrums aimed at achieving strategic and operational objectives in a defined time and space" [31]

An intervention in Syria which would allow them to coordinate with allied forces would give them such a scenario as to achieve "strategic and operational objectives in a defined time and space" and allow Third Army to see what needs work in their campaign plan.

It has been reported that that US and its allies are currently discussing with Middle Eastern allies about the situation in Syria.

**The United States, Britain and France have all been discussing contingency scenarios, potential training and sharing of intelligence about what is happening in Syria with neighboring countries including Jordan, Turkey and Israel.** But it is Jordan, so far, that is most seeking the help because of its relatively small military and potential need for outside help if unrest in southern Syria were to impact Jordan's security. (emphasis added) [32]

This is quite important to note as it implies that the Western forces may be preparing, at least partially, for some type of intervention into Syria.

**Russia**

Russia already has a naval base that it desperately wants to keep, however, that is not the full extent of Russia's military capability concerning Syria. According to Pavel Felgenhauer, an independent defense analyst based in Moscow, the Russian military is preparing "the 76th Pskov Airborne Division, the 15th Army brigade from Samara, as well as GRU special forces from the South Military District" and that "The Secretary General of the Collective Security Treaty Organization (CSTO) Nikolai Bordyuzha also remarked on the possibility of a CSTO peacekeeping force being deployed in Syria." [33]

Thus, it seems that Russia is ready and willing to defend its interests in Syria with military force, if the need arises.

This would present quite a problem for the US and its NATO and Arab allies if an intervention were to occur as a Russian military presence as well as Russian military backing for the Assad regime would make it much more difficult for their intervention to succeed. If Russia does go into Syria while the intervention was occurring, it could potentially make any place Russian soldiers reside a stronghold for the Assad regime as the US-NATO-Arab alliance would have to avoid killing Russian troops, even accidentally, lest it risk greatly escalating the conflict.

**Iran**

Iran has been doing much to support and prop up the Assad regime. It was reported in March 2012 that Iran was increasing its aid to Assad in the form of "[dispatching] hundreds of advisers, security officials and intelligence operatives to Syria, along with weapons, money and electronic surveillance equipment." [34]

The United States went so far as to state that it had "evidence of Iranian military and intelligence support for government troops accused of mass executions and other atrocities." [35] In May 2012, *The Guardian* reported that the Iranian government had sent members of its Quds force to aid government troops. [36] A reason this could be occurring is for the sake of Iran's national security as the Iranian government knows that if Assad falls, then it is almost only a matter of time before the US-NATO-Israeli alliance either attacks Iran's nuclear facilities or invades it outright.

**Syria**

The Syrian military is quite different from that of Mummar Gaddafi's Libya, with a larger army and air force, as well as advanced air defense capabilities.

The Syrian air defense system is composed of

• Major surface-to-air missiles (Sams) – 25 air defense brigades, 150 Sam batteries, 320 SA-2 missiles, 148 SA-3, 195 SA-6 and 44 SA-5

• Light Sams – 8,184+, including 4,000+ SA-7/SA-18 Igla Man-Portable Air Defense Systems (Manpads)

• Anti-aircraft guns – 1,225 guns [37]

The SA-2 has a ceiling range of 60,000 feet [38] which is the same as the flight ceiling of an F-22 Raptor [39], thus the US could potentially have a difficult time taking out Syria's anti- aircraft system with the F-22s that it has in the region. It is also important to note that in 2007 the Israeli Defense Force stated that Syria possessed "the most crowded antiaircraft system in the world" and that "According to one estimate, the Syrians hold more than 200 anti-aircraft batteries of different types." [40]

This only reinforces the notion that air power alone will not do the job if an intervention is to take place and that the intervening countries may have to send in special forces soldiers if they are to complete their objective of overthrowing the current regime. In addition to this, the Syrian military is actively preparing for an intervention by conducting large-scale exercises for such a scenario,[41] which will make an intervention all the more difficult.

**Post-Intervention Effects?**

If an intervention does occur, it is almost certain that there will be little to no similarities between the Syrian intervention and the Libyan one. Yet, there will be one major similarity in that there will be major effects on not just the nation of Syria but on the region as a whole.

The country that is most going to be affected by a fall of the Assad regime is Lebanon. Over the past month (March 2012) there has been a major flare-up in ethnic tensions between the Alawite and Sunni communities in Lebanon, which have resulted in major firefights between the two groups. [42]

This is quite problematic due to the fact that if there is already a considerable amount of violence in the country and there has been no intervention, then there is a possibility that the violence will explode if an intervention occurs.

Israel must also be taken into account as the two countries share a border and if there is large-scale violence in Lebanon then Israel will most likely beef up its military presence on its northern border.

Besides ethnic tensions, an ousting of Assad would hurt the Lebanese economy even more than it already has as the Lebanese economy is deeply connected with Syria and is affected by any political, economic, or social unrest that occurs there.

Pro-Syrian business interests are deeply influential within the Lebanese economy. The current unrest has significantly affected the Lebanese economy overall; the effects are particularly noticeable in trade relations, the banking industry, and tourism. Within Syria, the unrest has primarily impacted its oil and tourism industries. [...] According to the Lebanese Ministry of Tourism, tourism in Lebanon decreased by 25% in the first seven months of 2011. Approximately 25% of all tourist arrivals in Lebanon travel via Syria. Tourist activity on the Lebanese-Syrian border has decreased between 75%-90%. [43]

Greater economic distress on top of an already damaged economy and increased sectarian violence would most likely only increase violence in the country and make an already bad situation even worse.

Hezbollah would also be affected by regime change as "Without Syrian backing and without supply routes passing from Iran to Lebanon, through Syria, it is doubtful whether Hezbollah will continue to be the dominant player in Lebanon." [44] The supply routes are quite important as they allow Hezbollah to attain weapons and aid from Iran which in turn allows the group to maintain a powerful position in Lebanese politics.

Without the aid, the organization's position would be considerably weakened. A weakened Hezbollah also means a weakened Iran as "Under the new circumstances, these moderate forces will have a chance to finally put an end to the entrenchment of the armed militias, which serve Iranian, rather than Lebanese, interests" and Iran will no longer have an ally to aid in retaliation if Israel and its allies attack it.

Israel is also getting prepared for a potential backlash if the Assad regime falls. They are most concerned with Syria's biological and chemical weapons could fall into the hands of Hezbollah militants which would endanger the lives of Israelis living near the Israeli-Lebanese border.

Such a possibility has prompted Northern Command Chief Maj. Gen. Yair Golan to state that "The IDF has the capability to take over in a relatively short period of time the launching sites which threaten Israel's home front, and defeat Hezbollah terrorists at these sites," [45] as to reassure the populace that they would be safe.

Whether or not there is an intervention into Syria and to what extent no one knows, however, if there is one, the stakes will be high and the potential for catastrophe will be even higher. Overall, it seems that an intervention would do more harm than good. An intervention would only open up a Pandora's box that we may wish had stayed closed.

**Endnotes**

1: Fox News, *Turkey threatens Syria with retaliation over downed military jet*, June 26, 2012 (http://www.foxnews.com/world/2012/06/26/nato-will-likely-condemn-syria-downing-jet-but- not-respond-militarily-officials)

2: Jeremy M. Sharp, *Syria: Background and U.S. Relations*, Congressional Research Service http://fpc.state.gov/documents/organization/142735.pdf (April 26, 2010)

3: Ian Black, "Israel primed to attack a nuclear Iran," *The Guardian*, November 28, 2010 (http://www.guardian.co.uk/world/2010/nov/28/israel-primed-attack-nuclear-iran)

4: Jeremy M. Sharp, *Syria: Issues for the 112th Congress and Background on U.S. Sanctions*, Congressional Research Service http://assets.opencrs.com/rpts/RL33487_20110428.pdf (April 28, 2011)

5: Christopher M. Blanchard, Jeremy M. Sharp, *Syria: Unrest and U.S. Policy*, Congressional Research Service http://www.fas.org/sgp/crs/mideast/RL33487.pdf (May 24, 2012)

6: Greg Miller, "Al-Qaeda infiltrating Syrian opposition, U.S. officials say," *Washington Post*, February 16, 2012 (http://www.washingtonpost.com/world/national-security/al-qaeda- infiltrating-syrian-opposition-us-officials-say/2012/02/16/gIQA9LDJIR_story.html)

7: Eric Schmitt, "C.I.A. Said to Aid in Steering Arms to Syrian Opposition," *New York Times*, June 21, 2012 (http://www.nytimes.com/2012/06/21/world/middleeast/cia-said-to-aid-in- steering-arms-to-syrian-rebels.html?pagewanted=all)

8: Efraim Halevy, "Iran's Achilles' Heel," *New York Times*, February 7, 2012 (http://www.nytimes.com/2012/02/08/opinion/to-weaken-iran-start-with-syria.html?_r=1)

9: Giorgio Cafiero, "Syria: America versus Israel," *Asia Times*, June 6, 2012 (http://www.atimes.com/atimes/Middle_East/NF06Ak01.html)

10: *Asia Times*, June 6, 2012

11: Jonathan Steele, "Most Syrians back President Assad, but you'd never know from western media," *The Guardian*, January 17, 2012 (http://www.guardian.co.uk/commentisfree/2012/jan/17/syrians-support-assad-western- propaganda)

12: Mark Hosenball, Tabassum Zakaria, "Special Report: Intel shows Iran nuclear threat not imminent," *Reuters*, March 23, 2012 (http://www.*Reuters*.com/article/2012/03/23/us-iran-usa- nuclear-idUSBRE82M0G020120323)

13: James P. Rubin, "The Real Reason to Intervene in Syria," *Foreign Policy*, June 4, 2012 (http://www.foreignpolicy.com/articles/2012/06/04/the_real_reason_to_intervene_in_syria?page =full)

14: Yaakov Katz, "IDF tests siren for rogue non-conventional missiles," *Jerusalem Post*, July 3, 2012 (http://www.jpost.com/Defense/Article.aspx?id=276081)

15: Jadaliyya, *The Israeli Position Towards Events In Syria*, http://www.jadaliyya.com/pages/index/4336/the-israeli-position-toward-events-in-syria (February 11, 2012)

16: Dmitri Trenin, *Syria: A Russian Perspective*, Carnegie Endowment for International Peace, http://carnegieendowment.org/2012/06/28/syria-russian-perspective/ccln (June 28, 2012)

17: F. William Engdahl, "New Mediterranean oil and gas bonanza," *Russia Today*, February 26, 2012 (http://www.rt.com/news/reserves-offshore-middle-east-engdahl-855/)

18: James O'Toole, "Billions at stake as Russia backs Syria," *CNN Money*, February 10, 2012 (http://money.cnn.com/2012/02/09/news/international/russia_syria/index.htm)

19: Alexey Pilko, "The Syrian crisis and Russia's interests," *The Voice of Russia*, June 22, 2012 (http://english.ruvr.ru/2012_06_22/78965189/)

20: Scott Peterson, "Al Qaeda among the Chechens," *Christian Science Monitor*, September 7, 2004 (http://www.csmonitor.com/2004/0907/p01s02-woeu.html)

21: Yigal Schlefier, *From Endearment to Estrangement: Turkey's Interests and Concerns in Syria*, United States Institute of Peace, http://www.usip.org/files/resources/PB%20109.pdf (October 25, 2011)

22: *United States Institute of Peace*, October 25, 2011

23: Maria Fantanpple, "Turkey eyes Syrian crisis through lens of Kurdish stability*,"* *The National*, March 23, 2012 (http://www.thenational.ae/thenationalconversation/comment/turkey- eyes-syrian-crisis-through-lens-of-kurdish-stability)

24: Jessica Rettig, "Iran Has Much to Lose if Syria's Assad Falls," *US News*, September 2, 2011 (http://www.usnews.com/news/articles/2011/09/02/iran-has-much-to-lose-if-syrias-assad-falls)

25: *Asia Times*, June 6, 2012

26: Executive, *Syria – China – trade partners*, http://www.executive-magazine.com/getarticle.php?article=9819 (September 2007)

27: "John McCain & Joe Lieberman on AC360 talking Syria intervention," April 10, 2012, video clip, Youtube, http://www.youtube.com/watch?v=lwGhUZhhZOc

28: Dan Williams, "Israel accuses Syria of genocide, urges intervention," *Reuters*, June 10, 2012 (http://www.*Reuters*.com/article/2012/06/10/us-syria-crisis-israel-idUSBRE85902F20120610)

29: Global Security, *Fifth Fleet*, http://www.globalsecurity.org/military/agency/navy/c5f.htm

30: Ben Piven, "Map: US bases encircle Iran," *Al Jazeera*, May 1, 2012 (http://www.aljazeera.com/indepth/interactive/2012/04/2012417131242767298.html)

31: United States Army Central, *Third Army/ARCENT Campaign Plan Frequently Asked Questions (FAQ)*, http://www.arcent.army.mil/media/1287123/campaign%20plan.pdf

32: Barbara Starr, "US military completes initial planning for Syria," *CNN*, June 14, 2012 (http://security.blogs.cnn.com/2012/06/14/u-s-military-completes-planning-for-syria/)

33: Pavel Felgenhauer, *The Russian Military Prepares Expeditionary Forces, Allegedly for Deployment to Syria*, The Jamestown Foundation, June 14, 2012 http://www.jamestown.org/single/?no_cache=1&tx_ttnews%5Bswords%5D=8fd5893941d69d0b e3f378576261ae3e&tx_ttnews%5Bany_of_the_words%5D=benazir%20bhutto&tx_ttnews%5Bp ointer%5D=1&tx_ttnews%5Btt_news%5D=39494&tx_ttnews%5BbackPid%5D=7&cHash=30a 3cf9ebf0de90a68c6a031f1d85485 (June 14, 2012)

34: Liz Sly, John Warrick, "US officials: Iran is stepping up aid to Syria," *Washington Post*, March 3, 2012 (http://www.washingtonpost.com/world/national-security/us-officials-iran-is-       stepping-up-lethal-aid-to-syria/2012/03/02/gIQAGR9XpR_story.html)

35: *Washington Post*, March 3, 2012

36: Saeed Kamali Dehghan, "Syrian army being aided by Iranian forces," *The Guardian*, May, 28, 2012 (http://www.guardian.co.uk/world/2012/may/28/syria-army-iran-forces)

37: Jonathan Marcus, "Analysis: Options for military intervention in Syria," *BBC*, June 12, 2012 (http://www.bbc.co.uk/news/world-middle-east-17356556)

38: National Museum of the US Air Force, *SA-2 Surface-to-Air Missile*, http://www.nationalmuseum.af.mil/factsheets/factsheet.asp?id=334

39: Global Security, *F-22 Raptor Specifications*, http://www.globalsecurity.org/military/systems/aircraft/f-22-specs.htm

40: Alex Fishman, "IDF: Syria's antiaircraft system most advanced in world," *Ynet News*, August 13, 2007 (http://www.ynetnews.com/articles/0,7340,L-3436827,00.html)

41: Today's Zaman, *Assad military conducts large-scale exercises as fighting spills into Lebanon*, http://www.todayszaman.com/news-285903-assad-military-conducts-large-scale- exercises-as-fighting-spills-into-lebanon.html (July 8. 2012)

42: Nicholas Blanford, "In Lebanon, a worrying sectarian spillover from Syria," *Christian Science Monitor*, June 3, 2012 (http://www.csmonitor.com/World/Middle-East/2012/0603/In- Lebanon-a-worrying-sectarian-spillover-from-Syria)

43: Rebecca A. Hopkins, *Lebanon and the Uprising in Syria: Issue for Congress*, Congressional Research Service http://www.fas.org/sgp/crs/mideast/R42339.pdf (February 2, 2012)

44: Avigdor Lieberman, "The case of Syria could prove different," *Jerusalem Post*, March 13, 2012 (http://www.jpost.com/Opinion/Op-EdContributors/Article.aspx?id=261738)

45: Jacob Edelist, "Anticipating US Intervention in Syria, Israel, Iran, Prepare for Clash," *Jewish Press*, May 31, 2012 (http://www.jewishpress.com/news/breaking-news/in-face-of-us- intervention-in-syria-israel-iran-prepare-for-clash/2012/05/31/)

The ongoing situation in Mali is gaining traction in the media with the reporting of Al Qaeda members within the ranks of the Tuareg rebels. The situation is quite complicated and involves not only France, but also the US and partially Canada and links to the interests of these Western powers with not just Mali, but with the African continent as a whole.

**The Tuareg People**

In order to get a better handle on the situation, there must first be an understanding of the domestic actors, namely the Tuareg people, who presently "live across the Sahara Desert, including in the North African countries of Mali, Niger, Libya, Algeria and Chad."[1]

The Tuareg are a people that have lived in northern Mali "as early as the fifth century BCE" [2] according to Herodotus. After establishing the city of Timbuktu in the 11th century the Tuareg "traded, traveled, and conquered throughout Saharan" over the next four centuries, eventually converting to Islam in the 14th century, which allowed them to "[gain] great wealth trading salt, gold, and black slaves."[3]

This independence was swept away when the French colonized Mali after they "defeated the Tuareg at Timbuktu and established borders and administrative districts to rule the area until Mali declared independence in 1960."[4] The Tuareg people have consistently wanted independence and in pursuit of such goals have engaged in a number of rebellions.

The first was in 1916 when, in response to the French not giving the Tuareg their own autonomous zone (called Azawad) as was promised, they revolted. The French violently quelled the revolt and "subsequently confiscated important grazing lands while using Tuaregs as forced conscripts and labor – and fragmented Tuareg societies through the drawing of arbitrary boundaries between Soudan (Mali) and its neighbors."[5]

Yet, this did not end the Tuareg goal of an independent, sovereign state. Once the French had ceded Mali independence, the Tuareg began to push toward their dream of establishing Azawad once again with "several prominent Tuareg leaders [lobbying] for a separate Tuareg homeland consisting of northern Mali and parts of modern day Algeria, Niger, Mauritania. [...] [However,] black politicians like Modibo Keita, Mali's first President, made it clear that independent Mali would not cede its northern territories." [6]

**The First Tuareg Rebellion**

In the 1960s, while the independence movements in Africa were beginning, the Tuareg once again vied for their own autonomy, in an uprising known as the Afellaga rebellion. The Tuareg were greatly oppressed by the government of Modibo Keita, which came into power after the French had left, as they "were singled out for particular discrimination, and were more neglected than others in the distribution of state benefits," which may have been due to the fact that "most of the senior leadership of post-colonial Mali were drawn from the southern ethnic groups who were not sympathetic to the pastoral culture of the northern desert nomads."[7]

In addition to this, the Tuareg felt that the government's policy of 'modernization' was in reality an attack on the Tuareg themselves as the Keita government enacted policies such as "land reform that threatened [the Tuareg's] privileged access to agricultural products."[8] Specifically, Keita "had moved increasingly in the direction of [establishing a version of] the Soviet collective farm and had created state corporations to monopolize the purchase of basic crops."[9]

Keita also left customary land rights unchanged "except when the state needed land for industry or transport. Then the Minister of Rural Economy issued a decree of acquisition and registration in the name of the state, but only after publication of notice and a hearing to determine customary claims."[10] Unfortunately for the Tuareg, this unchanging of customary land rights did not apply to the subsoil that was on their land. Instead, this subsoil was turned into a state monopoly due to Keita's desire to ensure that no one became a capitalist based on the discovery of subsoil resources.

This had a major negative impact on the Tuareg as they had a pastoral culture and the subsoil helps to "determine what kind of crops can be grown in any area and, therefore, what livestock can be raised."[11] Thus, by creating a state monopoly on subsoil, the Keita government was effectively in control of what the Tuareg would be able to grow and therefore in control of their very lives.

This oppression eventually boiled over and became the first Tuareg rebellion, which began with small hit-and-run attacks on government forces. However, it was quickly crushed due to the Tuareg lacking "a unified leadership, a well-coordinated strategy or clear evidence of a coherent strategic vision."[12] In addition to this, the rebels were unable to mobilize the entire Tuareg community.

The Malian military, well-motivated and [well-equipped] with new Soviet weapons, conducted vigorous counterinsurgency operations. By the end of 1964, the government's strong arm methods had crushed the rebellion. It then placed the Tuareg-populated northern regions under a repressive military administration. [13]

Yet while the Malian military may have won the battle, they failed to win the war as their heavy-handed tactics only alienated Tuareg who didn't support the insurgency and the government failed to follow through on promises to improve the local infrastructure and increase economic opportunity.

To avoid the military occupation of their communities and also due to massive drought in the 1980s, many Tuareg fled to nearby countries such as Algeria, Mauritania, and Libya. Thus, the grievances of the Tuareg went unaddressed, only creating a situation in which a rebellion would once again occur.

**The Second Tuareg Rebellion**

The raging inferno that was the spirit of independence of the Tuareg people once again came back to life in 1990. It must be noted that Mali had greatly changed since the 1960s and moved from a socialist government to a military dictatorship that (due to massive pressure from the people) quickly changed to a transitional government with military and civilian leaders, finally fully becoming democratic in 1992. [14]

While Mali was transitioning to a democracy, the Tuareg people were still suffering under the boot of oppression. Three decades after the first rebellion, the occupation of Tuareg communities still had not ended and "resentment fueled by the harsh repression, continued dissatisfaction with government policies, and perceived exclusion from political power led various Tuareg and Arab groups to begin a second rebellion against the Malian government."[15]

The second rebellion was sparked due to "attacks on non-Tuareg Malians [at] the southernmost edge of the Tuareg regions [which led to] skirmishes between the Malian army and Tuareg rebels."[16]

Yet it did not last long as the first major step to peace was made in 1991 by the transitional government and resulted in the Tamanrasset Accords, which was negotiated in Algeria between the military government of Lt. Colonel Amadou Toumani Touré (that had taken power in a coup on March 26, 1991) and the two major Tuareg factions, The Azaouad Popular Movement and the Arabic Islamic Front of Azawad, on January 6, 1991.

In the Accords, the Malian military agreed to "disengage from the running of the civil administration," "avoid zones of pasture land and densely populated zones," to be "confined to their role of defense of the integrity of the territory at the frontiers," [17] and created a ceasefire between the two main Tuareg factions and the government.

However, not all of the Tuareg factions signed onto the Accords as many rebel groups demanded "among other concessions, the removal of current administrators in the north and their replacement with local representatives."[18]

The Accords represented a political compromise in which more autonomy was granted to Tuareg communities and local and regional councils made up of local representatives were established, yet the Tuareg still remained a part of Mali. Thus, the Accords didn't end the situation as tensions remained between the Tuareg and the Malian government.

The transitionary government of Mali that came about during the country's democratization process, attempted to negotiate with the Tuareg. This culminated in the April 1992 National Pact between the Malian government and several Tuareg factions. The National Pact allowed for the "integration of Tuareg combatants into the Malian armed forces, demilitarization of the north, economic integration of northern populations, and a more detailed special administrative structure for the three northern regions."[19]

After Alpha Konaré was elected president of Mali in 1992, he furthered the process of Tuareg autonomy by not only honoring the concessions made in the National Pact but by removing the structure of federal and regional governments and allowing authority to take hold at the local level. Yet, decentralization had a greater political purpose, as it "effectively co-opted the Tuareg by allowing them a degree of autonomy and the benefits of remaining in the Republic."[20]

However, this attempt to deal with the Tuareg did not hold as the National Pact only renewed debate about the unique status of Tuareg people and some rebel groups, such as the Arabic Islamic Front of Azawad, did not attend the National Pact talks [21] and the violence continued, eventually resulting in the deaths of 6,000-8,000 people before an peace agreement was signed by all factions.

It must be noted that the introduction the Arabic Islamic Front of Azawad to the Tuareg rebellion is also the introduction of radical Islam to the Tuareg fight for independence. The emergence of radical Islam was greatly aided by the Gaddafi regime. During the 1970s many Tuareg had fled to Libya and other countries, mainly for economic opportunity.

Once there, Gaddafi "welcomed them with open arms. He gave them food and shelter. He called them brothers. He also started training them as soldiers."[22] Gaddafi then used these soldiers to found the Islamic Legion in 1972. The goal of the Legion was to "further [Gaddafi's own] territorial ambitions in the African interior and advance the cause of Arab supremacy."[23]

The Legion was sent to fight in Niger, Mali, Palestine, Lebanon, and Afghanistan, among other countries. However, the Legion came to an end due to the price of oil declining in 1985, which meant that Gaddafi could no longer afford to recruit and train fighters.

Coupled with the Legion's crushing defeat in Chad, the organization was disbanded which left many Tuareg going back to their homes in Mali with large amounts of combat experience. The role of Libya played a role not only in the third Tuareg rebellion, but also in the fighting going on in 2013. [24]

**The Third Tuareg Rebellion**

The third rebellion was not so much a rebellion, but rather an insurgency in which members of the Malian military were kidnapped and killed. The insurgency began in May 2006, when "a group of Tuareg army deserters attacked [a] military barracks in Kidal region, seizing weapons and demanding greater autonomy and development assistance."[25]

The former general Amadou Toumani Toure had won presidential elections in 2002 and reacted to the violence by working with a rebel coalition known as the Democratic Alliance for Change to establish a peace agreement that restated the Malian government's commitment to improving the economy in the northern areas where the rebels lived.

However, many rebels such as Ibrahim Ag Bahanga, who was killed in 2012, [26] refused to abide by the peace treaty and continued to terrorize the Malian military until the government of Mali deployed a large offensive force to eliminate the insurgency.[27] Yet, the fight for Tuareg independence remains and leads us into the current 2013 rebellion.

**The Current Rebellion**

To understand this most recent rebellion, one must first go back to the 'humanitarian' intervention mission in Libya that was conducted by US-NATO forces in 2012. During the invasion of Libya, many Tuareg fighters fought in defense of the Gaddafi regime and once Gaddafi had been defeated, the majority of these fighters returned to Mali, armed with the weapons they had obtained while in Libya. [28]

Once there, some of the fighters joined the National Movement for the Liberation of the Azawad which again started up the call for Tuareg independence and on January 17, 2012, began to attack towns in northern Mali. [29]

From there, the rebellion spread and the Tuareg, making more and more headway in northern Mali, would eventually have an effect on the government of Mali itself, namely in the form of a coup. Time magazine noted that the coup began in March 2013 when "Sanogo [a captain in the Malian army] led a mutiny at the garrison in Kati — a sleepy commune of cinder- block bungalows just north of the capital" which later "intensified into a coup."[30]

The coup eventually resulted in Sanogo taking power. In December 2012, it was reported that "Soldiers arrested Mali's prime minister and forced him to resign before dawn on Tuesday" and that "coup leader Capt. Amadou Haya Sanogo had ordered the prime minister's arrest."[31]

It must be noted- and is extremely interesting- that Captain Sanogo had ties to the United States. Joshua E. Keating, an associate editor at Foreign Policy wrote in a 2012 article that "U.S. military officials have acknowledged that Sanogo 'participated in several U.S.-funded International Military Education and Training (IMET) programs in the United States, including basic officer training.'"[32]

The United States, however, condemned the coup [33] and eventually cut off all aid to the new military government.

From here, one can now analyze the interests of each of the actors involved in the ongoing violence in Mali.

**France**

As was noted, Mali was a former colony of the French and thus it was not surprising when the French decided to intervene in Mali on the grounds that "Mali's existence as a state was under threat" [34] and needing to protect the 6,000 French citizens living there. Airstrikes soon began to take place there, which was quite easy due to the proximity of French air bases near Mali. [35] Yet, there are more interests at stake than just protecting French citizens, such as oil.

**"In the long term, France has interests in securing resources in the Sahel – particularly oil and uranium, which the French energy company Areva has been extracting for decades in neighboring Niger," said [Katrin Sold of the German Council on Foreign Relations].**

But much time will pass before Mali's resources can be extracted, so Sold believes security interests really are at the forefront in France's current military strike.

Africa expert [Ulrich Delius of the Society for Threatened Peoples] agrees, noting that when it came to military involvement in Libya, many countries had an interest there, especially in oil. With Mali, he said, it's different, and Paris seems to be following a concrete set of goals. [36] (emphasis added)

While the myth that Mali has uranium has been debunked already [37], it must be realized that the focus isn't so much on Mali itself as it is on neighboring countries. Niger, for example, is right next to Mali and "has two significant uranium mines providing 7.5% of world mining output from Africa's highest-grade uranium ores" and "is the world's fourth-ranking producer of uranium."[38]

This uranium is quite important to the French as they get 75% of their electricity from nuclear energy. In addition to this, they are a net exporter of energy, which has become quite lucrative for them as they make £3 billion annually. [39]

It is also important to know that the French company operating in the uranium production business, Areva, is state-owned and it was noted earlier that the Tuareg people do also live in Niger, which is why if a Tuareg rebellion starts in Mali, it risks the possibility of to Niger, or vice versa. Thus, it is quite important to the French to put down any rebellion quickly.\

**The United States**

The US has its own personal interests in Mali, which is why they have been backing the French in the form of transportation assistance. [40] The official line is that the main US concern is Al Qaeda, with the Congressional Research Service reporting that "The prospect of an expanded safe-haven for AQIM [Al Qaeda in the Islamic Maghreb] and other extremists and criminal actors in Mali is a principal concern for U.S. policymakers examining the situation in Mali and the wider region."[41]

However, the real problem that the US has isn't Al Qaeda or Mali for that matter, but the US is concerned with China on a regional level. China's economic power within Africa has grown greatly within the past two years.

**China's trade with Africa reached $166 billion in 2011, according to Chinese statistics, and African exports to China – primarily resources to fuel Chinese industries – rose to $93 billion from $5.6 billion over the past decade. In July 2012** China offered African countries $20 billion in loans over the next three years, double the amount pledged in the previous three-year period.[42] (emphasis added)

Thus, we see not only the increasing economic influence of China via trade, but also their increasing political clout due to the economic aid that China is giving African countries.

This economic aid and investment definitely paid off it was noted by the *New York Times* in 2011 that China's image in Africa trumped that of the United States.

**A 2007 Pew Research Center survey of 10 sub-Saharan African countries found that Africans overwhelmingly viewed Chinese economic growth as beneficial. In virtually all countries surveyed, China's involvement was viewed in a much more positive light than America's; in Senegal, 86 percent said China's role in their country helped make things better, compared with 56 percent who felt that way about America's role.**

In Kenya, 91 percent of respondents said they believed China's influence was positive, versus only 74 percent for the United States. [43] (emphasis added)

The positive, albeit economically motivated, role that China was- and is- playing in Africa represents a threat to US interests. Thus, the US African Command (Africom) is paying much attention to the current events in Mali. It was noted in 2012 that Africom was meeting with Mauritania to discuss military intervention in Africa [44], thus the command could become involved in Mali in the future.

Despite US government officials stating that Africom isn't meant to counter Chinese influence in the region, it is quite the opposite. The BBC reported in 2008 that two of the main reasons for the creation of Africom was to "to secure oil supplies" and "counter China's growing influence on the continent,"[45] noting China's economic influence in the region.

**Canada**

Unfortunately, even our friends up north have their own interests in Mali, with Canadian Prime Minister Harper giving transportation aid to the French and former diplomat Robert Folwer wanting Canada to play a bigger role.[46]

Like the French, Canada's biggest interest in Mali is mining, mainly in the gold sector. The violence is currently hurting Canada's mining interests, with CTV News stating that the violence threw a "monkey wrench in the Harper government's ambitions for Canadian firms, especially in the mining sector" and that "The government is actively promoting Canadian business opportunities in Africa, but has no stomach for contributing troops to the French-led military campaign to drive al Qaeda-linked extremists out of northern Mali."[47]

Thus, while Harper are worried that the mining companies whom he has helped so much to make record profits will find themselves in trouble, he has no interests in getting his hands dirty to send troops to Mali.

It seems that the situation is only going to get worse as both rebels [48] and Malian soldiers [49] have been found committing atrocities and it is truly the people that are suffering as there are people who fear ethnic reprisals from Malian troops, over half a million people are in need of food assistance, and more than 400,000 people have fled the country. [50] While the powers, both internal and external duke it out, the people are the ones that pay the price.

**Endnotes**

1: Andrew Meldrum, "Tuaregs: 5 Things You Need to Know," *Global Post*, October 29, 2011 (http://www.globalpost.com/dispatch/news/regions/africa/111028/tuaregs-5-things-you-need- know)

2: Ann Hershkowitz, *The Tuareg in Mali and Niger: The Role of Desertification in Violent Conflict*, American University, http://www1.american.edu/ted/ice/tuareg.htm (August 2005)

3: http://www1..american.edu/ted/ice/tuareg.htm

4: Defense Language Institute Foreign Language Center, *Tamashek Cultural Orientation*, http://famdliflc..lingnet.org/products/Tamashek/co_tt/tamashek.pdf

5: Minority Rights, *Tuareg*, http://www.minorityrights.org/?lid=5315&tmpl

6: Aman Sethi, "Battle Reveals Islamists Riding Over Ethnic Fault lines," *The Hindu*, January 14, 2012 (http://www.thehindu.com/todays-paper/tp-international/battle-reveals-islamists-riding- over-ethnic-faultlines/article4305856.ece)

7: Global Security, *Tuareg – Mali – 1962-1964*, http://www.globalsecurity.org/military/world/war/tuareg-mali-1962.htm

8: Colonel Dan Henk, Lieutenant Colonel Kalifa Keita, *Conflict and Conflict Resolution in the Sahel: The Tuareg Insurgency in Mali*, Strategic Studies Institute, http://www.strategicstudiesinstitute.army.mil/pdffiles/pub200.pdf

9: John N. Hazard, "Marxian Socialism in Africa: The Case of Mali," *Comparative Politics* 2:1 (1969), pg 4

10: Hazard, pg 4

11: Forest Preserve District of Cook County, IL, *Topsoil and Subsoil*, http://www.newton.dep.anl.gov/natbltn/300-399/nb372.htm

12: http://www.strategicstudiesinstitute.army.mil/pdffiles/pub200.pdf

13: Ibid

14: Jaimie Bleck, *Countries at the Crossroads 2011 – Mali*, Freedom House, http://www.unhcr.org/refworld/publisher,FREEHOU,,MLI,4ecba6492f,0.html (November 10, 2011)

15: *Freedom House*, November 10, 2011

16: Jennifer C. Seely, "A Political Analysis of Decentralisation: Co-opting the Tuareg Threat in Mali," *The Journal of Modern African Studies* 39:3 (2001), pg 9

17: Uppsala Conflict Data Program, *Tamanrasset Accord*, http://www.ucdp.uu.se/gpdatabase/peace/mal19910106.pdf

18: Seely, pg 9

19: Seely, pg 10

20: Seely, pg 15

21: Katharine Murison, ed., *Africa South of the Sahara 2003*, 32 ed. (London, England: The Gresham Press, 2003) pg 640

22: Jeffrey Gettleman, "Libyan Oil Buys Allies for Qaddafi," *New York Times*, March 16, 2011 (http://www.nytimes.com/2011/03/16/world/africa/16mali.html?_r=0)

23: Andrew McGregor, *Can African Mercenaries Save the Libyan Regime?*, Jamestown Foundation, http://www.jamestown.org/programs/gta/single/?tx_ttnews%5Btt_news%5D=37551&cHash=4e 5f37dc8755b53452b6de6c97eef96a (February 23, 2011)

24: Glen Johnson, "Libya weapons aid Tuareg rebellion in Mali," *Los Angeles Times*, June 12, 2012 (http://articles.latimes.com/2012/jun/12/world/la-fg-libya-arms-smuggle-20120612)

25: Freedom House, *Mali, Freedom in the World 2009*,http://www.freedomhouse.org/report/freedom-world/2009/mali

26: France 24, *Tuareg leader's death linked to Libya arms trade*, http://www.france24.com/en/20110827-mali-tuareg-leader-death-linked-libyan-weapons (August 27, 2011)

27: France 24, *Army claims victory in clashes with Tuareg rebels*, http://www.france24.com/en/20090102-mali-army-clashes-tuareg-rebels-claims-victory (January 2, 2009)

28: *Los Angeles Times*, June 12, 2012

29: Martin Vogl, "Tuareg rebels attack towns in north Mali," *The Guardian*, January 17, 2012 (http://www.guardian.co.uk/world/feedarticle/10045305)

30: Julius Cavendish, "Mali's Coup Leader: Interview with an Improbable Strongman," *Time*, March 28, 2012 (http://www.time.com/time/world/article/0,8599,2110278,00.html)

31: Baba Ahmed and Rukmini Callimachi, "Mali coup leaders force prime minister to resign," *Mercury News*, December 11, 2012 (http://www.mercurynews.com/nation- world/ci_22168494/mali-coup-leaders-force-prime-minister-resign)

32: Joshua E. Keating, "Foreign Policy: Trained in The U.S.A.," *National Public Radio*, March 29, 2012 (http://www.npr.org/2012/03/29/149605074/foreign-policy-trained-in-the-u-s-a)

33: Voice of America News, *US Joins Condemnation of Mali Coup*, http://www.voanews.com/content/us-joins-condemnation-of-mali-coup–143839706/180850.html (March 21, 2012)

34: BBC News, *France confirms Mali military intervention*, http://www.bbc.co.uk/news/world- africa-20991719 (January 11, 2013)

35: Sun Degang & Yahia Zoubir, "Sentry Box in the Backyard: Analysis of French Military Bases in Africa," *Journal of Middle Eastern and Islamic Studies* 5:3 (2011), pgs 84-86

36: Rachel Baig, "The interests behind France's intervention in Mali," *Deutsche Welles*, January 16, 2013 (http://www.dw.de/the-interests-behind-frances-intervention-in-mali/a-16523792)

37: Mark Hibbs, *Uranium in Saharan Sands*, Carnegie Endowment For International Peace, http://carnegieendowment.org/2013/01/22/uranium-in-saharan-sands/f4ej (January 22, 2013)

38: World Nuclear Association, *Uranium In Niger*, http://www.world- nuclear.org/info/inf110.html

39: World Nuclear Association, *Nuclear Power In France*, http://www.world- nuclear.org/info/inf40.html

40: Alexis Arieff, *Crisis In Mali*, Congressional Research Service, http://www.fas.org/sgp/crs/row/R42664.pdf (January 14, 2013)

41: F. William Engdahl, "The War in Mali and AFRICOM's Agenda: Target China," *Global Research*, February 10, 2012 (http://www.globalresearch.ca/the-war-in-mali-and-africoms- african-agenda-target-china/5322517)

42: Dambisa Moyo, "Beijing, a Boon for Africa," *New York Times*, June 27, 2012 (http://www.nytimes.com/2012/06/28/opinion/beijing-a-boon-for-africa.html?_r=0)

43: Navy Times, *AFRICOM, Mauritania discuss Mali intervention*, http://www.navytimes.com/news/2012/09/ap-africom-mauritania-discuss-mali-intervention- 092712/ (September 27, 2012)

45: Adam Mynott, "US Africa command battles skeptics," *BBC*, October 1, 2008 (http://news.bbc.co.uk/2/hi/africa/7644994.stm)

46: CTV News, *Fowler warns of 'absolute chaos' if Mali violence escalates*, http://www.ctvnews.ca/canada/fowler-warns-of-absolute-chaos-if-mali-violence-escalates- 1.1113448 (January 14, 2013)

47: Mike Blanchfield, "Mali turmoil bad for Canadian mining ambitions in West Africa: analysts," *CTV News*, February 8, 2013 (http://www.ctvnews.ca/business/mali-turmoil-bad-for- canadian-mining-ambitions-in-west-africa-analysts-1.1148796)

48: Human Rights Watch, *Mali: War Crimes by Northern Rebels*, http://www.hrw.org/news/2012/04/30/mali-war-crimes-northern-rebels (April 30, 2012)

49: Al Jazeera, *Amnesty cites rights abuses in northern Mali*, http://www.aljazeera.com/news/africa/2012/05/2012516474946468.html (May 16, 2012)

50: Rick Gladstone, "U.N. Official Sees Desperation, Hunger and Fear on Visit to Mali," *New York Times*, February 26, 2013 (http://www.nytimes.com/2013/02/27/world/africa/un-official- sees-desperate-conditions-in-mali.html)

*Published on: June 17, 2013*

It has recently been announced that the Obama administration has decided to go ahead and arm the Syrian rebels on the grounds that they have "obtained proof the Syrian government used chemical weapons against fighters trying to overthrow President Bashar al-Assad."[1] Interestingly enough, up until this time, it has been noted by the UN that there is no clear evidence that either side had used chemical weapons. [2] While it may seem that the Obama administration is doing this to aid the rebellion, there may also be other factors at play.

It first needs to be noted that this announcement is only new in that the US government is actually admitting that they are arming the Syrian rebels. It has been known for quite some time that the US and its allies have been arming the Syrian rebels, mainly indirectly on the part of the US [3], but there has been direct aid on the part of America's allies. In February 2012, the International Business Times reported that "Syrian rebel forces are already being armed and supplied by Western powers" and that

Syrian National Council member Bassma Kodmani said unidentified countries were already providing communications equipment, body armor and night-vision goggles to the Free Syrian Army, a move previously denied by Western governments.

According to the paper, Kodmani refused to reveal which countries were helping, but [she] hinted that allies were also sending more lethal weapons such as rifles.

Defensive and light equipment are what they are doing on the ground, she told *The Telegraph*. [4]

Thus, the West has been arming the rebels for quite some time. Yet, at this moment the mainstream media is mainly discussing the admission that the US will openly be arming the Syrian rebels and stating that it is due to the "proof" the Obama administration has that the Assad regime has used chemical weapons.

While it is possible that the Assad regime did in fact use chemical weapons, we need to remain skeptical as the US has launched media wars before on governments that it opposed, such as the Gaddafi government, with the West stating that Gaddafi had bombed his own civilians and gave Viagra for his troops to rape women; when the conflict ended, it was found that Amnesty International "failed to find evidence for these human rights violations and in many cases has discredited or cast doubt on them. It also found indications that on several occasions the rebels in Benghazi appeared to have knowingly made false claims or manufactured evidence."[5] Thus, we should withhold judgment until the 'proof' is presented (if at all).

This sudden change in policy may have to do with much more than just the alleged use of chemical weapons. It may have been "prompted by the realization that Syrian President Bashar Assad was on the cusp of gaining a permanent advantage over rebel groups and the fear of imminent sectarian bloodshed further spilling into neighboring Iraq, Jordan and Lebanon."[6] It is quite evident that Assad may be gaining the upper hand in the conflict as Germany's foreign intelligence agency, the Bundesnachrichtendienst (BND; Federal Intelligence Agency in English), drastically changed its assessment of the Syrian conflict and they now believe that "the Syrian military of autocrat Bashar Assad is more stable than it has been in a long time and is capable of undertaking successful operations against rebel units at will."[7] The BND chief even stated that "Each new battle weakens the militias further."[8] The addition of Hezbollah is only enforcing this idea as it was reported on the week of June 10, 2013 that the Syrian military and its allies in Hezbollah not only retook the key city of Qusair, but were still pushing northward. [9]

Yet, there was also a question of perception as what Obama's aides were most concerned with "was the perception that world's sole superpower was standing by while European allies shouldered the burden of trying to stop a dictator from murdering thousands of his own people."[10] So it seems that partially the Obama administration may be more concerned with PR rather than the Syrian people, whom they claim to care so much about.

At the end of the day, it doesn't seem as if this will do any good for the Syrians as the rebels are extremely dependent upon radical Islamist groups, [11] and both the rebels and the Assad government have been accused of committing war crimes. [12] The US arming the rebels will only lengthen the conflict and make it much deadlier, and if the Assad regime does fall, it looks like the new one will be about the same.

The war has come to Syria and the people will continue to suffer.

**Endnotes**

1: *Reuters, U.S. considers no-fly zone after Syria crosses nerve gas "red line"*, http://www.*Reuters*.com/article/2013/06/14/us-syria-crisis-idUSBRE95C16L20130614 (June 14, 2013)

2: Al Jazeera, *UN: No clear proof of Syria chemical arms use*, http://www.aljazeera.com/news/middleeast/2013/05/201356135529534687.html (May 6, 2013)

3: Erich Schmitt, "C.I.A. Said to Aid in Steering Arms to Syrian Opposition," *New York Times*, June 21, 2012 (http://www.nytimes.com/2012/06/21/world/middleeast/cia-said-to-aid-in- steering-arms-to-syrian-rebels.html?pagewanted=all)

4: Oliver Tree, "Western Allies Arming Rebels in Syria, Opposition Claims, as Red Cross Reach Besieged Homs," *International Business Times*, February 24, 2012 (http://www.ibtimes.com/western-allies-arming-rebels-syria-opposition-claims-red-cross-reach- besieged-homs-415842)

5: Patrick Cockburn, "Amnesty questions claim that Gaddafi ordered rape as weapon of war," *The Independent*, June 24, 2011 (http://www.independent.co.uk/news/world/africa/amnesty- questions-claim-that-gaddafi-ordered-rape-as-weapon-of-war-2302037.html)

6: Reid J. Epstein and Glenn Thrush, "Syria chemical weapons: President Obama's forced hand," *Politico*, June 13, 2013 (http://www.politico.com/story/2013/06/president-obama-syria- chemical-weapons-92782.html?hp=t1_s)

7: Matthias Gebauer, "Syrian Rebels in Trouble: German Intelligence Sees Assad Regaining Hold," *Der Spiegel*, May 22, 2013 (http://www.spiegel.de/international/world/german- intelligence-believes-assad-regime-regaining-lost-power-a-901188.html)

8: Ibid

9: CBS, *Assad's troops in Syria, backed by Hezbollah, push rebels further north*, http://www.cbsnews.com/8301-202_162-57588210/assads-troops-in-syria-backed-by-hezbollah- push-rebels-further-north/ (June 7, 2013)

10: *Politico*, June 13, 2013

11: David Enders, "Al Qaida-linked group Syria rebels once denied now key to anti-Assad victories," *McClatchy DC*, December 2, 2012 (http://www.mcclatchydc.com/2012/12/02/176123/al-qaida-linked-group-syria- rebels.html#.UbtmbFSMKJD)

12: Zeina Karam, "Both Assad and rebels committing war crimes, atrocities a 'daily reality' in Syrian civil war: UN," *National Post*, June 4, 2013 (http://news.nationalpost.com/2013/06/04/both-assad-and-rebels-committing-war-crimes- atrocities-a-daily-reality-in-syrian-civil-war-un/)

The call for intervention in Syria has gone to a massive battle cry in just a couple of days following the chemical weapons attack allegedly committed by the Syrian government, though the information is dubious at best.[1]

The Obama administration as well as media pundits are calling for intervention, yet ignore their own hypocrisy- and in many cases irony- in regards to the entire situation.

In August 2013, Ian Hurd of the *New York Times* argued that the US should intervene in Syria because the alleged use of chemical weapons "[demands] an urgent response to deter further massacres and to punish President Bashar al-Assad."[2] It is quite fascinating that Hurd is so concerned with Assad's alleged use of chemical weapons, while ignoring the fact that the rebels very well may have used chemical weapons as well in May 2013. [3]

Nor do I see him and other pro-interventionists discussing that fact or the fact that the US and its allies have used chemical weapons before and not given a hoot. [4]

There is more hypocrisy when the argument of saving civilians is bought up. People such as Warren Kinsella at London Free Press claim to care about civilians. Kinsella states that "Inaction in the face of such terrible war crimes is complicity."[5] However he ignores the fact that if he and others so much about morality and protecting civilians from deadly state repression, why were they not pushing for intervention when civilians were getting killed and brutally repressed by their governments in Bahrain?[6] How about in Egypt?[7] Many of these same people were nowhere to be found.

There is also a rather large amount of irony in regards to Syria. There are those that criticize President Bush for his Iraq debacle, namely on the fact that Bush had based the war on fabricated evidence, however, they are willing to accept Kerry's assertion that "there's 'no doubt' the Assad regime was behind this 'crime against humanity.'"[8] This would be humorous if the consequences weren't going to be so horrific. Bush used the same 'just trust me' rhetoric that Obama is currently using, however, at least Bush presented evidence, albeit false evidence. In a way, it is even worse for Obama because he has not presented any evidence that the Assad regime committed the chemical attacks and there is evidence that the rebels were involved. [9]

Furthermore, the hypocrisy continues as there were critics that argued that the Iraq invasion was illegal, yet they back the intervention in Syria, with the aforementioned Ian Hurd having the audacity to say that we should "bomb Syria, even if it is illegal" and that "there are moral reasons for disregarding the law."[10] The fact that the US has no legal standing whatsoever for its intervention in Syria doesn't seem to matter at all.

A final touch of irony is that many are lamenting the federal sequestration which has wreaked havoc on local communities such as Salem, Oregon where "a Salem day center where the homeless went to get out of the heat and cold, do laundry and shower have severely cut hours and services"[12] and cuts in education which has resulted in

• Services cut or eliminated for millions of students.

• Funding for children living in poverty, special education, and Head Start slashed by billions.

• Ballooning class sizes.

• Elimination of after-school programs.

• Decimation of programs for our most vulnerable—homeless students, English language learners, and high-poverty, struggling schools.

• Slashing of financial aid for college students.

• Loss of tens of thousands of education jobs—at early childhood, elementary, secondary, and postsecondary levels. [13]

Yet, they will gladly spend more money on war, which is expected to cost $100 million [14] or perhaps even more if Assad falls.[15]

For all of their talk, the interventionists seem oblivious to the greatest irony of their cause: They may very well end up killing civilians so they can save civilians.[16] They have embraced the logic of empire.

**Endnotes**

1: Washington's Blog, *Point-By-Point Rebuttal of U.S. Case for War In Syria*, Global Research, http://www.globalresearch.ca/point-by-point-rebuttal-of-u-s-case-for-war-in-syria/5347826 (September 3, 2013)

2: Ian Hurd, "Bomb Syria, Even if Its Illegal," *New York Times*, August 27, 2013 (http://www.nytimes.com/2013/08/28/opinion/bomb-syria-even-if-it-is-illegal.html?_r=0)

3: Damien McElroy, "UN accuses Syrian rebels of chemical weapons use," *The Telegraph*, May 6, 2013 (http://www.telegraph.co.uk/news/worldnews/middleeast/syria/10039672/UN-accuses- Syrian-rebels-of-chemical-weapons-use.html)

4: Zoltan Grossman, "A Short History of Bio-Chemical Weapons," *Counterpunch*, September 2, 2013 (http://www.counterpunch.org/2013/09/02/a-short-history-of-bio-chemical-weapons/)

5: Warren Kinsella, "Five Reasons to Intervene in Syria," *London Free Press*, August 20, 2012 (http://www.lfpress.com/comment/2012/08/20/20119696.html)

6: Human Rights Watch, *World Report 2012: Bahrain*, http://www.hrw.org/world-report- 2012/world-report-2012-bahrain (2012)

7: Kareem Fahim and David D. Kirkpatrick, "Army Kills 51, Crisis Deepens In Egypt," *New York Times*, July 8, 2013 (http://www.nytimes.com/2013/07/09/world/middleeast/egypt.html?pagewanted=all)

8: Fox News, *Intel report cites evidence of Syria attack, Kerry says 'no doubt' Assad responsible*, http://www.myfoxdc.com/story/23301298/kerry-1429-killed-in-syrian-chemical- attack#axzz2e2SwUDPX (August 30, 2013)

9: Yahya Ababneh and Dave Gavlak, "Syrians In Ghouta Claim Saudi-Supplied Rebels Behind Chemical Attack," *Mint Press News*, August 29, 2013 (http://www.mintpressnews.com/witnesses-of-gas-attack-say-saudis-supplied-rebels-with- chemical-weapons/168135/)

10: *New York Times*, August 27, 2013

11: Eric Posner, "The U.S. Has No Legal Basis to Intervene in Syria," *Slate*, August 28, 2013 (http://www.slate.com/articles/news_and_politics/view_from_chicago/2013/08/the_u_s_has_no_ legal_basis_for_its_action_in_syria_but_that_won_t_stop_us.html)

12: Saerom Yoo, "Federal Sequester Means Cuts to Local Social Services," *Statesman Journal*, August 27, 2013 (http://www.statesmanjournal.com/article/20130827/UPDATE/130827028/Federal-sequester- means-cuts-local-social-services)

13: National Education Association, *Impact of Sequestration on Federal Education Programs – State-by-State*, http://www.nea.org/home/52610.htm

14: Mattea Kramer, *The Cost of Military Intervention In Syria*, National Priorities Project, http://nationalpriorities.org/en/blog/2013/09/05/cost-military-intervention-syria/ (September 5, 2013)

15: Kristina Wong, "Aftermath of US Intervention In Syria Would Cost Billions," *Washington Times*, August 30, 2013 (http://www.washingtontimes.com/news/2013/aug/30/aftermath-us- intervention-syria-would-cost-billion/)

16: Oliver Holmes and Khaled Yacoub Oweis, "Syria Army Defectors Say US Strikes Could Kill Assad Opponents," *Reuters*, August 30, 2013 (http://mobile.*Reuters*.com/article/idUSBRE97T0N820130830?irpc=932)

The Central African Republic (CAR) is currently awash in media coverage regarding the ongoing sectarian violence and general upheaval in the country. While many outlets have discussed the situation in the CAR, there have been few fully encompassing analyses of the violence that put the situation in a proper historical context and discuss the interests of some of the countries that are in the CAR such as France or Chad while others are watching from afar, yet still interested, such as the United States. The violence in the CAR is unprecedented and worrisome; however, historically this is nothing but another unfortunate and bloody chapter regarding the instability of the country.

**A History of Violence**

The CAR is a former French colony, with the country having gained its independence soon after a 1958 French constitutional referendum which dissolved France's African holdings. [1] The first president, Barthélemy Boganda, died in a March 1959 plane crash and power was transferred to David Dacko who oversaw the CAR's declaration of independence on August 13, 1960 and established a one-party state by 1962.

Unfortunately, Dacko's days were numbered. In 1965, Jean Bedel Bokassa, who was a colonel in the CAR military, "was plucked by France to overthrow the Central African Republic's first President, his cousin David Dacko, when Mr. Dacko began establishing close ties with China."[2] Bokassa was chosen due to this fierce devotion to France and his anti- Communist stance. After overthrowing Dacko in a bloodless coup, Bokassa quickly broke off relations with China and took on a multitude of titles, which would eventually culminate in his declaring himself king in 1977. In addition to changing the CAR's foreign policy, Bokassa also suspended the constitution and dissolved the National Assembly, allowing him free reign to do as he pleased.

Though he showed increasingly strange behavior as time passed, the French still maintained good relations with him, even going so far as to congratulate him when he declared the CAR an empire and took the title of emperor.

However, the French eventually turned their backs on him [3], due to his increased yearning to decide foreign policy on his own, and helped to put Dacko back into power via a coup against Bokassa in 1979.

In 1981, elections took place and Dacko emerged victorious over challenger Ange-Félix Patassé, but charges of fraud remained. Just months later in September, Army Chief of Staff General André Kolingba seized power in a military coup. While, there was a coup attempt against him involving Ange-Félix Patassé [4], the coup failed and Patassé fled to the Togo, eventually coming back in the early '90s.

Kolingba operated what was essentially a military dictatorship into the 1990s due to a new constitution in 1986, which "provided him a single-party state and six-year term as president."[5] This aided him in the 1988 elections as opposing political parties were not allowed to participate.

Following the fall of the Berlin Wall in 1990, a pro-democracy movement sprouted and blossomed in the CAR, with Kolingba's response being to detain many pro-democratic protesters. However, Kolingba eventually agreed to free elections, after having come under pressure from "countries like the United States and France, but also agencies and organizations like the UN."[6]

In 1993, Ange-Félix Patassé was elected president of the CAR. The instability of the country continued with three different army mutinies in April, May, and November of 1996. The first munity occurred when some 400 soldiers demanded paychecks, with soldiers "[entering] the homes of business executives, demanding money and vehicles and beating those who refused."[7] It would be proper to note here that the governments that have ruled over the CAR have generally been extremely corrupt, with the IMF/World Bank noting in 2013 that on a regional level, corruption was hindering the growth of many Central African states.[8] According to Transparency International, the CAR is near the bottom on a list of the least-corrupt states, ranking 150 out of 175.[9] It was, in part, due to corruption and larger economic problems, which led to army members not being paid.

In May of 1996, the army mutinied again as they accused Patassé "of transferring the army's armory to his presidential guard."[10] In order to put down the mutiny, Patassé requested aid from the French who eventually sent 1,000 soldiers and 100 special forces commandos. [11] The mutiny eventually died down with a ceasefire being negotiated.

After the April and May mutinies, Patassé "formed a new government that included Kolingba supporters, but the country's main opposition groups refused to join the coalition."[12] However, a third mutiny in November still occurred as soldiers took advantage of Patassé being out of the country. Once again, the French came to his aid as they "rapidly deployed patrols throughout the city to protect key points and provide support to the Presidential Guard. Additional French Foreign Legion troops were flown into CAR from Chad to supplement the 1,750 soldiers already stationed in the country."[13] The mutiny was eventually put down, but had threatened to devolve into ethnic conflict.

These mutinies were stirred up by ex-dictator Kolingba, who "is from the Yakoma group, which is part of the Ngbandi ethnic group found on the banks of the Obangui river in the south."[14] When Patassé first came to power, the military was mainly made up of soldiers from Kolingba's ethnic group. In response, Patassé "created militias favoring his own Gbaya tribe and did not bother to pay the Yakoma-dominated regular army," [15] which actively contributed to the mutinies. A final rebellion occurred in 1997, but was put down by a pan-African force.

The troubles didn't end for Patassé as in May 2001; Kolingba sponsored an unsuccessful military coup which set off a series of events that ultimately led to Patassé's removal. After the coup attempt, the president accused his Army Chief of Staff, François Bozizé, of involvement and fired him on October 26, 2001. Bozizé rallied troops to resist his sacking, but was ultimately forced to leave for exile in southern Chad. These events deeply split and weakened the CAR armed forces—the Central African Armed Forces—dividing it between Patassé and Bozizé loyalists. [16]

Overall, Patassé's time as president was problematic for the country, not only due to the mutinies and attempted coup, but also due to the fact that "the CAR underwent economic collapse, losing what was left of its institutional capacity to provide social services for its citizens, and increased its dependence on external aid for survival" and Patassé "built up the Presidential Guard at the expense of the army, further ethicizing the state security forces."[17]

In October 2002, Bozizé launched a coup; however Patassé was able to beat him back with the aid of Libyan forces. Gaddafi had backed the CAR government since 2001, "in return for a 99-year monopoly on extracting the republic's vast reserves of diamonds, gold and other minerals."[18]

However, in 2003 when Patassé was out of the country in Niger, Bozizé swept into the capital with 1,000 troops and took control. [19]

In December 2004, voters in the CAR accepted a new constitution which "provides for a five-year presidential term, renewable only once, and the appointment of the prime minister from the political party with a parliamentary majority."[20] Quickly following this change was the 2005 presidential elections in which Bozizé ran as an independent and won. Out of this election came the rise of the Peoples' Army for the Restoration of the Republic and of Democracy (APRD), led by Jean-Jacques Demafouth, and made up mainly of former Presidential Guard members. Another group that came out of the elections was the Union of Democratic Forces for Unity (UFDR), which "is made up largely of the mainly-Muslim Gula ethnic group" and "includes men who helped Bozizé overthrow Patassé in 2003 but who subsequently felt disgruntled with the lack of recompense."[21] Both of these groups are from the northern region of the CAR and began actively fought against the Bozizé government.

This rebellion had occurred due to economic and political weakness within the CAR government. Bozizé had little power outside of Bangui, the capital, "while extreme poverty and a lack of both strong government institutions and economic development have contributed to declining support for the government among CAR citizens."[22] Citizens from the north are generally anti- Bozizé and accuse him of "favoring southerners since taking power, of failing to uphold democratic commitments, and of delaying implementation of promised political and economic reforms." The aforementioned groups actively fought the CAR government, for example in 2006 it was reported that an escalation in fighting between the APRD and government troops caused 70,000 people to flee the country. [23]

In order to bring an end to the fighting, a comprehensive peace agreement was brokered in 2008 [24] and quickly followed up an Inclusive Political Dialogue that same year. The Dialogue "called for the creation of a government of national unity; the holding of municipal elections in 2009, and legislative and presidential elections in 2010, which actually took place in January and March 2011; the creation of a national human rights commission; the launch of program for the disarmament, demobilization and reintegration (DDR) of former combatants."[25]

However, the goals of the Dialogue never came to fruition:

> [Nearly] five years later [2013], the overwhelming feeling is bitter disappointment: the inclusive government was never put in place; the 2011 elections took place but, according to observers, were marred by many accusations of fraud; the state disintegrated further; the "grey zones" outside state control expanded; most of the agreed essential reforms were never implemented; and the attitude adopted by both the government and rebel groups meant the demobilization, disarmament and reintegration (DDR) program never saw the light of day for combatants in the north east.[26]

This, coupled with the fact that democratic rule had effectively ended due to Bozizé's authoritarian ways and "conditions inside the CAR rapidly declined as economic under- development, nepotism and corruption fostered dissent and emboldened political opponents,"[27] led to Bozizé's ousting in 2013 by rebel group Séléka and the installment of its leader, Michel Djotodia, as interim president.

However, to talk about Séléka, there needs to be a discussion regarding the ongoing sectarian violence involving Muslims and Christians.

**Sectarian Violence**

While the CAR is home to several different ethnic groups, historically speaking "the CAR has no significant history of sectarian conflict or deep-seated religious enmity."[28] So, then, why is this violence occurring? In order to discuss that, one must discuss Séléka and Michel Djotodia.

*The Guardian* reported in December 2012 that the group Séléka had formed and that among their demands was "the implementation of the recommendations of the inclusive political dialogue, which was held in 2008 among government, civil society, the opposition and the rebels; financial compensation for the rebels; the release of political prisoners; and the opening of an investigation into the disappearance of former CPJP (Convention of Patriots for Justice and Peace) leader Charles Massi and other 'crimes.'"[29] Thus, it can be seen that group formed, at least partially, in response to the failed political dealings with the CAR government.

Religiously, Séléka members "were recruited from Muslim communities settled in CAR or in the 'three border areas' (Chad, Sudan, and CAR)." The formation of the group aided in the heightening of sectarian tensions as

> **While Séléka fighters have notional inclinations for political Islam, they share a strong sense of communal identity and a will to avenge previous CAR regimes and their beneficiaries identified as Christians** (not much of a discriminating factor, as the CAR population is more than 75% Christian). **Lay Muslims in CAR today are less likely to be harassed by the Séléka, and most often, there is cooperation**. The whole Muslim community is therefore perceived as supporting the Séléka and hostile to the core Christian population. [30] (emphasis added)

This anti-Christian bias was revealed soon after the group took control of the capital. The Congressional Research Service reported in May 2014 that "once in power, Séléka leaders presided over the collapse of an already fragile state, and they oversaw brutal attacks on rural Christian communities in the northwest, Bozizé's home region."[31]

In response to this violence, the Christian communities formed anti-balaka (anti-machete) militias and began to fight Muslims. The Christian militias attacked the Muslims viscously, with "scenes of cannibalism and the dismemberment of Muslims by Christian mobs in Bangui" [32] prompting France to send 2,000 soldiers into the country and the UN to send 12,000 peacekeepers. [33]

In January 2014, Michel Djotodia stepped down as President [34], following pressure from Chadian president Idriss Déby. He was soon replaced with Catherine Samba-Panza, the former mayor of Bangui. [35]

However, this raises the question: What interest does Chad have in the Central African Republic? And for that matter, are there any other interested parties?


**Foreign Interests**

*Chad*

Chad is a neighboring country and has been involved in the internal politics of the CAR for quite some time.

President Déby sponsored Bozizé's rebel movement and "capitalized on this behind-the- scenes power grab by enabling his forces to operate in the north of the CAR to eliminate Chadian rebel groups using the territory as a staging ground for attacks."[36] A main reason for Déby's interest in the CAR is security reasons. There has been a large amount of activity of Chadian rebels in the CAR and "many [Chadian rebels] who took part in the attacks from 2008 to 2010 on N'Djamena and Abéché sought shelter in the north-west of the CAR, which was virtually untouched by Bangui's authority"[37] and some even linked up with CAR rebel groups, eventually forming Séléka. There were accusations that Chad backed Séléka in order to draw the Chadian elements of the group deeper into the CAR and thus stop them from launching attacks into Chad. [38]

Another interest of Chad is oil. "'Chad is drilling oil from that border region and it's actually a shared oilfield with CAR,' [Enough Project's field researcher Kasper Agger] said. While there is no drilling on the CAR side yet, Chad has high interest in keeping tight control over the area."[39]

Thus it is no wonder that Chad is keeping a close eye on the CAR, even if they did withdraw their troops earlier in 2014. [40]

*France*

The CAR's former colonial power also has interests at stake, which stem mainly from Bozizé's rule.

Right before he was overthrown, in 2012 Bozizé called on the French to aid him in beating back the Séléka rebels. [41] This call went unanswered of course and this was mainly due to problems with the CAR government and with CAR-China relations. A 2009 U.S. diplomatic cable noted that

The constant frustrations facing French commercial giants such as Total and AREVA are well known. While France used to count on the CAR as a valuable reserve of uranium, it is very clear that the double dealing of the Minister of Mines, among others, in renegotiating contracts is pushing the French beyond even their normally generous limits. [42]

While France does have "extensive interests in Africa, in oil, minerals, infrastructure projects, telecoms, utilities, banking and insurance," "its market share is being eroded by competition from China, Brazil, India and others."[43] Bozizé actively worked with the Chinese, to the ire of the French. It was reported in December 2012 that "in March and April 2012 [the] South African company DIG Oil had been awarded two exploration contracts and that a Chinese company had also obtained such authorization"[44] to explore for oil in the CAR. He was quite wary of the French, noting in a December 2012 speech that he was being attacked due the aforementioned Chinese oil contract, saying "We gave them [the French] everything. Before giving oil to the Chinese, I met Total in Paris and told them to take the oil; nothing happened. I gave oil to the Chinese and it became a problem. I sent counselor Maidou in Paris for the Uranium dossier, they refused. I finally gave it to the South Africans."[45] Due to his dealings with the Chinese and other problems, the French were disinterested in propping up Bozizé and thus let him fall.

In 2013, the French did send in troops to aid in the peacekeeping, along with African forces [46], but drew their forces down in January 2014 from 2,000 troops to 800 noting that UN peacekeepers had arrived. [47]

*United States*

The US sent their UN ambassador Samantha Power to the CAR in late 2013 to appeal for peace. [48] It should be noted that Power wants the US to intervene more and "has made a career out of scolding the U.S. for not intervening around the world enough,"[49] such as in her magnum opus where she lamented that the US didn't intervene to stop the Armenian genocide during the First World War. In fact, she is quite fond of the 'Responsibility To Protect' doctrine and "was one of the driving forces behind the United States intervention in Libya."[50] So an eye should be kept on her, knowing that she may push for further US intervention.

So far the US has sent delivered aid to peacekeepers [51], airlifted African troops into the CAR [52], and sent troops to support the US embassy resuming its activities [53], but not much else.

On a regional level, the US is interested in the CAR not just for any of its vast resources, but specifically oil. A 2013 Brookings Institution report entitled Top Five Reasons Why Africa Should Be a Priority for the United States noted that "significant new discoveries have prompted the [International Energy Agency] to anoint sub-Saharan Africa the 'new frontier' in global oil and gas" and "the emergence of new oil and gas producers in the region presents potential benefits for U.S. national security interests, if this new found wealth is managed appropriately [...] Several countries could also potentially become oil suppliers to the US, further diversifying the sources of US imported oil." [54]

The US concern with African oil is nothing new as it was noted in 2002 that

already, 15 percent of the United States' imported oil supply comes from sub-Saharan Africa. Oil experts predict that the amount of oil the United States receives from the prolific fields of Nigeria, Equatorial Guinea and Angola will double in the next five years.

**"African oil is of strategic national interest to us and it will increase and become more important as we go forward," Walter Kansteiner, assistant U.S. secretary of state for African Affairs, said during a July 2002 visit to Nigeria – the largest oil producer in West Africa with an estimated 24 billion barrels in reserve."[55] (emphasis added)**

Just as with the French, the Americans are also concerned about China. From that same Brookings report:

China's engagement in Africa has profound geopolitical implications for the U.S. global strategy. [...] China is looking beyond the traditional pursuit of economic benefits and aspires to increase and solidify its strategic presence through enhanced political, economic, diplomatic and academic resources. The failure to perceive and prepare for China's moves would be dangerous, unwise and potentially detrimental for the United States in the near future. [56]

So, the US is concerned with resources, but all the more so due to a major competitor that is actively making moves in the region.

More recently, in January 2015, the UN stated that it had found evidence of ethnic cleansing done by Christian militias against Muslims[57], giving confirmation to the alarms that had been raised in June 2014[58] and even before that in late 2013.[59] Unfortunately, the violence is only continuing.


## Endnotes

1: The Encyclopedia of Earth, *Central African Republic*, http://www.eoearth.org/view/article/150993

2: Howard W. French, "Jean-Bedel Bokassa, Self-Crowned Emperor of Central African Republic, Dies At 75," *New York Times*, November 5, 1996 (http://www.nytimes.com/1996/11/05/world/jean-bedel-bokassa-self-crowned-emperor-central- african-republic-dies-75.html)

3: Royal African Society, *Central African Republic*, http://www.royalafricansociety.org/countries/central-african-republic

4: Kaye Whiteman, "Ange-Félix Patassé Obituary," *The Guardian*, June 14, 2011 (http://www.theguardian.com/world/2011/jun/14/ange-felix-patasse-obituary)

5: J. Tyler Dickovick, *The World Series Today: Africa* 48th ed. (Lanham, Maryland: Stryker- Post Publications, 2013), pg 158

6: German School of Athens, *The Situation in the Central African Republic*, http://www.dsamun.gr/preparation/138-security-council-the-situation-in-the-central- african-republic/file

7: *New York Times, Central African Soldiers Continue Their Mutiny*, http://www.nytimes.com/1996/04/21/world/world-news-briefs-central-african-soldiers- continue-their-mutiny.html (April 21, 1996)

8: Moki Edwin Kindzeka, "Central African Growth Hindered by Vast Corruption," *Voice of America News*, December 2, 2013 (http://www.voanews.com/content/central-africa-growth- hindered-by-vast-corruption/1801782.html)

9: Transparency International, *Central African Republic*, http://www.transparency.org/country#CAF

10: Norman Kempster, "Americans Evacuated From Central African Republic," *Los Angeles Times,* May, 22, 1996 (http://articles.latimes.com/1996-05-22/news/mn-7063_1_central-african- republic)

11: CNN, *French Drawn Deeper Into Central Africa Mutiny*, http://web.archive.org/web/20050213012000/http:/www.cnn.com/WORLD/9605/22/ne wsbriefs.pm/index.html (May 22, 1996)

12: Portland Community College, *Central African Republic*, https://spot.pcc.edu/~mdembrow/Central%20African%20Republic.htm

13: Institute for Security Studies, *Crisis and Response in the Central African Republic: A New Trend in African Peacekeeping*, http://www.issafrica.org/pubs/ASR/7No2/McFarlaneAndMalan.html

14: BBC, *UN Steps into CAR Ethnic Tension*, http://news.bbc.co.uk/2/hi/africa/1385090.stm (June 12, 2001)

15: Global Security, *Central African Republic- Background*, http://www.globalsecurity.org/military/world/war/car-2.htm

16: Human Rights Watch, *State of Anarchy: Rebellions and Abuses Against Civilians*, http://www.hrw.org/reports/2007/car0907/4.htm

17: International Security Sector Advisory Team, *Central African Republic*, http://issat.dcaf.ch/Home/Community-of-Practice/Resource-Library/Country- Profiles/Central-African-Republic-Background-Note#introduction

18: The Economist, *Rebellion in Central Africa: No Pay, No Peace*, http://www.economist.com/node/1418716 (October 31, 2002)

19: The Economist, *Central African Republic: A Popular Coup*, http://www.economist.com/node/1648658 (March 20, 2003)

20: IRIN, *Central African Republic: New Constitution Adopted, 15 to Vie For Presidency*, http://www.irinnews.org/report/52467/central-african-republic-new-constitution- adopted-15-to-vie-for-presidency (December 20, 2004)

21: IRIN, *Central African Republic: Who's Who With Guns*, http://www.irinnews.org/report/84886/central-african-republic-who-s-who-with- guns (June 17, 2009)

22: Kelly Campbell, *Central African Republic, Chad, and Sudan: Triangle of Instability*, United States Institute of Peace, http://www.usip.org/publications/central-african-republic-chad-and- sudan-triangle-of-instability (December 1, 2006)

23: Angola Press, *70,000 Refugees Flee CAR Into Cameroon, Chad*, http://web.archive.org/web/20070929120427/http:/www.angolapress-angop.ao/noticia- e.asp?ID=480367 (October 15, 2006)

24: Uppsala University, *Comprehensive Peace Agreement*, http://www.ucdp.uu.se/gpdatabase/peace/CAR%2020080621.pdf

25: Global Security, *Central African Republic- Francois Bozize*, http://www.globalsecurity.org/military/world/war/car-3.htm

26: International Crisis Group, *Central African Republic: Priorities of the Transition*, http://www.crisisgroup.org/~/media/Files/africa/central-africa/central-african- republic/203-central-african-republic-priorities-of-the-transition.pdf (June 11, 2013)

27: Armada Global Inc, *Central African Republic: Conflict and Instability*, http://www.armadaglobalinc.com/docs/Central_African_Republic_Conflict_Instabilit y.pdf (October 2013)

28: Stephanie Burchard, "The Central African Conflict Is About Far More Than Religion," *Think Africa Press*, February 26, 2014 (http://thinkafricapress.com/central-african-republic/identity- politics-coding-religion)

---

29: *The Guardian, Rebel Union In Central African Republic Raises Humanitarian Concerns*, http://www.theguardian.com/global-development/2012/dec/21/rebel-central-african- republic-humanitarian (December 12, 2012)

30: News 24, *Fear Reigns In CAR's Capital Bangui*, http://www.news24.com/Africa/News/Fear- reigns-in-CARs-capital-Bangui-20121231 (December 31, 2012)

31: Congressional Research Service, *Crisis in the Central African Republic*, https://www.fas.org/sgp/crs/row/R43377.pdf (May 14, 2014)

32: Daniel Flynn, "Gold, Diamonds Feed Central African Religious Violence," *Reuters*, July 29, 2014 (http://www.*Reuters*.com/article/2014/07/29/us-centralafrica-resources-insight-idUSKBN0FY0MN20140729)

33: Euro News, *UN To Send 12,000-strong Peacekeeping Force to Central African Republic*, http://www.euronews.com/2014/04/10/united-nations-security-council-backs- resolution-to-send-12000-strong-force-to-/ (October 4, 2014)

34: *The Telegraph, CAR Leader Michel Djotodia Resigns Over Failure To End Sectarian Violence*, http://www.telegraph.co.uk/news/worldnews/africaandindianocean/centralafricanrepub lic/10564010/CAR-leader-Michel-Djotodia-resigns-over-failure-to-end-sectarian- violence.html (January 10, 2014)

35: Andrew Katz, "Central African Republic: Meet New President Catherine Samba- Panza," *Time*, January 23, 2014 (http://world.time.com/2014/01/23/meet-catherine-samba-panza- central-african-republics-new-interim-president/)

36: Frank Charnas, "The Chad Jihad Threat," *The National Interest*, June 21, 2013 (http://nationalinterest.org/commentary/the-chad-jihad-threat-8625)

37: Celeste Hicks, "Chad: Déby's Misstep in the Central African Republic," *Think Africa Press*, January 27, 2014 (http://thinkafricapress.com/chad/deby-overstretch-car-central-african- republic-seleka-djotodia)

38: Celeste Hicks, "Central African Republic a Crisis Too Far For Chad's Regional Security Ambition," *World Politics Review*, April 7, 2014 (http://www.worldpoliticsreview.com/articles/13681/central-african-republic-a-crisis-too-far-for- chad-s-regional-security-ambitions)

39: Priyanka Boghani, "Chad and France Are Really Not Helping the Central African Republic Right Now," *Global Post*, May 20, 2014 (http://www.globalpost.com/dispatch/news/regions/africa/140514/chad-france-not-helping- central-african-republic)

40: Al Jazeera, *Chad to Withdraw Troops From CAR Mission*, http://www.aljazeera.com/news/africa/2014/04/chad-withdraw-troops-from-car- mission-201443154748935527.html (April 3, 2014)

41: BBC, *Central African Republic's Bozize in US-France Appeal*, http://www.bbc.com/news/world-africa-20845887 (December 27, 2012)

42: Wikileaks, *French-CAR Relations Seriously Strained*, https://wikileaks.org/plusd/cables/09BANGUI120_a.html (June 17, 2009)

43: Brian Eads, "France Is Slowly Reclaiming Its Old African Empire," *Newsweek*, October 30, 2014 (http://www.newsweek.com/2014/11/07/france-slowly-reclaiming-its-old-african-empire- 280635.html)

44: Global Voices, *Who Wants to Overthrow the Central African Republic's Francois Bozize?* http://globalvoicesonline.org/2012/12/30/who-wants-to-overthrow-central-african- republics-president-francois-bozize/ (December 30, 2012)

45: Kumaran Ire, "French Troops Intervene in Central African Republic, Seize Bangui," *World Socialist Web Site*, December 9, 2013 (http://www.wsws.org/en/articles/2013/12/09/car- d09.html)

46: Nima Elbagir, Faith Karimi, Laura Smith-Spark, "French Troops Begin Operating In Central African Republic As Violence Worsens," *CNN*, December 8, 2013 (http://www.cnn.com/2013/12/06/world/africa/central-african-republic-unrest/)

47: Fox News, *France to Pull 1,200 Troops From Central African Republic*, http://www.foxnews.com/world/2015/01/14/france-to-pull-1200-troops-from-central- african-republic/ (January 14, 2015)

48: NPR, *CAR Atrocities Must Be Answered, Says U.N. Ambassador Samantha Power*, http://www.npr.org/2013/12/22/256224319/car-atrocities-must-be-answered-says-un- ambassador-samantha-power (December 22, 2013)

49: Richard Spencer, "Samantha Power and Paul Wolfowitz-Separated At Birth," *Taki's Magazine*, March 8, 2008 (http://takimag.com/article/samantha_power_and_paul_wolfowitzseparated_at_birth/print#axzz3 PxWX3DVK)

50: Alexander Abad-Santos, "Samantha Power Has It All," *The Wire*, June 5, 2013 (http://www.thewire.com/politics/2013/06/samantha-power-bio/65920/)

51: Jon Harper, "For US Forces, Delivering Peacekeepers To Central African Republic Is No Easy Task," *Stars And Stripes*, January 22, 2014 (http://www.stripes.com/news/for-us-forces- delivering-peacekeepers-to-the-central-african-republic-is-no-easy-task-1.263356)

52: Julia Barnes, Adam Entous, "US To Fly African Troops Into Conflict Zone," *Wall Street Journal*, December 9, 2013 (http://online.wsj.com/news/articles/SB10001424052702304744304579248351259511172?mod =djemalertEuropenews)

53: Hayes Brown, "Why There Are Now US Troops In The Central African Republic," *Think Progress*, September 12, 2014 (http://thinkprogress.org/world/2014/09/12/3566736/usa-return- car/)

54: Brookings Institution, *Top Five Reasons Why Africa Should Be a Priority for the United States*, http://www.brookings.edu/~/media/Research/Files/Reports/2013/04/africa%20priority%2 0united%20states/04_africa_priority_united_states.pdf (March 2013)

55: The Center for Public Integrity, *The Curious Bonds of Oil Diplomacy*, http://www.publicintegrity.org/2002/10/06/5685/curious-bonds-oil- diplomacy (October 6, 2002)

56: Brookings Institution, March 2013

57: *Reuters, Ethnic Cleansing In Central African Republic, No Genocide: UN Inquiry*, http://www.*Reuters*.com/article/2015/01/08/us-centralafrica-inquiry- idUSKBN0KH2BM20150108 (January 2015)

58: Al Jazeera, *UN Report Disputes Genocide Claims In CAR*, http://www.aljazeera.com/news/africa/2014/06/un-report-disputes-genocide-claims-car- 20146610611138683.html (June 6, 2014)

59: David Smith, "Unspeakable Horrors in a Country on the Verge of Genocide," *The Guardian*, November 22, 2013 (http://www.theguardian.com/world/2013/nov/22/central-african-republic- verge-of-genocide)

*Published on: July 8, 2015*

What occurred on September 11, 2012 in Benghazi, Libya has been mired in controversy, political agendas, stories appearing and disappearing and rumors. This report is an attempt to go past all of the political nonsense and the varying political opinions, to get to the heart of exactly what went on that night to the best that one can ascertain.

## Immediate Aftermath

Immediately after the attacks on the US embassy in Benghazi, the Obama administration began pushing a narrative based on a video. The official narrative was that "The violence began around 10 p.m. Tuesday amid a protest by the radical Islamist group Ansar Al-Sharia against a film mocking Islam's prophet. Four hours later, the consulate was destroyed, its walls blackened by shooting flames."[1] The following week on September 18, 2012, Press Secretary Jay Carney stated that "Our belief based on the information we had was that it was the video that caused the unrest in Cairo and the video that — and the unrest in Cairo that helped — that precipitated some of the unrest in Benghazi and elsewhere."[2] The idea was that the attack had been over a video insulting the Prophet Mohammed and that was it.

However, even then, there were some whispers that the attack may have been planned [3] and this only grew as more evidence came out. US officials and experts noted that the attack "involved the use of a rocket-propelled grenade and followed an al-Qaeda call to avenge the death of a senior Libyan member of the terrorist network."[4] Further evidence came out with regard to the protest that allegedly occurred before the attack with a Libyan guard saying that the assault **was a planned attack by armed Islamists and not the outgrowth of a protest over an online video** that mocks Islam and its founder, the Prophet Muhammad."[5] (emphasis added)

The nail in the coffin finally came when new Libyan president Mohammed Magarief said that "the controversial film that mocked Islam's Prophet Muhammad and ignited protests throughout the Muslim world had 'nothing to do' with the Sept. 11 attack on the U.S. Consulate in Benghazi, and that he [had] 'no doubt' it was an act of terrorism."[6] The evidence was so overwhelming that the Obama administration was forced to admit the following month (October 2012) that there were no protests before the attack.[7]

Early in October 2012, video evidence was added to the mix which "[showed] an organized group of armed men attacking the compound, according to two U.S. intelligence officials who have seen the footage and are involved in the ongoing investigation."[8] Later that month, *Business Insider* revealed that "Officials at the White House and State Department were advised two hours after attackers assaulted the US diplomatic mission in Benghazi, Libya, on Sept. 11 that an Islamic militant group had claimed credit for the attack, official emails show."[9] While the question of what caused the attack was put to rest, another question was raised: What about security?

## Security

The first discussions of security around the embassy came up in not soon after the attack occurred. *The Independent* reported that "American diplomats were warned of possible violent unrest in Benghazi three days before the killings of US Ambassador Christopher Stevens and three members of his team, Libyan security officials say" and that Libya's "interim President, Mohammed el-Megarif, said his government had information that the attack on the US consulate had been planned by an Islamist group with links to al-Qa'ida and with foreigners taking part."[10] The interim President's statement brings up the question: Were Al Qaeda-linked groups with the Libyan rebels?

There is a strong possibility AQ-linked groups were among the rebels. *The Guardian* reported in 2011 that while some individuals had left the Libyan Islamic Fighting Group, "Other top ex-LIFG figures remain in al-Qaida."[11] A 2011 *Telegraph* article quoted Libyan rebel leader Abdel-Hakim al-Hasidi as saying that the "members of al-Qaeda are also good Muslims and are fighting against the invader [Gaddafi]." There was even some background information on the relationship between the LIFG and Al Qaeda: "Even though the LIFG is not part of the al- Qaeda organization, the United States military's West Point academy has said the two share an 'increasingly co-operative relationship.'"[12] Thus, this creates the strong possibility that the attack was carried out by terrorists, as the Libyan president noted.

Furthermore, on the question of Al Qaeda-linked members to the embassy attack, *The Daily Beast* wrote in December 2013 that according to "two members of the House intelligence committee, Republican Mike Rogers and Democrat Adam Schiff" the "U.S. intelligence assessments concluded al Qaeda did play a role in the attack."[13] This was in response to a *New York Times* article published earlier that same month, which asserted that based on "extensive interviews with Libyans in Benghazi who had direct knowledge of the attack there and its context," there was "no evidence that Al Qaeda or other international terrorist groups had any role in the assault."[14]

According to both Rogers and Schiff, there was no talk of the Jamal Network, a group that "In October, the State Department [designated] as a terrorist group tied to al Qaeda" and that the *New York Times* itself reported information regarding their source, Ahmed Abu Khattala, that Khattala "was close to a leader of the militia the U.S. had entrusted to protect its facilities in Benghazi in light of an attack."[15] What was the name of the militia that the US had trusted its Benghazi facilities to? They were called the February 17th Martyrs Brigade.[16] The group is an affiliate of the organization Ansar al-Sharia.[17] It should be noted that "While both organizations are nominally independent, each has outwardly expressed either a direct or indirect affiliation with the terror brand known as Al Qaeda."[18]

So why were Al Qaeda affiliated terrorists protecting the embassy? According to a US Senate Committee report, this occurred due to the fact that the Libyan government itself wasn't strong enough to provide security. However, even then, "Throughout 2012, Department of State officials questioned the February 17 Brigade's competence and expressed concerns about its abilities."[19] In addition to this, "In early September [2012], a member of the February 17 Brigade told another [Regional Security Officer] in Benghazi that it could no longer support U.S. personnel movements. The RSO also asked specifically if the militia could provide additional support for the Ambassador's pending visit and was told no."[20] So not only were US personnel questioning the competence of the Brigade, but the Brigade had flatly told the Americans that they were not going to provide security support for J. Christopher Stevens.

The State Department can also be viewed as problematic as they admitted in early October 2012 that "it rejected appeals for more security at its diplomatic posts in Libya in the months before a fatal terrorist attack in Benghazi."[21] Later in October 2012, *Fox News* reported that there was "an urgent request for military help during last month's terrorist attack on the US consulate there 'was denied by the CIA chain of command" and "a Special Operations team had been moved to US military facilities in Sigonella, Italy – approximately two hours away – but were never told to deploy."[22] The Pentagon denied those assertions, stating that "The U.S. military did not get involved during the attack on the U.S. mission in Benghazi, Libya, last month because officials did not have enough information about what was going on before the attack was over" and then-Secretary of Defense Leon Panetta saying that "there was no 'real- time information' to be able to act on."[23]

In 2013, *NBC News* reported that "A small team of Special Forces operatives was ready to fly from Tripoli to Benghazi last year after Libyan insurgents attacked the U.S. mission there, but was told it was not authorized to board the flight by regional military commanders" and that the "flight [would not have arrived] in time for their presence to have had an impact in the fighting."[24] So, while it is true that the US could not have provided much aid during the actual attack, they could have acted proactively by providing an increase in security.

Yet, the journey does not end there as there are some questions surrounding the question of security surrounding the embassy. The CIA is bought into the mix as CIA members at a nearby annex stated "that they asked permission to leave for the consulate immediately and twice were told to wait. The CIA says the base chief was trying to arrange Libyan help."[25] This brings up the question of what exactly was the CIA doing in Libya.


**The CIA's Gun-Running**

According to a 2012 *Business Insider* article, "the State Department presence in Benghazi 'provided diplomatic cover' for the previously hidden CIA mission, which involved finding and repurchasing heavy weaponry looted from Libyan government arsenals,"[26] according to unnamed officials. While this may sound ludicrous on its face, this claim actually not only has some legs to it, but is true.

The allegations started earlier than 2012. In 2011, there were already reports of Libyan fighters going into Syria. *Russia Today* reported that the Libyan government "has sent 600 of its troops to support local militants against the Assad regime."[27] Jordanian news outlet Al Bawaba wrote that "Libyan sources conveyed in recent days that 600 rebel fighters have already gone from Libya to Syria in order to support the Syrian opposition" and that "there is coordination between the Libyan interim government and the Syrian opposition."[28]

In October 2012, *Fox News* wrote that "a source told Fox News that [US Ambassador Christopher Stevens] was in Benghazi to negotiate a weapons transfer, an effort to get SA-7 missiles out of the hands of Libya-based extremists." However, they also noted that "the Libyan- flagged vessel Al Entisar, which means 'The Victory,' was received in the Turkish port of Iskenderun -- 35 miles from the Syrian border -- on Sept. 6, just five days before Ambassador Chris Stevens, information management officer Sean Smith and former Navy Seals Tyrone Woods and Glen Doherty were killed during an extended assault by more than 100 Islamist militants."[29] The allegations went further into the mainstream in 2013 when it was reported that CNN "said that a CIA team was working in an annex near the consulate on a project to supply missiles from Libyan armories to Syrian rebels."[30] However, the hammer came down in 2015 when Judicial Watch, via a FOIA request, received documents which showed that weapons were shipped from Libya to Syria. Specifically the Defense Department documents noted that "Weapons from the former Libya military stockpiles were shipped from the port of Benghazi, Libya to the Port of Banias and the Port of Borj Islam, Syria. The weapons shipped during late August 2012 were sniper rifles, RPGs, 125mm and 155mm howitzers missiles."[31]

It is interesting to note, though, that the new Libyan government was also providing the Syrian rebels with weaponry. In November 2011, the *Sydney Morning Herald* reported that "Syrian rebels have held secret talks with Libya's new authorities, aiming to secure weapons and money for their insurgency against Bashar al-Assad's regime" and that "At the meeting, which was held in Istanbul and included Turkish officials, the Syrians requested assistance from the Libyan representatives and were offered arms and, potentially, volunteers."[32] So both the Libyan government and the US were aiding the Syrian rebels. So, what does this mean? It means that the US was actively aiding in the destabilization of Syria and the new government in Libya was more than happy to aid in the cause of helping their Islamist friends (the new Libyan government was extremely Islamist as Sharia law was to be the main source of legislation [33]).

However, it also raises the question: Why was the US government smuggling guns and fighters when the Libyans seemed to willing to do it? It may have to do with the fact that gun- running was overall aiding them in their regional plans and that the Libyan government just happened to also contribute as well.

Now it is time to look at the problems and revelations in the House and Senate Reports.


**US Government Reports**

In January 2014, the US Senate report on Benghazi came out and it was found that the Benghazi attack was preventable. [34] The report stated that in the months following up to the attack, "the [intelligence community] provided ample strategic warning that the security situation in eastern Libya was deteriorating and that US facilities and personnel were at risk in Benghazi."[35] It also noted a number of other aforementioned issues, such as security could have been beefed up and the like.

What is of real interest is the House report, which came out in November 2014, and the media claims that the report found that the Obama administration had done no wrong.[36] However, a further look at the report will reveal that some of the statements made are problematic.

There are two glaring problems with the House Benghazi report. The second conclusion of the report is that "there was no intelligence failure prior to the attacks. In the months prior, the [intelligence community] provided intelligence about previous attacks and the increased threat environment in Benghazi, but the [intelligence community] did not have specific, tactical warning of the September 11th attacks."[37] This is nothing more than a slight of hand. Given the fact that they did have warning of the attack, ten days to be specific according to newly released Defense and State Department documents [38], in addition to the fact that extra security was denied, there was definitely a mixture of intelligence and security problems.

The other claim made in the House report is that they "found no evidence that the CIA conducted unauthorized activities in Benghazi and no evidence that the [intelligence community] shipped arms to Syria."[39] Given all of the aforementioned information, including the newly disclosed documents, that argument is patently false. The CIA did in fact ship weapons from Libya to Syria.

Therefore, only one question remains which concerns a major political figure and presumed party presidential nominee: Hillary Clinton.


**Hillary Clinton**


In March 2015, Hillary Clinton made headlines regarding her emails as related to the assault on Benghazi. *Reuters* reported that "Huge gaps exist in the emails former U.S. Secretary of State Hillary Clinton has provided to a congressional committee investigating the 2012 attack on a U.S. consulate in Benghazi, Libya."[40] Due to this, Clinton was asked to hand over her email server, while she did this, she deleted more than 30,000 emails[42] and even wiped her server clean.[43] This only added more suspicion about her.

While the *New York Times* stated that the emails showed nothing incriminating; [44] that eventually turned out to be false as in February 2015, Judicial Watch obtained emails via a FOIA request that show that Clinton's advisers knew that the embassy attack was in fact a violent one.

An email from September 11, 2012, sent at 4:22 pm reads that the "[Diplomatic Security Command Center] received a phone call from [REDACTED] in Benghazi, Libya **initially stating that 15 armed individuals were attacking the compound and trying to gain entrance. The Ambassador is present in Benghazi and currently is barricaded within the compound.** There are no injuries at this time and it is unknown what the intent of the attackers is."[45] (emphasis added) This was also reported in the Wall Street Journal which noted that the emails "show at least some of the details about the worsening security environment in Benghazi that were presented directly to her."[46]

The lies and deception of the Obama administration have been unraveling since the day officials started making statements. Now is the time to push for the truth to be revealed.

**Endnotes**

1: Sarah Aarthun, "4 Hours of Fire and Chaos: How the Benghazi Attack Unfolded," *CNN*, September 13, 2012 (http://www.cnn.com/2012/09/12/world/africa/libya-consulate-attack- scene/)

2: *New York Times, Administration Statements on the Attack in Benghazi,* http://www.nytimes.com/interactive/2012/09/27/world/africa/administration-statements-on-the- attack-in-benghazi.html?_r=0

3: Michael Birnbaum, William Branigin, Karen DeYoung, "U.S. Officials: Attack on consulate in Libya may have been planned," *Washington Post*, September 12, 2012 (http://www.washingtonpost.com/world/news-agencies-us-ambassador-to-libya-killed-in-attack- outside-consulate/2012/09/12/665de5fc-fcc4-11e1-a31e-804fccb658f9_story.html)

4: Mark Hosenball, "US Intelligence Now Says Benghazi Attack 'Deliberate and Organized," *Reuters*, September 28, 2012 (http://www.*Reuters*.com/article/2012/09/28/us-usa-libya- intelligence-idUSBRE88R1EG20120928)

5: Nancy A. Youssef, Suliman Ali Zway, "No Protest Before Attack, Wounded Libyan Guard Says," *McClatchy DC*, September 13, 2012 (http://www.mcclatchydc.com/2012/09/13/168415/no-protest-before-benghazi-attack.html)

6: Dylan Stableford, "Libyan President: Benghazi Attack Was a 'Pre-Planned Act of Terrorism," Yahoo News, September 26, 2012 (http://news.yahoo.com/blogs/the-lookout/libya-president- benghazi-attack-terrorism-133154516.html)

7: Maggie Haberman, "Officials: No protests before Benghazi attack," Politico, October 10, 2012 (http://www.politico.com/blogs/burns-haberman/2012/10/officials-no-protests-before-       benghazi-attack-137978.html)

8: Eli Lake, "Video From Benghazi Consulate Shows Organized Attack," *The Daily Beast*, October 12, 2012 (http://www.thedailybeast.com/articles/2012/10/12/video-from-benghazi- consulate-shows-organized-attack.html)

9: Business Insider, *These Emails Make It Hard To Believe The White House Thought Benghazi Attackers Were Just Protesters*, http://www.businessinsider.com/white-house-officials-were- told-of-militant-gangs-two-hours-after-benghazi-attack-2012-10 (October 24, 2012)

10: Kim Sengupta, "Libya: We Gave Three-Day Warning of Benghazi Attack," *The Independent*, September 18, 2012 (http://www.independent.co.uk/news/world/africa/libya-we- gave-us-threeday-warning-of-benghazi-attack-8145242.html)

11: Ian Black, "The Libyan Islamic Fighting Group- from Al-Qaida to the Arab Spring," *The Guardian*, September 5, 2011 (http://www.theguardian.com/world/2011/sep/05/libyan-islamic- fighting-group-leaders)

12: Duncan Gardham, Nick Squires, Praveen Swami, "Libyan rebel commander admits his fighters have al-Qaeda links," *The Telegraph*, March 25, 2011 (http://www.telegraph.co.uk/news/worldnews/africaandindianocean/libya/8407047/Libyan-rebel-commander-admits-his-fighters-have-al-Qaeda-links.html)

13: Eli Lake, "Yes, There Is Evidence Linking Al Qaeda to Benghazi," *The Daily Beast*, December 29, 2013 (http://www.thedailybeast.com/articles/2013/12/29/yes-there-is-evidence- linking-al-qaeda-to-benghazi.html)

14: David D. Kirkpatrick, "A Deadly Mix in Benghazi," *New York Times*, December 28, 2013 (http://www.nytimes.com/projects/2013/benghazi/#/?chapt=0)

15: Ibid

16: Fred Burton, Samuel M. Katz, "40 Minutes in Benghazi," *Vanity Fair*, August 2013 (http://www.vanityfair.com/news/politics/2013/08/Benghazi-book-fred-burton-samuel-m-katz)

17: Lawrence Myers, "Source: Clinton Directly Involved In Terrorist Group 'Security Force' At Benghazi," *Townhall*, September 29, 2014 (http://townhall.com/columnists/lawrencemeyers/2014/09/29/source-clinton-directly-involved- in-terrorist-group-security-force-at-benghazi-n1897853)

18: Eric Draitser, "Benghazi, the CIA, and the War in Libya," *Global Research*, June 9, 2014 (http://www.globalresearch.ca/benghazi-the-cia-and-the-war-in-libya/5386266)

19: U.S. Congress, Senate, Committee On Homeland Security And Governmental Affairs, *Flashing Red: A Special Report On The Terrorist Attack At Benghazi* (Washington, D.C.: Committee On Homeland Security And Governmental Affairs, 2012), pg 11

20: Ibid

21: Anna Gearan, "State Dept. acknowledges rejecting requests for more security in Benghazi," *Washington Post*, October 10, 2012 (http://www.washingtonpost.com/world/national- security/state-dept-downgraded-security-in-libya-before-deadly-attack-ex-officer- claims/2012/10/10/d7195faa-12e6-11e2-a16b-2c110031514a_story.html)

22: Brad Knickerbocker, "Benghazi attack: Urgent call for military help 'was denied by chain of command," *Christian Science Monitor*, October 27, 2012 (http://www.csmonitor.com/USA/Military/2012/1027/Benghazi-attack-Urgent-call-for-military- help-was-denied-by-chain-of-command)

23: Chris Lawrence, "Panetta on Benghazi attack: 'Could not put forces at risk," *CNN*, October 26, 2012 (http://security.blogs.cnn.com/2012/10/26/panetta-on-benghazi-attack-could-not-put- forces-at-risk/)

24: Lisa Myers, "Official: US Special Forces Team Wasn't allowed to fly to Benghazi during attack," *NBC News*, May 6, 2013 (http://investigations.nbcnews.com/_news/2013/05/06/18086898-official-us-special-forces-team- wasnt-allowed-to-fly-to-benghazi-during-attack)

25: Jennifer Griffin, Adam Housley, "Military Timeline from night of Benghazi attack begs more questions," *Fox News*, November 11, 2012 (http://www.foxnews.com/politics/2012/11/11/military-timeline-from-night-benghazi-attack- begs-more-questions/)

26: Michael B Kelley, "There's A Reason Why All The Reports About Benghazi Are So Confusing," *Business Insider*, November 3, 2012 (http://www.businessinsider.com/benghazi- stevens-cia-attack-libya-2012-11#ixzz2Ea3tvDzg)

27: Russia Today, *Bomb voyage: 600 Libyans 'already fighting in Syria*, http://rt.com/news/libya-syria-fighters-smuggled-475/ (November 29, 2011)

28: Al Bawaba, *Libyan fighters join "free Syrian army" forces*, http://www.albawaba.com/news/libyan-fighters-join-free-syrian-army-forces-403268 (November 29, 2011)

29: Pamela Browne, Catherine Herridge, "Was Syrian Weapons Shipment Factor In Ambassadors Benghazi Visit?" *Fox News*, October 25, 2012 (http://www.foxnews.com/politics/2012/10/25/was-syrian-weapons-shipment-factor-in- ambassadors-benghazi-visit/)

30: Damien McElroy, "CIA 'running arms smuggling team in Benghazi when consulate was attacked," *The Telegraph*, August 2, 2013 (http://www.telegraph.co.uk/news/worldnews/africaandindianocean/libya/10218288/CIA- running-arms-smuggling-team-in-Benghazi-when-consulate-was-attacked.html)

31: Judicial Watch, *Defense, State Department Documents Reveal Obama Administration Knew that al Qaeda Terrorists Had Planned Benghazi Attack 10 Days in Advance*, http://www.judicialwatch.org/press-room/press-releases/judicial-watch-defense-state- department-documents-reveal-obama-administration-knew-that-al-qaeda-terrorists-had-planned- benghazi-attack-10-days-in-advance/ (May 18, 2015)

32: Ruth Sherlock, "Libya to arms rebels in Syria," *Sydney Morning Herald*, November 27, 2011 (http://www.smh.com.au/world/libya-to-arm-rebels-in-syria-20111126-1o088.html)

33: Al Jazeera, *Libya assembly votes for Sharia law*, http://www.aljazeera.com/news/africa/2013/12/libya-assembly-votes-sharia-law- 2013124153217603439.html (December 4, 2013)

34: Tom McCarthy, "Benghazi embassy attack was 'preventable,' US Senate report finds," *The Telegraph*, January 15, 2014 (http://www.theguardian.com/world/2014/jan/15/benghazi- embassy-attack-preventable-us-senate-report)

35: U.S. Congress, Senate, Select Committee on Intelligence, *Review of the Terrorist Attacks on U.S. Facilities in Benghazi, Libya, September 11-12, 2012 Together with Additional Views* (Washington, D.C.: Senate Select Committee on Intelligence, 2014), pg 9

36: Carolyn Lochhead, "House Panel: No Administration Wrongdoing in Benghazi Attack," *San Francisco Gate*, August 1, 2014 (http://www.sfgate.com/politics/article/House-panel-No- administration-wrongdoing-in-5663509.php)

37: U.S. Congress, House, Permanent Select Committee on Intelligence, *Investigative Report on the Terrorist Attacks on U.S. Facilities in Benghazi, Libya, September 11-12, 2012* (Washington D.C., Permanent Select Committee on Intelligence, 2014) pg 1

38: Judicial Watch, *Defense, State Department Documents Reveal Obama Administration Knew that al Qaeda Terrorists Had Planned Benghazi Attack 10 Days in Advance*, http://www.judicialwatch.org/press-room/press-releases/judicial-watch-defense-state- department-documents-reveal-obama-administration-knew-that-al-qaeda-terrorists-had-planned- benghazi-attack-10-days-in-advance/

39: Investigative Report on the Terrorist Attacks on U.S. Facilities in Benghazi, Libya, September 11-12, 2012, pg 2

40: Timothy Gardner, Lisa Lambert, "Huge Gaps' in Clinton email record, Benghazi probe chief says," *Reuters*, March 8, 2015 (http://www.*Reuters*.com/article/2015/03/08/us-usa-politics- clinton-emails-idUSKBN0M40US20150308)

41: Krishnadev Calamur, "Benghazi Panel Asks Clinton To Hand Over Her Email Server," *NPR*, March 20, 2015 (http://www.npr.org/sections/thetwo-way/2015/03/20/394355939/benghazi- panel-asks-clinton-to-hand-over-her-email-server)

42: Hunter Walker, "Why did Hillary Clinton Delete about 30,000 Emails?" *Business Insider*, March 10, 2015 (http://www.businessinsider.com/why-did-hillary-clinton-delete-about-30000- emails-2015-3)

43: Fredreka Schouten, "Clinton Wipes Server After Handing Over Emails," *USA Today*, March 28, 2015 (http://www.usatoday.com/story/news/politics/2015/03/28/hillary-clinton- emails/70583404/)

44: Michael S. Schmidt, "In Clinton Emails On Benghazi, a Rare Glimpse at Her Concerns," *New York Times*, March 23, 2015 (http://www.nytimes.com/2015/03/23/us/politics/in-clinton- emails-on-benghazi-a-rare-glimpse-at-her-concerns.html?_r=0)

45: Judicial Watch, *Documents Obtained by Judicial Watch Reveal Top Hillary Clinton Advisers Knew Immediately that Assault on Benghazi was Armed Attack*, http://www.judicialwatch.org/press-room/press-releases/documents-obtained-judicial-watch- reveal-top-hillary-clinton-advisers-knew-immediately-assault-benghazi-armed-attack/ (February 26, 2015)

46: Peter Nicholas, Byron Tau, "Emails Show Clinton Was Warned Over Security in Benghazi Ahead of Attack," *Wall Street Journal*, May 22, 2015 (http://www.wsj.com/articles/hillary- clintons-benghazi-emails-to-be-released-by-state-department-1432309888)

# Economics and History

In 2007, the world became engulfed in the largest economic slump since the Great Depression. The crisis was so damaging it was coined "the Great Recession" and there was much comparison of the recession to the Great Depression of the 1930s in the mainstream media. However, what many failed to do was an in-depth analysis of both the Great Depression and the Great Recession, to compare and contrast the two. Thus, this article will be a comparison of both economic downfalls, ending in an analysis of the current economic situation America finds itself in and asking the question if another Great Depression is possible.

The decade prior to the 1930s, the US was in a time of great economic boom known as "The Roaring Twenties." Yet while the nation's income rose about 20% (from $74.3 billion in 1923 to $89 billion in 1929), the majority of this wealth went to the richest as can be seen by the fact that "in 1929 the top 0.1% of Americans had a combined income equal to the bottom 42%" [1] and that the disposable income per capita rose 9% from 1920 to 1929 for the general public, while the top 1% enjoyed a massive 75% increase in per capita disposable income. This greatly increased wealth disparity led to an imbalance in the US economy where demand wasn't equal to supply and thus there was an oversupply of goods as "those [the poor and the middle class] whose needs were not satiated could not afford more, whereas the wealthy were satiated by spending only a small portion of their income." [2] This caused the US to become reliant on three things to keep the economy afloat: credit sales, luxury spending, and investment by the rich. However, all of this spending depended on the wealthy having confidence in the economy, if confidence were to lower, then their spending would come to a halt and with it the US economy.

The massive inequality in wealth was not solely in terms of socioeconomic status, but also extended to corporations as well. During the First World War, the federal government subsidized farms in earnest as they wanted to feed not only Americans, but also Europeans. However, once the war ended, so did subsidies for farms. The government began to support the automobile and radio industries, with help from then-President Calvin Coolidge in the form of pressuring the Federal Reserve to keep easy credit, as to allow for both industries to easily be heavily invested in.

In the 1920s, the profits of the automobile and its connected industries such as lead, nickel, and steel skyrocketed, so much so, that by 1929 "a mere 200 corporations controlled approximately half of all corporate wealth." [3] The automobile boom also led to the creation of hotels and motels which in turn led "Americans spent more than a $1 billion each year on the construction and maintenance of highways, and at least another $400 million annually for city streets." [4] In addition to the massive success of the automobile industry, the radio industry also performed exceptionally well as "Radio stations, electronic stores, and electricity companies all needed the radio to survive, and relied upon the constant growth of the radio market to expand and grow themselves." [5]

This dependence on two main industries to support the entire US economy led to quite serious problems as in the case of depending on the spending habits of the upper class to support the economy, if the expansion of either the radio or automobile industries slowed down or halted, the US economy would meet the same fate.

Still further, there was wealth inequality on the international banking scene. After World War 1, the Americans lent their "European allies $7 billion, and then another $3.3 billion by 1920" and by 1924 "the U.S. started lending to Axis Germany," eventually "climbing to $900 million in 1924, and $1.25 billion in 1927 and 1928" [6] The Europeans then used the loans to buy US goods and thus were in no shape to pay back the loans. One must realize that after World War 1, virtually all of Europe was hit hard economically by the war and thus unable to make any goods with which to sell, yet the US played a role as well due to its high tariffs on imports, thus increasing the difficulty in which Europe could sell goods and pay off its debt.

Yet, the massive wealth inequalities domestically were not the only problems that led to the stock market crash, financial speculation was rampant also, which allowed corporations to make huge amounts of money. As long as stock prices continued to rise, the corporation itself became near-meaningless. "One such example is RCA corporation, whose stock price leapt from 85 to 420 during 1928, even though it had not yet paid a single dividend." [7] This was a serious fundamental problem in the stock market as many forgot that if stock prices increase extremely quickly, a bubble is being created and sooner or later it will burst. This speculation greatly distorted the values of corporations. Usually, the stock price somewhat correlates with the performance of the company, but due to the rampant speculation, companies that were doing horribly could now seem as if they were great investments, all based on the increase in their stock price.

A factor that led to rampant speculation was the ability to buy stocks on margin, which allowed for one to buy stocks without actually having the money. Due to this, investors could potentially get extremely high returns on their investments. Buying stocks on margin was quite easy as the process

functioned much the same way as buying a car on credit. **Using the example of [the RCA corporation], a Mr. John Doe could buy 1 share of the company by putting up $10 of his own, and borrowing $75 from his broker. If he sold the stock at $420 a year later he would have turned his original investment of just $10 into $341.25** ($420 minus the $75 and 5% interest owed to the broker). That makes a return of over 3400%! [8] (emphasis added)

This massive speculation led stock prices to incredibly high levels, with "the total of outstanding brokers' loans [being] over $7 billion" [9] by mid-1929.

The stock market bubble soon burst as on October 21, 1929, prices began to fall so rapidly that the ticker fell behind. Prices fell even further due to investor's fears which led them to sell their shares. The speculation and wealth inequality caused a major undermining of the entire market which led to the wealthy ending their spending on luxury items and investing, as well as "[the] middle-class and poor stopped buying things with installment credit for fear of losing their jobs, and not being able to pay the interest," [10] and thus the US economy came to a grinding halt. The lack of spending led to a nine percent decrease in industrial production from October to December 1929. This led to job losses, defaults on interest payments, and the destruction of the radio and automobile industries as inventory grew due to no one having the ability to purchase anything.

Internationally, loaning had already come to an abrupt halt earlier in the decade because "With such tremendous profits to be made in the stock market nobody wanted to make low interest loans" [11] and trade quickly ended as the US increased already high tariffs and foreigners quit purchasing US goods.

A topic that is rarely mentioned in regards to the Great Depression is the role of the Federal Reserve. The Fed played a major role in why investment purchases collapsed dramatically. The main problem was that in the onset of the Great Depression, there was rampant deflation. This was caused by the fact that the M1 money supply [partially defined as "cash and assets that can quickly be converted to currency" according to Investopedia] had reached a peak in 1929 and went downhill from there, yet the Fed didn't see this. Instead, they saw "only the statistics on the monetary base, the currency in circulation plus the funds held as reserves by the banks with the twelve Federal Reserve Banks," [12] which showed that the monetary base had been steadily increasing since about 1929. Thus, since the Fed saw that the money supply was increasing, they found no reason to act, when in reality, the M2 money supply [partially defined as "cash and checking deposit [...] savings deposits, money market mutual funds and other time deposits by Investopedia] was decreasing rapidly. However, in the late 1920s, the Fed acted to end speculative banking and wound up applying more restrictive monetary policies.

This resulted in banks closing en masse, which the Fed initially welcomed, yet this caused "the banks and the banking public [to become] alarmed. Some people withdrew their funds from the banks. The [banks became worried about withdrawal of deposits and even bank runs and they] reacted by holding reserves in excess of what the Fed required." [13]

This massive withdrawal of funds emptied the coffers of banks, thus causing the aforementioned deflation. The Fed's actions, along with the stock market crash, led to a 90% decrease in investment purchases, cutbacks in the labor force due to business not being able to sell anything, and a downturn in consumer spending.

Thus, due to a mixture of socio-economic and industrial wealth inequality, high tariffs on foreign imports, a stock market bubble, and poor economic management by the Federal Reserve, the United States descended into the Great Depression.

Initially, in the onset of the Depression, then-President Hoover decided against the government taking action to help individuals on the grounds that "if left alone the economy would right itself and argued that direct government assistance to individuals would weaken the moral fiber of the American people." [14] However, when he was forced by Congress to intervene in the economy, Hoover focused his "spending [on stabilizing] the business community, believing that returning prosperity would eventually 'trickle down' to the poor majority," [15] and thus began the first implementation of what would later be called in the '70s, "trickle-down economics."

The public, being appalled by the lack of empathy from Hoover, voted Franklin D. Roosevelt (FDR) into office. Once in office, he began embarking on programs that would come to be known as "The New Deal." However, this was not a deal concerned with easing the pain of the Depression on ordinary people, rather FDR "sought to save capitalism and the fundamental institutions of American society from the disaster of the Great Depression." [16] While the popular view is that the New Deal was radically different from Hoover's plan, in reality the two plans didn't truly differ to much as while some social programs were implemented, overall FDR's plan "tended toward a continuation of 'trickle down' policies, albeit better-funded and executed more creatively." [17]

He never truly adopted Keynesian economics, which argued that the "government should use its massive financial power (taxing and spending) as a sort of ballast to stabilize the economy." [18] This can be seen in the Agricultural Adjustment Act which paid farmers to produce less, however, this "did little for smaller farmers and led to the eviction and homelessness of tenants and sharecroppers whose landlords hardly needed their services under a system that paid them to grow less" [19], while also not addressing the main problem of the Depression: weak consumer spending. Overall, the Act benefited mainly moderate and large agriculture operations. Another example is the National Industrial Recovery Act, which encouraged industries to avoid selling below cost to attract more customers, and while this was good for businesses in the short run, it "resulted in increased unemployment and an even smaller customer pool in the long-run." [20] FDR's overall goal, while he did aid in the creation of social programs such as Social Security and enacted many jobs programs, was to protect capitalism and the very institutions that led to the Great Depression.

Another topic that isn't mentioned in examinations of the Great Depression is the Depression's effect on home mortgages. During the 1920s and early 1930s, the US experienced a housing boom, whose peak was around 1924 for single-family houses and 1927 for multi-family houses. [21] In 1928, when the Fed began cracking down on speculation, housing investments then started to fall due to the sharp increase in interest rates. Housing debt had "increased rapidly during the 1920s and continued to grow even after housing starts had begun to decline and house prices had leveled off" [22] and due to deflation, housing debt continued to increase until 1932. While rising debt usually doesn't pose a problem for households as long as they could make their loan payments, household incomes and wealth decreased greatly during the Depression, thus leading "loan delinquencies and foreclosures [to soar], fueled by falling household incomes and property values." [23] It was extremely difficult for homeowners to keep their property as "Falling incomes made it increasingly difficult for borrowers to make loan payments or to refinance outstanding loans as they came due." [24] However, the situation would improve as unlike the experience with the financial industry, the government stepped in to remedy the situation with the creation of agencies such as the Federal National Mortgage Association and the Federal Home Loan Bank System which aided homeowners in financing their mortgages.

Unlike the Depression, where falling mortgages were a side effect of the overall economic crash, in this current recession, mortgages played a major role in facilitating a near collapse of the global economy. Ordinary Americans found themselves able to purchase homes as credit was easily available. Yet due to predatory lending on the part of banks, the majority of these houses were being bought by people who couldn't afford them and many homeowners would soon find themselves having underwater mortgages due to "one-year adjustable –rate mortgages (ARMs) with teaser rates for first 2-3 years of a mortgage" which "were set artificially low and then reset much higher." [25] Due to credit rating agencies lowering the requirements for having mortgages rated AAA, the majority of these mortgages "were packaged into opaque securities and sold to [the] public." From this "subprime loans increased from 9% of new mortgage originations in 2001 to 40% in 2006." [26] Yet at the end of 2006, events took a turn for the worse as mortgage payments decreased and with it the value of mortgage-backed securities.

The bursting of the mortgage bubble "destroyed household savings in the ensuring financial meltdown, forcing individuals to slash their spending," [27] which led to a massive decrease in consumer spending and a long, painful recession. The housing bubble burst also had larger consequences as the disappearance of cushion against future losses virtually froze the credit market." [28] In addition to this, several large financial institutions such as Lehman Brothers and Bear Stearns collapsed, thus prompting the government to intervene, though not on the behalf of the American people.

Just as in the Great Depression, the US government's main goal was to protect the very institutions that caused the financial crisis instead of dealing with them. There were cries from leaders of the financial and political elite that massive companies such as AIG were "too big to fail," thus the US government embarked upon a $700 billion bailout. However, the true cost of the bailout is more like $839 billion as

the $700 billion [was] in addition to an $85 billion agreement on a bailout of the insurance giant American International Group, plus $29 billion [was] support that the government pledged in the marriage of Bear Stearns and JPMorgan Chase. On top of all that, the Congressional Budget Office [said] the federal bailout of the mortgage finance companies Fannie Mae and Freddie Mac could cost $25 billion. [29]

This money was paid to the corporations by the US taxpayer. While the financial institutions stated that they needed to money to survive, once gotten, corporations used to bailout money to stabilize their corporations, but also to hand out massive bonuses to corporate executives. [30] This bailout did not address the root causes of the financial meltdown: incompetence of the US government in regulating the financial industry, massive financial speculation, and predatory lending.

As they had during the Depression, the Federal Reserve played a role in bringing about the recession. Their main goal was to try "to artificially prop up those markets [of bad debt and worthless assets] and keep those assets trading at prices far in excess of their actual market value." [31] To this end, the Fed provided $16 trillion to domestic and foreign banks in the form of secret loans and bought mortgage-backed securities that were in reality, completely and totally worthless. [32] In addition to this, many of the people on the board of directors at the Federal Reserve also had connections to corporations that received bailout money.

For example, the CEO of JP Morgan Chase served on the New York Fed's board of directors at the same time that his bank received more than $390 billion in financial assistance from the Fed. Moreover, JP Morgan Chase served as one of the clearing banks for the Fed's emergency lending programs.

In another disturbing finding, the GAO said that on Sept. 19, 2008, William Dudley, who is now the New York Fed president, was granted a waiver to let him keep investments in AIG and General Electric at the same time AIG and GE were given bailout funds. One reason the Fed did not make Dudley sell his holdings, according to the audit, was that it might have created the appearance of a conflict of interest. [33]

Thus, there was a very cozy relationship between the Federal Reserve and the banks that received bailout funds. This only serves to show the revolving door relationship between the two groups and how the Fed's actions were subject to the interests of the large banks.

However, these are not the only actions the Fed took that helped to create the financial crisis. Their role goes back even further, almost a decade. In the early 1990s, Congress played a large role in trying to increase the amount of homeowners by passing the Home Ownership & Equity Protection Act of 1994 (HOEPA), which planned to address concerns of "reverse redlining" which was "the practice of targeting residents of specific disadvantaged communities for credit on unfair terms, and in particular by second mortgage lenders, home improvement contractors, and finance companies." [34] To achieve these ends, the Act called for the establishment of residential mortgage loans which were fixed so that it would be easier for low- income home owners to repay their loans. The Act also gave the Fed the ability, not only to ensure that HOEPA was carried out, but also to

exempt specific mortgages or categories of mortgages from any or all of the HOEPA requirements, or prohibit additional acts or practices in connection with any mortgage (not just "high cost mortgages") that the Board determines are unfair, deceptive, or designed to evade HOEPA, or that are made in connection with a refinancing of a mortgage loan that the Board finds to be associated with abusive lending practices, or that are otherwise not in the interest of the borrower. [35]

However, then-Fed Chairman Alan Greenspan refused to curb predatory lending as he touted a kind of laissez-faire economics and argued that the market would take care of itself.

This refusal to attack predatory lenders would come back in later years in the form of the current financial crisis.

Many thought that with the election of Barack Obama, he would fulfill his much touted goals of "hope and change" to restore the US, yet this did not occur with America's foreign policy, nor did it occur with America's economic policy. Obama's economic team consisted of former Treasury Secretary Robert Rubin who was the "chairman of Citigroup Inc.'s executive committee when the bank pushed bogus analyst research, helped Enron Corp. cook its books, and got caught baking its own" and also "was a director from 2000 to 2006 at Ford Motor Co., which also committed accounting fouls and now is begging Uncle Sam for Citigroup- style bailout cash." [36] Two former Citigroup directors, Xerox Corp. Chief Executive Officer Anne Mulcahy and Time Warner Inc. Chairman Richard Parsons, were appointed to his economic team. Both Mulcahy and Parsons have shady pasts as not only were "Xerox and Time Warner got pinched years ago by the Securities and Exchange Commission for accounting frauds that occurred while Mulcahy and Parsons held lesser executive posts at their respective companies," [37] but both were directors at Fannie Mae when that company was breaking accounting rules. To round out the group, former Commerce Secretary William Daley was appointed and at the time of his appointment, Daley was "a member of the executive committee at JPMorgan Chase & Co., which, like Citigroup, is among the nine large banks that just got $125 billion of Treasury's bailout budget." [38] Thus, it was no surprise to anyone who was paying close attention to the financial crisis and Obama's economic team that instead of attacking the root causes of the crisis; instead these advisors opted for a massive stimulus package of almost $800 billion. The situation had long been one where the patients were running the asylum.

While the stimulus undoubtedly saved millions of jobs, it didn't fulfill its main objective: stimulate the economy. The debt ceiling debacle would serve to only make the situation worse as the Republicans wanted solely austerity measures implemented and the Democrats capitulated, almost without a fight. Both parties began to create in the public's mind the idea that the only way to rein in the deficit was for austerity measures to be implemented. However, these austerity measures will only serve to exacerbate the situation as the IMF stated that implementing austerity measures "will hurt income in the short term and worsen unemployment in the long term." [39] Thus, the $2 trillion that the government plans to cut in social programs will only serve to make an already horrid situation even worse.

Currently, America's fiscal situation is in tatters. While the stock market is doing well, the real problem is unemployment, which is on a level that hasn't been seen since the Great Depression [40] and things are not going to get better soon. This becomes a serious problem as without employment, people don't have money to spend and America's economy "is **predominantly driven by consumer spending, which accounts for approximately 70 percent of all economic growth.**" [41] (emphasis added)

Another Depression is possible due to the fact that while things may seem to have calmed down for now, the deep, structural problems within America's economy still exist, are still active and therefore still have the potential to do major damage in the future. Economist Nouriel Roubini stated that another crisis is already manifesting itself in developed nations. [42] The only thing that the bailouts served to do was delay the inevitable: the bailed out corporations will fail due to their own risky practices and they will bring the US and world economies down with them.


**Endnotes**

1: Paul Alexander Gusmorino, *Main Causes of the Great Depression,* https://web.archive.org/web/20030425092431/http://www.gusmorino.com/pag3/greatdepression/ index.html (May 13, 1996)

2-11: Ibid

12: San Jose State University Department of Economics, *The Great Depression of the 1930s and Its Origins,* http://www.sjsu.edu/faculty/watkins/dep1929.htm

13: Ibid

14: Collin College, *The Great Depression and the New Deal, 1929-1940s,* https://web.archive.org/web/20100709211032/http://iws.collin.edu/kwilkison/Online1302home/2 0th%20Century/DepressionNewDeal.html

15-20: Ibid

21: David C. Wheelock, *The Federal Response to Home Mortgage Distress: Lessons from the Great Depression,* Federal Reserve Bank of St. Louis, http://research.stlouisfed.org/publications/review/08/05/Wheelock.pdf (June 2008)

22-24: Ibid

25: Muhammad Mustafa, Matiur Rahman, *Genesis of Current US Great Recession And Its Global Transmission,* International Journal of Economics and Research, http://www.ijeronline.com/documents/volumes/vol1issue1/ijer2010010107.pdf

26-28: Ibid

29: David Stout, "The Wall Street Bailout Plan, Explained," *New York Times,* September 21, 2008 (http://www.nytimes.com/2008/09/21/business/21qanda.html)

30: CBS News, *Hard Times, But Big Wall Street Bonuses,* http://www.cbsnews.com/stories/2008/11/12/earlyshow/main4595179.shtml (November 12, 2008)

31: John Wallace, "The Financial Crisis and the Federal Reserve," *News Blaze,* September 27, 2008 (http://newsblaze.com/story/20080927140845tsop.nb/topstory.html)

32: Bernie Sanders, *The Fed Audit,* http://sanders.senate.gov/newsroom/news/?id=9e2a4ea8- 6e73-4be2-a753-62060dcbb3c3 (July 21, 2011)

33: Ibid

34: Raymond Natter, *Home Ownership Equity Protection Act of 1994,* American Bar Association, http://apps.americanbar.org/buslaw/committees/CL130000pub/newsletter/200708/natter.pdf

35: Ibid

36: Jonathan Weil, "Obama's Bailout Bunch Brings Us More of the Same," *Bloomberg*, November 11, 2008

37: Ibid

38: Ibid

39: Alexander Eichier, "IMF Report: Austerity Measures Hurt Income, Make Long-Term Unemployment Worse," *Huffington Post*, September 13, 2011 (http://www.huffingtonpost.com/2011/09/13/imf-austerity_n_960199.html)

40: Washington's Blog, *Great Depression-Level Unemployment in America*, Global Research, http://www.globalresearch.ca/index.php?context=va&aid=25098 (June 3, 2011)

41: Hale Stewart, "Consumer Spending and the Economy," *New York Times*, September 19, 2010 (http://fivethirtyeight.blogs.nytimes.com/2010/09/19/consumer-spending-and-the- economy/)

42: Investment News, *Roubini: Without Stimulus, Another Great Depression*, http://www.investmentnews.com/apps/pbcs.dll/article?AID=/20110911/REG/309119958 (September 11, 2011)

From the European Central Bank headquarters to the halls of the Senate floor in the United States, debt, deficits, and austerity measures are all on the minds of leaders all over the world due to the ongoing world-wide recession. Many facets of the economic crisis have been examined; however, the role of credit rating agencies has been largely ignored, with their being little to no in-depth analysis of the role of rating agencies in relation to the global economic downturn nor their influence on the global economy at large. It seems that while rating agencies can be used to rate the creditworthiness of a nation, they now have undue influence on countries and are able to hold them hostage, thus an examination needs to take place of how they wield such influence on the world at large.

**Sovereign Credit Ratings**

Credit rating agencies came into being due to the creation of railroad industry. In the 19th century "the growing investing class [wanted] to have more information about the many new securities – especially railroad bonds – that were being issued and traded" [1] and thus credit rating agencies filled that need. In the middle of the 19th century, railroads began to raise capital via the market for private corporate bonds as banks and direct investors were unable to raise the capital needed to construct railroads. This growth in the sale of the different private bonds led to a need for there to be "better, cheaper and more readily available information about these debtors and debt securities," thus Henry Varnum Poor responded by writing and publishing the Manual of the Railroads of the United States in 1868, containing the financial information of all major railroads companies and providing "an independent source of information on the business conditions of these corporate borrowers." [2]

With John Moody issuing the first credit ratings in the US in 1909, the credit rating agency had come into its own. Usually the entire process of "shaping investor perceptions of corporate borrowers" was dealt with by banks as they would be putting their reputations on the line by lending to corporations. Thus, if a venture succeeded, the bank's reputation would go up and if the venture proved a flop, the bank's reputation would be damaged, making it harder for them to attract new clients. Essentially the creditworthiness of a corporation was certified to the public via the reputation of the bank they had borrowed the money from. Due to this, "the bank as creditor would become more involved in the business of the corporation and become an insider," [3] yet bond investors would not have access to the same information that the banks did. Thus, rating agencies aided in a leveling of the playing field and improved the efficiency of capital markets.

However, in time rating agencies went from rating the bonds of railroads to rating the bonds of sovereign states. In the 1970s global bond markets were reviving, but the demand for bond ratings was slow to occur as most foreign governments didn't feel the need to have their credit rated since most already had good credit and for those that didn't, credit could be attained by other means. However, this changed in the '80s and '90s when countries with bad credit "found market conditions sufficiently favorable to issue debt in international credit markets." [4] These governments frequently tapped into the American bond market which required credit ratings, thus, "the growth in demand for rating services [coincided] with a trend toward assignment of lower quality sovereign credit ratings." [5] While this may have been good for investors as they would be able to now see if a nation was a financial risk, this ability to rate the credit of countries would give them the power to decide a countries economic fate.

**Ratings and Economic Policies**

Credit ratings, while they can be a potentially positive part of the financial industry, can also have a negative effect on the economic policy of countries. This is especially true for developing nations.

For countries that take out loans, "a rating downgrade has negative effects on their access to credit and the cost of their borrowing." [6] This could potentially force a government to have to borrow money at a higher interest rate and thus scale down its plans for economic development. The problem that this poses for developing nations is that the only way to increase their credit score is to follow the "orthodox policies [that focus] on the reduction of inflation and government budget deficits" [7] which is favored by such organizations as the IMF and the World Bank. The alternative, which would be to avoid a rating downgrade in the first place, is even worse as it could lead "borrowing countries [to] adopt policies that address the short-term concerns of portfolio investors, even when they are in conflict with long-term development needs." [8]

This entire state of affairs is rather unfair to the Developing World as they are forced to take on large amounts of debt as they try to industrialize and modernize. This is largely caused due to the fact that they are victims of neocolonialism and that the major means of production are owned mainly by foreigners who don't contribute much in terms of improving the long-term economic prospects of a country and getting them from under the weight of neocolonialism.

While rating agencies can have an effect on individual countries, they can also affect the global economic system at large as can be seen by their actions in the current global financial crisis.

**Global Recession**

As we all now know, the major reason for the near global economic collapse was due to a subprime mortgage lending bubble that occurred between the late '90s and 2007. The deep financial risk occurred due to the fact that financial corporations sold mortgages to families who could not pay them and used them to create collateralized debt obligations. This "encouraged subprime lending and led to the development of other financing structures, such as "structured investment vehicles," whereby a financial institution might sponsor the creation of an entity that bought tranches of the CDOs [collateralized debt obligation] and financed its purchase by issuing short-term 'asset-backed' commercial paper. (ABCP)" [9] Credit rating agencies came into play due to the fact that favorable ratings that the agencies gave allowed for high ABCP ratings.

It is quite crucial to note that the ratings agencies gave were extremely important as they "had the force of law with respect to regulated financial institutions' abilities and incentives (via capital requirements) to invest in bonds" and due to their friendly relationship with corporate and government bond ratings, many rating agencies were able to influence "many bond purchasers— both regulated and non-regulated—[to] trust the agencies' ratings on the mortgage-related securities, even (or, perhaps, especially) if the market yields on those securities were higher than on comparably rated corporate bonds." [10] Thus, the rating agencies were crucial in the economic calamity due to the fact that they were able to influence bond purchasers to bank on, what were in essence, junk investments.

Corporations may have had an effect on the ratings they were given due to the fact that the higher the ratings were, the larger the profits would be. Thus, corporations "would be prepared to pressure the rating agencies, including threats to choose a different agency, to deliver those favorable ratings." [11]

Eventually, when the house of cards that was precariously built upon high risk mortgage loans came tumbling down, the rating agencies were swift to pass judgment in the form of massive downgrades. These downgrades caused the rated securities to lose value in both the primary and secondary markets, quickening the pace of the economic downturn. However the downgrades revealed that the ratings system itself was quite flawed, being influenced by such things as "the drive for market share, pressure from investment banks to inflate ratings, inaccurate rating models, and inadequate rating and surveillance resources." [12]

Evidence reveals that in the years leading up to the economic meltdown both Moody's and S&P were quite aware of the increasing credit risks due to factors such as "higher risk mortgage products, increasingly lax lending standards, poor quality loans, unsustainable housing prices, and increasing mortgage fraud," [13] yet the agencies continued to ignore any and everyone's- even their own- assessment on the risks and refused to adjust the credit ratings to accurately reflect the risk of the investments. Interestingly enough, "Moody's and S&P began issuing public warnings about problems in the mortgage market as early as 2003, yet continued to issue inflated ratings for [mortgage] and CDO securities before abruptly reversing course in July 2007." [14] This leads one to wonder why they would continue to give good ratings to mortgages that they knew were junk.

The reason this occurred was due to the issuer-pays model under which the firm interested in profiting from a security is required to pay for the credit rating needed to sell the security. In addition to this, "it requires the credit rating agencies to obtain business from the very companies paying for their rating judgment" which results in "a system that creates strong incentives for the rating agencies to inflate their ratings to attract business, and for the issuers and arrangers of the securities to engage in 'ratings shopping' to obtain the highest ratings for their financial products." [15] Thus, the rating agency is forced to give inflated ratings if they want to stay in business. The ratings agencies are partially to blame for the financial crisis, but it is also the very system at large that needs to be uprooted and replaced. This entire fiasco brings up the question: Can the rating agencies be regulated?

**Regulation and the Revolving Door**

There has been some arguments for reform for CRAs, among these are switching to an investor pays model and promoting competition among rating agencies, however, each of these proposed solutions have their own problems.

Some argue for moving from the issuer-pays model to "an 'investor pays' model in which rating agencies would earn fees from users of the rating information." [16] While this may sound like a good solution, there are still problems as "it would not eliminate conflicts of interest but instead shift them from issuers to investors" [17] as it would now be in the interest of rating agencies to attract business from the very investors who are paying for their rating judgment, resulting, once again, in inflated ratings.

The proposal to promote competition among rating agencies is quite problematic due to the fact that "size and market recognition may be higher barriers to entry than regulatory status, turning the credit rating industry into an oligopoly." [18] On top of this, promoting competition could potentially lower the quality of the ratings due to the fact that new entrants would most likely offer higher ratings or lower prices as to compete with the three large rating firms, thus reducing both the level of effort in ratings and their reliability.

While these proposals may seem good, one must keep in mind that they are only reforms, which only make certain amendments to the overall system rather than creating an entirely new one. None of these reforms deal with the revolving door that exists between the Securities and Exchange Commission (SEC), the government institution that is supposed to regulate the ratings agencies among other financial markets, and the rating agencies themselves.

In May of 2011, the Project On Government Oversight announced that after completing a study from 2006 to 2010, they found some rather interesting facts concerning the revolving door, such as that the SEC Office of Inspector General had "identified cases in which the revolving door appeared to be a factor in staving off SEC enforcement actions and other types of SEC oversight, including cases involving Bear Stearns and the Stanford Ponzi scheme" and one empirical study "uncovered several significant and systematic biases in the SEC's enforcement patterns and found indirect evidence to support the contention that 'post-agency employment at higher salaries may operate as a quid pro quo in return for favorable regulatory treatment.'" [19] Yet while these actions were taking place and the role of rating agencies in causing the global recession were known by the US government, Congress and Obama did little to nothing to remedy the overall problem.

       Due to the major problems that rating agencies have caused in the recent years, it may lead some to ask the question are rating agencies even needed. The fact of the matter is that they are needed, but they need to play a much less influential role in the financial system than they do now. Instead of enacting small reforms that do nothing to solve the overall problem, a completely new way of interaction between the ratings agencies and the financial markets needs to be enacted. In addition to this, the revolving door between the SEC and members of the financial sector needs to end immediately. Without these changes the rating agencies may very well lead the world down another dark economic alley in the future.

**Endnotes**


1: Randall Dodd, Gautam Setty, *Credit Rating Agencies: Their Impact on Capital Flows to Developing Countries*, Financial Policy, http://www.financialpolicy.org/FPFSPR6.pdf (April 2003)

2: Ibid

3: Ibid

4: Richard Cantor, Frank Packer, *Sovereign Credit Ratings*, Federal Reserve Bank of New York, http://www.newyorkfed.org/research/current_issues/ci1-3.pdf (June 1995)

5: Ibid

6: United Nations Conference on Trade and Development, *Credit Ratings Agencies and Their Potential Impact on Developing Countries*, http://www.unctad.org/en/docs/osgdp20081_en.pdf (January 2008)

7: Ibid

8: Ibid

9: Lawrence J. White, *A Brief History of Credit Ratings Agencies: How Financial Regulation Entrenched this Industry's Role in the Subprime Mortgage Debacle of 2007-2008*, Mercatus Center, George Mason University, http://mercatus.org/sites/default/files/publication/59_CRA_history_%28web%29.pdf (October 2009)

10: Ibid

11: Ibid

12: US Congress, Senate, Permanent Subcommittee on Investigations, Committee on Homeland Security and Governmental Affairs, *Wall Street and the Financial Crisis: Anatomy of a Financial Collapse*, (Washington, D.C.: Committee on Homeland Security and Governmental Affairs, US Senate Permanent Subcommittee on Investigations, April 13, 2011) http://hsgac.senate.gov/public/_files/Financial_Crisis/FinancialCrisisReport.pdf

13-15: Ibid

16: Jonathan Katz, Emanuel Salinas, Constantinos Stephanou, *Credit Rating Agencies*, Global Indicators Group, http://rru.worldbank.org/documents/CrisisResponse/Note8.pdf

17: Ibid

18: Ibid

19: Project on Government Oversight, *Revolving Regulators: SEC Faces Ethics Challenges with Revolving Door*, http://pogoarchives.org/m/fo/revolving-regulators-20110513.pdf (May 13, 2011)

After the Civil War, the 13th, 14th, and 15th Constitutional amendments were passed which aided newly freed slaves in being equally treated under the law, or so the story goes. The fact of the matter is that slavery was- and still is- completely legal in the United States and not only that, but it took on a much different form. The institution of slavery changed as instead of having the direct enslavement of blacks with an entire apparatus that had to be created to keep slaves in their condition, elements of the state apparatus were used to enslave blacks, namely the legal and prison systems. Yet, the enslavement itself was changed as black convicts were no longer slaves to individual masters, but rather they were enslaved to the companies which they were leased out to. To create this system there not only had to be the involvement of the Southern judicial system and individual Northern and Southern elites, but also the involvement of the corporation and reinstitution of slavery within a corporate context.

**The 13th Amendment**

To attain a full understanding of the convict lease system, there must first be a reexamination of the 13th amendment. It has been stated in history books and in classrooms across America that this amendment ended slavery, yet this is quite false. The 13th Amendment states "neither slavery nor involuntary servitude, **except as a punishment for crime whereof the party shall have been duly convicted**, shall exist within the United States, or any place subject to their jurisdiction." [1] (emphasis added) Thus, slavery is completely and totally legal if it is part (or the whole) of a punishment for someone who was convicted of a crime.

When debating the 13th amendment, many in Congress were not thinking of slaves, but rather white labor, with Senator Henry Wilson saying "The same influences that go to keep down and crush down the rights of the poor black man bear down and oppress the poor white laboring man." [2] Senator Richard Yates of Illinois was much blunter, stating that he had "never had the negro on the brain" [3] when discussing the amendment. Such notions are in the absurd! Wilson is correct to an extent when he argues that both slave and white labor are oppressed by the same system; both are oppressed in that they are being manipulated and played off one another by the elite of both the North and South. Still, Wilson ignores the fact that white labor was very much less oppressed than black slave labor as white laborers were seen as human being, deserving of dignity and respect, rather than treated worse than animals. White laborers were free to do as they pleased, not having to worry about ensuring that they consistently had papers on their person as to prove their freedom.

The passing of the 13th amendment should be examined within the context of an economic competition between black slave labor and free white labor. The South's economy was built around slave labor and the ability to have the slaves produce more than they were 'worth,' seeing as how slaves were viewed as not just general property but a long-term economic investment which helped the Southern plantation elite. Yet, due to the existence of slavery, white labor suffered as not only did they lose out on the income they were making when slavery was first introduced as well as the potential future income, but also white labor was unable to make advances within the South as slave provided a source of labor that was less expensive in the long-term.

Senator Henry Williams illustrates these points and other problems that white labor had with slavery. He stated that slavery was evil because it destroyed much of the richest land in the South; **it degraded labor and the meaning of labor for poor white working men in the South; it robbed the South of culture by degrading the efforts of laborers; and it allowed southern aristocrats to further insult northern white workers by demeaning their laboring efforts as crabbed and mean. It was the association between labor and slavery in the minds of southern aristocrats that demeaned the efforts of industrious northern laborers.** Thus, slavery pulled white workers down in two ways: one, by direct competition with slave labor in the South, and two, by associating all the industrious efforts of workers with those of the degraded slaves. [4] (emphasis added)

Thus, the only way for white labor to triumph in their struggle for rights such as a fair wage and regular working hours was for the abolition of slavery. White labor had a direct interest in the nullification of slavery.

Yet, there was a difference of opinion in the minds of Southern elites who wanted to continue slavery, but on different terms.

**Southern Elites**

Before discussing the Southern elites, one must first examine it within the context of the Southern economy after the Civil War. It was utterly in shambles, one could make quite the argument that it had been decimated and demolished in virtually every conceivable way. The entire economy of the South was built upon the institution of slavery and agriculture. With the end of the Civil War, not only was the Southern economy damaged by the freeing of black slaves, but also the land was deeply scarred and hurt, thus creating an immediate economic problem. However, among all of this there was an opportunity reorient and reconstruct the economy around a new labor source as cheap labor would be needed to rebuild the region.

The social order must be examined as well. While the slaves were now free and able to do as they pleased, there was still a deeply embedded racism within the minds of Southern whites. Just because blacks had fought in the Civil War did not suddenly mean that the perception of blacks had changed; rather to the Southern elites, they still viewed blacks as inferior and only good for labor, longing to perpetuate the slave system but within a new industrial framework seeing as how the agricultural framework had been destroyed. This new system was to be found in the convict leasing.

The leasing out of state convicts to private hands has its basis in the minds of such people as John T. Milner of Alabama. Milner was no ordinary man, rather he was a Southern elite who "was in the vanguard of that new theory of industrial forced labor," writing in 1859 that "black labor marshaled into the regimented productivity of factory settings would be the key to the economic development of Alabama and the South." [5] Milner's idea of using regimented black labor can be seen in his involvement of a project for the Blue River, a railroad company, in Alabama. In 1859 he issued a plan for the laying of rail in Montgomery, "presenting statistical evidence to demonstrate the potential economic benefit to Montgomery of securing connections with Decatur," a city north of Montgomery. He argued that the Blue River could build its own track in nearby Jones Valley with the use of slave labor. Yet, in Milner's mind, this slave labor had to be managed by whites. He stated **"A negro who can set a saw, or run a grist mill, or work in a blacksmith shop, can do work as cheaply in a rolling mill**, even now, as white men do at the North, **provided he has an overseer, a southern man, who knows how to manage negroes."** [6] (emphasis added) After the end of the Civil War, Milner's plan changed, but he was convinced that "the future of blacks in America rested on how whites chose to manage them." [7] To this end, in the 1870s, he moved with purpose to acquire the black convict labor that Alabama's prisons were offering up. He took these convicts and put them to work in coal mines, treating them barbarically.

Records of Milner's various mines and slave farms in southern Alabama owned by one of his business partners- a cousin to an investor in the Bibb Steam Mill- tell the stories of black women stripped naked and whipped, of hundreds of men starved, changed, and beaten, of workers perpetually lice-ridden and barely clothed. [8]

Black Americans, many of them former slaves, were essentially re-enslaved but within the context of a corporate structure with an alliance between the state and the corporation. Yet, the judicial system was greatly involved in allowing this to occur, from the laws passed to sheriffs selling of convicts to companies.

## The Judicial System

In order to allow for the convict lease system to exist and for blacks to be reduced to their former state as a labor source, it required that the law limit the rights of blacks and criminalize black life to the point that blacks could be imprisoned on the most frivolous of offenses. Such laws took the form of Black Codes.

To understand the creation of Black Codes, it is necessary to understand the social order that motivated elites to push for such legislation. North Carolina is a prime example. After the war, the elite would have preferred the system to revert back to the status quo that existed under the slave system, yet this was not possible due to the liberation of blacks and free whites caused by the destruction of the slave system. This problem was greatly exacerbated by the fact that "in suppressing the war to dissolve the Union the whites were deprived of arms while many Negroes had easily obtained them," thus "A general feeling of insecurity on the part of the whites" resulted. [9] Armed blacks were a threat to elite interests as by being able to defend and protect themselves; blacks would be able to ensure that they would not be re-enslaved. Furthermore, it presented a problem to the overall white power structure as having weapons would empower blacks to stand up for themselves and assert their rights not only as Americans but also as human beings and such a situation bought the memories and worries of a slave revolt back to the forefront of the minds of elites.

To put blacks back 'in their place,' the elite pushed several laws that were passed in the state legislature such as defining "a Negro as any person of African descent, although one ancestor to the fourth generation might be white." [10] The fact that racial identity was dependent on the mother rather than the father made the situation all the worse as blacks who had white fathers, whether by marriage or by rape, were now considered to be black and thus would be subject to the worst aspects of living within a white supremacist society.

Another example of the law being used to punish blacks was those laws concerning vagrancy. In North Carolina there was a problem concerning labor as after the Civil War, blacks and whites were working on their own fields, yet

> Many others less energetic, white and black, were flooding the towns and refusing work of any sort, for in the days of bondage, master and slave had been taught that to labor with the hands was undignified: consequently, freedom to many Negroes meant a deliverance from hard labor. [11]

These workers proved a problem to North Carolinian industrialists and agriculturalists as few could afford to pay workers a wage until the crop had been grown, not to mention that neither employee nor employer were familiar with a wage system. A solution was found in creating vagrancy laws. Of the workers who refused to do any labor, vagrancy laws were passed that stated that a person who had no means of survival or refused to work would be regarded a vagrant and sent to court, however, a payment could be offered which would be conditional upon the good behavior of the vagrant for one year and thus would allow the person to get off scot free. Yet if the person was unable to make such a payment, they would be convicted a vagrant and fined, imprisoned, or both. When concerning now freed slaves, the laws was much harsher as many of them, once convicted, were apprenticed to their former owners under a contract or being leased to a corporation. In the contract, the owner was to feed, clothe, and instruct the freed slave in reading, writing, and arithmetic and, upon the end of the apprenticeship, they were to be given money, a new set of clothes, and a new Bible as payment for the work done. However, such repayment rarely occurred or was enforced by the state government.

Overall in the South, vagrancy laws were so vaguely defined that any free black that was not under the protection of a white person could be arrested. Such laws allowed for police to "round up idle blacks in times of labor scarcity and also gave employers a coercive tool that might be used to keep workers on the job." [12]

With the judicial system having established a means to ensure a continuous supply of cheap labor, the leasing could now begin.

**Convict Leasing**

The act of leasing out convicts isn't anything new as in states such as Alabama, where the government had no interest in caring for convicts; prisoners were leased out to companies. While this may have helped prisons get convicts off their hands, they made no extra revenue from it. After the Civil War, such leasing began to pick up steam as corporations had access to almost free labor.

Labor scarcity between states was a major problem and thus concerted efforts were made by each state to keep black prison labor within their borders. This was done be waging war on emigrant agents, people who specialized in moving labor from where it was abundant to where it was scarce. They had done this when slavery was still existent and it continued under the newly freed slaves. Such agents were viewed as a threat to white farmers as by moving black labor here and there, it threatened the establishment of a stable labor source. Though in the early months emigrant agents were ignored, many states established anti-emigrant agent laws due to their need to keep in black labor. One example is in 1876 when Georgia, "Hard hit by black movement to the West," passed legislation that "levied an annual tax of $100 for each county in which a recruiter sought labor. A year later she raised the amount to $500." [13]

Convict leasing, interestingly enough, resulted in power being taken from the state level and given to those on the local level to the point that sheriffs became quite powerful soon after the Civil War ended as "County sheriffs and judges had dabbled with leasing black convicts out to local famers, or to contractors under hire to repair roads and bridges, beginning almost immediately after the Civil War." [14] This economic empowerment of sheriffs created an incentive for them to convict and lock up as many freedmen as possible and keep a steady supply of labor. An entire economy eventually formed around the convict lease system, including a speculative trade system in convict contracts developed.

The witnesses and public officials who were owed portions of the lease payments earned by convicts received paper receipts- usually called scrips- from the county that could be redeemed only after the convict had generated enough money to pay them off. Rather than wait for the full amount, holders of scrips would sell their notes for cash to speculators at a lower than face amount. In return, the buyers were to receive the full lease payments- profiting handsomely from on those convicts who survived, losing money on the short-lived. [15]

While there was much profit to be made in the convict lease system, not everyone was happy with it, namely, white labor.

**Labor's Reaction to Convict Leasing**

Just as how white labor was against slavery due to it undermining their struggle for better working conditions, they were also against the convict lease system for the very same reasons. Never did they stop to consider the fact that both worker and freedman were being manipulated by the very same systems that governed them.

Labor's anti-convict leasing sentiments were felt long before the Civil War began. In 1823 in New York City, journey men cabinet makers conducted a mass meeting to discuss prison-made good being introduced to the market and how it threatened their trade. In that same year, also in New York City, mechanics petitioned the state legislature to end the use of prison labor. [16]

During the Civil War, labor unions were opposed to the use of convict labor, arguing that it "tended to lower the wages of thousands of laborers, and in some instances has virtually driven certain kinds of labor out of the field" and that" the contractor is seeking cheap labor and cares nothing for the welfare of the prisoner." [17] However it should be noted that unions were not opposed to all convict labor, as they stated that they were fine with prisoners building a state prison. Thus, the labor unions didn't truly care about the brutal, inhumane treatment of convicts, but whether or not the convicts were encroaching on their area of employment.

Yet this should not be examined as a separate battle between free labor and convict labor, but rather a continuation of the struggle between the two groups. Once again, the only way white labor's goals could be achieved was with the destruction of most of the convict lease system to protect their own industries.

While the convict leasing may have been profitable for a select few and a thorn in the side to many, eventually the system would have to end.

**The End of Convict Leasing**

Due to a mixture of the changes in economic and social landscape, convict leasing would eventually die out. However, it is important to first note that the economic and social justifications for such a system reinforced each other as not only was it "an expedient by which Southern states with depleted treasuries could avoid costly expenditures; it was also one of the greatest single sources of personal wealth to some of the South's leading businessmen and politicians." [18] The Southern elites benefitted greatly from the system and thus put all their efforts into perpetuating the system for as long as possible.

If one only looks on the surface at the abolition of convict leasing, they may assume that its demise was due to the public indignation that arose against the system yet this is not the case- far from it, rather it involved a combination of race, politics, and economics depending on the state. For example, in Louisiana, convict leasing was abolished due to it being "part of a reform package which had as its purpose the complete triumph of white supremacy in political affairs" whereas in Tennessee, its leaders

decided that the demands of fiscal responsibility dictated abolition when the expense of maintaining the militia at convict stockades-a cost incurred by an armed rebellion on the part of free miners who were displaced by convict gangs-proved greater than the income from the leasing contract. [19]

In this system was embedded racism, politics, and economics, but it was also just as much embedded in violence and brutality. Men and women were beaten, bloodied, bruised, and valued only so long as they were able to do labor. They were reduced to nothing more than human resources, human tools to do the bidding of and enrich white industrialists and agriculturalists from the North and the South. From the Civil War to World War Two, black Americans were re-enslaved under a new system that was no better than the first.


**Endnotes**

1: Legal Information Institute, *13th Amendment of the US Constitution*, http://www.law.cornell.edu/constitution/amendmentxiii

2: Lea S. VanderVelde, "The Labor Vision of the Thirteenth Amendment," *University of Pennsylvania Law Review* 138:2 (1989), pg 440

3: VanderVelde, pg 446

4: VanderVelde, pg 466

5: Douglas A. Blackmon, *Slavery by Another Name: The Re-enslavement of Black Americans from the Civil War to World War 2* (New York, New York: Anchor Books, 2008) pg 51

6: W. David Lewis, "The Emergence of Birmingham as a Case Study of Continuity between the Antebellum Planter Class and Industrialization in the 'New South'," *Agricultural History* 68:2 (1994), pg 67

7: Blackmon, pg 51

8: Blackmon, pg 52

9: James B. Browning, "The North Carolina Black Code," *The Journal of Negro History* 15:4 (1930) pg 462

10: Browning, pg 464

11: Browning, pg 466

12: William Cohen, "Negro Involuntary Servitude in the South, 1865-1940: A Preliminary Analysis," *The Journal of Southern History* 42:1 (1976) pg 34

13: Cohen, pg 39

14: Blackmon, pg 64

15: Blackmon, pg 65

16: Henry Theodore Jackson, "Prison Labor," *Journal of the American Institute of Criminal Law and Criminology* 18:2 (1927) pgs 244, 245

17: Theodore Jackson, pg 246

18: Matthew J. Mancini, "Race, Economics, and The Abandonment of Convict Leasing," *The Journal of Negro History* 63:4 (1978) pg 339

19: Mancini, pg 340

After the close of the Civil War, many assumed that the scar of slavery had been done away with, something to be put into the annals of American history and only to be bought up in classrooms. Yet, the situation in many ways couldn't have been farther from the truth. Slavery was still around; however it was in a much different form. Besides the convict lease system, which kept black people as slaves within the construct of leasing them out to corporations, there was also sharecropping, which kept blacks tied to the land they worked. In order to obtain a full understanding of sharecropping, the social, economic, and legal contexts under which sharecropping was instituted must first be examined.

**Reconstruction**

After the Civil War ended the rather short-lived era of Reconstruction came about which saw Union troops occupying former rebel states to ensure that blacks had equal rights and a large rise in the number of black politicians on both the local, state, and national levels. While this was good for black people, there was a dark undercurrent as Reconstruction "exacerbated sectional and political tensions and economic recovery problems."[1] Due to the Civil War, the entire South was engulfed in economic troubles as with physical slavery abolished; plantation owners now had to pay wages to their workers. Yet the implementation of a wage system was problematic as "the South's quasi-feudal plantation system was not well-suited for a modern, free labor force."[2] In addition to this, former slaves were quite reluctant to work in the fields for subsistence-level wages.

Having a wage labor economy was near futile as economically speaking; the entire South was in shambles, especially with regards to currency as "Circulating currency was in short supply," the Confederate currency was useless, "the banking system was practically destroyed and, crucially, planters, farmers and landowners could not borrow money to pay freedmen to work their land for them."[3] Planters were left in economic ruins as few were able to use their now ruined land as collateral for loans. Poor harvests only exacerbated the problems as planters found themselves unable to attain sufficient crops to gain enough money to hire wage laborers. Yet, the most important factor in this was that "freedpeople had altogether higher aspirations than being simply wage laborers on large centrally organized plantations."[4]

To address this problem, Congress established the Freedman's Bureau, whose purpose was to aid former slaves and refugees and to handle abandoned land. They were also given the task of supervising labor contracts. Initially, Congress envisioned "that the Bureau would undertake the role of umpire in ensuring that the contracts reflected the free interplay of market forces"[5] and gave Commissioner Major General Oliver Howard, explicit instructions as to what contracts and contractual terms could not be dictated by the Bureau.

Yet, this did not solve the South's labor problem as both planter and freedmen "had little initial idea of what the optimal labor arrangements would be. They had to be discovered by a process of experimentation."[6] The experimentation began when former slaves begrudgingly entered into labor contracts with planters who still expected them to work in ways quite similar to what they had experienced under slavery. Most planters still believed that blacks needed supervision, Whitelaw Reid noted that most Southerners held the belief that "'niggers wouldn't do more 'n half as much, now that the lash was no longer behind them."[7] To this end, in the name of ensuring that blacks would work, "they sought to restore gang labor, centralized plantations, and the close supervision of the work and social lives of their new laborers, which, to their mind, were central to the economics of plantation slavery."[8] While this new system was a compromise between worker and employer, a deal which neither group particularly was fond of, it was one in which blacks had some autonomy, an asset which they leveraged to make the system of sharecropping less oppressive.

**Black Autonomy**

During slavery, the black family was in a way nonexistent due to the bitter and bleak reality that a family member could be sold off at any time, for almost any reason whatsoever. Thus, when freedom came about, it made sense that former slaves went to great lengths to seek out and reestablish their families. "These attempts to restore families and redirect their labor to serve the needs of the household rather than the planter, were integral to the self-sufficiency that freedpeople sought from sharecropping."

For a time there existed sizable labor shortages, which gave more power to the former slaves and allowed them to "contribute decisively to the contours of the new labor system that was awkwardly being constructed."[9] Rather than large centralized plantations, blacks had them broken into smaller plots of land and chain gangs were replaced by family and kin-group labor that managed the land. This collective share arrangement was adopted by both planters and former slaves as planters considered it a group incentive scheme and the former slaves saw it as an opportunity to decrease the amount of outside supervision. The preference blacks had for family-level sharecropping lied "in the increased effectiveness of the incentives implicit in the share arrangement, more closely matching effort and reward at the individual family level, and in the preference that freedmen showed for family farming over collective arrangements."[10] Though for the little black autonomy that did exist, it was overshadowed by the economics and legal effects of sharecropping.

**Economics and the Law**

Sharecropping, while influenced by black autonomy, was overall negative for black farmers as such a system "allowed the exploitation of the small farmer by the monopolistic financial structure dominated by the local merchant," as the farmer (in this case the black family) was unable to access alternative sources of credit to acquire needed supplies and thus the farmer was forced to use his future crop as collateral to finance the loan which "bound the farmer to the merchant and restricted his options to buy elsewhere or dispose of his crop in the most advantageous manner."[11] Due to his need to pay back the loan, the farmer focused on growing a cash crop such as cotton, to the neglect of food production, thus forcing the farmer to borrow even more money from the merchant as to feed himself. This created a cycle where the farmer was constantly behind in his paying his debt. It also didn't help that the credit prices that the farmer was charged so he could purchase food "were exorbitant, reflecting not only the local merchant's inefficiency, but his exploitative powers as the sole source of rural credit."[12] Thus, the farmers stayed in perpetual debt and slavery perpetuated itself, but rather than a physical slavery, it was an economic bondage that held black people to the land.

Another factor in the economics of sharecropping was that the landowner could also provide loans to the sharecroppers. Once again, the future crop was used as collateral against the loan, yet in the 1870s, the Tennessee legislature legalized this practice which, in part due to the corrupt local authorities and the rulings of state courts, resulted in having horrid results for the sharecroppers.

Since 1825 a law had been in place allowing for future crops to be utilized as IOUs to landlords; however the law only applied to the collection of cash rent. In 1870 the legislature passed a law which stated "that under certain conditions a loan by the owner to the cropper for equipment and workstock constituted a lien against the cropper's share of the proceeds."[13] The legislation did not allow for liens to be carried over from the previous year and mandated that the transaction be in writing. The law was amended in 1875 as to include croppers' debts to their landlords for supplies used in family consumption. While the legislature did attempt to protect sharecroppers from fraud, they were quite ineffectual as "local authorities ignored violations of the laws and state courts stripped [fraud protection laws] of their legislative intent" which resulted in landowners having the ability to carry debts over year after year. This economic power not only gave them better security for their loans, but also "gave them greater control over their black croppers."[14]

Besides the law, contract provisions also hurt sharecroppers. Contract terms which assessed "penalties for noncompliance or neglect on the part of the cropper likewise enhanced the landowners' control"[15] as if croppers failed to cultivate the specified amount of land, consequences could be extremely damaging. One contract stated that such a failure would bind the sharecroppers "to pay for fifty acres of corn land at seven dollars per acre & ten (10) acres of tobacco land at twelve dollars & fifty cents per acre in money"[16] where another contract stipulated that the landowner had the privilege of dismissing him entirely. While such terms appeared in the contracts of both white and black farmers, they were more prevalent in the contracts of black farmers. By having the power to dictate the terms of the contract, landowners "could control black croppers during working hours and, perhaps, be situated to dominate them and their families during nonworking hours as well" and there is evidence, "both direct and inferential, that landowners sought to use the system for this purpose."[17] In some cases, if sickness or accident prevented sharecroppers from meeting their obligations, the landowner had the power to outsource the work at the sharecroppers' expense.

While such provisions reflected an assumption that blacks were unable to manage a commercial enterprise, it is maintained by many historians that the provisions were an "effort by white southerners in general to hold freedmen, the large majority of whom became sharecroppers, in a subordinate status after emancipation."[18] Yet, while black sharecroppers in many ways remained subordinate to white landowners, the situation was worse for black women as for them, sharecropping combined the oppression of debt peonage and black patriarchy within the family.

**Black Women**

While slavery was brutal, there was actually gender equality among black men and women. Though the plantation system was based on patriarchy, "the domesticity in the enslaved cabin at the quarters was, ironically, about as close an approximation to equality of the sexes as the nineteenth century provided. An androgynous world was born, weirdly enough, not out of freedom, but out of bondage."[19] Yet, with sharecropping, black gender relations changed with the empowering of the black male to create a patriarchal family model.

While black female labor played a large role in producing income for families under the sharecropping model, their work was subjugated to the interests of black men as "male croppers controlled the labor of family members and, hence, held more power than women held over income and property."[20]

Family sharecropping was not just the preferred model for the black family as a whole, but also for black women. Many times freedwomen rejected field work as they were paid less than men, but also due to gang and squad labor putting them in close proximity to white landowners and overseers who would abuse them.

However, while family sharecropping benefited black women, it was also used as a form of control by white landowners as many held the view that "Where the Negro works for wages, he tries to keep his wife at home. If he rents land, or plants on shares, the wife and children help him in the field."[21] In their view, by allowing family sharecropping the landowner could ensure the stability of their labor and add to the labor pool by having the entirety of the black family work in the fields.

Black patriarchy was rather problematic for black women as "fathers could legally use corporal punishment to discipline their wives and children."[22] In some cases, such discipline was contractually specified. Thus, not only was the black woman afflicted by the negative economic effects of sharecropping in the form of debt peonage, but also the social affects were harmful to them, especially due to sharecropping empowering and upholding black patriarchy.

Sharecropping eventually ended due to mechanization and the Great Migration [23], yet the effects of sharecropping, compounded with slavery and the convict lease system had a negative multi-generational impact on the black community as a whole as rather than being able to work and obtain and pass down capital as to aid in the economic growth of the black community, it resulted in economic stagnation that would only increase racial economic disparity.

**Endnotes**

1: John J. McDermott, "Reconstruction and Post-Civil War Reconciliation," *Military Review* 89:1 (2009) pg 67

2: McDermott, pg 68

3: Ian Ochiltree, "Mastering the Sharecroppers: Land, Labor and the Search for Independence in the US South and South Africa," *Journal of Southern African Studies* 30:1 (2004), pg 43

4: Ochiltree, pg 43

5: Ralph Shlomowitz, "The Origins of Southern Sharecropping," *Agricultural History* 53:3 (1979), pg 588

6: Shlomowitz, pg 568

7: Ochiltree, pg 44

8: Ibid

9: Ibid

10: Shlomowitz, pg 572

11: Roger L. Ransom and Richard Sutch, "Debt Peonage in the Cotton South After the Civil War," *The Journal of Economic History* 32:3 (1972), pg 642

12: Ibid

13: Donald L. Winters, "Postbellum Reorganization of Southern Agriculture: The Economics of Sharecropping in Tennessee," *Agricultural History* 62:4 (1988), pg 10

14: Winters, pg 11

15: Winters, pg 13

16: Ibid

17: Winters, pg 14

18: Ibid

19: Willie Lee Rose, *Slavery and Freedom* (New York, Oxford University Press, 1982) pg 29

20: Susan A. Mann, "Slavery, Sharecropping, and Sexual Inequality," *Signs: Journal of Women in Culture and Society* 14:4 (1989), pg 7

21: Mann, pg 11

22: Mann, pg 12

23: PBS, *People and Events: Sharecropping in Mississippi,* http://www.pbs.org/wgbh/amex/till/peopleevents/e_sharecrop.html

The ongoing conflict in the Democratic Republic of the Congo is a long one, marked with political intrigue among nations, outside influences, ethnic tensions, and staggering amounts of violence. It is something that is often ignored in the mainstream media - even among the Obama- era 'humanitarian interventions' - even though it is the theater of the deadliest post-WW2 conflict (over three million people have died and many are still dying). [1] The Congo has become a hell on earth; and to understand how the situation became as it is, a historical examination of the nation is needed and overdue.

## Colonial Rule

Having been quite late getting into the Great Game, Belgium moved with purpose in the early 1900s in trying to acquire an African colony. In 1906, the Belgians annexed the Congo, making two separate zones: Belgian Congo and the Congo Free States, the latter of which became King Leopold's own personal fiefdom where he had complete control. His forces engaged in horrific acts such as holding "the [families] of [men] hostage until they returned with their rubber quota. Those who refused or failed to supply enough rubber often had their villages burned down, children murdered, and their hands cut off." [2] Leopold's main concern was the ivory and rubber trades. Eventually, the atrocities that occurred under his watch became widely known and he was forced to fold the CFS into the Belgian Congo. It was among this time that Congolese became politically awakened and active, namely in Leopoldville.

Before discussing the political awakening in Leopoldville, it would be pertinent to first understand the economic situation of the Congo. During World War 2, the Congo was "an important source of raw materials, especially of copper, tin, industrial diamonds, rubber, and palm oil." Afterward, due to the ever-increasing price of raw materials, the Congo economy expanded greatly: "In 1952 the value of exports was put at 20,000 million francs - an increase of 88 per cent as compared with 1948 - and by 1956 it had reached 28,000 million francs."[3] However, almost a decade later, a global decrease in the prices of the same raw materials caused the economy to stagger and created a large increase in unemployment (from 4,300 in September 1957 to 16,000 in March 1958), particularly in the Katanga region, a significant mining location.

While this economic downturn contributed to the political awakening of the Congolese, they had already become politically active. In January 1945, the first indigenous newspaper, La Voix du Congolais (The Voice of Congo), appeared in Leopoldville; and in 1955, Conscience Africaine was introduced. In July of the following year, the Conscience published a manifesto which suggested that within 30 years the Congo should be independent. Several weeks later, "a cultural association of the Lower Congo, known as ABAKO (founded in 1950), led by M. Joseph Kasavubu, improved on the 'manifesto', demanding complete and immediate emancipation and entirely rejecting the idea of a thirty-year preparatory period." [4] This political awakening soon manifested itself in the Leopoldville riots.

Though the riots became political, they were economic in origin. Due to the decline in the prices of raw materials, the budget dropped to a 5 million-pound deficit in 1957, and tripled to 15 million pounds in 1958. In the face of runaway unemployment, the government denied there were any problems. On January 4, 1959, following economic turmoil and the government's refusal to recognize such, riots ensued and lasted for three days. The force publique (the gendarmerie) was used to prevent the rioters from entering the European town.

These riots forced the Belgian political establishment to acknowledge that there were in fact a multitude of problems, and to embrace reform. In seven months, "from January to August, forty acts and ordinances containing discriminatory regulations were abolished or changed," although discrimination still remained in the European towns.

The Congo was given a charter of freedom and, "for the first time, freedom of assembly, of the press, and of speech was finally recognized."[5] Local elections formed and the first municipal elections took place in Leopoldville and several other towns in late 1957 and early 1958. Also in 1958, the Congolese National Movement political party was formed by Patricia Lumumba. The Movement focused on Congolese nationalism and created a large political rift in domestic Congolese politics, "[dividing] those who [wished] for a strong unitary state from those wanting a federal system of largely autonomous provincial governments based on primary [ethnic] alliances." [6] After the riots, three Abako leaders, including Kasavubu, were arrested and flown to Belgium to face trial - a trial that would only worsen the racial tensions in the colony.

## Independence

The move to reform forced a decision by the Belgian government to hold a roundtable conference in January 1960, which allowed for face-to-face meetings with Congolese political leaders. At the conference, "the Congolese delegates had presented a common front in their desire for immediate independence, no matter how divided they were on other issues," and the Belgians awarded the Congo full independence on June 30, 1960. However, the Belgian government limited this independence to the political realm. Economically, the intent was to retain the Congo "as a neo-colonial country whose resources would be exploited for the development of Belgian and West European economies, and the continued underdevelopment of the Congo." [7]

Nevertheless, the announcement resulted in a scramble to form political parties. The result was that in May 1960, "Of the seven major 'parties' in the Congo, none gained enough seats in the election to assure it of even 30 percent of the votes in the Chamber of Representatives. Patrice Lumumba, whose MNC party won some 38 of the 137 seats, emerged as leader of the largest single bloc." Of the other parties, "the Abako, under Joseph Kasavubu, the Conakat party of Katanga, led by Moise Tshombe, and a dissident wing of the MNC led by Albert Kalondji in Kasai Province, together garnered about 27 votes, but were allied chiefly by their growing opposition to a tightly centralized, unitary type of government."[8] Ultimately, the philosophical conflict between having a centralized government versus a nation of largely autonomous provinces was a major source of division in the formation of the new Congolese government.

A spat between Kasavubu's Abako party and Lumuba's MNC quickly escalated. Based on the weak elections of the MNC, the Belgian Resident Minister allowed Lumumba to look into forming a coalition government. However, Lumumba was unsuccessful as he was unable to persuade Kasavubu and his Abako party to join him, thus the offer was given to Kasavubu. Lumuba refused to work with the Abako party. On June 20th, it was reported that "a 'deal' was apparently taking shape, whereby Mr. Lumumba would head the Government as Premier and Mr. Kasavubu would become Chief of State." [9] Lumumba would eventually become Premier of the Congo, after being offered the Premiership by the Belgians; however, more drama was to come in the form of a military mutiny, two secessions, and a UN intervention.


## Endnotes

1: Integrated Regional Information Networks, *DRC: Conflict Deadliest Since World War II - Aid Agency*, http://www.irinnews.org/report/42969/drc-conflict-deadliest-since-world-war-ii-aid- agency (April 8, 2003)

2: Yale University Genocide Studies Program, *Congo Free State, 1885-1908*, http://www.yale.edu/gsp/colonial/belgian_congo/index.html (2010)

3: Majory Taylor, "The Belgian Congo Today: Background to the Leopoldville Riots," *The World Today* 15:9 (1959), pg 354

4: Taylor, pg 358

5: Colin Legum, Congo Disaster (Baltimore, Maryland: Penguin Books, 1961, pg 59

6: Legum, pg 66

7: Omajuwa Igho Natuf, "The Cold War and the Congo Crisis, 1960-1961," *Africa: Quarterly Review of Studies and Documentation of the Italian Institute for AFRICAE the East* 39:3 (1984), pg 358

8: Byron Fairchild, *The Congo 1960*, Historical Division Joint Chiefs of Staff, http://www.dod.mil/pubs/foi/International_security_affairs/africa/415.pdf (July 1961)

9: Ibid

After the Congo had been under a brutal colonization by Belgium, it finally seemed that their independence was at hand. However, there were a number of hindrances which created the Congo Crisis, a situation that had the characteristics of a secessionist war, a proxy war between the United States and the Soviet Union, and a UN peacekeeping operation with the backdrop being the fight for Congolese independence.

## Military Mutiny

It must first be noted that in the Congo, the military had only whites in command positions, even though there were "three African sergeant-majors in an army of 24,000 soldiers and non-commissioned officers, 542 officers, and 566 junior officers." This was because due to a limited education, few Congolese officers had the proper experience to lead the military and thus the European officers needed to be retained. Even nationalist Patrice Lumumba "felt the need for continuity in the army-that is to say, for the retention of European officers" and stated as such to the Congo Executive College two months before the Congo became independent. Specifically, he stated that the military must stay "exactly as it is-with its officer class, its junior officers, its traditions, its discipline, its unique hierarchy and above all its morale unshaken."[1]

With the average soldiers realizing that they would remain in the same situation of obedience, rather than having opportunities for advancement, they rose up in a rage, seeking not only increased authority, but also an increase in pay. The mutiny began at the Thysville military base and quickly spread across the country. Once the mutiny had started, "stories of atrocities against whites surfaced in newspapers around the globe" and due to the fact that mainly Belgians were fleeing the Congo, the Belgian government brought in troops to restore order[2], even though Lumumba had denied a request from the Belgians to do so. This violated the friendship treaty between the two nations which stated that Belgian troops "may be used on Congolese national territory only upon the specific request of the Government of the Republic of the Congo, in particular, on the specific request of the Congolese Minister of Defense."[3] It was around this time that the situation became even more unstable with the secession of the Katanga region.

## Katanga Secession

As has been noted beforehand, the Katanga was quite an important part of real estate in the Congo due its large mineral wealth. Yet, there were much greater problems than just natural wealth at play.

Economically speaking, while the Katanga region did have a large amount of mineral wealth, the capital was held in the hands of one company: the Union Miniere du Haut Katanga (translated as Mining Union of Upper Katanga, UMHK). Having immense economic resources that are controlled by one company would have serious political implications both generally but especially for secession, namely, that Belgian aid was needed as the region was so dependent on Belgian technicians and investments.[4] Some sectors of the Katangan population viewed the province as "' the cow that the other territories never tired of milking.'"[5]

The economic status of the province played into the ethnic tensions of the population. Industrialization of the Congo was mainly within the southern region of the province, where the three major mining centers were located, creating a rather large amount of uneven regional development. This was reflected in the uneven distribution "of social overhead capital- commercial centers, communication facilities, schools, hospitals, etc."[6] This uneven development created ethnic tensions as the UMHK received much of its labor from neighboring Kaisai province. For example, the Luba of Kaisai, even though they were ethnically related to the Luba people of the Katanga, formed their own unique culture and this presence of 'aliens' helped to make both groups more conscious of their differences.

Besides the ethnic tensions between Congolese, another factor was the presence of Belgian settlers who had their own agenda. The interests of the settlers lined up with those of the economic elite as the settlers formed the Special Committee of Katanga, "whose principal function was to promote, in every possible way, the development of an agricultural colony. To serve this purpose, a [Frontier Syndicate of Katanga] had been set up in 1920, thanks to the financial backing of the UMHK, [the Congo Company for Trade and Industry] and several other large-scale capitalist enterprises." In addition to this, besides the corporate interests, the settlers themselves had personal political and economic interests as they desired the special administrative status with a Vice Governor General, which acted as a representative of the Belgian monarchy.

Economically, they felt that "the proportion of public expenditures devoted to the Katanga appeared minute when compared with the over-all contribution of its taxpayers to colonial revenues."[7] Thus, through a combination of ethnic tensions and economic interests, when the province finally decided to secede, it was "supported by a Belgian mining company and was backed by Belgian troops almost from the very beginning."[8] Moïse Tshombé, a pro-Western anticommunist, was elected to lead the breakaway province and Katanga officially seceded on July 11, 1960. It was due to this secession and the Belgian intervention due to the military mutiny that Patrice Lumumba appealed to the UN to intervene.

Both Premier Patrice Lumumba and President Kasavubu went to the UN Security Council to plead their case for military intervention, with the goal of "[protecting] the national territory of the Congo against the present external aggression which is a threat to world peace." They also alleged that "the Belgian Government of having carefully prepare the secession of the Katanga with a view of maintaining" [9] a hold on the Congo. The Council voted in favor of intervention, with there being only three abstentions of China, France, and the United Kingdom out of concern for Belgian interests.

From there, "contingents of a United Nations Force, provided by a number of countries including Asian and African States began to arrive in the Congo" and "United Nations civilian experts were rushed to the Congo to help ensure the continued operations of essential public services."[10] The UN force would remain in the country for the next three years. However, it is rather interesting that both the USSR and the US would even agree on something like this, thus it is time to explore each of their respective interests in the Congo.

**Foreign Interests**

On a regional level, the US and Soviet Union both viewed Africa as important as "The question of independence for the colonies was championed by the USSR," while the US and its allies can up with ways to "either delay the granting of independence and/or to involve the newly independent countries in their [the West's] global anti-communist crusade." Demands for freedom by colonized populations were viewed as "a communist inspired movement, thus implicitly suggesting that the colonized peoples preferred to remain colonized."[11]

The focus on independence allowed for the Soviets to gain a foothold in Africa as it could be seen as wanting equality and independence for oppressed peoples around the globe. The Soviets viewed the liberation movements sweeping Africa and Asia as "damaging to the West and therefore beneficial to World Communism—if it could be properly exploited."[12] Thus, their goal in Africa was to aid the expansion of Communism. When Lumumba turned to the Soviet Union in August 1960 for aid to battle the Katanga secession after the UN refused to intervene [13], he was immediately seen as a Communist sympathizer or a useful fool for the Soviets in the eyes of the West, though it aided the Soviets in expanding their influence and building a reputation as supporting independence for oppressed peoples. While this would come back to haunt him, for the Soviets, it worked quite well to boost their credibility in the eyes of countries fighting colonialism.

The United States had a number of interests in the Congo. From the very start the West had been hostile to Lumumba as they saw him as over-nationalistic and an unreliable ally in the East-West conflict. When he accepted aid from the Soviet Union, this view only intensified. The US also had a number of economic interests in the region as well, with there being a number of high-level connections to corporations and the US State Department and other organizations.

For example, the Liberian-American Mineral Company was led by "Bo Gustav Hammarskjöld, brother of the U.N. Secretary General" and "Under-Secretary of State George Ball, who was directly in charge of making U.S. policy in the Congo,"[14] was a former member of Fowler Hamilton's law firm, which represented the International African American Corporation, a UN mineral syndicate in the Congo. The aforementioned Mining Union of Upper Katanga had stock held in it by "American companies like Lazard Freres, the New York investment house" and "Allan A. Ryan, an American, [who] was director of the Belgium- American Banking Corporation" held 25% of the shares in Mining Union and "the Rockefeller Brothers [held] less than 1% of [Mining Union] shares."[15] While Howard Kersher, a newspaper reporter, did not find a smoking gun linking these people to the problems in the Congo, it was quite obvious that they all had financial interest in the Congo and thus a stake in what was going on in regards to the Katanga secession.

From a geostrategic perspective, the Congo was important to the US as Congo could have a serious influence upon its neighbors, Cameroon, Gabon, the Central African Republic, and Sudan. US officials were worried that if a pro-Communist government came to power, it could set the tone that other African nations would follow and on a larger level, aid the Soviet Union in spreading Communist ideology. The Congo was valuable from a military perspective in that a key front in WW3 would be the Middle East and they assumed that Soviets would attempt to block routes to that theater and "Soviet generals and planners would understand the importance of the Mediterranean Sea, the Suez Canal and even the waters surrounding the coasts of South Africa" to overall US strategy and that "any Soviet attack would make security of these routes integral to its plan."[16]

Overall, the US "detested Lumumba and were determined to overthrow him, and this became the principal objective of US policy during the first six months of the Congo Crisis."[17] CIA Director Allen Dulles warned of a "communist takeover of the Congo with disastrous consequences ... for the interests of the free world" and "authorized a crash-program fund of up to $100,000 to replace the existing government of Patrice Lumumba with a 'pro-western group.'"[18] While the superpowers did have their respective interests in the Congo, the situation would intensify with the secession of South Kasai.

*South Kasai*

The South Kasai region, like the Katanga region, was rich with mineral wealth, mainly diamonds. Until the mid-1970s, it produced one-third of global output of industrial diamonds. Though mineral wealth was important due to the economics of the Congo, it was mainly ideological differences and ethnic conflict that caused the secession.

Ideologically, the secession was led by Albert Kalonji, who had been prominent figure in the Congolese National Movement party, but later split off from Lumumba to help form a more moderate wing of the nationalist party, which came to be known as MNC-Kalonji. Like the Abako political party, the Kalonji wing of the MNC preferred a centralized system in favor of autonomous provinces based on ethnic lines.

With regards to ethnicity, the secession "can be traced to the territorial expansion of the Baluba beyond southern Kasai to the Lulua area in the late-nineteenth century, which created animosities between the Baluba and the Lulua."[19] This territorial expansion of Baluba peoples due to lack of cultivable land saw the Baluba move permanently into the region and attain most of the clerical colonial jobs. "The fear of domination by the Baluba prompted the creation of the Association of Lulua-Frères in 1951 by a Lulua chief, Sylvain Mangole Kalamba."[20] Tensions eventually reached a crisis when "the local administration proposed to resettle Baluba farmers from Lulua land (an economically booming center province) back to their impoverished homeland in southern Kasai."[21] Kalonji exploited these ethnic tensions for political gain and declared secession of South Kasai.

*The Rise of Mobutu*

While the country was wracked with political turmoil, it provided the perfect atmosphere for a coup. On September 6, 1960, President Kasavubu dismissed Lumumba and appointed Joseph Ileo as the new Premier. However, his reign was not to last as the Army Chief of Staff, Joseph Mobutu, would soon take power in a coup with foreign help.

Mobutu already had ties with the CIA that dated back to "his role in the pre- independence negotiations in Brussels where he both reported to the Belgian Sûreté and made his first contacts with Lawrence Devlin,"[22] the CIA station chief in the Congo. These ties only grew during the Congo Crisis when the US and other Western powers funded Mobutu, who, in turn "distributed large amounts of money to the officers and men under his command; through this arrangement he was able to establish bonds of loyalty among his soldiers." It also didn't hurt that his unit "was virtually the only really functioning element of the Congolese National Army."[23] The US aided Mobutu's rise to power as, has previously been mentioned, they viewed Lumumba as a Communist sympathizer and they needed to get rid of him in order to ensure that the Soviets would not gain a sphere of influence in Africa.

The first time Mobutu took power was regarding a constitutional dispute. Kasavubu had dismissed Lumumba. Though, both the US and the UN had influence on this action. Andrew W. Cordier, a UN official, and Dag Hammarskjöld, the UN Secretary-General, "coordinated their activities with the State Department" overall and Cordier for September 6, "arranged for UN troops to close the airport -- to preclude any airlift of loyal troops to the capital by Lumumba" and then "ordered UN forces to close the radio station as well, which prevented Lumumba from broadcasting an appeal for support."[24] This encouraged Kasavubu to act against Lumumba, however his plan would backfire as Lumumba would receive full vote of confidence from the Congolese Parliament whereas Kasavubu's appointment, Joseph Ileo, would not.

Due to this situation, the US became even more focused on getting Mobutu into power and advocated for a military coup. On September 14, Mobutu removed Lumumba from office, dissolved Parliament, but quickly "turned the government over to a College of Commissioners composed of the few college graduates the country possessed."[25] He placed Lumumba under house arrest, but Lumumba was soon freed by loyal Congolese troops. Mobutu then again captured Lumumba and placed him under house arrest with a UN guard.

Upon hearing that Lumumba had been place under house arrest, Vice Prime Minister Antoine Gizenga set up a rival government in the eastern city of Stanleyville with the help of pro-Lumumba forces. On December 12, 1960, Gizenga declared the nation of Stanleyville, with its capital of Oriental City, to be the only legitimate government of the Congo.

Gizenga quickly turned to the Soviet Union for aid. In a telegram, he asked the Soviets to "immediately, without delay, to help us in military equipment and foodstuffs' in order to repel the invasion of Mobutu's troops 'who unleashed the civil war against soldiers and units loyal to the legitimate government."[26] Factoring in that they had attempted to aid the Lumumba government and failed, the Soviets took their time in replying to Gizenga. When they did respond, they sent $500,000 in aid as due to the blockade on Stanleyville, they could not transport aid directly to the fledging government and due to infighting among the USSR and its regional allies, and little else was done.

The situation was then where there were four competing governments in the Congo: Joseph Mobutu and Joseph Kasavubu in Léopoldville, supported by Western governments, Antoine Gizenga in Stanleyville, Albert Kalonji in South Kasai, and Moise Tshombe in Katanga.

*The Assassination of Patrice Lumumba*

As has been previously mentioned, the West had never been particularly fond of Lumumba, especially after he sought aid from the Soviet Union. His assassination came as a surprise to many, but it had already been planned from the very beginning as the US was determined to get him out of the picture, as were the Belgians.

With regards to the assassination, on November 27, 1960, Lumumba left UN custody to make a break for Stanleyville and join his supporters there. However, he was captured by Mobutu's forces only days later and imprisoned him. In early January 1961, forces loyal to Lumumba invaded "northern Katanga to support a revolt of Baluba tribesmen against the Tshobme government." Due to 'security' reasons, "the CIA and Mobutu decided to transfer Lumumba from Leopoldville to Katanga,"[27] where he and two aides were subsequently killed.

The United States had plans to eliminate Lumumba that went as high as the President himself. In August 25, 1960, a subcommittee of the National Security Council, known as the Special Group, met; Thomas Parrott, the secretary of the Group, began the meeting by outlining the CIA operations that had been undertaken in 'mounting an anti- Lumumba campaign in the Congo,' with the meeting ending with the group "not necessarily rule out of any particular kind of activity which might contribute to getting rid of Lumumba."[28] The very next month, CIA Station Officer Victor Hedgman received a cable from Bronson Tweedy, the Deputy Director of the CIA, in which "he advised [Hedgman], or [his] instructions were, to eliminate Lumumba" and that the orders came from the President himself.[29]

While a Senate report did that there was "no evidentiary basis for concluding that the CIA conspired in this plan or was connected to the events in Katanga that resulted in Lumumba's death," some doubt still remains as the CIA did have a plan to poison Lumumba and possessed "advance knowledge of the central government's plan to transport Lumumba into the hands of his bitterest enemies, where he was likely to be killed."[30] The US government, at the very least, played a role in the killing of Lumumba.

The Belgians also had wanted to kill Lumumba and were somewhat involved with his assassination. Specifically, they were involved in "weapon deliveries; supporting the arrest of Lumumba; action 58316, (the outline of which is unclear but within which an attack on Lumumba could be relevant); and the kidnapping of Lumumba."[31] They also had information that the leader's life was in danger due to being in the Katanga, but the Belgian government did not take any action to protect him; in fact, when Lumumba was executed, it was in the presence of "a Belgian police commissioner and three Belgian officers who were under the authority, leadership and supervision of the Katangan authorities."[32]

With Lumumba dead, it was only a matter of time before the Congo would be reunited under the rule of Mobutu.

*The Fall of the Revolution*

During late 1960 and early 1961, it became obvious to the Western powers that "the provisional government of Kasavubu would not last without reconciliation with Katanga, and the U.S. pressed for a federated Congo government which would include Katanga."[33] The US pushed for the UN Security Council to pass a resolution demanding an end to the Katanga secession. This was passed in the form of UNSC Resolution 161, which stated in part that the UN should "take immediately all appropriate measures to prevent the occurrence of civil war in the Congo."[34]

However, this was undermined by Belgium and other involved American interests, which didn't want the secession to end. Thus, they formed an organization called 'The Committee to Aid Katanga Freedom Fighters," which allowed Tshombe to "build an army which could resist the UN, financed by Belgium," yet this armed force also had reactionary forces within it from a number of places. They came from "the United States (Cuban exiles), Britain, France (ex- Foreign Legionnaires), West Germany (ex-SS men), South Africa (fascists), Rhodesia--and, of course, Belgium."[35]

In February 1961, Kasavubu put an end to the Mobutu reign and appointed Joseph Ileo and Cyrille Adoula heads of the new government, with him remaining as president.. The very next month, Gizenga attempted to make peace with the Congo, but he was arrested by Kasavubu and imprisoned, while Tshombe was forced into exile. Three years later, in 1964, the UN left the Congo Tshombe came back to rule the Congo. During his leave of absence, Tshombe "conferred in Brussels with Foreign Minister Paul-Henri Spaak and the U.S. Ambassador,"[36] which allowed him to return to the Congo and replace Adoula as Prime Minister. Yet, this government would not last. Mobutu would take power in November 1965, once again with the aid of the CIA.

The US became worried in 1964 regarding the competition between Tshombe and Kasavubu, both of whom hoped to rule the Congo after the civil war ended. This concern heightened when Kasavubu "sought 'an opening to the left' by dismissing Tshombe and appointing a government ready to consider not only the dismissal of mercenaries, but also the recognition of Communist China and improved relations with left-nationalist African states"[37] and the CIA backed Mobutu as to ensure that no leftist groups gained power.

However, there was also internal politicking as well. The coup itself was a collective decision by senior officers of the Congolese military. They backed Mobutu as "they believed that the army was above partisan politics and their immediate demand after the coup was an increase in the fighting power of the army."[38] In order to satisfy the military, Mobutu would increase the size of the military and enhance is prestige. Yet, while it seems that Mobutu had finally become the ruler of the Congo, there were internal struggles that he would have to deal with.


**Endnotes**

1: Claude E. Welch, "Soldier and State in Africa," *The Journal of Modern African Studies* 5:3 (1967), pgs 307-308

2: US Department of State, Office of the Historian, *The Congo, Decolonization, and the Cold War, 1960–1965*, https://history.state.gov/milestones/1961-1968/congo-decolonization

3: Africa Today Associates, "Conflict in the Congo," Africa Today 7:5 (1960), pg 8

4: Rene Lemarchand, "The Limits of Self-Determination: The Case of the Katanga," *American Political Science Review* 56:2 (1962), pg 405

5: Lemarchand, pg 406

6: Ibid

7: Lemarchand, pg 409

8: M. Rafiqul Islam, "Secessionist Self-Determination: Some Lessons from Katanga, Biafra, and Bangladesh," *Journal of Peace Research* 22:3 (1985), pg 213

9: Joseph Kasavubu, Patrice Lumumba, *UN Security Council Resolution S/4382*, United Nations Security Council, http://www.un.org/en/ga/search/view_doc.asp?symbol=S/4382 (July 13, 1960)

10: United Nations Department of Peacekeeping Operations, *Republic of the Congo- ONUC Background*, http://www.un.org/Depts/DPKO/Missions/onucB.htm

11: Natuf, pg 355

12: William G. Thom, "Trends in Soviet Support for African Liberation," *Air University Review* 25 (1974), pg 36

13: BBC, *The Congolese Civil War, 1960-1964*, http://news.bbc.co.uk/dna/place-lancashire/plain/A1304803

14: Kiama Mutahi, "The United States, The Congo, and the Mineral Crisis of 1960-64: The Triple Entente of Economic Interest, Electronic Thesis or Dissertation. Miami University, 2013. https://etd.ohiolink.edu/, pg 33

15: Mutahi, pg 32

16: Davis, Erik M., "The United States and the Congo, 1960-1965: Containment, Minerals, and Strategic Location" (2013). Theses and Dissertations--History. Paper 8. http://uknowledge.uky.edu/history_etds/8, pg 578

17: David N. Gibbs, "Secrecy and International Relations," *Journal of Peace Research* 32:2 (1995), pg 220

18: William Blum, *Killing Hope: US Military and CIA Interventions Since WW2* (London, United Kingdom: Zed Books, 2003), pg 156

19: Emizet Kisangani and Léonce Ndikumana, "The Economics of Civil War: The Case of the Democratic Republic of Congo," *Political Economy Research Institute Working Papers* 47 (2003), pg 8

20: Ibid, pg 9

21: Ibid

22: Götz Bechtolsheimer "Breakfast with Mobutu: Congo, the United States and the Cold War, 1964-1981," PhD Diss., *The London School of Economics and Political Science* (2012), pg 64

23: Gibbs, pg 220

24: Gibbs, pg 221

25: Michael G. Schatzberg , "Beyond Mobutu: Kabila and the Congo ," *Journal of Democracy* 8:4 (1997), pg 72

26: Sergei Mazov, "Soviet Aid to the Gizenga Government in the Former Belgian Congo (1960– 61) as Reflected in Russian Archives," *Cold War History* 7:3 (2007), pg 429

27: Tom Cooper, *Congo, Part 1: 1960-1963*, Air Combat Information Group, http://www.acig.org/artman/publish/article_182.shtml (September 2, 2003)

28: U.S. Congress, Senate, Select Committee to Study Governmental Operations With Respect to Intelligence Activities, Alleged Assassination Plots Involving Foreign Leaders, 1975, 94th Congress, 1st Session, November 20, 1975 (Washington D.C.: GOP 1975), pg 60

29: Alleged Assassination Plots Involving Foreign Leaders, pgs 24, 26

30: Alleged Assassination Plots Involving Foreign Leaders, pg 48

31: Belgian House of Representatives, *Parliamentary Inquiry on the Circumstances of the Assassination of Patrice Lumumba and on the Possible Involvement of Belgian Politicians*, Report of the Commission of Inquiry http://www.dekamer.be/commissions/LMB/indexN.html, pg 6

32: http://www.dekamer.be/commissions/LMB/indexN.html, pg 8

33: Dick Roberts, "Patrice Lumumba and the Revolution in the Congo," *The Militant*, http://www.themilitant.com/2001/6528/652850.html (July 23, 2001)

34: United Nations Security Council, *UN Security Council Resolution S/4741*, http://daccess-dds-ny.un.org/doc/RESOLUTION/GEN/NR0/171/68/IMG/NR017168.pdf?OpenElement (February 21, 1961)

35: Roberts, July 23, 2001

36: Ibid

37: Stephen R. Weissman, "CIA Covert Action in Zaire and Angola: Patterns and Consequences," *Political Science Quarterly* 94:2 (1979), pg 273

38: Kisangani N. F. Emizet, "Explaining The Rise And Fall of Military Regimes: Civil-Military Relations in the Congo," *Armed Forces & Society* 26:2 (2000), pg 211

## The Rule of Mobutu

Mobutu encountered two main problems once he became the ruler of the Congo: legitimacy and an underdeveloped military. To deal with his military, he "began modernizing the army with new equipment to provide prestige to the military and to accommodate the senior officers with whom he seized power in 1965, and the acquisition of modem equipment paralleled the enlargement of military spending."[1] Mobutu also sent large amounts of officers to Western military schools. All of this was done with the goal of building an apolitical institution in the Congo.

To gain legitimacy, he absorbed 22 civilians from all over the country and across political parties into his government and appropriated Lumumba's nationalism by declaring him a national hero and nationalizing the Mining Union of Upper Katanga, which, to the ordinary Congolese, looked like a revival of nationalist principles. Politically, he created a political party called the Popular Movement of the Revolution and amended the constitution to institutionalize it as the only legal political party.

The Mobutu regime was marked by massive corruption, with the ruling elite using the state for self-enrichment. During Mobutu's 32 year reign (1965 to 1997), the country "accumulated an external debt of roughly US\$ 14 bn. At the same time the living standards of the vast majority of Congo's people deteriorated from an already low base" and by the 1980s, 70 percent of the population was impoverished.[2] While all this was going on, "Mobutu and his associates amassed remarkable personal fortunes" with "Mobutu's own assets reportedly [peaking] in the mid-1980s at US\$ 4 bn."[3] Mobutu and his cronies were not the only ones to benefit. The US benefitted greatly as while they gave Zaire more than \$1.5 billion in economic and military aid, US companies "increased their share of the ownership of Zaire's fabulous mineral wealth" and on a geopolitical level, Mobutu "a stabilizing force and a staunch supporter of U.S. and Western policies."[4] The regime was also aided by the French as they "contracted for a number of prestige infrastructure projects- major contributary factors to Zaire's national debt which would top \$8 billion by I 996 - in exchange for guaranteed French protection for Mobutu."[5] However, Mobutu's ill-gotten gains would not last long as he in 1997 he would be disposed.

## Civil War and the End of Mobutu

The fall of Mobutu occurred due to a number of factors. Externally, due to a withdrawal of US support and a war between the joint forces of Uganda, Rwanda and the Alliance of Democratic Forces for the Liberation of Congo-Zaire (ADFL) led to the collapse of the regime.

With the collapse of the Soviet Union in 1991, the Cold War, and with it the threat of Communism, officially ended. The US began to change its foreign policy in order to encourage democratization around the world. With regards to Africa, the US "announced that future foreign assistance to Africa would be conditioned upon democratization"[6] and made good on this promise by cutting Mobutu off in 1992. The US further withdrew from Africa due to "Somalia Syndrome" regarding the Black Hawk Down incident. "Reeling from the debacle in Somalia, and with the Rwandan genocide already unfolding, Clinton issued Presidential Decision Directive 25, which sought to strictly limit future U.N. missions, and especially U.S. participation in them."[7] Thus, with the lack of US support, Mobutu was left to fend for himself. Yet, he was soon to be affected by outside forces within the region.

Around this time the genocide in Rwanda was already well under way and the "genocidal forces made up of the remnants of the army of the ancien régime and the extremist Interahamwe militias" fled to the Congo. The Rwandan military pursued them, but needed Congolese allies to give its incursion into the Congo some legitimacy. This alliance was found in the form of "Laurent-Désiré Kabila, a retired revolutionary involved in cross-border business ventures, and among the Congolese Tutsi, who were fighting for recognition of their citizenship."[8]

A number of nations in addition to Rwanda, including Uganda, wanted Mobutu out of power as the Congo "served as a rear base for attacks by armed movements against Uganda, Rwanda and Burundi; and the support offered by Mobutu to the Angolan rebel movement UNITA had not ceased with the 1994 Lusaka peace accord."[9]

There was an ethnic component to the war as well. The Congolese Tutsi were viewed by Mobutu as being more loyal to Rwandan Tutsis than to the Congo. This led to pogroms and a small level of ethnic cleansing in the Kivu region, which is directly west of Rwanda. The Tutsi resisted with the aid of the Rwanda Patriotic Front. The Congolese Tutsi took part in the 'rebellion of the Banyamulenge' which started in September 1996 and was the start of the campaign that put Kabila into power.

Yet, it was not just the Tutsis that aided Kabila, but also the United States due to the strategic location and natural resource wealth of the Congo. Kabila was visited by the Political Counselor to Kinshasha, the capital of the Congo, and US Ambassador Peter Whaley. The leader of the Rwandan rebels, Paul Kagame, "was trained at the US Army's Command and General Staff College at Fort Leavenworth in Kansas."[10] Soon economic ties were established with the rebels as soon as the rebels took Kisangani, the capital of Orientale Province, North American mining companies rushed to get generous contracts; among them was the "Canadian-owned Tenke Mining Corp, which in May 1997 won a contract of $50 million to exploit the world's largest copper and cobalt deposits" and "America's Mineral Fields which signed a contract of $1 billion with the ADFL."[11] Thus, a Kabila victory was also a victory for the United States.

The fight against Mobutu's forces was not difficult as they were unpaid and Mobutu had "kept [them] weak and divided so that it would not pose a threat."[12] This resulted in the swift overthrow of his fleeing to Morocco, where he died in September 1997. In his place, Kabila came to power.

**Second Congo War**

Rather than establish the democracy that many had hoped for, Kabila quickly established a one man rule and used public enterprises to "rapidly generate finances through indiscriminate concession granting;" overall his rule was marked by "corruption, patronage, and lack of accountability." [13]

The Kabila regime was quickly drawn into conflict, however, as rebel groups from Uganda, Rwanda, and Burundi continued to use Congolese territory to launch attacks from into their respective countries. Rwanda did not take these attacks lying down as then-Vice President of Rwanda stated that "if the international community was unable or unwilling to stop the delivery of weapons to the ex-FAR and Interahamwe and the military training in the refugee camps, the Rwandan government could decide to take preventive military action."[14] The final split between Kabila and the Rwandan government came when Kabila dismissed a Rwandan military chief of Tutsi descent as the chief of staff of the military and sent all of his Rwandan allies packing in July 1998 in order to avert the possibility of a military coup against him.

In the very next month, August, troops from Rwanda and Uganda entered the Congo and the Second Congo War began, with Rwanda, Uganda, and Burundi on one side and the Congo, Angola, Chad, Nambia, Sudan, and Zimbabwe on the other.

The war lasted from 1998 to 2003, even though a ceasefire had been brokered in 1999 and UN troops deployed the year after. The war finally ended with the signing of the Pretoria Peace Accords in 2003 which called for an end to hostilities between Rwanda and the Congo and the rise of a transitional government, which was formed in July of that year.

During the Second Congo War, Kabila was assassinated in January 2001. His son, Joseph Kabila, took over and was even elected President in 2006. Unfortunately, the violence in the Congo would continue as the Kivu conflict arose.

**Kivu Conflict**

While the Second Congo War officially ended in 2003, there was still resistance in the aforementioned Kivu region. At the end of the Second Congo War, Laurent Nkunda, who had been an officer in the rebel group Rally for Congolese Democracy (RCD), was made a colonel in the transitional government and promoted to general in 2004. Yet he soon turned against the government to support the RCD.

Starting on May 26, 2004, clashes took place "between soldiers loyal to Colonel Jules Mutebutsi, a commander from the Rally for Congolese Democracy" and "pro-government forces of the newly created Tenth Military Region under the command of General Mbuza Mabe."[15] Nkunda was stationed in the north Kivu region and sent 1,000 soldiers to support Mutebutsi. There was an ethnic aspect to this as Mabe's forces had been killing Congolese Tutsis and thus Nkunda, being a Congolese Tutsi himself, sent forces to protect his fellow Tutsis. From there a number of atrocities have occurred, from rape to the wholesale slaughter of civilians.

While the fighting continued until 2009 and ended with the capture of Nkunda in January[16], it is a wonder that they were able to sustain themselves for that long and thus the resources within the Kivu region and foreign companies played a role in sustaining the conflict must be bought up.

The main minerals that are exploited are "gold, cassiterite, wolframite, and columbite- tantalite (coltan)."[17] These minerals, especially coltan, are "needed to manufacture everything from lightbulbs to laptops, from MP3 players to Playstations" [18] and often change hands numerous times so that it is virtually impossible for the average consumer to find out if their devices are being powered by conflict minerals.

Even though many companies are attempting to clean up their act by avoiding the use of conflict minerals, there are still problems as "while major US-registered electronics firms are outwardly pledging to end the use of conflict minerals some of these same firms belong to industry associations that are seeking to water down the disclosure requirements under Dodd-Frank," [19] which would force corporations to disclose the fact that they are utilizing conflict minerals. The situation has not fully been worked out yet and thus the violence- and suffering- continues.


**Endnotes**

1: Kisangani N. F. Emizet, "Explaining The Rise And Fall of Military Regimes: Civil-Military Relations in the Congo," *Armed Forces & Society* 26:2 (2000), pg 209

2: James K. Boyce, Leonce Ndikumana, "Congo's Odious Debt: External Borrowing and Capital Flight in Zaire," *Development and Change* 29:2 (1998), pg 195

3: Ibid

4: Ellen Ray, "US Military and Corporate Recolonization of the Congo," *Covert Action Quarterly* (2000), pg 6

5: Mel McNulty, "The Collapse of Zaire: Implosion, Revolution, or External Sabotage?" *Journal of Modern African Studies* 37:1 (1999), pg 62

6: Letitia Lawson, "US Africa Policy Since The Cold War," *Strategic Insights* 6:1 (2007), pg 1

7: Lawson, pg 3

8: Georges Nzongola-Ntalaja, "The International Dimensions of the Congo Crisis," *Global Dialogue* 6:3 (2004), pgs 1-2

9: Filip Reyntjens, "The Second Congo War: More Than A Remake," *African Affairs* 98:391 (1999), pg 241

10: Francois Ngolet, "African and American Connivance in Congo-Zaire," Africa Today 47:1 (2000), pg 70

11: Ngolet, pgs 70-71

12: Heather Congdon Fors, Ola Olsson, "Congo: The Prize of Predation," *Journal of Peace Research* 41:3 (2004), pg 325

13: Ibid

14: Christian R. Manahl, "From Genocide to Regional War: The Breakdown of International Order in Central Africa," *African Studies Quarterly* 4:1 (2000), pg 19

15: Human Rights Watch, *D.R. Congo: War Crimes in Bukavu*, http://www.hrw.org/sites/default/files/reports/2004_DRCongo_WarCrimesinBukavu.pdf (June 2004)

16: Matthew Weaver, "Congo and Rwandan Forces Arrest Rebel Leader Laurent Nkunda," *The Guardian*, January 23, 2009 ( http://www.theguardian.com/world/2009/jan/23/laurent-nkunda- congo-rwanda )

17: Relief Web, *Democratic Republic of the Congo: Mineral Exploitation by Armed Groups & Other Entities*, http://reliefweb.int/map/democratic-republic-congo/democratic-republic-congo- mineral-exploitation-armed-groups-other (June 7, 2013)

18: Elizabeth Dias, "First Blood Diamonds, Now Bloods Computers?" *Time*, July 24, 2009 ( http://content.time.com/time/world/article/0,8599,1912594,00.html)

19: Nick Heath, "How Conflict Minerals Funded A War That Killed Millions, And Why Tech Giants Are Finally Cleaning Up Their Act," *Tech Republic*, April 1, 2014 ( http://www.techrepublic.com/article/how-conflict-minerals-funded-a-war-that-killed-millions/ )

Currently, the world is facing a major political, social and economical crisis. While we may be paying attention to important stories such as the Islamic State's movements in Iraq and the ongoing fighting in the Gaza Strip which are extremely important, there are dealings being made behind closed doors of which we know virtually nothing about. There are major international trade deals in the works and the government seems to be getting prepared for the fallout.

**The Trans-Pacific Partnership**

The Trans-Pacific Partnership (TPP) has its roots in the Asia Pacific Economic Cooperation (APEC) organization. In 1994, APEC stated in its Bogor Declaration that:

> **With respect to our objective of enhancing trade and investment in the Asia-Pacific, we agree to adopt the long-term goal of free and open trade and investment in the Asia-Pacific.** This goal will be pursued promptly by further reducing barriers to trade and investment and by promoting the free flow of goods, services and capital among our economies.
>
> [...]
>
> **We further agree to announce our commitment to complete the achievement of our goal of free and open trade and investment in the Asia-Pacific no later than the year 2020.**[1] (emphasis added)

Furthermore, in the free trade agreement between the US and Singapore both leaders made a statement in 2000 in which they stated that both countries "are committed to APEC's Bogor Goals of free and open trade and investment by 2010 for industrialized economies and 2020 for developing economies."[2] Thus we can see that some sort of trade deal has been sought after for quite some time and logically, it would be much easier to have a regional trade deal between APEC nations rather than individual trade deals among the many countries in the region.

The TPP itself, originally had nothing to do with the United States, rather it was a trade deal between Chile, New Zealand and Singapore and Brunei which was signed in 2005. The US became involved three years later and officially joined the TPP in 2009.[3] However, this leads to the question: If the trade deal was originally between four Asia Pacific nations, why did the US feel the need to become involved?

According to Deborah Elms, head of the Temasek Foundation Centre for Trade & Negotiations, the US became involved for three reasons:

1) A trade agreement between the European Union and South Korea bolstered the argument for greater US economic intervention in the region.

2) Alternative trade configurations were starting to be discussed such as ASEAN plus China, Japan and Korea. If these were to become a reality, the US would end up being sidelined from Asian markets.

3) "The TPP gave the United States a seat at the economic table in Asia in a way that these alternatives did not. It represented a better platform for meaningful engagement than the only remaining configuration— somehow coaxing APEC to do more."[4]

The last point is further backed up when one looks at the US President's 2008 Annual Report on the Trade Agreements Program, which read that "US participation in the TPP could position US businesses better to compete in the Asia-Pacific region, which is seeing the proliferation of preferential trade agreements among US competitors and the development of several competing regional economic integration initiatives that exclude the United States."[5]

However, there is also much more to the story than just not wanting to be locked out from Asian markets. US geopolitical interests are also involved as well. The aforementioned annual report also stated that "Apart from economic considerations, there are also geopolitical concerns, **particularly with regard to the growing power and influence of China, something which became clearer with the Obama administration's policy announcement of a military and diplomatic 'pivot' or 'rebalance' towards Asia**" and a US Congress research paper noted that the TPP would have regional effects for the US, especially when one factors in that "**the region has served as an anchor of US strategic relationships, first in the containment of communism and more recently as a counterweight to the rise of China.**"[6] (emphasis added)

Jane Kelsey, a professor of law at the University of Auckland, argued that the TPP had "very little to do with commercial gain and everything to do with revival of US geopolitical and strategic influence in the Asian region to counter the ascent of China" and that the US wanted to "isolate and subordinate China in part through constructing a region-wide legal regime that serves the interests of, and is enforceable by, the US and its corporations – and in the TPPA context, what the US wants is ultimately what counts."[7] Many in China seem believe that the TPP indeed is meant to harm China, with it being reported that "official media have suspected that the deal has more insidious goals than simply forging a trade alliance, accusing the US of corralling Pacific nations against Beijing's interests."[8]

While many praise the Trans-Pacific Partnership as free trade, one must be wary not only due to the geopolitical aspects, but also due to it being so secret that "often times, members of Congress and Parliament are denied access to them, even though the agreement will set out legal obligations that these elected officials will be expected to meet."[9] However, the TPP is not the only secretive trade deal currently being discussed. There is also the Transatlantic Trade and Investment Partnership.

**Transatlantic Trade and Investment Partnership**

A transatlantic partnership between the US and Europe has been in the works for quite some time. In 1995, the US mission to the European Union stated that it wanted to "create a New Transatlantic Marketplace by progressively reducing or eliminating barriers that hinder the flow of goods, services and capital" and that the US and EU would "carry out a joint study on ways of facilitating trade in goods and services and further reducing or eliminating tariff and non-tariff barriers."[10]

The idea of focusing on Europe economically was pushed by those who thought that, due to the Cold War being over, the US should shift away from examining Europe through a military lens. Robin Gaster and Alan Tonelson wrote in The Atlantic that the military-view of Europe "completely misreads the nature of America's post–Cold War interests in Europe, and has resulted in a deepening transatlantic rift on both the security and the economic front" and that "the United States and Europe urgently need to develop a NATO-like forum for handling economic issues."[11] While this argument isn't for a US-EU free trade agreement, it still signals that to some, there needed to be a shift in the US relationship with Europe.

However, that quickly changed as some began to argue for a deeper economic integration between the transatlantic partners. In 1997, Ellen L. Frost, a then-senior fellow at the Peterson Institute for International Economics, proposed to the to the House Subcommittee on Trade (part of the House Ways and Means Committee) the creation of a North Atlantic Economic Community which would be "a framework combining APEC-like trade and business initiatives with a NATO-like strategic, political-economic orientation" and would "establish a deadline for free and open Transatlantic trade and investment (say, 2010) on a Most Favored Nation Basis." She argued that the Community "should span not only trade and investment but also macroeconomic coordination, monetary policy, exchange rates, and other financial aspects of the transatlantic relationship, as well as trade and investment."[12]

The very next year, in May 1998, Bill Clinton and Tony Blair announced in a press conference that "we have launched a major new transatlantic trade initiative, the Transatlantic Economic Partnership, which will further add momentum to the process of developing what is already the most important bilateral trade relationship in the world. We've also agreed to work ever more closely together to promote multilateral trade liberalization."[13]

The push for a transatlantic economic partnership has continued into the present day, both by individuals and organizations. In 2006, an article was penned in *Der Spiegel* which argued that "The role NATO played in an age of military threat could be played by a trans-Atlantic free- trade zone in today's age of economic confrontation" and that such a partnership would "help reduce the slope of Asia's ascent and prevent our flight paths from crossing too frequently."[14]

In 2012, "Business Europe released a report to contribute to the EU-US High Level Working Group entitled, Jobs and Growth: Through a Transatlantic Economic and Trade Partnership, in which it was recommended to eliminate tariffs and barriers, to trade in services, ensure access and protection for investments, 'opening markets,' to establish 'global standards' for intellectual property rights, and to build on the Transatlantic Economic Council (TEC) for regulatory cooperation."[15]

While both of these 'free trade' partnerships are quite worrisome, there is still the Trade in Services agreement which has recently come to light.

**Trade in Services Agreement**

The TiSA is so new and so secretive that barely any information can be found about it. Public Services International, a global trade union federation, issued a report in April 2014 discussing the origins of TiSA, stating

The TISA appears to have been the brainchild of the U.S. Coalition of Service Industries (CSI), specifically its past president Robert Vastine. After his appointment as CSI President in 1996, Vastine became actively involved in services negotiations. The CSI initially endorsed the Doha Round and seemed to be optimistic in the early stages of negotiations, but when the target deadline passed in 2005, the CSI became increasingly frustrated. Vastine personally lobbied developing countries for concessions in 2005 and continued to try and salvage an agreement until at least 2009.

By 2010, however, it was clear that the WTO services negotiations were stalled. In mid- 2011, Vastine declared that the Doha Round "holds no promise" and recommended that it be abandoned. Vastine was also one of the first to suggest, as early as 2009, that plurilateral negotiations on services should be conducted outside the framework of the WTO. Working through the Global Services Coalition (GSC), a multinational services lobby group, the CSI then garnered the support of other corporate lobbyists for the TISA initiative. The TISA is a political project for this corporate lobby group.[16]

Some of the actual effects TiSA would have were released in June 2014 by Wikileaks. In the leak, it explained that TiSA would have horrendous effects on public services. TiSA would **"lock in the privatizations of services-even in cases where private service delivery has failed-meaning governments can never return water, energy, health, education or other services to public hands,"** "restrict a **government's right to regulate stronger standards in the public's interest,"** "restrict a government's ability to regulate key sectors including financial, energy, telecommunications and cross-border data flows," and **"limit the ability of governments to regulate the financial services industry at exactly the time when the global economy is still recovering from a crisis caused by financial deregulation."**[17] (emphasis added) This trade agreement not only has the power to allow corporations free rein and to truly be unrestricted in doing whatever they please, but also to put the public in massive danger via permanently privatizing public goods.

However, this brings up the questions of what exactly is the Coalition of Services Industries, what involvement do they have with TiSA, and who is Robert Vastine?

According to its website, the Coalition of Services Industries is an organization representing the interests of the US service economy and aims at "expanding the multilateral trading environment to include more countries and more services, enhancing bilateral services trading relationships, and ensuring competitive services trade in the global marketplace."[18] Among its board of directors are people such as Zubaid Ahmad, the Vice Chairman of Institutional Clients Group and Member of Senior Strategic Advisory Group of Institutional Clients at Citigroup and Jake Jennings, Executive Director of International External Affairs at AT&T. It represents companies ranging from Walmart to JP Morgan Chase and Citigroup to Google, Verizon, and AIG. In many ways it represents a variety of interests, virtually all of whom benefit from worker subjugation and/or economic deregulation.

The Coalition of Services Industries is part of the TiSA Business Coalition (aka Team TiSA) which is "dedicated to promoting and advocating for an ambitious agreement which eliminates barriers to global services trade, to the benefit of services providers, manufacturers and farmers, and consumers globally."[19]

Now, with regards to Robert Vastine, in 2012 he retired from the presidency of the Coalition of Services group and is currently a senior industry fellow at the Center for Business and Public Policy at the McDonough School of Business at Georgetown University.[20] He is quite known for having stated in 2011 at the Doha Round, a round of negotiations among the members of the World Trade Organization with the aims of achieving "major reform of the international trading system through the introduction of lower trade barriers and revised trade rules,"[21] that the talks were a waste of time and "hold no promise."[22] However, he already had problems with the Doha Round talks as he stated in 2005 in the Global Economy Journal that "High expectations for substantial reductions in barriers to services trade emerged from the 1997 negotiations, but thus far remain unfulfilled" and that "a Doha Round that does not contain substantial benefits for services is a Round that will have failed."[23] Thus, it is no wonder that he is a supporter of TiSA.

The effects of these trade agreements will be horrendous for millions of people around the world, but especially the poor and working-class, much of whom are more vulnerable to these agreements as few have the money needed to learn new skills and adapt to the changing economy. For them and many in what remains of the middle class, if these trade agreements become a reality, it will result in a global race to the bottom in which, among them, there are no winners.

All of these trade agreements, however, are being done all the while the police are becoming increasingly militarized and the Pentagon is preparing for a mass breakdown in society.

**Police Militarization**

We have recently been seeing an increase in coverage of the militarization of the police and a number of stories reveal this. It was reported in July 2014 that the Albuquerque police purchased 350 AR-15 rifles[24] and the American Civil Liberties Union released a report in which they found that the police are often being used incorrectly and actually creating violence as "SWAT teams today are overwhelmingly used to investigate people who are still only suspected of committing nonviolent consensual crimes. And because these raids often involve forced entry into homes, often at night, they're actually creating violence and confrontation where there was none before."[25]

Police are also acquiring military-grade weaponry. A *New York Times* article written in June 2014 noted that "the former tools of combat — M-16 rifles, grenade launchers, silencers and more — are ending up in local police departments, often with little public notice" and that "During the Obama administration, according to Pentagon data, police departments have received tens of thousands of machine guns; nearly 200,000 ammunition magazines; thousands of pieces of camouflage and night-vision equipment; and hundreds of silencers, armored cars and aircraft."[26] The situation also has the potential to get increasingly strange as it was reported that a drone which can shoot pepper spray bullets at protesters had been developed by a company in South Africa. [27] Unfortunately, however, police militarization isn't anything new.

A study was conducted in 1998 which "found a sharp rise in the number of police paramilitary units [PPUs], a rapid expansion in their activities, the normalization of paramilitary units into mainstream police work, and a close ideological and material connection between PPUs and the U.S. armed forces. These findings provide compelling evidence of a national trend toward the militarization of U.S. civilian police forces and, in turn, the militarization of corresponding social problems handled by the police."[28] The study found that this increased militarization would lead to three problems:

1. It would reinforce "the cynical view that the most expedient route to solving social problems is through military-style force, weaponry, and technology."[29]

2. The militarist-feel could potentially infect the police on an institutional level, noting that many police departments have specific paramilitary units to deal with patrolling, drugs, and suppressing gangs.

3. Most PPUs don't solely react to already existing emergencies which require their level of skill, but also "proactively seek out and even manufacture highly dangerous situations" and these "units target what the police define as high crime or disorderly areas, which most often are poor neighborhoods."[30]

Furthermore, police militarization in many ways doesn't make sense as we have seen a decrease in the amount of crime, but it does make sense when we acknowledge the fact that most of the victims of police militarization are the poor.

According to the 2003 Federal Bureau of Investigation's (FBI) annual crime report, violent crime in America has declined by 3 percent since 2002, and declined some 25 percent since 1994. Aggravated assaults, which make up two-thirds of all reported violent crimes, reportedly declined for the tenth consecutive year. The 2003 annual crime report also revealed that property crimes had declined 14 percent since 1994.

Similar findings of a historic decline in the violent crime rate in America over the past decade were also reported in other government studies. One such study that provided supporting evidence of this declining violent crime rate was the United States Justice Department's annual survey of crime victims, released in September 2004. **This report revealed that the nation's violent crime rate was at its lowest point since their study of crime victims began, in 1973. However, even with this reported decline in violent crime there still remained throughout suburban communities a perceived threat of being victimized by violent acts of crime, perpetrated by the urban underclass.**[31] (emphasis added)

We can further see that there is a war on the underclass in the form of police militarization as a study in 1997 found that SWAT teams "were characterized by the deployment of military special operation weapons, such as Heckler and Koch MP5 submachine guns, diversionary devices, and the wearing of tactical body armor and camouflage uniforms" and that often those resources were used "in daily and routine policing activities against the urban underclass." One can even go so far as to say that "the use of special weapons, military tactics, and the wearing of combat style uniforms in the course of routine urban policing by street-level law enforcement officers would suggest that they are engaged in an actual urban war with the enemy being the urban underclass."[32]

This increased cooperation between the police and military should have us wonder: What exactly is the Pentagon up to?

**The Pentagon**

The Pentagon is actively preparing for civil unrest and a breakdown of society. The organization currently has a research program which "is funding universities to model the dynamics, risks and tipping points for large-scale civil unrest across the world, under the supervision of various US military agencies" and earlier in 2014 awarded a project to the University of Washington which "seeks to uncover the conditions under which political movements aimed at large-scale political and economic change originate,' along with their 'characteristics and consequences."[33] However, like with police militarization, this has been going on for a while.

In 2008, it was noted that "A U.S. Army War College report [warned that] an economic crisis in the United States could lead to massive civil unrest and the need to call on the military to restore order."[34] The use of the military to quell civil unrest was also discussed in Directive No. 3025.18, the Defense Support of Civil Authorities.

The directive was rather interesting in that it stated that "Federal military forces shall not be used to quell civil disturbances unless specifically authorized by the president in accordance with applicable law or permitted under emergency authority," however, later the document reads that federal military commanders are able, **"in extraordinary emergency circumstances where prior authorization by the president is impossible and duly constituted local authorities are unable to control the situation, to engage temporarily in activities that are necessary to quell large-scale, unexpected civil disturbances,"**[35] under two conditions. (emphasis added) The two conditions are when the military has "to prevent significant loss of life or wanton destruction of property and are necessary to restore governmental function and public order" and "when federal, state and local authorities are unable or decline to provide adequate protection for federal property or federal governmental functions."[36] This is quite vague in the sense of who defines what "significant loss of life" or "wanton destruction of property" is? What exactly does "adequate protection" for federal property and/or governmental functions mean?

Unfortunately, this isn't just occurring in the US, but also in Europe as well. It was reported in July 2014 that "European governments are working together to prepare to militarily suppress social unrest. This effort—involving legal, technical, as well as military plans—is in an advanced stage of development, according to a report by Aureliana Sorrento that aired on June 20 on Germany's Deutschlandfun k radio station."[37] Just like the US, the Europeans also utilize vague language, saying that a disaster "is defined as 'any situation that has harmful repercussions on human beings, the environment or wealth assets.'"[38]

However, among all of this preparation and secrecy, there is mounting resistance to these trade deals. In December 2013, 30 protests were held across the US and Mexico, with people voicing their opposition against the Trans-Pacific Partnership.[39] The World Development Movement, a UK-based group fighting poverty and inequality, noted that "Campaign groups and trade unions announced plans for Europe-wide protests on 11 October against the deal, known as the Transatlantic Trade and Investment Partnership (TTIP). Campaigners also launched a 'Citizens' Initiative' petition to the European Commission with the aim of gathering one million signatures against the deal."[40]

We are beginning to resist against the secretive trade deals and police militarization, but we must go further. We have to also reject the governments, no matter how large are small their facilitation or complicity may be, as they are being used as tools in a corporate agenda meant to oppress us even further. The calamity may soon be coming, the question is, will you resist?


**Endnotes**

1: Asia Pacific Economic Cooperation, *1994 Leaders' Declaration Bogor Declaration*, http://www.apec.org/Meeting- Papers/Leaders-Declarations/ 1994/1994_aelm.aspx (November 15, 1994)

2: US Government Printing Office, *Joint Statement by President Bill Clinton and Prime Minister Goh Chok Tong on a United States-Singapore Free Trade Agreement*, http://www.gpo.gov/fdsys/pkg/ WCPD-2000-11-20/pdf/WCPD-2000- 11-20- Pg2885.pdf (November 16, 2000)

3: Office of the United States Trade Representative, *TPP Statements and Actions to Date*, http://www.ustr.gov/about-us/ press-office/fact-sheets/2009/ december/tpp-statements-and- actions-date

4: Deborah Elms, *US Trade Policy In Asia: Going For The Trans-Pacific Partnership?* East Asia Forum, http://www.eastasiaforum.org/ 2009/11/26/u-s-trade-policy- in-asia-going- for-the-trans- pacific-partnership/ (November 26, 2009)

5: T. Rajamoorthy, "And Then There Were Twelve: The Origins and Evolutions of the TPPA," *Third World Resurgence*, July 2013, pg 4

6: Ibid

7: Jane Kelsey, "TPP As A Lynchpin of US Anti-China Strategy," *Scoop*, November 19, 2011 (http://www.scoop.co.nz/ stories/HL1111/S00171/tpp-as- a-lynchpin-of-us-anti-china- strategy.htm)

8: Shawn Donnan, David Pilling, "Trans-Pacific Partnership: Ocean's Twelve," *Financial Times*, September 22, 2013 (http://www.ft.com/intl/cms/s/ 0/8c253c5c-2056-11e3-b8c6- 00144feab7de.html?siteedition= intl#axzz37adFOqTN)

9: Cory Doctorow, "Trans Pacific Partnership Meeting Switched From Vancouver to Ottawa, Ducking Critics," Boing Boing, July 2, 2014 (http://boingboing.net/2014/ 07/02/trans-pacific- partnership-meet.html)

10: United States Mission to the European Union, *Transatlantic Relations*, http://useu.usmission.gov/new_ transatlantic_agenda.html(December 5, 1995)

11: Robin Gaster, Alan Tonelson, "Our Interests In Europe," *The Atlantic*, August 1995, pgs 28, 31

12: Peterson Institute for International Economics, *Transatlantic Trade: Towards a North Atlantic Economic Community*, http://www.iie.com/ publications/testimony/print. cfm?ResearchId=286&doc=pub (July 23, 1997)

13: The American Presidency Project, *The President's News Conference With European Union Leaders in London, United Kingdom*, http://www.presidency.ucsb. edu/ws/?pid=55983 (May 18, 1998)

14: Gabor Steingart, "A NATO for the World Economy: An Argument for a Trans-Atlantic Free-Trade Zone," *Der Spiegel*, October 20, 2006 (http://www.spiegel.de/ international/a-nato- for-the- world-economy-an-argument-for- a-trans-atlantic-free-trade- zone-a-443306.html)

15: Andrew Gavin Marshall, *Large Corporations Seek U.S.–European 'Free Trade Agreement' to Further Global Dominance*, http://andrewgavinmarshall. com/2013/05/12/large- corporations- seek-u-s- european-free-trade-agreement- to-further-global-dominance/ (May 12, 2013)

16: Public Services International, *TISA Versus Public Services*, http://www.world-psi.org/ sites/default/files/documents/ research/en_tisaresearchpaper_ final_web.pdf (April 28, 2014)

17: CNBC, *Secret Trade Deal Puts Public Services at Risk Around the World*, http://www.cnbc.com/id/ 101773881 (June 19, 2014)

18: Coalition of Services, *Who We Are*, https://servicescoalition.org/ about-csi/what-is-csi

19: Coalition of Services, *The TiSA Business Coalition*, https://servicescoalition.org/ about- csi/team-tisa

20: Georgetown University, *J. Robert Vastine*, http://cbpp.georgetown.edu/ staff/j-robert-vastine/

21: World Trade Organization, *The Doha Round*, http://www.wto.org/english/ tratop_e/dda_e/dda_e.htm

22: Claude Barfield, "It's Time To Dump The Doha Development Round," *Real Clear Markets*, August 25, 2011 (http://www.realclearmarkets. com/articles/2011/08/25/time_ to_dump_the_doha_development_ round_99212.html)

23: Robert Vastine, "Services Negotiations in the Doha Round: Promise and Reality," *Global Economy Journal* 5:4 (2005), pg 1

24: Travis Gettys, "Highly-criticized Albuquerque police militarize with $350,000 purchase of 350 AR-15 rifles," *Raw Story*, July 11, 2014 (http://www.rawstory.com/rs/ 2014/07/11/highly- criticized- albuquerque-police-militarize- with-350000-purchase-of-350- ar-15-rifles/)

25: Radley Balko, "New ACLU Report Takes a Snapshot of Police Militarization in the United States," *Washington Post*, June 24, 2014 (http://www.washingtonpost. com/news/the- watch/wp/2014/06/ 24/new-aclu-report-takes-a- snapshot-of-police- militarization-in-the-united- states/)

26: Matt Apuzzo, "War Gear Flows to Police Departments," *New York Times*, June 9, 2014 (http://www.nytimes.com/2014/ 06/09/us/war-gear-flows-to- police-departments.html?_r=0)

27: Hack Read, *"Riot Control" Drone Will Shoot Pepper Spray Bullets At Protesters*, http://hackread.com/riot- control-drone-shoots-pepper- bullets/ (June 22, 2014)

28: Peter B. Kraska and Victor E. Kappeler, "Militarizing American Police: The Rise and Normalization of Paramilitary Units," *Social Problems* 44:1 (1998), pg 12

29: Ibid

30: Ibid

31: Daryl Meeks, "Police Militarization in Urban Areas: The Obscure War Against the Underclass," *The Black Scholar* 35:4 (2006), pg 37

32: Ibid, pgs 37-38

33: Nafeez Ahmed, "Pentagon Preparing For Civil Breakdown," *The Guardian*, June 12, 2014 (http://www.theguardian.com/ environment/earth-insight/ 2014/jun/12/pentagon-mass- civil-breakdown?CMP=twt_gu)

34: Diana Washington Valdez, "Unrest Caused By Bad Economy May Require Military Action Report Says," *El Paso Times*, December 29, 2008 (http://www.elpasotimes.com/ ci_11326744)

35: Bill Girtz, "Inside the Ring: Directive Outlines Obama's Plan to use the Military Against Citizens," *Washington Times*, May 28, 2014(http://www.washingtontimes. com/news/2014/may/28/inside- the-ring-directive-outlines- obamas-policy-t/?page=all)

36: Ibid

37: Dennis Krassnin, "European Governments Prepare For Military Suppression of Popular Opposition," *World Socialist Web Site*, July 10, 2014 (http://www.wsws.org/en/ articles/2014/07/10/euro-j10. html)

38: Ibid

39: Truthout, *30 Cities Across US Protest Toxic Free Trade Agreements*, http://www.truth- out.org/ speakout/item/20457-30-cities- across-us-protest-toxic-free- trade- agreements (December 5, 2013)

40: Miriam Ross, *Opposition to EU-US Trade Deal Gathers Negotiation as Talks Falter, World Development Movement*, http://www.wdm.org.uk/trade/ opposition-eu-us-trade-deal- gathers- momentum-negotiations- falter (July 17, 2014)

The Bank for International Settlements (BIS) is an organization that is shrouded in mystery, mainly due to the fact that the majority of people don't even know of its existence. According to the BIS itself, the main purpose of the Bank is to "to promote the cooperation of central banks and to provide additional facilities for international financial operations" and "act as trustee or agent in regard to international financial settlements entrusted to it under agreements of the parties concern."[1] This means that the BIS is to have the central banks work with one another to facilitate international operations and to oversee any international financial settlements.

The Bank has a Board of Directors, which "may have up to 21 members, including six ex officio directors, comprising the central bank Governors of Belgium, France, Germany, Italy, the United Kingdom and the United States. Each ex officio member may appoint another member of the same nationality. Nine Governors of other member central banks may be elected to the Board."[2] BIS also has a management wing in the form of a General and Deputy General Manager, both of whom are responsible to the board and supported by Executive, Finance, and Compliance and Operational Risk Committees.[3]

However, its purpose has changed and evolved over the decades, however, it has always been a club for central bankers, yet in many ways it can aid some countries more than others.

The origins of the BIS lie in the United States, specifically New York City. The individuals involved were international bankers who, despite past differences, "worked together to establish a world financial order that would incorporate the federal principle of the American central banking system."[4] Specifically among them were people such as "Owen D. Young, J. Pierpont Morgan, Thomas W. Lamont, S. Parker Gilbert, Gates W. McGarrah, and Jackson Reynolds, who, in conjunction with the Federal Reserve Bank of New York, sought to extend the principle of central bank cooperation to the international sphere."[5]Before delving any further into the creation of the Bank, it is necessary to examine some of the more notable of these individuals to better understand why they would be involved in the creation of an international bank.

Owen D. Young was already in good with the US government as he, "with the cooperation of the American government and the support of GE, organized and became chairman of the board of the Radio Corporation of America" and "in subsequent years he engineered a series of agreements with foreign companies that divided the world into radio zones and facilitated worldwide wireless communication"[6] Young had a strong belief that global radio service and broadcasting were important for the advancement of civilization. In 1922, Young became chairman of General Electric, and along with GE President Gerard Swope, "urged closer business-government cooperation and corporate self-regulation under government supervision."[7]

During the 1920s, Young became involved in international diplomacy as the foreign affairs spokesman for the Democratic Party. At the behest of then-Secretary of State, Charles Evan Hughes, Young and Charles Dawes, a banker, were recommended to the Allied Reparations Commission in order to deal with the breakdown in Germany's reparations payments following the First World War. The Commission resulted in the Dawes Plan which allowed for "Germany's annual reparation payments would be reduced, increasing over time as its economy improved; the full amount to be paid, however, was left undetermined. Economic policy making in Berlin would be reorganized under foreign supervision and a new currency, the Reichsmark, adopted."[8] Young viewed improving the world financial structure as important to "the very survival of capitalism" and furthermore he "sought rather the 'economic integration' of the world which would prepare the way for 'political integration' and lasting peace."[9]

John Piermont Morgan, Jr. was already ensconced in the world of international banking, having inherited the JP Morgan Company from his father. During World War One, the House of Morgan worked hand-in-hand with the British and French governments, engaging in a number of tasks such as floating loans for the two countries, handling foreign exchange operations, and advising officials of each respective country.[10]

Both these individuals were heavily involved in politics and banking therefore had a personal interest in the creation of a global bank. It should be noted, this fits into the US government's own policies as they wanted to "[keep] aloof from the political entanglements in Europe while safeguarding vital American interests by means of unofficial observers or participants."[11] The Federal Reserve also was interested in the creation of the BIS as it would "[promote] both the ascendancy of New York City in world banking and the reconstruction of a stable and prosperous Europe able to absorb American exports."[12]

This idea of an international bank didn't occur in a vacuum. The creation of the bank "was inextricably tied to the problem of German reparations in the context of Germany's overall debt burden during the 1920s."[13] A slowdown in international lending to Germany began in 1928 as markets became extremely worried about the internal politics of the Weimar Republic. Due to the breakup of a center coalition government and the Social Democrats needing support from right-wing parties, the political situation began to fall apart with "government stability [being] threatened whenever budget debates exposed the basic social divide of unemployment insurance and increased industrial taxation on the one hand versus spending austerity and tax cuts on the other."[14] The budget problems came on the heels of the Reparations Committee having determined that Germany's total reparations came to $33 billion, which was twice the size of the country's total economy in 1925. As long as foreign capital kept coming into Germany, things were fine, however as was aforementioned, that situation changed in 1928.

Between February 1929 and January 1930, negotiations were made to reschedule Germany's reparations payments. "These negotiations were initiated by central bankers and private actors, who were the first to link problems in the capital market with the need to reorganize Germany's financial obligations."[15] Thus, it should be no surprise that many of the main individuals involved in the creation of the BIS were central bankers or engaged in international affairs/finance to some extent.

The idea for an international bank had already been explored to some extent by people such as John Mayard Keynes [16], however the idea truly took off during the Young Conference in 1929 when the Allies were attempting to deal with Germany's reparations debts for World War One. Belgian delegate Emile Franqui bought up the possibility of having a settlement organization to administer the reparations agreement and the very next day, Hjalmar Schacht, president of the Reichsbank and chief German representative at the conference, presented a proposal to establish such an organization to as a direct financier of global economic development and trade. The bank would act as a lender to the German central bank in case the Germany currency weakened and the government found itself unable to make the reparations payment. In addition, it would give steps for how to proceed in the case of German default as if "Germany did not resume payments within two years, the BIS would propose revisions collectively for the creditor governments (which would only go into effect with their approval)" and "the bank was responsible for surveillance and informing the creditor countries about economic and financial conditions in Germany."[17]

While the US State Department was concerned with having a settlement as State Department "economic adviser Arthur N. Young observed, 'a final reparations settlement' would 'promote both political and economic stability in Europe, and thus tend to be of advantage to the United States," the US government as a whole didn't want any type of linkage between reparations and war debts due to the fact that because each of the Allied nations was demanding reparations from Germany large enough to cover the debts it owed to the US, having such a linkage would mean that "Germany's refusal or inability to pay that amount would put Washington in the position of having to agree to a debt reduction or bear the opprobrium and suffer the consequences of opening the door to financial chaos."[18] However, several other countries had their own interests as well in the creation of the BIS. The French Prime Minister, Raymond Poincare, promised the French public that the reparations would cover the country's debts to both the US and Britain as well as cover the war damages. France was also interested in reaching an agreement on German debts as they were developing trade interdependence with the Germans and stability was needed.[19]

The British wanted to use the BIS as a means to ensure that the Germans would pay on their debts as scheduled. The Bank of England itself supported the creation of the BIS "because of its potential role in stabilizing the position of the pound in the international monetary system. Britain's relatively small gold reserves made it difficult to defend the pound without international monetary cooperation and the willingness of smaller powers to hold foreign exchange as reserves instead of gold."[20]At the meeting in Baden, Germany in October 1929 to draw up the final plans for the BIS saw the heavy presence of US finance in the form of Melvin Traylor of the First National Bank of Chicago and Federick Reynolds of the First National Bank of New York. There, the two nominated Gates W. McGarrah, chairman of the board of the New York Reserve Bank for the officer of President. Later, his assistant, "Leon Fraser, a legal counselor at Gilbert's reparations office, the Young conference, and Baden," [21] would become president of the Bank in 1935. When the Bank of England expressed anger and that the European public wouldn't find American domination of the Bank acceptable, they were effectively told that if they wanted American participation in the BIS it would have to be on American terms. However, they did agree to appoint Pierre Quesnay of the Bank of France as the general manager of the BIS. The Bank was officially founded on May 17, 1930.

The role of the BIS quickly changed as with the onset of the Great Depression, it was unable to "play the role of lender of last resort, notwithstanding noteworthy attempts at organizing support credits for both the Austrian and German central banks in 1931" and due to the Depression, the issue of reparations was off the table due to Germany's inability to pay. The problem was further compounded when countries such as Britain and the US began to devalue their currencies (i.e. print more money) and the BIS attempted numerous times to end the exchange rate instability by restoring the gold standard, "the BIS had little choice but to limit itself to undertaking banking transactions for the account of central banks and providing a forum for central bank governors to help them maintain contact."[22] During the Second World War, all operations were suspended for the duration of the conflict, yet the situation became rather dicey for the Bank once the guns stopped firing.

Immediately after World War Two, the global economic landscape had massively changed and thus a new system was needed, In July 1944 over 700 delegates from the Allied nation met in Mount Washington Hotel in Bretton Woods, NH for the United Nations Monetary and Financial Conference which "agreed on the creation of the International Monetary Fund (IMF) and an International Bank for Reconstruction and Development (BRD), which became part of the World Bank,"[23] where the IMF would pay attention to exchange rates and lend reserve currencies to nations in debt. A new global currency exchange system was created in where all currencies were linked to the US dollar and in exchange the US agreed to fix the price of gold at $35/ounce.

All of this meant that there would be no need for currency warfare or manipulation. This proved a threat to the BIS as if the IMF was to be the center of this new global financial order, what need would there be for the BIS? Wilhelm Keilhau, a member of the Norwegian delegation, even went so far as to propose a notion to eliminate the BIS. However, the Bank was to continue as several other European nations noted its importance to the financial matters of the European continent and soon the move to eliminate the Bank was rescinded. The situation was stable until the 1960s and '70s as while the Bretton Woods system of "free currency convertibility at fixed exchange rates" coincided with a massive increase of international trade and economic growth, cracks began to show as the British currency was weak and, more importantly, the gold parity on the US dollar was straining due to "an insufficient supply of gold and from the weakening of the US balance of payments."[24] However, the Bretton Woods system collapsed on August 1971; however the system of 'managed floating' was created in its place which allowed for flexibility of exchange rates within certain parameters.

Later in the 1970s, the situation became all the more dire due to the creation of OPEC and the subsequent rise in oil prices and the Herstatt Bank failure. The Herstatt Bank was central in processing foreign exchange orders (people exchange currencies, such as trading in dollars for yen) and when German regulators withdrew the bank's license forcing the bank to close up shop on June 26, 1974. Meanwhile, "it was still morning in New York, where Herstatt's counterparties were expecting to receive dollars in exchange for Deutsche marks they had delivered"[25] and when Hersttat's clearing bank Chase Manhattan refused to fulfill the orders by freezing the Herstatt account, it caused a chain of defaults. It was this problem that led to the creation, in conjunction with the G-10 countries and Switzerland, of the Basel Committee on Banking Supervision in which the goal was to set the global standard for bank regulation and to provide a forum for bank supervisory matters.

Yet, this newly created stability was short-lived as in the 1980s and '90s saw serious economic problems involving Latin America and Asia.

Oil prices quadrupled in November 1973, leading to stagflation, an increase in balance of payment imbalances, and major shocks in international banking. The Euro-currency markets were growing as they began to be utilized by OPEC countries more and more as the oil- producing nations invested in European money markets, greatly increasing the money European banks had and thus could lend. Thus, the European Coal and Steel Community began loaning money to developing nations at a faster and faster peace and while this was largely beneficial to the world economy at the start, "it also implied that the international banking system was faced with an increase in country risk,"[26] as many of the countries that were being loaned to were getting more and more into debt. This concerned then-BIS Economic Advisor Alexandre Lamfalussy who warned of a threat of a crisis and was specifically focused on credit, saying in a 1976 speech that from" '[looking at]... the continuous growth of credits, the spread of risks to a large number of countries, and the change in the nature of credits – I draw the conclusion that the problem of risks has become a very urgent one."[27]

While real interest rates (the difference between yearly interest rates on savings and inflation rates) were negative in the 1970s, meaning that borrowers lost a percentage of every dollar they loaned, allowed for an increase in credit, it quickly came to a halt in 1979 as the US Federal Reserve tightened US monetary policy which led to an increase in debts which many Latin American countries were unable to pay off.

The BIS was worried about debt that matured in less than a year as by early 1982, such debt would amount to half of Mexico's and Argentina's debt respectively. On August 12, 1982, Mexico alerted the US that its financial reserves were exhausted. This prompted the BIS to work to get financial assistance to Mexico in the form of loans, as the Mexican government negotiated with the IMF. Specifically, the BIS "offered a US$ 925 million loan, backed by the G10 central banks and the Bank of Spain" and both the US Federal Reserve and Treasury "matched this with an equal amount, so that a total of US$ 1.85 billion was made available for an initial period of three months."[28] While there were some last-minute problems, Mexico eventually accepted the loan and made a promise to pay it back, "[consisting] of a gold pledge by the Bank of Mexico and advance claims on future revenues of the Mexican state oil company Pemex."[29] The first loan was paid out on August 30, 1982.

However, the loans were tied to the Mexican government enacting austerity measures.[30] This had serious effects as the cutback in public spending "set back many development programs, including poverty alleviation programs"[31] and the overall economic effects harmed "especially the lower and middle classes. For Mexican workers, real wages in 1986 were at virtually the same level they had been at in 1967; for many, a generation of economic progress had been wiped out by the 'lost decade' of the 1980s."[32]

In the late 1990s in Asia, a new crisis would emerge. There were extremely robust GDP rates in the Asian markets, ranging from "more than 5 percent in Thailand to 8 percent in Indonesia. This achievement continued a pattern existing since the early 1980s. Rapid growth was fueled by high rates."[33] However, the growth began to slow down in 1996, which "[reflected] slower growth of demand in the region's principal export markets, a slowdown in the global electronics industry, and competition from Mainland China."[34] This slowdown led to an increase in deficit rates, especially with Thailand, whose deficits grew eight percent of GDP. In an attempt to prevent fluctuations in the Thai currency, the baht, the government tied the value of the baht to a basket of foreign currencies, heavily leaning on the US dollar. However, because the dollar was gaining strength, the strength of the baht also grew, making the export of goods more difficult.

Thailand, as well as Indonesia, the Philippines, and Malaysia devalued their currencies 25 to 33 percent in the middle of 1997 and when Taiwan began to devalue its currency, it led to a speculative currency attack on Hong Kong the in which people sold off their Hong Kong dollars, expecting them to fall in value. This caused the Hong Kong stock market to crash in October 1997 while at the same time the South Korean won was weakening in value. From there the crisis grew to global proportions and spread to a number of countries such as Russia and Jakarta.

Thailand, South Korea, and Indonesia went so far as to request assistance from the IMF, which the IMF granted of course, but only in exchange for brutal austerity measures. Much of this led to violence and even deaths in Indonesia and protests in South Korea.[35]

What is most interesting about the crisis is how the leaders of some of the affected countries spoke about it. Dr. Mahathir Bin Mohamad, the former Prime Minister of Malaysia, said in a speech on September 26, 2008 that "in 1997-98 American hedge funds destroyed the economies of poor countries by manipulating their national currencies." It should be noted that this isn't a simply 'blame America' attitude as Dr. Mohamad is "recognized as an authority on the role of hedge funds in financial crises, given his experience managing the Asian currency crisis as it engulfed his nation."[36] The Reserve Bank of Australia "produced two reports in 1999 on the potentially destructive role of highly leveraged institutions such as hedge funds." The reports claimed that "hedge funds contributed to the instability of its exchange rate in 1998, and it describe how hedge funds can have a destabilizing impact on not only the currencies of emerging economies but also on currencies such as the Australian dollar which has the eighth largest global trading volume."[37]

In a paper written in early 1999 after the crisis ended, William R. White, then-Economic Adviser and Head of the Monetary and Economic Department at the Bank for International Settlements, wrote that "Many Asian-Pacific authorities (including representatives from Australia, Hong Kong and Malaysia) feel strongly that hedge funds set out systematically to destabilize their currencies and their financial markets. However, other evidence is less compelling in support of this hypothesis and, even if accepted, would not necessarily lead to the conclusion that such funds should be regulated."[38] So he is not only denying the evidence that not only have Dr. Mohamad produced, but also the Reserve Bank of Australia produced, but effectively saying that even if he did accept the information, so what? However, years later, in a turn of the ironic, White had warned of the global crisis as he and his team had been paying attention to the growing US real estate bubble and they "criticized the increasingly impenetrable securitization business, vehemently pointed out the perils of risky loans and provided evidence of the lack of credibility of the rating agencies."[39] He started warning people back in 2003, "[imploring] central bankers to rethink their strategies, noting that instability in the financial markets had triggered inflation, the 'villain' in the global economy."[40] White retired from the BIS on June 30, 2008 with his advice having been ignored.

This was due to the fact that the Federal Reserve was attempting to "artificially prop up those markets [of bad debt and worthless assets] and keep those assets trading at prices far in excess of their actual market value"[41] which led to them providing "$16 trillion to domestic and foreign banks in the form of secret loans and bought mortgage-backed securities that were in reality, completely and totally worthless"[42] as well as the fact that many of the people on the board of directors at the Federal Reserve also had connections to corporations that received bailout money.

Even still, after the financial crisis seemed to be over, the BIS was sounding the alarm about debt, in June 2010 the organization "delivered a stern message to central banks and governments that keeping interest rates low for too long, or failing to act quickly to cut budget deficits, could sow the seeds for the next crisis."[43] Earlier that year, the organization was warning of a sovereign debt crisis and noted that "Drastic austerity measures will be needed to head off a compound interest spiral, if it is not already too late for some."[44] It seems that from the austerity measures that have been enacted in Europe and the US, the call has been heeded. The question is this: how much devastation will this have and will it result in a 'lost generation' such as in 1980s Mexico?


**Endnotes**

1: Roger Auboin, *The Bank for International Settlements, 1930-1955*, Princeton University, https://www.princeton.edu/~ies/IES_Essays/E22.pdf

2: Bank for International Settlements, *Board of Directors*, http://www.bis.org/about/board.htm

3: Bank for International Settlements, *Management of the BIS*, http://w ww.bis.org/about/officials.htm

4: Frank Costigliola, "The Other Side of Isolationism: The Establishment of the First World Bank, 1929-1930," *The Journal of American History* 59:3 (1972), pg 602

5: Ibid, pg 603

6: Steven Schoenherr Home Page, *Owen D. Young*, http://www.sunnycv.com/steve/ar/dd5/young.html7: Ibid

8: US State Department, *The Dawes Plan, the Young Plan, German Reparations, and Inter- allied War Debts*, https://history.state.gov/milestones/1921-1936/dawes

9: Costigliola, pg 605

10: Martin Horn, "A Private Bank At War: J.P. Morgan & Co. and France, 1914-1918," *Business History Review* 74:1 (2000), pg 86

11: Costigliola, pg 603

12: Ibid

13: Beth A. Simmons, "Why Innovate? Founding the Bank for International Settlements," *World Politics* 45:3 (1993), pg 370

14: Simmons, pg 375

15: Simmons, pg 377

16: J. Keith Horsefield, *International Monetary Fund 1945-1965 Twenty Years of International Monetary Cooperation*, vol. 1 Chronicle (Washington D.C.: International Monetary Fund, 1986)

17: Simmons, pg 383

18: Costigliola, pg 610

19: Simmons, pgs 384-385

20: Simmons, pg 389

21: Costigliola, pg 616

22: Bank for International Settlements, *BIS Archive Guide*, http://www.bis.org/about/arch_guide.pdf

23: Adam Lebor, *Tower of Basel* (New York: Public Affairs, 2013) pg 87

24: Bank for International Settlements, *BIS Archive Guide*, http://www.bis.org/about/arch_guide.pdf

25: Gregana Koleva, *Icon of Systemic Risk Haunts Industry Decades After Demise*, American Banker, http://www.americanbanker.com/bankthink/bankhaus-herstatt-icon-of-systemic-risk- 1039312-1.html (June 23, 2011)

26: Piet Clement, Ivo Maes, "The BIS and the Latin American Debt Crisis of the 1980s," National Bank of Belgium, Working Paper 247, December 2013, pg 3

27: Ibid, pg 4

28: Ibid, pg 17

29: Ibid

30: Paul Lewis, "Mexico to Receive $1.85 Billion In Loans," *New York Times*, August 31, 1982 (http://www.nytimes.com/1982/08/31/business/mexico-to-receive-1.85-billion-in-loans.html)

31: Bhuvan Bhatnagar, Aubrey C. Williams, eds. *Participatory Development and the World Bank: Potential Directions for Change*, http://www-wds.worldbank.org/external/default/WDSContentServer/WDSP/IB/1999/10/21/000178830_9810 1903552081/Rendered/PDF/multi_page.pdf (October 31, 1992), pg 103

32: Robert M. Buffington, Don M. Coerver, Suzanne B. Pasztor, *Mexico Today: An Encyclopedia of Contemporary History and Culture* (Santa Barbara, CA: ABC-CLIO, 2004), pg 137

33: Barry Eichengreen, *Understanding Asia's Financial Crisis*, Saint John's University, https://www.csbsju.edu/Documents/Clemens%20Lecture/lecture/Book98.pdf (November 2, 1998)34: Ibid

35: PBS, *Timeline of the Crash*, http://www.pbs.org/wgbh/pages/frontline/shows/crash/etc/cron.html

36: Stephen J. Brown, "The Role of Hedge Funds in Financial Crisis," The EconoMonitor, October 20, 2008 (http://www.economonitor.com/blog/2008/10/the-role-of-hedge-funds-in- financial-crisis/)

37: Hedge Funds, *Hedge Funds Studies*, http://www.fundshedge.co.uk/hedgefundsreports.htm

38: Bank For International Settlements, *Mr. White discusses the Asian crisis and the Bank for International Settlements*, http://www.bis.org/review/r990331a.pdf

39: Beat Balzi, Michaela Schiessl, "The Man Nobody Wanted To Hear: Global Banking Economist Warned Of Coming Crisis," *Der Spiegel*, July 8, 2009 (http://www.spiegel.de/international/business/the-man-nobody-wanted-to-hear-global-banking- economist-warned-of-coming-crisis-a-635051.html)

40: Ibid

41: John Wallace, "The Financial Crisis and the Federal Reserve," *News Blaze*, September 27, 2008 (http://newsblaze.com/story/20080927140845tsop.nb/topstory.html)

42: Bernie Sanders, *The Fed Audit*, http://www.sanders.senate.gov/newsroom/press-releases/the- fed-audit (July 21, 2011)

43: Brian Blackstone, "International Finance: BIS Warns Countries About Risks of Debt," *Wall Street Journal*, June 29, 2010

44: Ambrose Evans-Pritchard, "Sovereign Debt Crisis At 'Boiling Point,' Warns Bank for International Settlements," *The Telegraph*, April 8, 2010 (http://www.telegraph.co.uk/finance/economics/7564748/Sovereign-debt-crisis-at-boiling-point- warns-Bank-for-International-Settlements.html)

*Please note that this article contains graphic descriptions of lynchings. Discretion is advised.*


In 1918 Brook County, Georgia, a local plantation owner was killed by Sidney Johnson, a black man who had been leased out to the plantation via the convict lease system, in a dispute over unpaid wages. Upon hearing this, the white community went on a rampage and lynched not only Johnson, but anyone they thought to even be remotely involved in Johnson's decision. One of these men was Hayes Turner. Not only was he lynched, but also castrated.

Turner's wife, Mary, who was eight months pregnant at the time, began to speak out against her husband's lynching; unfortunately, she too, became a victim. A white mob "hanged her by her feet, set her on fire, sliced her stomach open, and pulled out her baby, which was still alive." They stomped on the child's head, killing it. Then the mob "[took] the time to sew two cats in Mrs. Turner's stomach and making bets as to which one would climb out first." [1]

This can be described as nothing short of demonic. In many ways, even that fails to fully encompass the horror and pure wickedness of this event. Though, the only thing more horrid is that in a way, lynchings continue in the form of police murder.

Before delving into the connections between the aforementioned violence, it is imperative to first understand lynching. The origins of lynching truly lie in slavery where "there were numerous public punishments of slaves, none of which were preceded by trials or any other semblance of civil or judicial processes. Justice depended solely upon the slaveholder." [2] Punishment ranged from lashings to family separation to mutilation and branding. The overall idea behind these actions were that black people were not human beings, in a way, they weren't even property, they were just things, lesser than both humans and animals. This mindset continued in the post chattel slavery era, where slavery took on the form of both the convict leasing and sharecropping systems respectively. Yet, it also took place in the form of mob violence against blacks.

There have been many explorations as to the reasoning behind lynching. E.M. Beck, a professor of sociology at the University of Georgia, posited the argument that lynching was linked to the cotton markets. He argued that lynchings "[increased] during times of sparse cotton revenues, and declining with increasing cotton profits." The lack of profit from cotton led unemployed whites to want to replace black workers and that "Mob violence was a form of intimidation to facilitate this labor substitution." [3] While further studies have shown that fluctuations in cotton pricing don't explain lynching [4], it should be noted that white elites would have an interest in fueling white angst into hatred against blacks, effectively utilizing poor whites as foot soldiers in their mission to maintain the current racial and economic hierarchy.

The cause of lynching was first and foremost the culture of white supremacy that had existed for the past two centuries or so. Blacks became scapegoats for many of the problems that were going on and thus a subculture of violence that had arguably already taken root in the days of slavery, took on new form. "The existence of a subculture presupposes a complex pattern of norms, attitudes and actions" which "reflects 'a potent theme of violence current in the cluster of values that make up the life-style, the socialization process, [and] the interpersonal relationships of individuals living in similar conditions." [5] Effectively, violence becomes normalized and is used as a tool of to socialize and condition people as to how the society operates.

This normalization and conditioning can be seen in the form of the lynching. Lynchings were very much a community affair in which legal authorities seldom if ever got involved as "the judge, prosecutor, jurors and witnesses—all white—were usually in sympathy with the lynchers" and "local police and sheriffs rarely did anything to defend Negro citizens and often supported lynchings." [6] Newspapers as well were extremely biased in covering lynchings. "Southern editors often used sympathetic language in describing lynch mobs while reserving callous damnation for lynch victims. The southern press was extremely creative when it came to providing moral, if not legal, justification for the action of lynch mobs."

We can see the affect that journalists had on the public's view of lynching in the case of the murder of the Hodges family in Statesboro, Georgia. [7]

Henry and Claudia Hodges lived on a remote farm, near a black community, some of whom were the employees of the Hodges. Late on the night of July 28, 1904, two men saw the Hodges home aflame. They went to investigate and found the mutilated, charred remains of the entire family. The suspected motive was robbery as it was known that Hodges was better off than most farmers and it was even rumored that he possibly had several hundred dollars stashed away on his property.

The following morning, Bulloch County sheriff John Kendrick formed a group to hunt down the killers. After discovering strands of hair, a knife, a shoe, and tracks of mud, they were led to a small shack occupied by Paul Reed, a black laborer. While Paul denied involvement, he, along with his wife Harriet, were arrested and taken to jail. When being interrogated, Harriet broke down and revealed that her husband and another black man, Paul Cato, had planned to rob the Hodges. The shoe matched the one found on the Hodges farm and blood stains on his clothing seemed to seal the deal with regards to Paul Reed's guilt, however, no money was found. The sheriff also arrested thirteen other blacks who lived in the general vicinity.

Despite the lack of hard evidence in the form of money, newspapers assumed Reed's guilt. The Macon Telegraph wrote "The wholesale butchery . . . of the Hodges family near Statesboro by dehumanized brutes adds another to the long list of horrors perpetrated in this state since the emancipation of the African slaves in 1865" and noted that "the people of [Statesboro] ... displayed great moral courage and forbearance in permitting the perpetrators to escape summary punishment without the forms of law," [8] a statement clearly hinting that lynching was on the table as an option. Others went even further in their demonization of the alleged perpetrators, such as the editor of Statesboro News who penned "Good farmers awoke to the fact that they are living in constant danger, and that human vampires live in their midst, only awaiting the opportunity to blot out their lives." [9] Language such as this only served to heighten white anxiety and fears that a black uprising had occurred in response to white mistreatment, something that had been the in the backs of their minds since the institution of slavery began.

The media actively went and pushed erroneous and misleading evidence, such as was with Morning News which stated that Reed had made a 'partial confession' to the murders, despite there being a lack of legal evidence to support the assertion. The Statesboro News continued to utilize inflammatory language, publishing an article which said in part "Their guilt has been established beyond a doubt - every chain has been traced and all lead to their door." [10] Additional stories argued that the rape of both Mrs. Hodges and their daughter Katy, where the real motives for the motive for the murders, again without the slightest shred of evidence.

Newspapers also noted that Reeds and Cato belonged to a distinct subset of blacks who were lazy and shiftless. This contrasts with the blacks who 'know their place' in society and often work on white farms. The only reason this was even discussed was because there were rumors floating around that the Hodges family may have been killed due to Mr. Hodges being too friendly with blacks, something that only aided to reinforce the region's racial caste system and conjure images of murderous black people who would attack whites were they to let their guard down.

An Atlanta News editorial minced few words in its character analysis: "It is true that the negroes in the turpentine campus of south Georgia are in the main a lot of irresponsible and half-savage vagabonds, apparently hopeless to the redeeming efforts of civilization, and that their presence makes a continual menace and threat to the peace and safety of the people." [11]

On August 15, the court case finally got underway. Superior Court Judge Alexander Daley was forbidden by Georgia law to request a change in court venue, despite his wanting to as to possibly give people time to 'cool off.' This was actually dangerous in some ways as such changes were often used by mobs as an excuse to lynch blacks on the grounds that they may have a chance to 'escape justice.'

When the trial began, the press continued to present rumor as fact. The Statesboro News reported that Reed had admitted to being part of a gang of blacks who were roaming the Bulloch County countryside, robbing, raping, and killing whites. Once again this increased the amount of fear in whites and put them more dead-set on lynching. It didn't help that throngs of whites were milling about outside the courthouse.

The actual trial was incredibly brief, lasting less than a day and a half, with Reed's and Cato's respective defenses lasting barely eight minutes, both men plead innocent. Still, the court sentenced them to hanging. As soon as this was done, the white mobs that had been surrounding the courthouse burst in and took both men, making no effort to hide their identities, despite the fact that soldiers (without any ammunition) had been dispatched to protect the men. Both men were beaten and eventually doused in kerosene and set ablaze and dead by 3:30 pm.

Many newspapers actively defended the lynching. *The Forest Blade* published an editorial which argued "While we will not say we are in favor of lynching principles, there are crimes - and this is one of them - that fully justified the act," similarly another editorial in the Sparta Ishmelite wrote "What society does not do for them [Georgia's whites], efficiently, they do for themselves." [12] The press played a major role in increasing tensions and outright encouraging lynchings, a serious act which helped to normalize the very act itself.

The normalization of lynching was rampant in Southern society. In 1893 in Paris, Texas, a black man by the name of Henry Smith was lynched for allegedly killing and raping the sheriff's daughter. Smith's lynching was in that a spectacle was made of it. It was the first "blatantly public, actively promoted lynching of a southern Black by a large crowd of southern whites with features such as 'the specially chartered excursion train, the publicly sold photographs, and the wide circulated, unabashed retelling of the event by one of the lynchers.'" [13] It should be examined in detail that there were a number of "event-like themes, such as a float, carnival, and parade" all of which indicates "that within the act of justice, the structures of entertainment were organized. [...] In addition, the souvenir scrambling for burnt remains as well as promotional materials for acquisition or purchase provides a similar semblance to paraphernalia purchased at modern-day sporting events." [14]

Thus, what we see is within the context of lynching, there was also an aspect of entertainment and even revelry, as if it was something to be celebrated and loved. The squabbling over Smith's remains reinforces the unbroken idea from slavery that black people aren't human beings, but rather just things, in this case a trophy.

The situation went even further in the case of Jesse Washington, a 17 year old mentally disabled boy who was accused of murdering a white woman and subject to a kangaroo court. Children were even bought to view his horrific lynching:

Fifteen thousand men, women and children packed the square. They climbed up poles and onto the tops of cars. . . . Children were lifted up by their parents in the air. Washington was castrated, and his ears were cut off. A tree supported the iron chain that lifted him above the fire of boxes and sticks. Wailing, the boy attempted to climb the skillet hot chain. For this the men cut off his fingers. The executioners repeatedly lowered the boy into the flames and hoisted him out again. With each repetition, a mighty shout [from the crowd] was raised. [15]

It is in acts such as this, with the involvement of children and, as with Smith's lynching, the selling of Washington's remains as if they were memorabilia, that the murder of black people becomes normalized and something beyond a source of maintaining racial hierarchy, something akin to a form of entertainment. Among this murderfest, though, there were those who fought back such as Ida B. Wells.

Wells was a black woman who was mainly focused on battling racial discrimination and penning articles. This changed in 1892, "when a close childhood friend of hers, Thomas Moss, was lynched" in Memphis [16] Wells was of the mindset that lynching was an overreaction by whites against rapists, however, her views quickly changed given the fact that Moss was lynched for defending his grocery store from armed whites and being lynched for the simple act of self-defense. On top of this, Memphis law enforcement didn't even bother to lift a finger to arrest the lynchers, who were publicly known.

Wells took a bit of an academic-esque approach to the situation, thinking that if lynching were exposed as the incarnation of racial hatred it was, it would no longer be socially acceptable. For three months, she traveled around the South investigating lynchings and interviewing witnesses. She found that not only were Black men lynched for having consensual relationships with white women, but also virtually all lynchings became about rape after the lynching went public. She took her information and published a pamphlet entitled Southern Horrors: Lynch Law in All Its Phases. Eventually due to threats on her life, she fled Memphis and moved to Chicago, where she continued to write and speak out against lynching. Still, there were others who took a more hands on, self-defense approach to lynching as took place in Decatur, IL.

On June 3, 1893, in Decatur, IL, a black day labor by the name of Samuel L. Bush who had been accused of rape, was taken from the Macon County jail and lynched by a white mob after they had went on a rampage searching for him from March 31 to June 2. During this time, rather than meet with members of the black community to discuss Bush's situation, "State's Attorney Isaac R. Mills, Decatur Mayor David Moffett, Deputy Sheriff Harry Midkiff, and Decatur Marshal William Mason were meeting with Charles B. Britton and Charles M. Fletcher, the leaders of the vigilantes." They attempted to appease the leaders, with Mills stating that if Bush wasn't sentenced to death, "it would then be time to resort to extreme measures." [17]

Despite days of lynching rumors floating around, the authorities allowed for nearly one thousand people to gather across from the jail where Bush was being held and made no effort to move or in any way ensure Bush's safety. Just before 2 AM, "a mob composed of some of the county's leading citizens broke Sam Bush out of jail and lynched him." [18]

In response to the lynching, Wilson B. Woodford, the only black lawyer in town that Bush had hired, published an open letter to blacks living in Decatur, urging them to attend a mass meeting where a strategy for dealing with the lynching would be formed. At the meeting, Woodford advocated taking the legal route, pushing the state attorney, the same one who had been complicit in Bush's lynching, to take action. Some, such as Edward Jacobs, rejected it and pushed for armed blacks to go themselves and arrest Bush's murderers. The resolutions committee backed Woodford's strategy and messages were sent to both the governor and state attorney.

Woodford and Jacobs were coming from two separate worlds. Woodford, having a legal background, "was predisposed to distinguish between the law and enforcers of the law. Woodford, like other liberal race men and women, believed that racial prejudice and contempt for law and order were the twin causes of lynching" whereas Jacobs questioned this method of thinking. Jacobs acknowledged the cozy relationship between lynchers and the police and knew that "knew the authorities had mobilized the vigilantes to help them in capturing Bush but had rejected African-American support either to protect Bush or to arrest his murderers." [19]

Interestingly enough, the two strategies would merge as both Woodford and Jacobs were members of the National Afro-American League, an organization that push for black development and fight against white responses to said development. NAAL "combined the pre-eminent philosophy of self-help and racial solidarity with the protest tactics of legalism, direct action, and violent self-help." [20]

A year later, James Jackson, a black male porter, was accused of raping a white woman under questionable circumstances. The father of the woman was pushing for Jackson's lynching and stated that help was coming from Mt. Zion. This situation would turn out rather differently than Bush's.

Blacks controlled the streets surrounding the jail. They could be seen in doorways, under stair wells and behind wagons, armed and ready for action. Other African-Americans patrolled the streets scrutinizing whites who happened to be out at that late hour. And unlike at the protest meeting, at least two black women participated. [21]

They continued to patrol the streets around the courthouse, the police didn't attempt to intervene, and there were no attempts to lynch Jackson.

As the case with Bush shows, the police themselves were many times the very ones who were, at best, complicit (not that that truly matters), and at worst, active participants in lynchings. This shouldn't be surprising as not only were the police entrenched in the same racial mindset as the lynchers, but also the purpose of the police was (and is) a tool of social control, especially against black people.

The police themselves came out of slavery as "slave patrols and night watches, which later became modern police departments, were both designed to control the behaviors of minorities." [22] In fact, in 1871 Congress passed the Ku Klux Klan Act, "which prohibited state actors from violating the Civil Rights of all citizens in part because of law enforcements' involvement with the infamous group." [23] (emphasis added) The police themselves oftentimes were directly involved in lynchings such as with the case of Austin Callaway, a sixteen year old boy.

Callaway was shot and killed in LaGrange, Georgia on September 8, 1940, having just a day earlier been accused of assaulting a white woman. He was arrested and taken to the local jail. Later that night, six men, one of them armed, went into the jail, forced the jailer to open the door, and murdered Callaway. [24] Though the killers were never found, it is known that the police were personally involved. It was noted in 2017 by LaGrange's police chief, Louis M. Dekmar, in an apology regarding Callaway's murder. Specifically, Dekmar said "I sincerely regret and denounce the role our Police Department played in Austin's lynching, both through our action and our inaction." [25] Callaway's story is just one in many [26] where police were directly or indirectly involved in lynchings. It is this historical backdrop in which police actively murder black people that today's police murders continue.

With lynchings, the body would hang for days as both a reminder to other blacks to 'stay in their place' but also a part of the aforementioned spectacle. This spectacle continues as can be seen with "the fact that Michael Brown's body was left on the street for hours after he was killed by police officer Darren Wilson," something "that points to just how little has changed in American race relations since the days of Jim Crow." [27] Leaving Brown's body out to languish was an illustration of the lack of concern and decency the Ferguson police department had for him and is reminiscent of leaving a lynch victim's body out for all to see, to remind everyone where black people stood on the racial hierarchy: the bottom.

The media, too, plays a role in police killings as they did during lynchings. Once again, the Michael Brown case puts this in stark view. Darren Wilson, the police officer who killed Brown, described him in disproportionate and even inhuman terms.

> "When I grabbed him, the only way I can describe it is I felt like a five-year-old holding onto Hulk Hogan," Wilson, who is 6' 4" and 210 lbs., said of Brown, who was 6' 4" and 292 lbs. at the time of his death. [...]He said Brown tried to get his fingers inside the trigger. "And then after he did that, he looked up at me and had the most intense aggressive face. The only way I can describe it, it looks like a demon, that's how angry he looked." [28]

Not only are black people described in nonhuman terms, but there is a constant implication that they deserve to be shot due to past transgressions. In the case of Akai Gurley, "The New York Daily News ran a headline, Akai Gurley had criminal record, innocent when shot by cop, which they later switched out for 'Protesters call for arrest of rookie cop who shot Akai Gurley as victim's sister says he didn't deserve to die.'" [29] There is also guilt by association. When twelve year old Tamir Rice was killed by the police, the media bought up the fact that the family's lawyer had "also defended the boy's mother in a drug trafficking case" [30] and that Rice's father had a history of domestic violence. [31] Regularly, the media brings up information that has nothing to do with the actual incident in question, but actively works to defame and sully the victim's name.

Where there once were slave owners and slave catchers, the KKK, and lynch mobs, they have all now "become largely replaced by state agencies such as the criminal justice system, and local and federal police." [32] In August 2016, the United Nations Working Group of Experts on People of African Descent went on a mission to the United States. In their conclusion on their findings, they wrote: "Contemporary police killings and the trauma that they create are reminiscent of the past racial terror of lynching. Impunity for State violence has resulted in the current human rights crisis and must be addressed as a matter of urgency." [33]

This assessment is quite correct, especially within the ideas of the spectacle and normalization. While there may not be a sports theme to current police murders, there is a spectacle in and of itself in the near constant sharing of videos of black people dying at the hands of police and the footage being played again and again on the nightly news. While one shouldn't discount that videos are being shared to raise awareness and may very well get people involved in activism, at the same time by the videos being shared and viewed over and over, it can very well create a situation where it the death of black people is normalized and an immunity of sorts built up to it. As writer Feliks Garcia notes

> To witness the final moments of someone's life is not supposed to be a regular experience, yet it feels like every week, we're presented with a new video of a different unarmed black man—or child—killed by police.

> With the reach of social media, each of these videos is viewed ad nauseum, and you have to ask what purpose this serves. Who needs to see these videos at this point? [34]

Due to the constant viewing of black people dying at the hands of the police, coupled with the media's twisted narratives, seeing black people die becomes a normal occurrence.

The ongoing police murders of black people draws strong parallels to lynchings: from the involvement of the police to the utter dearth of justice to the larger social implications. It is both a tragedy and a nightmare, an endless horror.

**Endnotes**

1: This American Life, *Suitable For Children*, https://www.thisamericanlife.org/627/transcript

2: Robert L. Zangrando, *About Lynching*, http://www.english.illinois.edu/maps/poets/g_l/lynching/lynching.htm

3: E. M. Beck, "The Killing Fields of the Deep South: The Market For Cotton and the Lynching of Blacks, 1882-1930," *American Sociological Review* 55:4 (August 1990), pg 526

4: James W. Clarke, "Without Fear or Shame: Lynching, Capital Punishment and the Subculture of Violence in the American South," British Journal of Political Science 28:2 (April 1998), pg 272

5: Clarke, pg 275

6: Robert A. Gibson, The Negro Holocaust: Lynching and Race Riots in the United States, 1880-1950, Yale-New Haven Teacher's Institute, http://teachersinstitute.yale.edu/curriculum/units/1979/2/79.02.04.x.html

7: Richard M. Perloff, "The Press and Lynchings of African Americans," Journal of Black Studies 30:3 (January 2000), pg 320

8: Reed W. Smith, "Southern Journalists and Lynching: The Statesboro Case Study," Journalism and Communication Monographs 7:2 (2005), pg 63

9: Ibid

10: Ibid, pg 64

11: Ibid, pg 65

12: Ibid, pg 70

13: Rasul A. Mowatt, "Lynching as Leisure: Broadening Notions of a Field," *American Behavioral Scientist* 56:10 (August 2012), pg 1371

14: Ibid

15: Ibid, pg 1376

16: Amii Larkin Barnard, "The Application of Critical Race Feminism to the Anti-Lynching Movement: Black Women's Fight against Race and Gender Ideology, 1892-1920," *UCLA Women's Law Journal* 3:1 (January 1993), pg 15

17: Sundiata Keita Cha-Jua, "A Warlike Demonstration,' Legalism, Armed Resistance, and Black Political Mobilization in Decatur, Illinois, 1894-1898," *The Journal of Negro History* 83:1 (Winter 1998), pg 54

18: Ibid

19: Cha-Jua, pg 57

20: Ibid

21: Cha-Jua, pg 59

22: Victor E. Kappeler, *A Brief History of Slavery and the Origins of American Policing*, http://plsonline.eku.edu/insidelook/brief-history-slavery-and-origins-american-policing

23: Ibid

24: Northeastern University Law School, *Austin Callaway*,
http://nuweb9.neu.edu/civilrights/georgia/austincallaway/

25: Alan Binder, Richard Fausset, "Nearly 8 Decades Later, an Apology for a Lynching in Georgia," *New York Times*, January 26, 2017 (https://www.nytimes.com/2017/01/26/us/lagrange-georgia-lynching-apology.html)

26: State Sanctioned, *Police and State Involvement with Lynching*, https://statesanctioned.com/police-and-state-involvement-with-lynching/

27: David G. Embrick, "Two Nations, Revisited: The Lynching of Black and Brown Bodies, Police Brutality, and Racial Control in 'Post-Racial' Amerikkka," *Critical Sociology* 41:6 (June 2015), pg 837

28: Josh Sanburn, "All The Ways Darren Wilson Described Being Afraid of Michael Brown," *Time*, November 25, 2014 (http://time.com/3605346/darren-wilson-michael-brown-demon/)

29: Simple Justice, *The Outrage of the Victim's Rap Sheet Must End*, http://blog.simplejustice.us/2014/11/23/the-outrage-of-the-victims-rap-sheet-must-end/ (November 23, 2014)

30: Brandon Blackwell, "Lawyer representing Tamir Rice's family defended boy's mom in drug trafficking case," *Cleveland*, November 24, 2014 (http://www.cleveland.com/metro/index.ssf/2014/11/lawyer_representing_tamir_rice.html)

31: Brandon Blackwell, "Tamir Rice's father has history of domestic violence," *Cleveland*, November 26, 2014 (http://www.cleveland.com/metro/index.ssf/2014/11/tamir_rices_father_has_history.html)

32: Embrick, pg 838

33: United Nations General Assembly, *Report on the Working Group of Experts on People of African Descent on its mission to the United States of America*, https://documents-dds-ny.un.org/doc/UNDOC/GEN/G16/183/30/PDF/G1618330.pdf?OpenElement (August 18, 2016)

34: Feliks Garcia, "Police brutality is modern lynching- and you may be a part of it," *Daily Dot*, April 20, 2015 (https://www.dailydot.com/via/black-men-police-violence-lynching-internet/)

# Social Movements, Issues, and Commentary

For quite some time now the United States has had a mountain of debt which has grown to the point where it is now unpayable. Only recently, (since Obama came into office and the Tea Party came about) has the federal government been paying attention to its spending rates. The main solution that has been pushed by the Republicans is austerity. Those in power act as if these cuts will suddenly cure all the nation's economic woes, while ignoring the massive 'defense' budget. It seems that our representatives either are not aware of or are ignoring just how inhumane and ironic austerity is.

## Education

In February 2011, Providence, the capital of Rhode Island, sent a message to all of its public teachers telling them that they could potentially be laid off by year's end. The local government reasoned that it was necessary "because of the dire fiscal straits that both Providence and its school system are in."[1] This puts the education of many school children at risk. The effects of these cuts will most likely be larger class sizes and a lower quality of education for attendees of public schools

Also, the federal government is planning to cut Pell Grants, which aid many low-income college students in paying for their education. This proposal is actually unfair in that it "hurts Pell Grant funding more severely than other budget items" [2] and the current increase is only to make up for the increases that should have happened during the Bush administration. Due to these Pell Grant cuts and increases in college tuition costs, many low-income college students may very well be forced to drop out.

These cuts are not only inhumane in that they make the suffering of the poor the solution to the current problems, but is also ironic. The right-wing wants to see an economically and militarily strong America, yet how does one expect America to be either when its young are uneducated?

## Social Security

Many Republicans on Capitol Hill are up in arms, arguing that Social Security has to be cut in order to balance the budget. They completely ignore the importance Social Security to the elderly, especially those of color. Social Security provides most retirees with about two-thirds of their income, but with people of color, it provides 90% of all income. [3] In advocating cuts to Social Security, both political parties are advocating a war on not only poor people, but a war that mainly targets people of color.

Yet, the most shocking part is that Republicans and the Democrats are not only willing to let other people's parents and grandparents suffer, but are willing to let the young suffer as well. The people who will suffer the most from an increase in the retirement age is this generation of young people, who will find that they will have to work more and more years just to be eligible for Social Security benefits.

When taking into account the employment situation of those who receive Social Security, the predicament for those affected becomes even more ironic. One proposal virtually forces the elderly to go and find a job in order to be able to support themselves, while the other proposal forces younger people to work for more years. Yet both are going to have to deal with the Great Recession and its main effect: little to no job growth. What this essentially does is subject both old and young to a meager existence, at the beck and call of corporations who can fire them at any moment, knowing that they (the corporations) have a virtually limitless labor pool to draw from.

## Medicare and Medicaid

Everyone, from the President to the newest House member has been pressing for cuts in Medicare and Medicaid. They say that it is the main problem with our budget and that, just like with all other social programs, we just can't keep funding them, lest we eventually go bankrupt. According to the latest information, 15% of the population is on Medicare while 19% is on Medicaid. [4] Even if only a small amount of the funding is affected, this will have serious effects as the health care of both seniors and the poor is taken out from under their feet. Once again, as with Social Security, we see the irony in this. Since the poor and elderly will have no health insurance, the only way they'll be able to get health insurance is by going back to work, yet there are so few jobs available.

## Food Assistance

With assisting the poor in getting access to food, it seems that in this too, the government has decided that it would be best to cut funding. An article in the Iowa Independent states "The cliff in food stamps means that one month, **a family will receive a set amount of money, about $4.50 per person per day. The next month, they will get less**." (emphasis added) [5] In good economic conditions, that amount would barely feed a family for a month and this is even truer today, when one looks at rising food costs! It is impossible for anyone to survive on such a meager income. The irony is that this may very well create criminal elements in society where there were none before, as people turn to crime to fill their stomachs. This irony becomes stronger when one considers that there was a 14% increase in the number of food stamp recipients last year. [6]

The most ironic part of austerity measures, though, is how they create a situation where the public is willing to fight back and rally against the destruction of their lives. The elite have a perception that they are invulnerable and that their intelligence is second to none, yet they are unable to realize that the very things they are doing to shore up revenues in the short-term will be their long-term downfall.


## Endnotes

1: Tami Luhby, "All Providence Teachers Receive Dismissal Notices," *CNN Money*, February 24, 2011 (http://money.cnn.com/2011/02/23/news/economy/Providence_teachers_layoff_notices/index.ht m)

2: Mark Kantrowitz, *Congress Proposes Big Cuts In Pell Grants*, Fastweb, http://www.fastweb.com/financial-aid/articles/congress-proposes-big-cuts-in-pell-grants (February 13, 2011)

3: National Senior Citizens Law Center, *Social Security Cuts Would Hurt Low-Income Older Adults*, http://web.archive.org/web/20120910183702/http://www.nsclc.org/index.php/social- security-cuts-would-hurt-low-income-older-adults/ (December 2, 2010)

4: The Henry J. Kaiser Family Foundation, *Medicare Beneficiaries as a Percent of Total Population*, http://kff.org/medicare/state-indicator/medicare-beneficiaries-as-of-total-pop/

5: Annie Lowrey, "The Real Impact of Cutting Food Stamps," *Iowa Independent*, September 29, 2010 (http://web.archive.org/web/20120910183658/http://iowaindependent.com/44131/the-real- impact-cutting-food-stamps)

6: Walter Smolarek, "Number of Food Stamp Recipients Increased 14 Percent In 2010," *Liberation*, February 17, 2011 (http://web.archive.org/web/20140311062837/http://pslweb.org/liberationnews/news/food- stamp-recipients-2010.html)

*The Threat of Private Military Companies*

*Published on: May 22, 2011*

## Introduction

Private Military Companies (PMCs) have been in the national and international spotlight in recent years, most famously known are the actions of the PMC Blackwater (now renamed Xe Services) in Iraq. There are many mixed feelings about PMCs, some say that they are a "good thing" and that they help countries to save money while others argue that they are not regulated and many times go about killing innocent people.

PMCs are a major problem in that they are a threat to state sovereignty as they threaten the role of the state in overseeing its armed forces. They also have major legality issues that need to be addressed, threaten democracy, and aid in continuing the influence of multinational companies in the third world.

While I will delve into the above issues, I will not be able to give the full picture of the effect that PMCs have on states nor how they operate, thus I recommend that anyone who finds themselves wanting to know more about PMCs read the book Servants of War: Private Military Corporations and the Profit of Conflict by Rolf Uesseler (translated by Jefferson Chase; it also provided the research for this essay), as it provides a comprehensive analysis of PMCs and the manner in which they do business, from interviewing owners of PMCs to discussing how PMCs effect international conflicts and concluding by exploring if there is way to properly handle PMCs.

## State Sovereignty

PMCs threaten state sovereignty because they threaten the state's monopoly on "the use of force". In the German Parliament, the conservative faction submitted a proposal in 2004 which stated that the privatization of the military "could lead to a fundamental shift" between a nation's armed forces and its government as "the state's monopoly on force could be called into question or even possibly eradicated." [1] By bringing PMCs into the picture, it creates a "hollowing out of the state," where the military itself can become weakened due to its reliance upon private organizations to do things such as gather intelligence.

> A third emphasis of the modern military companies is the area of intelligence, which includes everything from information collecting to outright spying. In the wake of the electronics revolution, many firms have developed techniques for information gathering and analysis that only they are able to master and offer as a service. [2]

The effect that having PMCs gather intelligence for the military is that people then realize that the real intelligence jobs are with PMCs and use government institutions like the military and the CIA as resume-builders for when they go to apply for a position at a PMC. It also creates a dependency on PMCs to do the intelligence work for the government and thus the influence of PMCs in the Pentagon increases.

This dependence is not only in the area of intelligence gathering, but also extends into what is arguably the most important aspect of warfare: logistics. Companies offer services "from the procurement of toilet paper to the organization of diverse types of vehicles." Also maintenance of military equipment "represents a huge portion of this spectrum, be it the upkeep and repair of motor vehicles, transport vans, helicopter warships, or other types of military aircraft." [3]

By supplying US troops, private corporations have increased their influence within the Pentagon to levels in which they hold major sway. Private corporations deeply undermine state authority because due to the fact that they build and supply weapons to our military as well as supply them with the needed materials so that the military can fight wars, they profit from when the US goes to war and may be likely to encourage American military action abroad.

## Legality Issues

There are major problems with the legality of private companies and how they operate in countries where they are deployed. One example pertains to Iraq in 2004 when Blackwater employees entered into the city of Fallujah and "under the pretense of looking for terrorists, [they] had carried out nighttime raids, mistreated women and children, and tortured and murdered local men and teenage boys." [4] Due to this, the local Iraqis took the law into their own hands and killed the Blackwater employees. However, whether one agrees with what the Iraqi people did or not, what occurred would have been the only justice the employees received for their crimes.

It is extremely hard to investigate PMCs due to the secrecy that is guaranteed by government contracts, as well as the fact that they are not accountable to the US military and "receive their orders directly from the Pentagon, and both the Department of Defense and the headquarters of the companies concerned keep their lips strictly sealed." [5]

The secrecy begins with the contracts themselves where the government leaves out certain legal passages that specify exactly what the companies are supposed to do, how they are supposed to go about doing it, and if they will be held legally responsible for anything that occurs under their watch. Uesseler cites an example of this, one that should be quoted at length:

DynCorp received a contract for more than a million dollars from the US State Department to organize the Iraqi criminal justice system. In June 2004, four of their employees, heavily armed and in battle gear, led Iraqi police on a raid of the former Iraqi leader in exile, Ahmed Chalabi. It is doubtful whether this action was in keeping with the spirit of the original contract. But that fact that DynCorp did not receive an official warning suggests that the contract is vague enough to allow for such "violations." [6]

The fact that the contracts are so vague as to the point where companies can virtually decide what they want to do has the potential to create serious problems, one example private companies doing night raids which result in the deaths of civilians and thus aggravating the local population and whipping up anti-American sentiment. That would make the job of US solders that much harder because they would bear the brunt of the backlash, not the employees that created the situation in the first place.

The situation gets worse, however, when one goes to the national levels. In the United States, no one is able to hold any private companies accountable. The parties that "issue the contracts are barely capable of doing much in the way of monitoring, because, for example, they are tied down in Washington, and the state military, which would have the capabilities, has little interest in babysitting private soldiers that aren't part of its chain of command." [7] Thus the military cannot do it and Congress isn't much better as they don't allocate funds to the oversight of private companies. This allows them to "exist in a state of near anarchy and arbitrariness."

Private companies and their personnel are not "subject to strict regulations that determine to whom they are ultimately accountable." Private corporations only have to go as far as declarations of intent in which they "maintain that they instruct their personnel to respect national laws and international human rights standards." [8] Even if major crimes are done, the state cannot do anything as mercenaries enjoy significant protection. "In passing Coalition Provisional Authority Order 17 of June 2003, the Iraqi provisional government granted exemption from prosecution to all personnel action on behalf of the coalition- including PMC employees." [9] This allows for PMCs to go about and do literally whatever they please, without fear of any consequences whatsoever and could potentially have the employees do things that they wouldn't have done so before if they were under the law, like torturing and killing civilians for example.

Internationally, things have the potential to get complicated quickly. The Geneva Convention clearly distinguishes between civilians and armed combatants. However, the employees of private companies aren't civilians "since they are involved in the machinery of war, are employed by governments, and frequently carry arms." Combatants are defined by the Geneva Convention "as people directly and actively involved in hostilities," yet new forms of warfare muddle this definition. "To take an illustrative question: Is a private solider in Florida who presses a button launching a carpet bomb attack in Afghanistan only indirectly involved in war, while a regular soldier delivering supplies there is directly engaged in hostilities?" [10]

The legality issues of private soldiers need to be solved on an international level as they currently occupy a gray area in the legal system. However, the US government needs to hold these companies accountable for any crimes that their employees are involved in, if not, then situations like the one mentioned at the beginning of this topic will continue.

## Democracy

Private military corporations threaten democracy solely because they are not accountable to anyone and can do as they please. By not having any accountability, private companies undermine democratic institutions.

One of the many roles of government is "to maintain security, which includes democratic control over the use of force." However, PMCs undermine this because citizens do not have any influence over the services offered by PMCs. For example, "The standards that govern the military, the police, customs officials, border guards, and state intelligence agencies do not apply at all to contracts given to PMCs." [11]

Due to citizens having no control over the actions of private companies, democracy is put on the line because in a democratic society, there is a need for checks and balances on all forms of power. By not having this, PMCs are able to go and do as they please due to having no restrictions and, as was noted earlier, this could lead to potential problems.

## The Third World

PMCs will do business for anyone who has the money to hire them, from governments, to non-governmental organizations, to rebel movements. However, PMCs will also gladly work for other companies and in the process, have aided in US corporations maintaining undue influence in the third world.

One major example is Colombia. From the viewpoint of US corporations, unions, the FARC, and the ELN threaten the status quo. In order to remedy this, "Lobbyists for US firms active in Colombia- above all oil, arms, and military companies- made $6 million in campaign contributions to convince the US Congress to approve of Plan Colombia, which was sold to the public as a humanitarian assistance program for the crisis-ridden Andean nation. Yet of the $1.3 billion initially approved for the program, only 13 percent went to the Colombian government to improve its security infrastructure. The rest flowed into the coffer of US firms." [12]

Since the majority of the money went to American firms, the question that must be asked is: Exactly what did those PMCs do in Colombia? They did a variety of things that were connected with one another, which all ended up aiding US corporations maintain their influence in Colombia. For example PMCs would "collect via satellite or reconnaissance flights information about guerilla troop movements that they then pass onto the military. They plant informants within the workers' movement or village populations and share what they learn with the police and paramilitary groups." [13] This has led to workers being killed, wages decreasing, increased unemployment, and human rights violations, all of which are sanctioned or supported by foreign companies. [14]

A counterargument would be that the FARC and ELN are recognized as terrorist organizations by the US and thus it is in American interests to aid in their destruction, however, this ignores the reasons why the FARC attacks US corporations. "Their attacks against business are largely directed at transnational oil companies and are, they say, aimed at ensuring that some of the profits from Colombia's petroleum reserves go to the country in general, instead of being siphoned off by oligarchs, members of the government, and high-ranking military leaders." [15]

By maintaining US corporate interests in Colombia, PMCs are aiding in the destruction of left-wing movements and backing right-wing governments. The situation is reminiscent of how the US, during the Cold War, overthrew left-wing governments and installed and backed military dictators that allowed US corporations to move in, this is just a new version of it.

## Conclusion

In conclusion, PMCs are a threat on multiple levels and need to be dealt with. Most pressingly are the legal issues and the international community as well as governments within nations need to establish a new classification in their laws specifically for the employees of PMCs so that they will be held liable for any crimes committed. PMCs, without a doubt, need massive reform as to lead to a better society at large.

## Endnotes

1: Rolf Uesseler, *Servants of War: Private Military Corporations and the Profit of Conflict*, trans. Jefferson Chase (Brooklyn, New York: Soft Skull Press, 2008) 146.

2: Ibid, pg 24

3: Ibid, pgs 25-26

4: Ibid, pg 160

5: Ibid, pg 161

6: Ibid, pg 163

7: Ibid, pg 164

8: Ibid, pgs 168-169

9: Ibid, pg 169

10: Ibid, pgs 170-171

11: Ibid, pg 207

12: Ibid, pg 149

13: Ibid, pg 151

14: Ibid, pg 152

15: Ibid

*Published on: April 21, 2012*

The state itself is a form of oppression. In a modern-day context this may seem like a false statement, however it is quite true. The state oppresses and restrains us every day, keeping us back from our full potential through its laws and security apparatus that enforce the whims of the state. Yet, this is not only done on a physical and economic level, but is also done based on one's sexuality and gender identity. Yet, to get a fuller understanding of how the state oppresses us based on sexuality or gender identity, it is first necessary to ask the question: What is the state?

The state can be defined in many ways; however there are several definitions that are accepted such as Max Weber's definition that the state is "a human community that successfully claims the monopoly of the legitimate use of physical force within a given territory." It can also be defined in a geographical sense using borders. However, at its heart, the state is made up of people. While these people may be of different genders or racial/ethnic groups and hold different positions in the state apparatus, they still make up the state itself. Merriam-Webster defines the state as "a politically organized body of people usually occupying a definite territory." This "politically organized body of people," in a modern context, refers to what is called the federal government.

However, we must take a deeper look at Weber's definition. He states in his definition that the state has a "monopoly of the legitimate use of physical force." What does that say about the state, that it needs the use of physical force in order for its creation? It says that the state itself is inherently violent and that it needs the consistent use of force in order to maintain its validity, for without the use of force, the state will no longer exist. In this, there comes the realization that the concept of the state is in many ways forced down the throats of the individual and they are forced to accept it.

In the United States and Western nations in general, the federal government has the power to create laws and initiatives that may seem as if they are in the best interest of the public, but are in reality much more about continuing the power of the state. In order to better understand this, one must look at the state not as some faceless entity, but rather as a gang of political elites and their financiers. The entire purpose of these political elite is to further their own power. One may be familiar with this in the examples that can be seen under the Bush and Obama administrations.

After 9/11 Bush used the tragedy as an excuse to further centralize power in the Executive Branch, but on a larger level to expand the power of the state, allowing for the state to intrude on the lives of private citizens and to begin the creation of the surveillance state that is so prevalent today. Obama furthered the power of the state when he signed the National Defense Authorization Act which allows for the indefinite detention of US citizens and argued that the President has the power to engage in extrajudicial assassinations of US citizens. Yet, while the state is biased towards expanding its own power, it must also be examined in the framework of sexuality and gender identity and how that plays into the role of oppressing others.

The state recognizes and validates the relations of heterosexual couples by allowing them to get married and giving with them a number of benefits. [1] The state have even gone so far as to define heterosexual marriage as the legal marriage, one only need to look at the Defense Of Marriage Act (which is still in effect) to see this. This oppresses queer people in a legalistic and psychological sense. queer s are oppressed psychologically as not only are they viewed in a negative manner and ostracized on a regular basis and by not allowing queer marriage (this also includes polyamorous relationships), it only serves to reinforce the notion that they are underprivileged citizens and alienates them from the larger society.

There is economic oppression in the form of wage gaps and hiring discrimination. As of April 2012, it is legal in 29 states to fire an employee based on sexual orientation and the number increases to 34 if they are transgender. [2] While there is a law that aims to end this so far nothing has been put into place and actually the situation is getting worse. A 1995 study revealed that "between 16% and 46% of [lesbian, gay, or bisexual people surveyed] reported having experienced some form of discrimination in employment (in hiring, promotion, firing, or harassment)." [3] Today the situation has little changed. [4]

This has a major negative impact on queers on both an individual and group level as their earnings are lower than a heterosexual person's would be, thus contributing to them being more likely to be poor, especially if they are same sex couples. [5] In the state now enacting legislation to deal with this problem, they are, at most, engaging in oppressing queers, or, at least, acting as an accessory to their oppression.

The state is further oppressing queers in the form of voter suppression, especially transgendered individuals.

Georgia, Indiana, Kansas, Mississippi, South Carolina, Pennsylvania, Tennessee, Texas, and Wisconsin have all passed laws requiring voters to present a government-issued photo identification before casting a ballot. But the laws impose unique barriers on transgender individuals, since many do not have an updated identification — such as a driver's license — that lists their correct gender. [6]

This would deter queer individuals from making attempts to end their oppression in a manner consistent with the current status quo, that of legalistic reform than actual radical change.

Yet, this oppression by the state is not only in the West but can be seen all over in the world. In the African country of Uganda, there was originally a bill bought up in Parliament that argued that anyone who was caught engaging in homosexual activity should receive the death penalty. While this particular part of the bill was retracted, the bill still generally criminalized the "promotion" of homosexuality. In the country of Indonesia, an LGBT rights advocacy website was banned, with the government deeming it "pornographic." [7] Even the much-touted Europe isn't safe for all members of the queer community as 17 European countries force transgender sterilization. [8]

Throughout the world, members of the queer community are actively under attack by the state. The state has always betrayed us and continues to be a source of oppression for the queer community. We need to realize that while it seems that the oppression may end with the passing of same sex marriage or the criminalization of discriminatory practices against queers, it will only be a first step in a battle against the state. The oppression could still take different forms, such as institutionalizing discrimination. The only way we may every truly be free is with the destruction of the state.


## Endnotes

1: Nolo, *Marriage and Rights Benefits*, http://www.nolo.com/legal-encyclopedia/marriage-rights-benefits-30190.html

2: Human Rights Campaign, *Pass ENDA Now End Workplace Discrimination*, http://sites.hrc.org/sites/passendanow/index.asp

3: M. V. Lee Badgett, "The Wage Effects of Sexual Orientation Discrimination," *Industrial and Labor Relations Review* 48 (July 1995) pg 728

4: Crosby Burns, Jeff Krehely, *Gay and Transgender People Face High Rates of Workplace Discrimination and Harassment*, Center for American Progress, http://www.americanprogress.org/issues/2011/06/workplace_discrimination.html (June 2, 2011)

5: Lauren Keiper, "Children of gay families more like to be poor: study," *Reuters*, October 25, 2011 http://www.*Reuters*.com/article/2011/10/25/us-gays-families-idUSTRE79O7MC20111025

6: Eric W. Dolan, "Voter ID laws could disenfranchise more than 25,000 transgender voters: study," *Raw Story*, April 15, 2012 http://www.rawstory.com/rs/2012/04/15/voter-id-laws-could-disenfranchise-more-than-25000- transgender-voters-study/

7: International Gay and Lesbian Human Rights Commission, *IGLHRC Website Banned*, http://www.iglhrc.org/cgi-bin/iowa/article/pressroom/pressrelease/1481.html (February 7, 2012)

8: Nicole Pasulka, "17 European Countries Force Transgender Sterilization," *Mother Jones*, February 16, 2012 http://motherjones.com/mojo/2012/02/most-european-countries-force-sterilization-transgender-people-map

We are in a time of crisis, a time of austerity, a time the where poor are getting poorer and the rich are getting richer at a faster pace than at any other time in recent US history. We have gone from having a well-functioning economy to a real unemployment rate of 14.5% as of May 2012 [1]. During all of this, the situation has greatly affected college students, who are taking on massive debt just to further their education. With student debt at over $1 trillion, an examination is underway of how we have gotten into this scenario and how we can get our way out of it.

The situation began in 1964 when Lyndon B. Johnson established a task force to examine the role of federal government in student aid, headed by John W. Gardener. The taskforce firmly believed that cost shouldn't be a barrier in attaining a college education and to this end they concerned themselves with how lack of funds contributed to students being unable to attend college. Gardener

> **focused on a study which revealed that one out of six students who took the National Merit Scholarship test in high school did not attend college**. Of the students who did not attend college and who had families who could contribute only $300 or less to their education, about 75 percent of the men and 55 percent of the women indicated that they would have attended college if they had had more money available. [2] (emphasis added)

Upon seeing this information, Johnson was shocked as he viewed the situation as a loss in human capital. This drove him to sign the Higher Education Opportunity Act of 1965 into law. The bill included the recommendations put forth by the Gardener taskforce that the federal government should aid student in their journey to attain a higher education by providing loans, remedial classes, and grants to college-aspiring students as well as special programs and projects for low-income students who have an interest in attending college. This allowed for low-income and middle-class students who have an opportunity to go to college.

There was an uphill battle, though, as the American Bank Association was against the loan guarantee provision. The ABA was mainly concerned about possible government encroachment in their business, arguing that "the federal government could not replicate the working relationships that locally-owned financial institutions had with state and private non- profit guarantee programs" and "the federal government would end up taking over the industry because there would be little incentive for the state and private non-profit agencies to establish their own programs." [3] To solve this problem, the Johnson administration met with the ABA and worked to "[assure] the bankers the loans would pay them back handsomely over time because they were investing in young people who would become their best customers in the future," [4] as well as telling the banks that the government would be the ultimate loan guarantor if there was no one else available. Thus, with the banks placated, the bill could be passed.

There were several reauthorizations of the Higher Education Opportunity Act, but one of the most important reauthorizations was in 1972. In the 1972 bill, there were several new programs created, yet one of the most important ones was the Basic Educational Opportunity Grant which sends "a payment directly from the federal government to undergraduate students based on their financial need," yet this act also "tied institutional aid to the number of students receiving federal student aid at the given institution." [5] Tying institutional aid in this manner only served to increase costs. According to the Bennett hypothesis, first proposed in the 1980s by Secretary of Education William J. Bennett, colleges absorb federal student aid by increasing tuition costs. (This was proven in a paper done by two economics professors at the University of Oregon. [6]) While these increases in tuition were not seen in the 1970s, they began to be felt substantially during the 1980s, thus causing students to increase their debt levels. However there was another factor involved that led to student debt increase: President Ronald Reagan.

During the presidency of Ronald Reagan, he launched a massive attack on federal student aid. Reagan's budget included a proposal that would

**cut deeply into the two major student assistance programs, the Pell grants and the Guaranteed Student Loans, to reduce sharply or eliminate a series of categorical programs in higher education,** and to eliminate a group of social or economic programs which either directly or indirectly affect higher education. With rare exception, every college campus would be affected by the proposed cuts beginning in academic year 1981-82. [7] (emphasis added)

In cutting these student assistance programs, Reagan went against the spirit of the 1965 Higher Educational Opportunity Act, in which the main goal was to ensure that a college education was both accessible and affordable. In addition to this, he was effectively targeting low-income and middle class people who needed that assistance in order to afford a college education. Congress attempted to enact amendments to the Higher Education bill that would allow for both programs to continue until 1985 and expanded programs such as Guaranteed Student Loans to middle-class families.

Yet, there were complaints from the Reagan administration, specifically Secretary of Education Terrence Bell, that the expanding such programs "had the potential for eroding the traditional roles of the student and the family in the financing of educational costs" [8] and that the Guaranteed Student Loans program was actually an entitlement program as its costs couldn't be constricted without Congressional approval. Rather than actually allow students greater access to education, the Reagan administration was able to pass a plan that would gut federal student aid assistance by cutting the amount of aid per Pell Grant from $1,900 to $1,750, limiting Guaranteed Student Loans to remaining need, and eliminating the in-school interest subsidy and the subsidy to lenders on Parent Loans.

This decrease in federal aid only served to disenfranchise millions of potential college students from attaining an education. Student debt also increased. A survey done by the College Scholarship Service and National Association of Student Financial Aid Administrators showed that "those students at public institutions who borrow will graduate with an average debt of $6,685, while their counterparts at private colleges and universities will assume $8,950 in debt on average."

The decrease also hit minority students quite hard as in 1987 there was a seven percent decline in college enrollment for Native Americans and eleven percent for blacks. Many minority groups depended on grants and scholarships to go to college, but now their only option was to borrow money or just not go at all. This would have a major ripple effect as "Many studies have shown that one of the most important factors influencing the decision to go to college is parental educational level" and that "If today's minority high school graduates choose not to participate in further education, out of concern for loan burdens or for other reasons, their children may not be as likely to go to college as the next generation of white and Asian students." [9] This would only serve to further increase educational- and with it economic- disparities between races.

The situation did not get any better in the next decade as the median student loan debt more than doubled in a 10 year period, increasing from $4,000 in 1990 to about $11,000 in 1999. [10] It was to become even worse with the passing of the Higher Education Amendments of 1998, which stated that student loans could no longer be forgiven under bankruptcy. Thus, if one found themselves in bankruptcy, but had student loans, they would be in debt bondage until the loans were paid. In such a situation, the only possible out is to default on one's student loans, however, that would not only worsen your credit but your entire financial life can potentially be destroyed as if you default

• Your entire loan balance will be due in full, immediately.

• Collection fees can be added to your outstanding balance.

• Up to 15% of your paychecks can be taken.

• Your Social Security, disability income, and state and federal tax refunds can be seized.

• You will lose eligibility for federal aid, including Pell grants.

• You will lose deferment or forbearance options.

• Outstanding fees and unpaid interest can be capitalized (added) onto your principal balance. [11]

Thus, by the very circumstances, a situation of 'damned if you do, damned if you don't' is created and students are put into de facto debt slavery.

This brings us to our current situation where student debt nationwide is over $1 trillion. Student debt can potentially turn into a major problem by threatening economic growth due to the fact that people are defaulting on their student loans as they cannot find jobs. A recent article came out from the Associated Press which stated that 53% of college graduates are either unemployed or underemployed and that when "underemployment [is taken] into consideration, the job prospects for bachelor's degree holders fell last year to the lowest level in more than a decade." [12] This is an even further economic threat when one realizes that the current level of student is unsustainable and that there will be major ripple effects on the economy when this house of cards comes crashing down.

In order to deal with the situation, there are some in Washington who favor rewriting bankruptcy laws as to allow for a return for student debt to be cleared in bankruptcy, however, this would only apply to private student loans, thus the student would still be on the hook for any federal loans owed. Yet, allowing federal loans to be absolved in bankruptcy is quite a thorny issue as taxpayers would have to pick up the tab. Once again, just as in 1965, the American Bankers Association is against such a proposal "saying it would tempt students to rack up big debt that they won't repay [and that] 'The bankruptcy system would be opened to abuse.'" [13] It will be interesting to see whether or not the government can once again placate the banks.

The only way to get out of this mess is forgiving loans. There is already some support in Congress as bill H.R. 4170 also known as The Student Loan Forgiveness Act is currently being proposed. The bill would fully forgive the loans of those who have been making payment for the past decade or will be able to do so in the coming years. It also "caps interest rates on federal student loans at 3.4 percent and enables existing borrowers to break free from crushing fees by converting many private loans into federal loans." Such a bill would free students from debt slavery and "would give Americans greater purchasing power, helping to jumpstart our economy and create jobs." [14]

This is what needs to be done in order to aid getting our economy back on track. If the government can spend over $1 trillion on wars and billions to bailout corrupt banks, hopefully they can spare a couple billion to bailout America's college graduates.

The alternative is to have the student debt bubble explode in our faces and the economy slump into even more dire straits and banks tighten up the flow of credit.

America now has a choice before it concerning its young people: they can either set them free, aiding in economic regrowth or risk shattering the economic recovery and maintain their children in the shackles of debt slavery.

## Endnotes

1: Portal Seven, *Unemployment Rate U-6*, http://portalseven.com/employment/unemployment_rate_u6.jsp

2: TG Research and Analytical Services, *Higher Education Opportunity Act*, http://www.tgslc.org/pdf/hea_history.pdf (November 2005)

3: Ibid

4: Ibid

5: Thomas R. Wolanin, "Federal Policy Making in Higher Education," *American Association of University Professors* 61:4 (1975), 309

6: Larry D. Singell, Jr., Joe A. Stone, "For Whom the Pell Tolls: The Response of University Tuition to Federal Grants-in-Aid," University of Oregon, September 2005 (http://web.archive.org/web/20081011160038/http://darkwing.uoregon.edu/~lsingell/Pell_Bennet t.pdf )

7: Alfred D. Sumberg, "The Reagan Budget: Attacks on Student Assistance," *American Association of University Professors* 67:2 (1981), 102

8: Sumberg, 103

9: Kathryn Mohrman, "Unintended Consequences of Federal Aid Student Policies," *The Brookings Review* 5:4 (1987) 24, 26

10: Department of Education, *Student Loans Overview: Fiscal Year 2012 Budget Request.* http://www2.ed.gov/about/overview/budget/budget12/justifications/s-loansoverview.pdf, pg 19

11: American Student Assistance, *Default Consequences*, http://www.asa.org/in-default/consequences/default.aspx

12: Hope Yen, "Half of recent college grads underemployed or jobless, analysis says," *Associated Press*, April 23, 2012 (http://www.cleveland.com/business/index.ssf/2012/04/half_of_recent_college_grads_u.html )

13: Josh Mitchell, "Trying to Shed Student Debt," *Wall Street Journal*, April 27, 2012 (http://online.wsj.com/article/SB10001424052702303978104577364120264435092.html?mod=WSJ_WSJ_US_News_5 )

14: Hansen Clarke, "Trillion Dollar Crisis: The Case for Student Loan Forgiveness," *Huffington Post*, April, 25, 2012 (http://www.huffingtonpost.com/rep-hansen-clarke/student-loan- forgiveness_b_1454241.html )

*Published on: July 30, 2012*

Colonialism is a word associated with the 19th and 20th centuries, with an outside force (usually European) coming into a country and destroying and uprooting the culture and people, with the main goal being the extraction of resources for the gain of the 'mother' country. It is defined as "the policy or practice of acquiring full or partial political control over another country, occupying it with settlers, and exploiting it economically."[1] Yet this definition of colonialism can be expanded from examining the external to examining the internal. For what may be the first time in US history, internal colonialism is occurring as the very facades of democracy and the economic system begin to fall apart and the elites begin to colonize internally.

The internal colonization of America by elites can be seen most starkly in the financial sector, specifically in the ongoing economic crisis. There was mass panic about the near global economic collapse which the government responded to by bailing the corporations out to the tune of $12.8 trillion,[2] yet, once the dust cleared, the very banks (with much help from the US Congress and the Federal Reserve) that caused the crisis only grew larger. Bloomberg noted in April 2012 that Bank of America, JP Morgan Chase, Wells Fargo, Goldman Sachs, and Citigroup had combined assets that "amounted to 43 percent of US output" in 2007, but after the crisis those same banks now "held $8.5 trillion in assets at the end of 2011, equal to 56 percent of the U.S. economy," [3] meaning that their combined percentage of the economy had increased by thirteen percent.

While the near collapse of the economy led to large amounts of growth for the banks and the banksters getting massive bonuses for their supposed 'good work,' it had a devastating impact on average Americans. While one can go and generalize about the number of jobs and houses lost, it is much more telling to go and look at the actual numbers. After the crisis ended, it was stated that the entire fiasco "cost the U.S. an estimated $648 billion due to slower economic growth" which translated into "an average of approximately $5,800 in lost income for each U.S. household."[4] It was also found that 5.5 million more jobs were lost than were predicted in the Congressional Budget Office forecast of 2008.

The effects of this recession have not only resulted in droves of Americans being left destitute and unemployed to the point where in 2011 one million people applied to McDonalds, [5] but has also left towns and cities almost utterly destroyed. A 2011 IHS report revealed that there were "37 metropolitan areas which are not expected to return to peak employment until after 2021" and that many of these metropolitan areas are part of the "Rust Belt," an area covering portions of the Mid-Atlantic and Midwest that was once an international center for heavy manufacturing. Cities such as Canton and Youngstown, Ohio were once hubs of the steel industry. Detroit and Flint, of course, were at the heart of the US automobile industry. [6]

This is a prime example of internal colonialism, where the banks and automobile companies have sucked the economic life out of towns and cities, exploiting them to the fullest extent possible, and then when they are done and no more can be used, the banks and companies leave these areas and move elsewhere in the world to exploit other people, leaving in their wake only destruction and devastation. This combination of greedy banksters along with the Federal Reserve not only created a global economic crisis, but also a situation where half of the US population is now either impoverished or low-income. [7]

Yet, this internal colonization happens on an even more horrendous scale environmentally. Mining companies such as Massey Energy, now owned by Alpha Natural, engage in a horrid practice called mountaintop mining which is defined as "a surface mining practice involving the removal of mountaintops to expose coal seams, and disposing of the associated mining overburden in adjacent valleys"[8] Mining practices such as these allow corporations to get at the resource faster and thus extract more easily and cheaply as well as it allows miners more safety since they do not have to actually go down into the mines. While this may be good for the corporations, it is nothing but horrible for the environment. A 2007 *Wired* article stated that

In just two decades, hundreds of mountaintops, more than a thousand miles of stream, and hundreds of square miles of forests have been obliterated....

According to the Environmental Protection Agency, MTR destroyed more than 1,200 miles of Appalachia's streams and 7 percent of its forests between 1985 and 2001. Approximately 800 square miles of mountains were leveled....

According to a rough estimate by West Virginia University bio-geochemist William Peterjohn, the deforestation could add as much as 138 million tons of carbon dioxide into the atmosphere and that's not even counting the even-larger CO2 emissions from burning the coal. [9]

There is also a human factor involved also as removal of the mountaintops in such a manner causes water resources to become contaminated which can lead to "Balkan endemic nephropathy (BEN), an irreversible kidney disease has been related to the leaching of toxic organic compounds in groundwater." Contaminated drinking water can affects children quite negatively as "An Eastern Kentucky University study found that children in Letcher County, Kentucky, suffer from an alarmingly high rate of nausea, diarrhea, vomiting, and shortness of breath, symptoms related to blue babe syndrome,"[10] which was found to be caused by contaminated minerals find their way into nearby streams.

This is yet another prime example of internal colonialism. As the corporations abuse the planet and push the environment to its breaking point, their careless exploitation and sole concern for profits results in a decimated, uninhabitable environment and people who become sickly and weak. As with the bankers, once there is no one and nothing left to exploit, they flock to the next location and start the process anew.

This internal colonialism is not only destroying people, but also the very environment that everyone—including the bankers and industrialists—live on. While we may be suffering currently, the colonizers may be in for a surprise as they destroy the environment and with it, themselves.


## Endnotes

1: Oxford Dictionaries, *Colonialism*, http://oxforddictionaries.com/definition/english/colonialism

2: PBS, *The true cost of the bank bailout*, http://www.pbs.org/wnet/need-to-know/economy/the- true-cost-of-the-bank-bailout/3309/ (September 3, 2010)

3: David J. Lynch, "Banks Seen Dangerous Defying Obama's Too-Big-To-Fail Move," *Bloomberg*, April, 16, 2012 (http://www.bloomberg.com/news/2012-04-16/obama-bid-to-end- too-big-to-fail-undercut-as-banks-grow.html)

4: Pew Charitable Trusts, *The Impact of the 2008 Economic Collapse*, http://www.pewtrusts.org/our_work_report_detail.aspx?id=58695 (April 28, 2010)

5: Andy Kroll, "How the McEconomy Bombed the American Worker," *Truthout*, May 9, 2011 (http://truth-out.org/index.php?option=com_k2&view=item&id=998:how-the-mceconomy- bombed-the-american-worker)

6: 24/7 Wall St, *Ten Cities That Will Take A Decade To Recover From The Recession*, http://247wallst.com/2011/06/22/ten-cites-that-will-take-a-decade-to-recover-from-the-recession/ (June 22, 2011)

7: ABC News, *Census date: Half of US poor or low income*, http://www.cbsnews.com/8301- 201_162-57343397/census-data-half-of-u.s-poor-or-low-income/ (December 15, 2011)

8: U. S. Environmental Protection Agency, *Mid-Atlantic Mountaintop Mining*, http://www.epa.gov/region3/mtntop/

9: Brandon Keim, "Blowing The Top Off Mountaintop Mining," *Wired,* September 10, 2007

(http://www.wired.com/science/planetearth/news/2007/09/mountaintop_mining?currentPage=all

10: University of South Carolina, *Mountaintop Removal: Effects on Human Health and the Environment,* http://law.sc.edu/environmental/papers/200841/eas/chhotray.pdf

Given the current conflict in Syria, there are many in the alternative media whose main focus when reporting on the fighting is the actions of the rebels. This has earned such media outlets and writers the taunts and attacks of others who label them "regime apologists." I have personally had such labels thrown at me when I've posted work in other places. Yet, such accusations are quite untrue and the reasons for such baseless accusations must be explored. Generally speaking, the media has portrayed the Syrian conflict (as well as the Libyan conflict and many others) in stark, almost comic book-esque terms where the side of the US and its allies are portrayed as the 'good guys' and whoever is the enemy at the moment, portrayed as a 'bad guy.'

This can lead to a situation where one immediately thinks in absolutist terms and assumes that anything that isn't criticism of the 'bad' side is actually support of it. On a somewhat deeper level, this shows just how much power the mainstream media has in shaping the opinions of people, rather than the 'objective' journalism that is supposed to occur where simply the facts are presented and people are left to look more into the situation and make up their own minds.

While people and sites that are accused of being 'regime apologists,' the fact of the matter is that what they are doing is actually quite logical and helpful. For example, during the war in Libya, the mainstream media was reporting stories to the effect that that Gaddafi was giving his soldiers Viagra [1] to engage in mass rape. And more recently with regards to Syria, the mainstream media has been reporting that there is a "high probability" that Assad used chemical weapons [2] against Syrian civilians. However, the Viagra story turned out to be false [3] and there is no conclusive evidence that government forces in Syria used chemical weapons. [4]

In this context, it is important to realize that these so-called regime apologists are actually providing the reader with more information and aiding to show a more balanced view of current events. Articles focusing solely on the atrocities that rebels have committed is positive as the crimes that despotic regimes commit can be found rather easily as they are reported on exhaustively, whereas the war crimes of rebels are often ignored.

There are those that argue that sites such as Global Research, which published articles discussing Gaddafi's social programs [5] and questioning such incidents as the Houla massacre[6], support the dictatorial regimes of Gaddafi and Assad. Yet, this ignores the fact that such outlets are rightfully questioning these events as the mainstream media has been shown to get such stories quite wrong.

In addition to this, outlets that question the general narrative are needed as many times they analyze the situation within a much larger framework, allowing for a more complete understanding of a conflict. Essentially what such outlets do is ask questions that others won't or can't ask, even if they do seem extreme.

We must always ask questions; for that is the only way we will get to the truth.


## Endnotes

1: Louis Charbonneau, "US envoy: Gaddafi troops raping, issued Viagra," *Reuters*, April 29, 2011 (http://www.*Reuters*.com/article/2011/04/29/us-libya-troops-rape- idUSTRE73S74B20110429)

2: Michael Martinez, Joe Sterling, Nick Paton Walsh, "Game-changer: Syria's 'probability of using chemical warfare," *CNN*, March 20, 2013 (http://www.cnn.com/2013/03/19/world/meast/syria-civil-war)

3: Eric Garris, "Susan Rice's Viagra Hoax: The New Incubator Babies," *Antiwar*, April 30, 2011 (http://antiwar.com/blog/2011/04/30/susan-rices-viagra-hoax-the-new-incubator-babies/)

4: Marc Ambinder, "Why Would Assad Use Chemical Weapons?" *The Week*, March 19, 2013 (http://theweek.com/articles/466501/why-assad-use-chemical-weapons)

5: Mahdi Darius Nazemroaya, "Who Was Muammar Gaddafi? Libya's Wealth Redistribution Project," *Global Research*, October 27, 2011 (http://www.globalresearch.ca/who-was-muammar- qaddafi-libya-s-wealth-redistribution-project/27327)

6: Global Research, *The Houla Massacre: The Disinformation Campaign*, http://www.globalresearch.ca/the-houla-massacre-the-disinformation-campaign/31399 (June 13, 2012)

Even doing so much as glancing at the occasional headline or ticker feed can make one feel as if the world is going to hell in a hand basket. From the economic crisis in Europe to the bombings in Boston, to the continuing news about the false economic recovery, the world can seem like a dangerous and terrifying place, yet we must realize that the people and forces behind these problems and realize that solutions are in fact possible.

Children are starving in Greece due to the fact that Greece's economy "is in free fall, having shrunk by 20 percent in the past five years" [1] and in the United States, the amount of suburban poverty is increasing, [2] with neither situation seeming to change anytime soon. The entire global economy looks like it may come apart at the seams. [3] Governments from the US to China are engaging in a massive currency war [4] which is backed by the G20 and will hurt the average person. [5]

The governments of the world are hiding the economic downturns by fiddling with the indicators, such as the levels of unemployment and inflation. Generally, "the way these numbers are calculated sometimes doesn't reflect the true economic landscape at all," [6] however this is unsurprising when we realize that the market has been manipulated time and again. [7]

Due to these economic problems, one would think that many nations would be busy attempting to fix their wrecked economies, yet Western nations such as France [8] have found the time to fund and arm radical Islamists in an attempt to overthrow Assad, the Chinese government is making "increased military spending a top priority,"[9] and the threat of regional wars from Israel-Iran to North and South Korea.

The corruption of governments around the world and how they do not care for their people has been shown time and time again. The fact that the Greek government is allowing for austerity to occur even if it means children starve is a crime in and of itself. What is occurring is the bastardization of the so-called First World countries by their own governments and in the case of Europe, the IMF and World Bank are helping in cannibalizing Europe, allowing for poor euro countries such as Greece to essentially become a corporate colony for the major EU countries like Germany. What has happened to the so-called Third World countries is now happening to the 'First World,' where "areas of education and health care as well as other public enterprises are dismantled, privatized and sold off to mega corporations and banks for pennies on the dollar," [10] resulting in a type of neo-feudalism [11] where corporations are in control of our entire society, from the government to the very food that you eat.

While the situation may seem dismal and it seems as if all hope is gone, we must fight. People have been fighting all over the globe, from anti-austerity protests [12] in Europe to the number of protests planned for May 2013 [13] across the US to labor strikes and social protests being on the rise in Egypt. [14]

These protests are a sign that people are realizing that the power to change their reality doesn't like in the halls of government nor in the offices of a corporate office, the power is—and always has been—inside of them. If we are to stop this madness, we must fight and not just for our own sake, but for the sake of those who have yet to be born.


**Endnotes**

1: Liz Alderman, "More Children in Greece Are Going Hungry," *New York Times*, April 17, 2013 (http://www.nytimes.com/2013/04/18/world/europe/more-children-in-greece-start-to-go-hungry.html?_r=2&)

2: Allison Linn, "Sprawling and Struggling: Poverty Hits America's Suburbs," *NBC*, March 22, 2013 (http://www.nbcnews.com/feature/in-plain-sight/sprawling-struggling-poverty-hits-americas-suburbs-v17404578)

3: Michael Sivy, "Is the Global Economy Slowly Falling Apart?" *Time*, April 5, 2013 (http://business.time.com/2013/04/05/is-the-global-economy-slowly-falling-apart/)

4: Gregory McKenna, "War, what war? Don't mention the (currency) war,"*News*, April 9, 2013 (http://www.news.com.au/finance/markets/war-what-war-dont-mention-the-currency-  war/story-fn6t6wad-1226611800434)

5: Paddy Hirsch, "Why A Currency War Could Hurt You," *Marketplace*, March 11, 2013 (http://www.marketplace.org/topics/business/whiteboard/why-currency-war-could-hurt-you)

6: Global Europe Anticipation Bulletin, *Uncertain Financial Markets: The Global Systemic Economic Crisis 2013*, Global Research, http://www.globalresearch.ca/uncertain-financial-  markets-the-global-systemic-economic-crisis-2013/5327633 (March 20, 2013)

7: GlobalResearchTv, "Systemic Economic Collapse: A Brief History of Market Manipulation," https://www.youtube.com/watch?v=5i7Q4Mm7t5w (March 6, 2013)

8: Gearóid Ó Colmáin, "France's Media Admits That The Syrian 'Opposition' Is Al Qaida. Then Justifies French Government Support to the Terrorists," *Global Research*, April 14, 2013 (http://www.globalresearch.ca/frances-media-admits-that-the-syrian-opposition-is-al-qaida-then- justifies-french-government-support-to-the-terrorists/5331289)

9: William Wan, "China makes increased military spending a top priority as People's Congress meets," *Washington Post*, March 5, 2013 (https://www.washingtonpost.com/world/china-to- boost-military-spending-107-percent/2013/03/05/aaa62f10-8565-11e2-9d71- f0feafdd1394_story.html)

10: Andrew Gavin Marshall, "Western Civilization and the Economic Crisis: The Impoverishment of the Middle Class," *Global Research*, March 30, 2010 (http://www.globalresearch.ca/western-civilization-and-the-economic-crisis-the- impoverishment-of-the-middle-class/18386)

11: John W. Whitehead, *The Age of Neo-Feudalism: A Government by the Rich, and for the Corporations*. The Rutherford Institute https://www.rutherford.org/publications_resources/john_whiteheads_commentary/the_age_of_ne o_feudalism_a_government_of_the_rich_by_the_rich_and_for_the_c (January 28, 2013)

12: Kerin Hope, Miles Johnson, Peter Spiegel, "Europe May Day Protests Target Austerity," *Financial Times*, May 1, 2013 (http://www.ft.com/intl/cms/s/0/8b50c3d4-b263-11e2-a388-00144feabdc0.htmlhttp:/www.ft.com/intl/cms/s/0/8b50c3d4-b263-11e2-a388-00144feabdc0.html?siteedition=intl#slide0)

13: Margaret Flowers, Kevin Zeese, "Popular Resistance and Protest Movements across America," *Global Research*, May 4, 2013 (http://www.globalresearch.ca/popular-resistance-and- protext-movements-across-america/5333891)

14: Ahmed Aboulnei, "Labor strikes double under Morsi," *Daily News Egypt*, April 28, 2013 (http://www.dailynewsegypt.com/2013/04/28/labour-strikes-and-protests-double-under-morsi/)

From early in one's life, an American is taught the law and American institutions of justice are great equalizers within our society, ensuring that everyone is treated the same, no matter one's class, race, or ethnicity. Yet, what has been happening quite recently, especially within the past decade or so, is that we have been seeing an increasing breakdown in the rule of law and the use of the justice system to enforce injustices.

President Obama rode in on a high horse in the 2008 presidential elections, specifically on his slogan of hope and change. He rightly criticized the Bush administration on a number of issues, from the economy to the wars abroad, as well as the use of drones. [1]

Yet, Obama subsequently went and not only increased the use of drones, but used them to kill Anwar Al-Awlaki, an alleged member of Al Qaeda who was legally an American citizen at the time of his death.[2] However, the story gets even more shocking as not only does such as act create a legal precedent where the President can kill any US citizen that he deems a terrorist[3], but the Obama administration's attorney general argued that such assassinations of American citizens on US soil "would be legal and justified in an extraordinary circumstance.'"[4] Some would argue that Attorney General Eric Holder cleared the entire domestic drone debacle when he sent a letter to Senator Rand Paul which read:

It has come to my attention that you have now asked an additional question: "Does the President have the authority to use a weaponized drone to kill an American not engaged in combat on American soil?" The answer to that question is no. [5]

However, the problem with that answer is the vagueness of the phrase "engaged in combat." While it may seem obvious to someone what that phrase means, it becomes murky when one sees that the Defense Department has labeled protests as a form of low-level terrorism [6] and that environmental activists are being prosecuted as terrorists. [7] Does this means that protesters and environmental activists are "engaged in combat on American soil" and thus it is OK to attack them with armed drones?

This is deeply problematic as it essentially nullifies the due process clause of the Fifth Amendment and paves the way for future Presidents to potentially label their political opponents as terrorists or an enemy combatant (both have vague definitions), assassinate them with a drone, and hide the evidence under the guise of national security.

The breakdown of the rule of law has been furthered in the economic sphere as the wealthy elites are able to crash the economy and receive no jail time whatsoever, even though crimes were committed. [8] These economic elites are so powerful that even "the Department of Justice fears bringing criminal charges against them because of the possible repercussions such proceedings would have on the greater economy."[9] The fact that these corporate fatcats can crash the economy without fear of prosecution is only a testament to their political and economic clout. They have established institutions that are so firmly entrenched within the American economy that even the Department of Justice fears the effects of bringing them to court.

These corporations have cheated the government out of what they owe by using tax havens or shell companies, as was the case with Apple.[10] This corporate tax evasion does not only send money overseas, but these corporations can tap that money at will "simply by taking out loans and using foreign cash as collateral."[11] Activity such as this reveals our two-tiered justice system where individuals get prison time for tax evasion, while bankers run free. [12]

A final- and perhaps the most disturbing of all of these examples- in the breakdown of the rule of law in America is that those who reveal injustices are harshly punished. Chelsea Manning revealed information of US war crimes and was demonized as a traitor even though he had a legal duty to tell of these war crimes as "in the US Army Subject Schedule No. 27-1 is 'the obligation to report all violations of the law of war.'"[13] Manning was treated with such harshness that the UN Torture Chief classified Manning's treatment as being in "violation of [her] right to physical and psychological integrity as well as of [her] presumption of innocence."[14] More recently, Edward Snowden released information that the US has been spying on its citizens and he has been deemed a traitor even though

Treason is the only crime specified in the Constitution, and here is what our founding document says about it, from Article Three, Section Three:

**Treason against the United States, shall consist only in levying War against them, or in adhering to their Enemies, giving them Aid and Comfort.**

**The Supreme Court has interpreted this to mean that no one can commit treason unless it's with a country against whom our Congress has declared war.** This means that neither the Vietnam War nor the Korean War nor the War on Terror can yield treasonous Americans, as none of these wars were declared by Congress.[15] (emphasis added)

The actual law is being ignored in order to demonize and prosecute those who go against the state.

Yet, what does this the breakdown of the rule of law mean for the United States? For one it means that the US is a nation where "there are two sets of laws: one set for the government and the corporations, and another set for you and me," [16] yet on a deeper level it signals that the US is becoming more and more of an authoritarian state. There are many characteristics of authoritarianism that the US is currently engaged in or has shown since the dawn of the 21st century. They include

• Constraints on political institutions (Think the political constraints on third parties[17])

• Constraints on the mass public

• Ill-defined executive power[18]

The descent of the US to an authoritarian nation signals the destruction of the rule of law. Yet, there is hope. We the people can reverse this situation, but we will have to work outside the system. We are our only hope.


**Endnotes**

1: Tom Curry, "Obama Continues, Expands Some Bush Terrorism Policies," *NBC News*, June 6, 2013 (http://nbcpolitics.nbcnews.com/_news/2013/06/06/18804146-obama-continues-extends- some-bush-terrorism-policies?lite)

2: Joshua Keating, "Was Anwar Al-Awlaki Still A US Citizen?" *Foreign Policy*, September 30, 2011 (http://blog.foreignpolicy.com/posts/2011/09/30/was_anwar_al_awlaki_still_a_us_citizen)f

3: Adam Serwer, "Obama's Dangerous Awlaki Precedent," *Mother Jones*, September 30, 2011 (http://www.motherjones.com/mojo/2011/09/al-awlakis-innocence-beside-point#13725235717251&action=collapse_widget&id=3279092)

4: Jon Swaine, "Barack Obama 'has authority to use drone strikes to kill Americans on US soil," *The Telegraph*, March 6, 2013 (http://www.telegraph.co.uk/news/worldnews/barackobama/9913615/Barack-Obama-has- authority-to-use-drone-strikes-to-kill-Americans-on-US-soil.html)

5: Amy Davidson, "Rand Paul Gets a Letter from Eric Holder," *The New Yorker*, March 7, 2013 (http://www.newyorker.com/online/blogs/closeread/2013/03/rand-paul-gets-a-letter-from-eric- holder.html)

6: American Civil Liberties Union, *ACLU Challenges Defense Department Personnel Policy To Regard Lawful Protests as "Low-Level Terrorism,"* http://www.aclu.org/national-security/aclu-challenges-defense-department-personnel-policy-regard-lawful-protests-%E2%80%9Clow-le, June 10, 2009

7: Kevin Gosztola, *Environmental Activist, Prosecuted as If He Was Terrorist, Was Held in Isolation for Political Speech*, Firedoglake, http://dissenter.firedoglake.com/2013/04/01/environmental-activist-prosecuted-as-if-he-was- terrorist-was-held-in-isolation-for-political-speech/ (April 1, 2013)

8: All Gov, *Why No Prison for Banksters Who Caused Financial Crisis...Yet?,* http://www.allgov.com/news/top-stories/why-no-prison-for-banksters-who-caused-financial-crisisyet?news=842515, April 15, 2011

9: Halah Touryalai, "The Real Reason Wall Street Always Escapes Criminal Charges? The Justice Dept Fears The Aftermath," *Forbes*, June 3, 2013 (http://www.forbes.com/sites/halahtouryalai/2013/03/06/the-real-reason-wall-street-always- escapes-criminal-charges-the-justice-dept-fears-the-aftermath/)

10: Brendan Sasso, "Senate report: Apple using shell companies to dodge taxes," *The Hill*, May 20, 2013 (http://thehill.com/blogs/hillicon-valley/technology/300791-senate-report-accuses- apple-of-using-shell-companies-to-dodge-taxes)

11: Christopher Matthews, "The Next Big Thing In Corporate-Tax Avoidance," *Time*, April 3, 2013 (http://business.time.com/2013/04/03/the-next-big-thing-in-corporate-tax-avoidance/)

12: Jamie Satterfield, Ex-lawyer Sentenced to Prison For Tax Evasion," *Knoxnews,* June 24, 2013 (http://www.knoxnews.com/news/2013/jun/24/ex-lawyer-sentenced-to-prison-for-tax- evasion/)

13: Marjorie Cohn, "Bradley Manning's Legal Duty to Expose War Crimes," *Truthout*, June 3, 2013 (http://www.truth-out.org/news/item/16731-bradley-mannings-legal-duty-to-expose-war- crimes)

14: Kim Zetter, "UN Torture Chief: Bradley Manning Treatment Was Cruel, Inhuman," *Wired*, March 12, 2012 (http://www.wired.com/threatlevel/2012/03/manning-treatment-inhuman/)

15: Evan Puschak, "Lawrence O'Donnell: Why Edward Snowden Cannot Be A Traitor," *MSNBC*, June 25, 2013 (http://tv.msnbc.com/2013/06/25/why-edward-snowden-cannot-be-a- traitor/)

16: John W. Whitehead, *The Age of Neo-Feudalism: A Government of the Rich, by the Rich, and for the Corporations*, The Rutherford Institute, https://www.rutherford.org/publications_resources/john_whiteheads_commentary/the_age_of_ne o_feudalism_a_government_of_the_rich_by_the_rich_and_for_the_c, (January 28, 2013)

17: Roy L. Behr, Edward H. Lazarus, Steven J. Rosenstone, *Third Parties in America* 2nd edition (Princeton, NJ: Princeton University Press, 1984), Chapter Two "Constraints on Third Parties"

18: Gretchen Casper, *Fragile Democracies: The Legacies of Authoritarian Rule* (Pittsburgh, PA: University of Pittsburgh Press, 1995), pg 40

On September 11th, I will be attending an anti-drone demonstration in Union Square, NYC. This will be my first protest and I am quite excited. Obviously, the main goal of this demonstration is to protest against the use of drones around the world which kill innocents under the guise of attacking terrorists. While I welcome this protest, we must realize that this demonstration is not enough; that focusing on drones is not enough. We must battle the 'War On Terror' overall, as drones are only a small part of that.

The global drone attacks started under Bush and have continued and massively expanded under Obama, with Obama going so far as to assassinate four US citizens (officially speaking). Yet, while this is extremely problematic, it is a symptom of America's global militarism. Contrary to popular thinking, this global militarism didn't start in the Bush era, but rather in the time of FDR, with World War Two, and has continued and intensified since then. The US has, overtly, either already been involved in or started new wars/conflicts every single decade since the 1940s. This has created destruction all over the world, not just physically in terms of destroyed infrastructure, but mentally [1], historically [2], economically [3], and socially [4].

However, the problems go beyond just the military sphere. It has leaked into American society, and specifically into the social realm and how the American people relate to our government. Socially, this militarism has gone and allowed Islamophobia and anti-Arab racism to flourish in American society. It can be seen in everything, from attacks on mosques [5] to anti- Muslim ads [6]. This hatred and racism has heavily infected every part of our society to the point where it is seen as "OK" for TV pundits to spew anti-Muslim hatred.

Americans' relationship with their government has greatly changed ever since the 'War on Terror' was launched. While the government had previously spied on American citizens [7] (and even assassinated some [8]), it was mainly on those whom the government deemed a threat to the status quo. Now, the situation has become much more drastic, with the government spying on all US citizens [9], and has given itself the legal authority to not only indefinitely detain them without trial [10], but also to assassinate them (Assassination on US soil is still possible, given the fact that there are problems with Attorney General Holder's letter to Rand Paul. [11]). At every level, the very people who are supposed to represent Americans have been complicit in allowing Americans to be spied upon and their civil liberties to be destroyed. [12] There has been such a breakdown in the rule of law that there are even secret interpretations of law [13] that the American people can be subjected to, but not know of. This growing authoritarianism must be confronted as well.

Economically, corporations have profited quite handsomely [14] from the continuous wars of aggression around the world, as well as from the business of spying on Americans [15]. They are only able to do this because there is an economic incentive to create weapons of war and espionage, and to use those to great effect. In order to fight against militarism more broadly, such companies should be targeted for boycotts, and information campaigns should reveal to the public exactly who these companies are and how they are profiting off exploiting their customers' information.

There is a psychological battle to be held as well. The American people have become accustomed to their country being in a perpetual state of war. In many ways, some have become complacent at best, and, at worst, will actually support the 'humanitarian interventions' launched by the Obama administration. Just like with the drone debate, we should also work to have people realize that, while the names and terminology may have changed, the death and destruction have remained the same. This is especially important for those on the left, as there are many liberals whose hypocrisy has been revealed by condemning Bush's wars of aggression, but support interfering in the affairs of sovereign nations now that Obama is at the helm. We must combat these hypocritical and uninvolved minds, lest we allow these problems to perpetuate.

We must combat what Martin Luther King Jr. called "the giant triplets of racism, militarism, and economic exploitation" if we are to mount a truly successful attack on the drone war. The drone wars are a byproduct of the 'War on Terror' and its associated effects at home and abroad. If we do not look at this interconnected system, we will, in a way, be wasting our time as we will only be cutting off a branch of a tree rather than getting to the roots. We must go beyond drones.


**Endnotes**

1: Michelle Castillo, "Study: Suicide Rates Among Army Soldiers Up 80 Percent," *CBS News*, July 10, 2012 ( http://www.cbsnews.com/8301-504763_162-57394452-10391704/study-suicide- rates-among-army-soldiers-up-80-percent/ )

2: Robert Fisk, "It Is The Death of History," *The Independent*, September 17, 2011 (http://www.independent.co.uk/voices/commentators/fisk/robert-fisk-it-is-the-death-of-history-402571.html)

3: Jim Lobe, "Iraq, Afghanistan Wars Will Cost U.S. 4-6 Trillion Dollars: Report," *Inter Press Service*, March 30, 2013 ( http://www.ipsnews.net/2013/03/iraq-afghanistan-wars-will-cost-u-s- 4-6-trillion-dollars-report/ )

4: Forbes, *The True Costs of the Iraq and Afghanistan Wars*, http://www.forbes.com/2010/08/31/costs-war-military-iraq-afghanistan-business- oxford.html (September 1,2010)

5: Kari Huus, "Mosque in Missouri Burns to the Ground One Month After Arson Attack," *NBC News*, August 6, 2012 ( http://usnews.nbcnews.com/_news/2012/08/06/13146671-mosque-in- missouri-burns-to-the-ground-one-month-after-arson-attack?lite )

6: CBS News, *New anti-Muslim ads up In NYC Subway Stations*, http://www.cbsnews.com/8301-201_162-57562947/new-anti-muslim-ads-up-in-nyc- subway-stations/ (January 9, 2013)

7: NPR News, *COINTELPRO and the History of Domestic Spying*,http://www.npr.org/templates/story/story.php?storyId=5161811 (January 18, 2006)

8: Democracy Now, *The Assassination of Fred Hampton: How the FBI and the Chicago Police Murdered a Black Panther*,http://www.democracynow.org/2009/12/4/the_assassination_of_fred_hampton_how (December 4, 2009)

9: Dell Cameron, "Yes, The NSA Can Spy on Every US Citizen," *Vice,* June 2013 (http://www.vice.com/read/the-fbi-wants-to-wiretap-every-us-citizen-online )

10: Russia Today, *Obama Wins Back the Right to Indefinitely Detain under NDAA*, http://rt.com/usa/obama-ndaa-appeal-suit-229/ (July 17, 2013)

11: Guy Benson, "WH Official: Holder's Letter to Rand Paul Was An Intentional Non- answer," *Town Hall*, March 11, 2013 ( http://townhall.com/tipsheet/guybenson/2013/03/11/wh- official-holders-letter-to-rand-paul-was-a-nonanswer-n1531213 )

12: Kevin Collier, "Senate Votes to let NSA, FBI, Keep Spying On Your Email," *The Daily Dot*, December 28, 2012 ( http://www.dailydot.com/politics/senate-nsa-monitor-emails-five-years/ )

See Also: Jason Mick, "US House Backs Obama's Drone Strikes, NSA Spying," *Daily Tech*, July 25, 2013 (http://www.dailytech.com/US+House+Backs+Obamas+Drone+Strikes+NSA+Spying/article320 42.htm )

13: Alexander Abdo, *Government Confirms That It Has Secret Interpretation of Patriot Act Spy Powers*, American Civil Liberties Union, http://acludev.aclu.org/blog/national- security/government-confirms-it-has-secret-interpretation-patriot-act-spy-powers (March 16, 2012)

14: Bill Quigley, "Corporations Profit From Permanent War: Memorial Day 2010," *Huffington Post*, May 24, 2010 ( http://www.huffingtonpost.com/bill-quigley/corporations-profit- from_b_586896.html )

15: Laurence Marvin, "80 Major Corporations Profit From NSA Global Spying Network," *The Examiner*, July 4, 2013 ( http://www.examiner.com/article/80-major-corporations-profit-from- nsa-global-spying-network )

It has been known for quite some time that technocratic governments have taken hold in Europe, with the most prominent examples being in Greece, where "Lucas Papademos, a former vice president of the European Central Bank, interim prime minister of a unity government charged with preventing the country from default"[1] and Italy, which had Mario Monti take over, with the argument for imposing an undemocratic government being the economic problems of both countries respectively. However, it seemed that the technocracy was going to be contained within the realm of Europe, yet it has come to America.

Currently, in Detroit, there is a battle between residents and Michigan Governor Rick Snyder, over sending an emergency manager (EM) to Detroit whose goal it would be to "repair the deeply troubled finances of Detroit."[2] Specifically, the financial problems in Detroit are that the city has "more than $14 billion in long-term liabilities, including underfunded pensions. The city is also poised to end the fiscal year more than $100 million in the red without an infusion of cash."[3] Currently, residents of Detroit are actively resisting the appointment of an EM via protests. [4]

The people of Detroit are understandably worried as emergency managers "have sweeping powers to overrule the mayor and city council, as well as unilaterally amend or cancel public sector collective bargaining agreements" and "EMs across Michigan have used their authority to privatize public services and eliminate public sector jobs"[5] More specifically, the powers that an EM has is that they can

• Hire/fire local government employees

• Renegotiate, terminate, modify labor contracts with state treasury approval

• Sell, lease, or privatize local assets with state treasury approval

• Revise contract obligations

• Change local budgets without local legislative approval

• Initiate municipal bankruptcy proceedings

• Hire support staff[6]

Thus, what essentially occurs is austerity and a war against the public sector to the detriment of the people.

Yet, this is not the first time EMs have been used. In January 2012 it was reported the Flint, Michigan was put under the direction of an emergency manager to deal with Flint's deficit, however, it was pointed out that "the pay of Michigan's five emergency managers — ranging from $132,000 to $250,000 — is set by the state, **but the money actually is paid by the local communities they're in charge of.**"[7] (emphasis added) Thus, this brings up the question: How can the deficit of a town be lowered when the people overseeing that operation are getting six- figure salaries?

It is also important to know how these emergency managers came to be. Michigan has had an emergency management system since 1988, due to Public Act 101 which "allowed an emergency financial manager to assess and manage the finances of Hamtramck."[8] Public Act 101 gained greater strength in 1990 via Public Act 72[9], which allowed the state government to appoint emergency financial managers to towns which were having financial troubles. Yet, the modern- day emergency manager came about in 2011 when Public Act 4[10] not only gave emergency managers full-range of a town's finances, but also surpassed and overrode Public Acts 101 and 72. It is in Public Act 4 that the EMs truly came to embody the technocratic like governments found in Europe.

In addition to being undemocratic, the question of whether or not the strategy of using emergency managers' work remains. In 2002, Flint was put under EM Ed Kurtz from 2002- 2004. Upon his leaving, Kurtz claimed to have left Flint "$6.1 million budget surplus in 2005. However, the prosperity didn't last and the city struggled with a deficit of $6.8 million by 2008."[11] This resulted in Kurtz being put back as Flint's EM in 2012. So, EMs may not even work.

What has essentially occurred is that technocracy has come to America on the state level. The state government declares a location to have financial problems and appoints someone to enact austerity, ignoring whether or not the deficit is actually caused by runaway public spending or not. The emergency manger is for Detroit is rumored to Kevyn Orr, "a bankruptcy expert who collected more than $1 million in fees helping to manage Chrysler's restructuring"[12] and he could potentially have the city file for bankruptcy.

When a town goes bankrupt, "in one sense, life goes on as usual. Police and fire departments still respond to 911 calls; the garbage is still collected. But don't expect that new bridge or school to be built."[13] However, the problem in this situation is that the police and fire departments may not respond to 911 calls as they have been cut both departments down to a skeleton crew that will only answer the most urgent of calls. This, coupled with privatization and certain powers emergency managers have such as being able to fire government employees, will allow for creditors, which are in many cases corporations, to come in and buy the towns up for cheap.

Technocracy has come to America. Let us hope it doesn't spread.


**Endnotes**

1: Rachel Donadio, "Greece and Italy Seek a Solution From Technocrats," *New York Times*, November 10, 2011 (http://www.nytimes.com/2011/11/11/world/europe/greece-and-italy-ask- technocrats-to-find-solution.html?pagewanted=all&_r=0)

2: Monica Davey, "Michigan Naming Fiscal Manager to Help Detroit," *New York Times*, March 1, 2013 (http://www.nytimes.com/2013/03/02/us/michigan-appoints-emergency-manager-for-detroit.html?pagewanted=all)

3: Huffington Post, *Rick Snyder, Michigan Gov., Declares Detroit Financial Emergency Exists*, http://www.huffingtonpost.com/2013/03/01/rick-snyder-detroit-financial- emergency_n_2789782.html (March 1, 2013)

4: Journal Gazette, *Emergency manager protest ties up Detroit traffic*, http://www.journalgazette.net/article/20130311/NEWS03/130319889/1066/NEWS03 (March 11, 2013)

5: Ned Resnikoff, "Detroit officials beg state to reconsider Emergency Manager appointment," *MSNBC*, March 12, 2013 (http://tv.msnbc.com/2013/03/12/detroit-officials-beg-state-to- reconsider-emergency-manager-appointment/)

6: Michigan Radio, *7 things to know about Michigan's emergency manager law*, http://www.michiganradio.org/post/7-things-know-about-michigans-emergency-manager-law (December 6, 2011)

7: Kristin Longley, "State-appointed emergency managers make six figures at local community's expense," *Flint Journal*, December 27, 2011 (http://www.mlive.com/news/flint/index.ssf/2011/12/state-appointed_emergency_mana.html)

8: Michigan Radio, December 6, 2011

9: Michigan Legislature, *Local Government Fiscal Responsibility Act*, http://www.legislature.mi.gov/%28S%28mqd5jmnth0yapg55meffow55%29%29/mileg.aspx?pag e=GetObject&objectname=mcl-Act-72-of-1990

10: Michigan Legislature, *Public Act 4*, http://www.legislature.mi.gov/documents/2011-2012/publicact/htm/2011-PA-0004.htm

11: Michigan Daily, *From the Daily: Misguided management*, http://www.michigandaily.com/opinion/03daily-emergency-manager11 (March 10, 2013)

12: Steve Neavling, "Chrysler bankruptcy lawyer is pick for Detroit manager: source," *Reuters*, March 12, 2013 (http://www.*Reuters*.com/article/2013/03/12/us-usa-detroit-manager- idUSBRE92B0J720130312)

13: Eric Weiner, "What Happens When City Hall Goes Bankrupt?," *NPR*, February 28, 2008 (http://www.npr.org/templates/story/story.php?storyId=60740288)

The alternative media began and in many cases still is a platform upon which one can gain access to views, narratives, and analyses of current and historical events that are separate from the mainstream discourse, media, academic, or otherwise. Yet, there is a major problem in the alternative media; namely the fact that there are so many voices saying so many different (and in several cases, contradictory) views on the issues of the day that it is rather difficult to create alliances to combat the current power structures.

There are a number of different ideologies and ideas within the alternative media. Some, like Addicting Info, push a partisan agenda, others like Common Dreams push a progressive agenda, whereas shows like the Infowars are motivated by conspiracies and a disdain for government. Essentially, no matter where one goes in the alternative media, there is virtually always an agenda being pushed. However, it is positive that such groups and organizations are open about their bias as it allows for the information presented to be taken with a grain of salt. However, this is a major problem as creates a situation where it is rather difficult to build coalitions, as one group will almost always be contradicting someone else. For example, right after the Boston Bombing, you had Infowars arguing that it was a false flag and Democracy Now's Amy Goodman stating that "no one [should] jump to any conclusions."

This creates a situation where groups and individuals that agree on major issues such as being against wars of aggression, wanting to protect the environment, and wanting to respect the Constitution (among other issues), wind up walling themselves off from one another, each group in their respective bubble. These bubbles create echo chambers of confirmation bias and don't allow us to challenge ourselves. Yet, the greater problem is that they keep us from building coalitions and challenging the real enemy, the current political, economic, and social systems that harm us all.

The question that then poses itself is: How do we overcome these barriers, burst these bubbles, and create coalitions and alliances. We need to begin a dialogue among one another, specifically the grassroots organizers and everyday individuals who get their information from the alternative media. From this dialogue, we can begin to work together and hammer out a pathway to combating the system. The attention should not focus on who each person gets their information from, as that would create the grounds for disagreement and a shattering of the coalition rather than a creation of an alliance. In addition to this, to include the 'stars' would be unbeneficial as the discussion would focus on them and their views rather than the actual goal of working together.

Without a doubt there will be disagreements and problems, it will be both a chance to air out grievances and to see who among us is truly as open-minded as they claim to be. It will allow for a chance to get the facts straight and for questions to be answered. But most importantly, it will be a way for people to unite.

As of April 2014, it is currently being debated by the Senate, but rarely discussed on mainstream television: the Shield Law. While on the surface it may seem to be rather innocuous, some of the language in it and its implications are quite problematic for journalists.

A Shield Law is a law which "provides statutory protection for the 'reporters' privilege'— legal rules which protect journalists against the government requiring them to reveal confidential sources or other information."[1] Generally, this is a positive occurrence as journalists are much more able to conduct their work and bring information to public light if they do not need to worry about having to reveal their sources. While Shield Laws have occurred in the past, they have only been on the state level. This currently proposed Shield Law is the first one to reach the federal level and the main goal is to protect journalists from having to reveal confidential sources in federal cases.[2]

However, there are certain instances in which journalists will have to reveal sources, such as "(1) The party seeking disclosure has exhausted all reasonable alternative sources of the information; (2) The requested information is essential to resolving the matter; (3) Disclosure of the requested information would not be contrary to the public interest; and (4) In criminal cases, if the requesting party is the federal government, the government must show that there are reasonable grounds to believe that a crime has occurred."[3]

While overall it may seem like a good bill, there are a number of problems with this Shield Law, officially known as the Free Flow of Information Act of 2013. For starters, this law would "allow the government to seize reporters' records without notifying them for 45 days – a period of time that could be renewed by a judge 45 additional days – if investigators convince a judge pre-notification 'would pose a clear and substantial threat to the integrity of a criminal investigation.'"[4] (emphasis added) This power of seizing records without notifying reporters was used most recently in regards to the Associated Press, when the federal government seized their phone records in May of last year, with the government only saying that "they were needed for investigation of an unspecified criminal matter."[5] Oh yes! What transparency and accountability! Infringing upon the First Amendment rights of reporters and then only giving what is essentially a BS, purposefully vague explanation.

In addition to this, the government can force journalists to give up information in the name of national security. [6] This is quite worrying as the US government has time and time again been involved in operations of entrapment. [7,8] Due to this, they could potentially have a scenario where they create a case of entrapment, label it terrorism, and then force all journalists to give up information on any and all sources as well as seize their records under the guise of national security.

Yet in this current bill, not only can the government continue to engage in the above behavior, but they are also defining who is and who is not a journalist. Initially, the bill defined a journalist as "a person who has a 'primary intent to investigate events and procure material' in order to inform the public by regularly gathering information through interviews and observations" and added the stipulation that "The person also must intend to report on the news at the start of obtaining any protected information and must plan to publish that news."[9] This seems to be rather fine as it would include mainstream and independent journalists. However, the situation became problematic when in September 2013, an amendment to the bill was proposed that- let's just say- 'more clearly' defined who and who was not a journalist.

Kevin Gosztola of Firedoglake discussed this amendment last year and it would be appropriate to quote him now at some length:

**A "covered journalist," under the amendment, would be the following: an employee, independent contractor, or agent of an entity or service that disseminates news or information by means of newspaper; nonfiction book; wire service; news agency; news website, mobile application or other news or information service (whether distributed digitally or other wise); news program; magazine or other periodical, whether in print, electronic, or other format; or through television or radio broadcast, multichannel video programming distributor** (as such term is defined in section 602(13) of the Communications Act of 1934 (47 U.S.C. 522(13)), or motion picture for public showing

[...]

**That person must also have the "primary intent to investigate events and procure material in order to disseminate to the public news or information concerning local, national, or international events or other matters of public interest."** Or, that person should be engaged in the "regular gathering, preparation, collection, photographing, recording, writing, editing, reporting or publishing on such matters." A person would also qualify as a "covered journalist" if they had experience in journalism and had "substantially contributed, as an author, editor, photographer, or producer, to a significant number of articles, stories, programs, or publications" in the past twenty years.

As Feinstein said, it would "cover a legitimate journalist such as a Dan Rather who leaves his media entity and takes to publishing freelance stories on the web."[10] (emphasis added)

Now, let's begin to take those paragraphs apart and analyze them, bit by bit.

In the first paragraph, the law defines a journalist as "an employee, independent contractor, or agent of an entity or service that disseminates news or information" and then goes on to define the many mediums by which the news can be disseminated. Some of this language seems to be problematic. What exactly do they mean by "independent contractor?" Do they mean a freelancer? Do they mean someone like myself who researches and writes independently?

In the next paragraph, it adds a caveat to the definition of journalist, stating that the individual in question must also "have the 'primary intent to investigate events and procure material in order to disseminate to the public news or information concerning local, national, or international events or other matters of public interest.'" Well, how do you prove that this is one's primary intent? Do you just have to state as such? And what do they even mean by the term "primary intent?" Isn't the main goal of most if not all journalists to disseminate news to the public?

The final paragraph offers an alternative if one is not with a mainstream source by stating that they are covered if "they had experience in journalism and had 'substantially contributed, as an author, editor, photographer, or producer, to a significant number of articles, stories, programs, or publications' in the past twenty years." Does this mean that contributing to sites such as Truthout and Alternet could qualify one as a journalist under this law?

Apparently, in an earlier version of the bill, the law defined "journalists so narrowly that it excludes bloggers, citizen reporters and even some freelancers,"[11] and thus the amendment was added. However, this amendment seems to leave more questions than answers.

In addition to this, many supporters of this bill have been using some rather bellicose language. For example, Senator Dianne Feinstein has been quoted as saying that "real journalists draw salaries" [12] and stating that the First Amendment is "a privilege,"[13] which is rather worrying.

On top of all these other problems, former U.S. Attorney General Michael Mukasey, has written that this bill would "give judges too much power to decide on their own whether the disclosure of the information would be contrary to the public interest and thus not protected."[14] This means the issue of deciding whether or not information that is being withheld by journalists, say, sources for example, violates the public interest in the form of national security would be decided by judges. If the judges do decide that the information being withheld does violate the public interest, then the journalist would be forced to hand over that information.

While judges do from time to time uphold the rights of the people, they seem to have often sided with the national security state as of recent. For example in 2010, a federal appeals court "ruled that former prisoners of the C.I.A. could not sue over their alleged torture in overseas prisons because such a lawsuit might expose secret government information,"[15] last year, the US Supreme Court decided to "allow the National Security Agency's surveillance of domestic telephone communication records to continue."[16]

In 2014 it was reported that the US Supreme Court "rejected [the Center for Constitutional Rights] lawsuit against Bush-era warrantless surveillance, which "guarantees that the federal courts will never address a fundamental question: Was the warrantless surveillance program the NSA carried out on President Bush's orders legal?"[17] Thus, it seems that the situation of on whose side the courts would rule in a case regarding national security is rather iffy. This is made all the more strenuous by the fact that if a case were to make it up all the way to the Supreme Court and they ruled in favor of the US government, it has the potential to set a precedent which could only be overturned by an entirely new Supreme Court case.

As of now, there are conflicting reports about whether or not Chuck Shumer (D.-N.Y.) has the votes to pass the bill in the Senate, with Schumer saying he does and Sen. John Cornyn (R-Texas) saying he doesn't.[19] However, if it does pass, there is no doubt about it going into law as Obama has already voiced his support for it.[20]

By essentially giving the government the power to define what a journalist is, it has the potential to hurt independent media when it is needed now more than ever. The mainstream media consistently sits on stories to please the US government. It was reported in 2006 that the *New York Times* made a decision to "[withhold] a story about the Bush administration's program of illegal domestic spying until after the 2004 election."[21] More recently, the US media reported again and again that the Syrian government had used chemical weapons in Ghouta and that the UN report confirmed it[22], when in reality, the question is still up in the air as new information has come to light that puts the official narrative in doubt.[23]

We need independent alternatives to the mainstream media like Corbett Report, Citizen Radio, and Black Agenda Report to allow people to get a glimpse behind the wall of misinformation that permeates much of the mainstream and get an idea of what is truly going on in the world. If this law gives the government the power to define who a journalist is, we may just lose that.


**Endnotes**

1: Society of Professional Journalists, *Shield Law 101: Frequently Asked Questions*, https://www.spj.org/shieldlaw-faq.asp

2: Rem Reider, "Media Shield Law Moves Forward," *USA Today*, http://www.usatoday.com/story/money/business/2013/09/12/senate-judiciary-committee- approves-media-shield-bill/2807045/ (September 12, 2013)

3: Chris Palmer, Josh Stearns, *The Journalism Shield Law: How We Got Here*, Free Press, http://www.freepress.net/blog/2013/08/06/journalism-shield-law-how-we-got-here (August 6, 2013)

4: Steven Nelson, "Holes in Media Shield Law Worry Opponents, and Even Some Supporters," *US News*, http://www.usnews.com/news/articles/2013/09/18/holes-in-media-shield-law-worry- opponents-and-even-some-supporters (September 18, 2013)

5: Roger Yu, "Feds Seize AP Phone Records For Criminal Probe," *USA Today*, http://www.usatoday.com/story/news/2013/05/13/justice-department-associated-press-telephone-records/2156521/ (May 13, 2013)

6: Zoë Carpenter, "Flawed Media Shield Law Goes to the Senate Floor," *The Nation*, http://www.thenation.com/blog/176166/flawed-media-shield-law-goes-senate-floor (September 13, 2013)

7: Alex Newman, "FBI Celebrates Foiling Its Own Terrorist Plot, Again," *The New American*, http://www.thenewamerican.com/usnews/crime/item/13263-fbi-celebrates-foiling-its-own-terror- plot-again (October 18, 2012)

8: Glenn Greenwald, "The FBI Again Thwarts Its Own Terror Plot," *Salon*, http://www.salon.com/2011/09/29/fbi_terror/ (September 29, 2011)

9: Tim Cushing, "Sen. Feinstein During 'Shield' Law Debate: 'Real' Journalists Draw Salaries," *Techdirt*, https://www.techdirt.com/articles/20130807/13153224102/sen-feinstein-during-shield-     law-debate-real-journalists-draw-salaries.shtml (August 8, 2013)

10: Kevin Gosztola, *Media Shield Law, Which Aims to Protect Only 'Real Reporters,' Moves Onward to the Senate*, Firedoglake, http://dissenter.firedoglake.com/2013/09/12/media-shield- law-which-defines-covered-journalists-moves-onward-to-the-senate/ (September 12, 2013)

11: Free Press, August 6, 2013

12: Morgan Weiland, *Why Sen. Feinstein Is Wrong About Who's a 'Real Reporter*,' Electronic Frontier Foundation, https://www.eff.org/deeplinks/2013/08/why-sen-feinstein-wrong-about- whos-real-reporter (August 9, 2013)

13: Mark Whitney, "Dianne Feinstein First Amendment Is A Special Privilege," https://www.youtube.com/watch?v=bywtn9RIDRw

14: Jacob Gershman, "Mukasey: Beware the Proposed Media-Shield Law," *Wall Street Journal*, http://blogs.wsj.com/law/2013/12/02/mukasey-beware-of-the-proposed-media-shield-law/ (December 2, 2013)

15: Charlie Savage, "Court Dismisses a Case Asserting Torture by C.I.A.," *New York Times*, http://www.nytimes.com/2010/09/09/us/09secrets.html?pagewanted=all&_r=0 (September 8, 2010)

16: Bill Mears, "Supreme Court allows NSA to continue looking at telephone records for now," *CNN*, http://www.cnn.com/2013/11/18/politics/supreme-court-nsa-phone-records/ (November 8, 2013)

17: Kevin Gosztola, *Supreme Court Declines to Hear Case That Would Have Challenged NSA Warrantless Surveillance of Lawyers*, Firedoglake, http://dissenter.firedoglake.com/2014/03/04/supreme-court-declines-to-hear-case-that-would- have-challenged-nsa-surveillance-of-lawyers/ (March 4, 2014)

18: Fox News, *Schumer: Senate Has Votes for Media Shield Law*, http://www.foxnews.com/politics/2014/03/21/schumer-senate-has-votes-for-media-shield-law/ (March 21, 2014)

19: Hadas Gold, "Cornyn: Schumer Doesn't Have Votes for Shield Law," *Politico*, http://www.politico.com/blogs/media/2014/03/cornyn-schumer-doesnt-have-votes-for-shield- law-185862.html (March 27, 2014)

20: David Jackson, "Obama backs 'Shield Law' for Reporters," *USA Today*, http://www.usatoday.com/story/news/politics/2013/05/15/obama-schumer-associated-press- shield-law/2161913/ (May 15, 2013)

21: Barry Grey, David Walsh, "A Damning Admission: *New York Times* Concealed NSA Spying Until After 2004 Election," *World Socialist Web Site*, http://www.wsws.org/en/articles/2006/08/nyti-a22.html (August 22, 2006)

22: Bill Chapel, "U.N. Report Confirms Chemical Weapons Were Used In Syria," *NPR*, http://www.npr.org/blogs/thetwo-way/2013/12/12/250572623/u-n-report-confirms-chemical- weapons-were-used-in-syria (December 12, 2013)

23: Matthew Schofield, "New Analysis of Rocket Used In Syria Chemical Attack Undercuts U.S. Claims," *McClatchy DC*, http://www.mcclatchydc.com/2014/01/15/214656/new-analysis- of-rocket-used-in.html (January 15, 2014)

A number of occurrences have taken place of the past 13 years since the rise of the new millennium; we have seen and are seeing the rise of popular movements all over the world and a resistance to the forces of imperialism, crony capitalism, and subjugation, from the most recent Arab Spring to the world's largest coordinated anti-war protest in history with the global protests against the Iraq War[1], to the rise of the Occupy Movement and the rise of indigenous resistance as can be seen in the Idle No More campaign of Canada's First Nations population. While not all movements are pushing for the elimination of the state, or even anarchistic in nature, they are rebelling against the current societal structures and creating an opportunity for radical change. What we are seeing around the world is a global resistance that, in some cases, has anarchist undercurrents. We are witnessing the new politics of the 21st century.

While many movements such as the Occupy Movement and the Arab Spring had anarchists and anarchist influences within them, anarchism as a political philosophy is quite misunderstood and some time should be taken to understand it.

Anarchism is defined by the American Heritage Dictionary as "The theory that all forms of government are oppressive and should be abolished."[2] While it does advocate the abolition of the state, anarchism also includes "a heightened and radical critique and questioning of power and authority: if a source of authority cannot legitimize its existence, it should not exist."[3] This has led to anarchism being critiqued by a number of individuals and an increase in anarchist thought to the point today where there are a large number of anarchist ideas being championed, from anarcho-feminism to queer anarchism to black anarchism.

In the United States, anarchism has had a rather interesting history with regards to not only Occupy, but also the 19th century labor movement as well. Anti-statism isn't anything new in the US as there have been a large number of crusaders who "condemned [the government] as an oppressive tyranny" when slavery wasn't abolished in the newly founded country, as Charles A. Madison notes. This abhorrence of slavery and hypocrisy caused "Men like William Lloyd Garrison and Wendell Phillips renounced their allegiance to it, John Brown openly declared war upon it, and thousands of others regarded it as unfit to command their respect and loyalty."[4] The anti-statism only increased in the 19th century with the inclusion of anarchists in the labor movement.

The International Working Men's Association (IWMA) put forward in its 1866 Congress that the 8-hour day should be advocated for. The IWMA "had influence amongst the German-speaking immigrant anarchist and socialist workers of Chicago," [5] and after it was disbanded, the International Working People's Association, being founded in 1881 by anarchists, took up the struggle.

This struggle for better working conditions culminated is what is known as the 1886 Haymarket Square Riot in which 40,000 workers went on strike to fight for an 8-hour day. The strikes beget protests which beget police confrontation. "On May 3, police fired on strikers who were menacing the strikebreakers at McCormick Harvester, and several strikers were injured. Labor leaders then convened a mass meeting for the following evening at the city's Haymarket Square."[6] As the peaceful rally ended, the police demanded that it be shut down and someone threw a dynamite bomb towards a group of police to which the police responded with gunfire. The result: seven dead cops and several workingmen injured. A total of eight anarchists were charged, which resulted in seven people being sentenced to death and one life sentence. Two death sentences were commuted to life imprisonment by Illinois governor Richard J. Oglesby, one committed suicide and four were hung.

While anarchism continued until World War One with massive anti-war protests occurring, it was eventually forced underground. However, the Occupy movement breathed new life into anarchist ideas. OWS's focus on "direct action and leaderless, consensus-based decision-making,"[7] embodied into the General Assembly, was an anarchistic aspect of Occupy. It also was anarchistic in its refusal to "recognize the legitimacy of existing political institutions," "accept the legitimacy of the existing legal order," and its "embrace of prefigurative politics."[8] This refusal to recognize the political institutions is anarchistic in nature as usually when protests occur, they appeal to political powers to alleviate their suffering. By rejecting the two-party system and rather than fighting for a third-party, creating a small, autonomous community, OWS rejected the state and worked to create a community based on horizontal as opposed to hierarchical organization. By rejecting the legal order in the form of ignoring "local ordinances that insisted that any gathering of more than 12 people in a public park is illegal without police permission," [9] OWS refused to subjugate itself to the very forces that worked to establish and uphold the current status quo. Occupy embraced political ideas and experimented with them, which resulted in the creation of new institutions, from kitchens to clinics to media centers, but they were consistently built around the ideas of working together, horizontal organization, and voluntary cooperation, all of which are central to anarchist thought.

The Occupy movement is still alive as while the encampments may no longer exist, it has created a number of offshoots and the activists that made up Occupy didn't disappear, rather they have moved on into other forms of resistance[10], though just not under the Occupy banner. They have even been involved in organizations that have provided large amounts of aid to damaged communities, such as Occupy Sandy, which stepped in when the federal government could not.[11]

Yet, this resistance to the status quo has not just been taking place in America, but also all over the world. In 2008, Zbigniew Brzezinski warned of a global political awakening. In a *New York Times* op-ed, he stated "**For the first time in history almost all of humanity is politically activated, politically conscious and politically interactive**. Global activism is generating a surge in the quest for cultural respect and economic opportunity in a world scarred by memories of colonial or imperial domination"[12] (emphasis added). This "global activism" is quite real and very well may upend the entirety of the current political, social, and economic systems.

In Brazil, protests have been occurring over issues ranging from inflation to education reform to forced evictions. Among all of this, teachers went to the streets to "demand better wages and school conditions when police decided to disperse the demonstration."[13] There had already been violent clashes between teachers and police as nights before the protest, several striking teachers that were occupying a city council building in Rio de Janiero were beaten and dragged out by the police. During the demonstration in late October, the police decided to repress the teachers by using heavy-handed tactics such as shooting tear gas canisters. Brazilian anarchists came to the aid of striking teachers by protecting them from state violence, as one teacher Andrea Coelho said, "It was the Black Bloc that protected me in that protest."[14] This protection of teachers has caused the teachers union to declare unconditional support for the black bloc protesters.[15]

These protests in Brazil come amidst a time where, according to Time Magazine, there was "less than 1% growth last year and less than 3% forecast this year [2013] compared to 7.5% in 2010" and where its political leaders convinced the world that it "was developed enough to host the soccer World Cup next year and the Summer Olympics in Rio de Janeiro in 2016, yet seemed so unwilling to show their own people they could improve the country's pathetically underfunded schools, staffed by just as woefully underpaid and undertrained teachers."[16] Just last year, a UN study indicated that wealth inequality was increasing with "the richest 20% of the population on average earn 20 times more than the poorest 20%."[17] It is among this massive increase in wealth inequality on a regional level, along with a corrupt government and lack of educational investment that the people have finally decided that enough is enough and are demanding there be massive changes to the current system.

In Europe, where in Greek children are starving in order to repay banks, revolt is taking place there as well. In Bulgaria, around 4,000 people demonstrated "calling for an end to the 'reign of the oligarchy' and demanding that the nation's government steps down to make way for early elections."[18] They argue that the country is still unstable, unprosperous, and not well governed 24 years after Communist rule was ended. The protest was part of a five-month old anti-government movement that alleges that government has mafia ties. Such accusations are in part true as back in 2008, the European Union's anti-fraud office was investigating the Nikolov- Stoykov group, a conglomerate with businesses from meat processing and storage to a Black Sea Resort, whose leading partners had connections to the government and has been accused of being a front for a criminal company network comprised of over 50 Bulgarian companies as well as other European and offshore companies.[19] More recently, the European Commission issued a report last year discussing the government-mafia ties in Bulgaria, with puts the blame on "both the executive and the judiciary in Bulgaria, which have been engulfed by power struggles, with each accusing the other of serving the mafia."[20]

In Italy there have been anti-austerity protests going on for quite some time and the violence has erupted as late last month, police fired tear gas at anti-austerity protesters and at least 16 people, including four officers, were injured and eight protesters were arrested. The protesters were "calling for more affordable housing, better wages and improved conditions for immigrants and refugees, tens of thousands of whom live in a twilight zone of semi-legality in Italy, with many forced to squat in disused buildings or sleep rough."[21] More protests are continuing in Italy where there have been cuts in education spending, and they continue all over Europe as the EU proposes spending cuts in its 2014 budget.[22]

Amidst the talk and fervor of the Arab Spring, anarchist activists were heavily involved in organizing after Mubarak's ousting. Egyptian anarchist Mohammed Hassan Aazab noted that after Mubarak was gone, they "started gathering, talking to people, printing up writing about our ideas, and organizing meetings in downtown cafes in front of whoever was there."[23] The organizing continues and the fight against the oppressive Egyptian regime goes on, even as the Egyptian government bans protests of more than ten people without a police permit, effectively an attempt to end all protests.

In Bahrain, the protests against the Sunni monarchy continue as Shiites protest "repression against the opposition amid an ongoing crackdown on the largely peaceful demonstrations."[24] These protests occur even though the Bahraini government has a history of using violence against peaceful demonstrators, even going so far as killing children.[25] The majority Shiite nation has been repressed for years; they face employment and educational discrimination, have little political representation, and are barred from most government and military positions.[26]

Protests have even hit nations in sub-Saharan Africa, such as Sudan. There, protesters have taken to the street, initially to protests a cut in fuel subsidies, but since the demonstrations have evolved "to wider dissent against the country's leadership after security forces killed at least 50 people [in late September], according to the African Center for Justice and Peace Studies and human rights watchdog Amnesty International."[27] The Sudanese government so far admits "that 87 people were killed, while activists and rights groups say the number was at least 200."[28] A main reason why the people began protesting was the fuel subsidies were cut due to the separation between Sudan and South Sudan, which was home to about 75% of Sudan's oil production. All of this is occurring when "the Sudanese pound hit an all-time low on the key black market on [September 21, 2013] as people sought to shift their savings into hard currency in anticipation of higher inflation."[29] This increase in inflation, couple with the cut in fuel subsidies, will lead to a situation in which everything is more expensive, but especially food as Sudan is a major food importer.

While quite sparse in certain areas of the region, protests have spread to Asia as well. Overall, "Strikes have become increasingly frequent at privately owned factories in recent years, often involving workers demanding higher wages or better conditions" and technology has helped grow this protest movement as "the explosive growth in the use of home-grown versions of Twitter has made it easy for protesters to convey instant reports and images to huge audiences."[30] These protests are in response to having low wages and unsafe conditions as the number of millionaires and billionaires in China increases and China has become the world's second largest economy. Most recently, after the July 2013 floods, the government seems to have taken a rather slow response to addressing the problem, causing flood victims to protest. The Chinese government has responded to these protests by sending out riot police which may have used violence to quell the protesters as "Photographs showed several residents [of Yuyao city] bleeding from the head."[31]

There are also protests in Thailand, as Thais seek to oust current Prime Minister Yingluck Shinawatra, the sister of former premier Thaksin Shinawatra, who protesters say control her. Shinawatra's older brother was wildly unpopular as in 1998 he used his American connections to boost his political image and after coming into office committed Thai troops to aiding the US invasion of Iraq amid protest from both the military and the public[32] and allowed for the CIA to use Thailand for its extraordinary rendition program.[33] More than just this though, Yingluck Shinawatra has also been criticized for "her alleged ignorance, lack of political experience, and tendency to stay adrift of key issues."[34] Thus, on literally every continent there is resistance to the current political power structures and while many may not be pushing for the end of the state, they are pushing for radical change to the society where the many will benefit rather than the few.

Yet, for all of these protests and uprisings, it would not be complete without a group that has been exploited, ignored, stereotyped, and have been victims of genocide: the indigenous population.

In Canada, Elsipogtog First Nation members located in New Brunswick province have been fighting against fracking plans as neither the government nor industries discussed the issue with them, despite the fact that "Rulings by the Supreme Court of Canada and lower courts have established a duty to consult and accommodate aboriginal people when development is considered on their land, even non-reserve traditional lands."[35] The First Nations argue that they have never ceded their lands and that the treaties signed in the 1700s were only to acknowledge peace and friendship between the immigrants and the indigenous population. This revolt has culminated in the Idle No More movement which is aimed to protect not only indigenous lands, but also the larger environment in Canada from corporations which aim to use the land for the sole purpose of extracting its resources using harmful techniques such as fracking.

Indigenous resistance is also occurring in Israel. In November 2013, the Israeli parliament moved to begin debating and possibly approving the Prawer Plan. The Prawer Plan, if passed, will result in "the destruction of 35 'unrecognized' Arab Bedouin villages, the forced displacement of up to 70,000 Arab Bedouin citizens of Israel, and the dispossession of their historical lands in the Naqab."[36] On November 30, 2013, it was reported that "In the Negev village of Houra, clashes broke out at the main demonstration where about 1,200 protesters had gathered," with protesters eventually throwing stones at Israeli security forces and the police responding with "tear gas, stun grenades and water cannon."[37] The Arab Bedouins are fighting for the survival of their culture. It is rather interesting that even though they are citizens of Israeli, the Bedouins are still subjugated to the interests of the Jewish majority.

Yet, Canada and Israel are not the only places where the indigenous population is fighting back. In addition to be wracked by protests in regards to education, corruption and a generally inefficient government, Brazil is also witnessing protests from indigenous people. In October, 500 people set up camp in front of Congress to "oppose a constitutional change that would let lawmakers participate in the demarcation of territories. Indigenous people and their supporters say the proposal would allow agricultural interests to encroach on their lands."[38] The fight of Brazil's indigenous population to protect their lands has been going on for over a year now, with many of the conflicts resulting in deaths. According to a 2012 report done by the Indigenist Missionary Council, "54 Indians were murdered in 2012, most of them as a result of land conflicts," [39] and the problem only continues into 2013, with a total of three murders occurring.

Yet, what does this all mean? Why does it even matter? This global resistance is extremely important as it reveals to the elites that their façade of democracy and consumerism is falling rapidly a part in the face of lagging economies, high unemployment rates, and a political class that is more concerned with its own personal needs rather than that of the people who they have charge over. It shows the people that they can and must fight back against the current political, social, and economic systems if they are to survive, that they can create new communities and new institutions that don't rely on the current systems of power and are organized horizontally rather than hierarchically. These protests show that the people will not sit idly by and let the government serve them on a platter to corporations, or, even worse, neglect to uphold the promises they took to protect the population. These movements represent a mass awakening of humanity which has the potential to radically change the entire landscape of society on a global scale.

We must be willing to fight for as long as it takes to alter society so that rather than serving industry or a small societal elite at the expense of the many, society fosters a climate of peace: peace with each other, peace with the environment, and encourage education and cooperativeness for the good of all while respecting the autonomy of the individual. Most importantly though, we must foster peace within ourselves and not be afraid to engage with those in our immediate area on the issue, for if not, we will risk the continuation of this broken system and lose what may have been a great chance to change the current situation for the better.


**Endnotes**

1: Phyllis Bennis, *February 15, 2003. The Day the World Said No to War*, Institute For Policy Studies, http://www.ips-dc.org/blog/february_15_2003_the_day_the_world_said_no_to_war (February 15, 2013)

2: American Heritage Dictionary, 5th edition, s.v. "anarchism"

3: Devon Douglas-Bowers, *On Anarchism: An Interview with Andrew Gavin Marshall*, Hampton Institute, http://www.hamptoninstitution.org/onanarchism.html#.UpatMVQ9La8 (October 2, 2013)

4: Charles A. Madison, "Anarchism in the United States," *Journal of the History of Ideas* 6:1 (1945), pg 50

5: International Workers Association, *The 8 Hour Day, the Anarchists and the IWPA: Haymarket and the Radicalization of Labour Demands in the 1880s*, http://www.iwa- ait.org/content/8-hour-day-anarchists-and-iwpa-haymarket-and-radicalization-labour-demands- 1880s (May 6, 2013)

6: David Greenberg, "Anarchy in the US: A Century of Fighting The Man," *Slate*, April 28, 2000 (http://www.slate.com/articles/news_and_politics/history_lesson/2000/04/anarchy_in_the_us.ht ml)

7: Dan Berrett, "Intellectual Roots of Wall St. Protest Lie in Academe," *The Chronicle of Higher Education*, October 16, 2011 (http://chronicle.com/article/Intellectual-Roots-of- Wall/129428/)

8: David Graeber, "Occupy Wall Street's Anarchist Roots," *Al Jazeera*, November 30, 2011 (http://www.aljazeera.com/indepth/opinion/2011/11/2011112872835904508.html)

9: Ibid

10: Democracy Now, *Two Years After Occupy Wall Street, a Network of Offshoots Continue Activism for the 99%,* http://www.democracynow.org/2013/9/19/two_years_after_occupy_wall_street (September 19, 2013)

11: Alan Feuer, "Occupy Sandy: A Movement Moves to Relief," *New York Times*, November 9, 2012 (http://www.nytimes.com/2012/11/11/nyregion/where-fema-fell-short-occupy-sandy-was- there.html?_r=0)

12: Zbigniew Brzezinski, "The Global Political Awakening," *New York Times*, December 16, 2008 (http://www.nytimes.com/2008/12/16/opinion/16iht- YEbrzezinski.1.18730411.html?pagewanted=all)

13: Bradley Brooks, "Anarchist Tactics Grow Among Brazil's Protests," *Associated Press*, October, 22, 2013 (http://news.yahoo.com/anarchist-tactics-grow-amid-brazils-protests- 040814619.html)

14: Ibid

15: Revolution News, *Brazil: Teachers Union Officially Declares Unconditional Support for Black Bloc*, http://revolution-news.com/brazils-teachers-union-officially-declares-unconditional- support-for-black-bloc/ (October 9, 2013)

16: Tim Padgett, "What Brazil's Protests Say About Latin America's Fumbling Elites," *Time*, June 19, 2013 (http://world.time.com/2013/06/19/what-brazils-protests-say-about-latin-americas- fumbling-elites/)

17: BBC News, *UN Study Says Wealth Gap in Latin America Increases*, http://www.bbc.co.uk/news/world-latin-america-19339636 (August 21, 2012)

18: Al Jazeera, *Bulgarians Protest Against Government Policy*, http://www.aljazeera.com/news/europe/2013/11/bulgarians-protest-against-government- policy-2013111015288976392.html (November 10, 2013)

19: Doreen Carvajal, Stephen Castle, "Mob Muscles Its Way Into Politics in Bulgaria," *New York Times*, October 15, 2008 (http://www.nytimes.com/2008/10/16/world/europe/16bulgaria.html?pagewanted=all&_r=0)

20: Turkish Weekly, *EC Draft Report Slams Bulgaria over Govt-Mafia Ties*, http://www.turkishweekly.net/news/138606/ec-draft-report-slams-bulgaria-over-govt- mafia-ties.html (July 17, 2012)

21: Nick Squires, "Anti-austerity Protesters Clash With Police in Rome," *The Telegraph*, October 31, 2013 (http://www.telegraph.co.uk/news/worldnews/europe/italy/10418497/Anti- austerity-protesters-clash-with-police-in-Rome.html)

22: BBC, *Students Protest Over Austerity Cuts in Italy*, http://www.bbc.co.uk/news/world- europe-24956693 (November 15, 2013)

23: Joshua Stephens, *Anarchism in Egypt: An Interview From Tahrir Square*, Waging Nonviolence, http://wagingnonviolence.org/2013/07/anarchy-in-egypt-an-interview-from-tahrir- square/ (July 2, 2013)

24: Russia Today, *Thousands Protest in Bahrain Capital, Demand 'torturers be brought to justice,'* http://rt.com/news/bahrain-protests-opposition-repression-194/ (November 23, 2013)

25: Huffington Post, *Bahrain: Hundreds Mourn After Boy Is Killed In Demonstration*, http://www.huffingtonpost.com/2011/11/19/bahrain-hundreds- mourn_n_1102730.html (November 19, 2011)

26: Rannie Amiri, *Bahrain: Days of Rage, Decades of Oppression*, Antiwar, http://original.antiwar.com/rannie-amiri/2011/02/20/bahrain-days-of-rage/ (February 21, 2011)

27: Henry Austin, "Is The Arab Spring Moving South? Violent Anti-government Protests Hit Sudan," *NBC News*, October 1, 2013 (http://worldnews.nbcnews.com/_news/2013/10/01/20769020-is-the-arab-spring-moving-south- violent-anti-government-protests-hit-sudan)

28: BBC, *Sudan Feels The Heat From Fuel Protests*, http://www.bbc.co.uk/news/world-africa- 24938224 (November 14, 2013)

29: Khalid Abdelaziz, Ulf Laessing, "Sudan to Lift Fuel Subsidies Posing 'Great Risk' For Economy-Bashir," *Reuters*, September 22, 2013 (http://www.*Reuters*.com/article/2013/09/22/sudan-economy-idUSL5N0HI0OG20130922)

30: The Economist, *Unrest In China: A Dangerous Year*, http://www.economist.com/node/21543477 (January 28, 2012)

31: Sui-Lee Wee, "China Sends Riot Police to Block New Protests by Flood Victims," *Reuters*, October 16, 2013 (http://www.*Reuters*.com/article/2013/10/16/us-china-protest- idUSBRE99F0BN20131016)

32: Fox News, *Thailand Vows to Keep Troops in Iraq*, http://www.foxnews.com/story/2003/12/28/thailand-vows-to-keep-troops-in- iraq/ (December 28, 2003)

33: Max Fisher, "A Staggering Map of the 54 Countries That Reportedly Participated in the CIA's Rendition Program," *Washington Post*, February 5, 2013 (http://www.washingtonpost.com/blogs/worldviews/wp/2013/02/05/a-staggering-map-of-the-54- countries-that-reportedly-participated-in-the-cias-rendition-program/)

34: Samudcha Hoonsara, Somroutai Sapsomboon, Kittipong Thavevong, "Yingluck Enters 2013 A Survivor," *The Nation*, January 1, 2013 (http://www.nationmultimedia.com/politics/Yingluck- enters-2013-a-survivor-30197064.html)

35: Mark Gollom, Daniel Schwartz, "N.B. Fracking Protests and the Fight for Aboriginal Rights," *CBC News*, October 19, 2013 (http://www.cbc.ca/news/n-b-fracking-protests-and-the- fight-for-aboriginal-rights-1.2126515)

36: Adalah: The Legal Center for Minority Rights in Israel, *Demolition and Eviction of Bedouin Citizens of Israel in the Naqab (Negev) – The Prawer Plan*, http://adalah.org/eng/?mod=articles&ID=1589

37: Russia Today, *'Day of rage': Police, protesters clash in Israel at plans to evict 40,000 Bedouins*, http://rt.com/news/britain-protest-prawer-plan-511/ (November 30, 2013)

38: Fox News, *Indigenous Groups Stage Protests Across Brazil to Press For Demarcation of Their Lands*, http://www.foxnews.com/world/2013/10/01/indigenous-groups-stage-protests- across-brazil-to-press-for-demarcation-their/(October 1, 2013)

39: David Dudenhoefer, "Brazil's Natives Protest Threats to Their Rights From Congress," *Indian Country*, October 8, 2013 (http://indiancountrytodaymedianetwork.com/2013/10/08/brazils-natives-protest-threats-their- rights-congress-151644)

*The Politics of Abandonment: Abandoning Chelsea Manning and Siding with the State and Heteronormativity*

*Published by: QED: A Journal in GLBTQ Worldmaking*

*Published in: Spring 2014*

Chelsea Manning is a hero. She stood up for American values and for the American people when she leaked classified documents to Wikileaks. Due to her courageous actions, we became aware of a number of issues, from unsavory diplomatic backdoor dealings to war crimes committed by the US military. Yet, when the time came to defend her, the American people failed. They were told by a media that has sided time and time again with the government that Manning was a traitor and that she had endangered the security of the nation and other soldiers (something that was proven false by the Pentagon no less), the American people turned their back on her. Yet, the worst betrayal came from the LGBT community. We betrayed Manning, we allowed her to be fed to the wolves. It even went so far that other trans* people such as Christine Howey referred to Manning as a "trans traitor" and stated that it was "disheartening to see the transgender community saddled with another negative image" [1] in the form of Chelsea Manning.

Manning was stigmatized by the LGBT community early last year. In May at the San Francisco Pride Parade, plans were made to have Manning nominated as the grand marshall of the parade, however, after "LGBT military groups from outside of San Francisco began to bombard San Francisco Pride's office with phone calls and emails," [2] the Pride Board removed her from the list and a press release was published in which it was stated that Manning's nomination was a "mistake" and "should never have been allowed to happen."[3]

There is also something deeper at work here, specifically an attitude that seeks to conform. It is a mindset which plays out in one's actions in their daily life. It is an attempt to be blend in with and assimilate to the larger culture. To this end, one may even betray members of their own community and side with the group(s) of the larger culture. In certain communities, it is called respectability politics, in the LGBT community, it is called heteronormativity. It is this heteronormativity that has become a part of the LGBT community and has resulted in the betrayal of Chelsea Manning. It is in this context that Chelsea was betrayed, that the LGBT community sided with the US government, a government that has historically oppressed them into modern times, not just in civilian life, but also in the military.

**The US Government**

While many were infuriated at Manning for leaking classified information and sided with the government in condemning Manning as a traitor, they failed to realize or acknowledge the fact that the US government has a history of oppressing the LGBT community.

LGBT persecution first came about most prominently after World War 2, in the late 1940s. In 1947, the Senate Appropriations subcommittee sent with a list of "admitted homosexuals and suspected perverts" to the State Department and in 1950, "a State Department official testified before that subcommittee that 91 'sex perverts' had been allowed to resign in the previous three years, and that some had subsequently been reemployed by other federal agencies."[4] This resulted in Republicans launching attacks against President Truman for not only employing gay people, but also a full scale inquiry led by Clyde Roark Hory (D-NC) to discover why federal employment of gays was unwanted. The committee found that

The behavior of homosexuals was criminal and immoral; they lacked emotional stability because "indulgence in acts of sex perversion weakens the moral fiber"; they frequently attempted to seduce normal people, especially the young and impressionable; and they had a "tendency to gather other perverts" around them. Probably most importantly, homosexuals were seen as security risks. On the one hand, their emotional instability and moral weakness made them "vulnerable to interrogation by a skilled questioner and they seldom refuse to talk about themselves." On the other hand, "the pervert is easy prey to the blackmailer." (emphasis added) [5]

Thus, from the very start, gays were seen as a threat to the United States and very likely to be traitors to their country due solely to their sexuality. This fear of gays came from the fear that they could "[hide] their true natures, allowing them to 'infiltrate' government in a way other out-groups could not," yet some took this fear to the extreme with one right-wing columnist "[charging] that 'an all-powerful, super-secret inner circle of highly educated, socially highly placed sexual misfits in the State Department" controlled foreign policy."[6]

The effects of this manner of thinking were quite detrimental to the country as the government began to go on a massive witch hunt for gays, even going so far as to use entrapment in the case of William Dale Jennings.[7] The FBI even went to so far as to create a Sexual Deviates Program. The program was created by J. Edgar Hoover to "purge any suspected homosexual from the federal payroll" as well as "sex deviates employed either by institutions of higher learning or law-enforcement agencies."[8] It was amid this persecution and increased hostility that gays began to organize and fight back against a government that demonized them.

*The Mattachine Society*

During this turbulent and worrisome time for the gay community, some believed that it was time to organize and promote gay rights. This was during the time of the Lavender Scare, which "saw increased gay bar raids, homosexuals ferreted out of the military, gays being purged from government jobs, and the enactment of state and municipal sexual psychopath laws, all of which made living an openly gay life seemingly impossible."[9] In Los Angeles in 1950, former Communist Party members Harry Hay, Chuck Rowland, and Bob Hull created the Mattachine Society. The Society was "named for an obscure medieval French group that satirized the French aristocracy from behind the safety of face masks,"[10] the trio believed that the name fit quite well, given the situation of the gay community which had to remain in the shadows of American society.

The FBI quickly learned of the Society and began to investigate it to discern whether or not it was Communist-led or had been infiltrated by Communists, yet they were unable to find anything despite the fact that the Society had been founded by three former Communists. The Society's first victory came in the case of the aforementioned William Dale Jennings who had been caught in a case of homosexual entrapment, but the charges were dismissed in court when the jury deadlocked over the issue of acquittal. The court case resulted in an increase in membership, but also the group became the subject of an intense FBI investigation.

Los Angeles Mirror reporter Paul Coates, "obtained copies of Mattachine's lobbying questionnaires [and] published an article questioning the legitimacy of the group."[11] He even raised the specter that Mattachine was a possibly dangerous group and speculated that a "well- trained subversive could move in and forge that power into a dangerous political weapon."[12] Coates fed on the popular narrative that gays were susceptible to blackmail. This actually played into the FBI investigation of the Society as the FBI interviewed an informant from the group who gave them additional information to Coates' article.

While all of this was going on in Los Angeles, the fight to protect gay federal employees was occurring in Washington D.C. Frank Kamney, an astronomer with a doctorate from Harvard, lost a three-year legal battle to keep his job with the US Army Mapping Service. He and Bruce Scott, a former federal employee who has been forced to resign in 1956 due to his homosexuality, founded the Mattachine Society of Washington D.C. and launched efforts to discuss with government officials the employment ban on gays.

The Society of DC argued that "homosexuals were a minority group and that federal employment policies toward gays were equivalent to racial discrimination," [13] with Kameny testifying before a congressional committee in August 1963 and the group protesting the White House on numerous occasions in the summer of 1965. The Society finally got a meeting with a Civil Service Commission committee in the fall of 1965 in which "Commission Chairman John W Macy, Jr., wrote to the Mattachine Society completely [rejected] their contention that the exclusion of homosexuals constituted discrimination against an oppressed minority and [claimed] that there was no such thing as a homosexual" and that "the attempt to define people with homosexual inclinations as a minority group was an attempt to excuse them from taking responsibility for their immoral actions."[14]

Thus, we see a history of where the US government has, in civilian life, oppressed, ridiculed, demonized and overall shown a complete and utter disdain for gays. From cases of entrapment and spying, to outright being labeled as traitors to their country, the anti-gay tendencies of the US government were quite strong. However, the problems didn't stop there. They went into the realm of the military and culminated in the well-known Don't Ask, Don't Tell (DADT) policy. While the policy is infamous, the effects on LGBT service members are not well known.

**The US Military**

The DADT policy had a horrendous effect on LGB service members. "For instance, over 19,000 service members (active-duty enlisted or officer members of the military service, including the National Guard and Reserve) experienced sexual-orientation- based discharges from 1980 to 1993 and 13,000 more were discharged from 1993 to 2009 following initiation of 'Don't Ask, Don't Tell.'"[15] The military is a space in which heterosexuality and masculinity are the norm and are strictly enforced. If one does not adhere to those standards, then one is victimized and intimidated. Assaults of all types were used as enforcement mechanisms in the military. In a 2004 survey of anonymous LGB service members revealed that "Experiences of discrimination and victimization in the military as related to sexual orientation were reported by almost half of respondents, with 47.2% indicating at least one experience of verbal, physical, or sexual assault."[16] More recently, in 2010, the Department of Defense did a study on sexual orientation and US military personnel policy and found that

> **The majority of LGB respondents (91%) indicated that DADT puts gay service members at risk for blackmail or manipulation, as well as negatively affects their personal (86%) and unit (76%) relationships.** Seventy-two percent indicated experiencing stress and anxiety in their daily lives because of DADT. Twenty-nine percent indicated having been teased or mocked and 7% indicated previous threats or injuries by other individuals in the military because of their own LGB sexual orientation. (emphasis added) [17]

While some may argue that DADT is over, it actually isn't as the policy does not include transgendered individuals such as Chelsea Manning. In fact, "the U.S. military disqualifies transgender troops for health reasons" and "for now, the Pentagon has no plans to cross that line."[18] The military's policy in regards to trans* people are quite wretched. According to Outserve-SLDN, an organization for LGBT military members, trans* people are rejected not just if they have had any type of genital surgery, but even if they only identify as transgender as "the military considers this to be a mental health condition." In regards to active duty military members, the military "is unlikely to provide the medical support necessary for transitioning service members" and if one seeks outside help, "they are at risk because they have a duty to report such treatment to the military. Failure to abide by these regulations could result in criminal prosecution by the military."[19] Many Americans viewed the fall of DADT as a victory and rightfully so, however, there is a serious problem for trans* people that is largely being ignored by mainstream LGBT groups

**Heteronormativity**

When Manning's case gained mainstream attention, many groups that should have went to bat for her and supported her, instead remained mute and allowed the vilification of Manning to continue unabated and some, such as the aforementioned San Francisco Pride Parade Board, even went so far as to participate in it themselves. Such activity on the part of the LGBT community constitutes not just a betrayal of Manning, but of ourselves as well.

Two major LGBT rights groups, the Human Rights Campaign and GLAAD, stayed silent about Manning for the entire fiasco of her trial and never once came out in support of her. On the day of her sentencing, HRC released a statement in which they stated that Manning's transition deserved to be respected and that she deserved to be protected from violence, yet it slighted her when the message read:

What should not be lost is that there are transgender service members and veterans who serve and have served this nation with honor, distinction and great sacrifice. We must not forget or dishonor those individuals. Pvt. Manning's experience is not a proxy for any other transgender man or woman who wears the uniform of the United States. [20]

This is essentially a message which seeks to separate Manning from the rest of the military community. It turns Manning into a black sheep of the trans* military community, implies that she did not serve her country honorably and only continues the campaign to isolate and ostracize her.

However, her abandonment should not come as a surprise to anyone, especially when one factors in who groups such as HRC and GLAAD are connected to. It was reported in July 2014 that HRC had "the financial backing of major military industrial corporations, including Lockheed Martin, which is sponsoring the HRC's upcoming national gala in Washington DC and Booz Allen Hamilton, a corporate partner for the national event, as well as Northrop Grumman a sponsor of their Los Angeles gala."[21] On GLAAD's website, they list the AT&T Foundation as one of their sponsors. [22] AT&T is paid by the NSA to provide the government agency with the communications of their customers.[23] We see that the one of the main reasons that neither of these major groups made even the slightest defense of Manning was due to the fact that they were directly connected to the military complex and if a defense of Manning had been mounted; their funding may very well have dried up rather quickly.

There is also another reason as to why a defense of Manning did not occur and that is because of her background. Manning didn't "conform to these upwardly mobile, white, polished, virile male stereotypes" of LGBT people that both of these groups attempted to portray. Rather, her "slight frame, lower-class background, questioning of [her] gender identity, inability to hold down a typical job, general dorkiness and dysfunctional family life"[24] created a situation in which she did not fit the image that either GLAAD or HRC wanted to promote.

At its heart, what this speaks to is two problems within the LGBT community: 1) that there is a split between the lesbian and gay branches of the community and everyone else and that 2) there is only one type of person that mainstream LGBT groups want to promote.

The split between the lesbian and gay branches with everyone else in the LGBT community is quite problematic as the political effects for members of the LGBT community are quite real, specifically with the separation of the GL portion, which came with ignoring other members of the community. Essentially, gays and lesbians succeeded by distancing themselves from other LGBT people.

Over time, the "GL" portion of the platform became increasingly acceptable to the population at large, both through increased education and desensitization of the public and by disavowing the more unacceptable elements of the movement. At the same time, this political success fueled a separatist culture, which bisexuals and transgenders threatened to dilute and homogenize.[25]

By fighting solely for their own rights, lesbians and gays were able to attain mainstream acceptance by the larger American culture, but at the expense of other members of the community, which includes bisexuals and trans* and queer people.

Yet, what must also be examined is that lesbians and gays were able to go gain acceptance due to aligning their interests with the view of the overall American culture. Pushing for marriage equality doesn't upset the apple cart for most people. Many LGBT rights groups want to promote a certain image of the community as was described above. This selective portrayal can be seen on a regular basis with people being interviewed about LGBT issues largely being white, middle and upper class, cisgendered men.

However, this all comes at a cost. The cost of focusing on only one type of person means that the experiences of people are lost and ignored. The experience of the black gay man, the poor white bisexual, the transgendered high school student, and countless other stories are forgotten and laid to the wayside.

At the end of the day, by betraying Manning, the LGBT community has betrayed itself as Manning is "actually what many, if not most, LGBT people have been at one point or another – an outsider, a loner, a person who does not fit in or conform."[26] All LGBT people were like that at some point in their lives or are currently in that situation. The betrayal must end and Chelsea Manning's story must be heard.


**Endnotes**

1: Christine Howey, "First Person: 'Trans Traitor' Manning Adds to Transgender Perception Problem," *NBC News*, August 23, 2013 (http://usnews.nbcnews.com/_news/2013/08/23/20153443-first-person-trans-traitor-manning- adds-to-transgender-perception-problem?lite)

2: Kevin Gosztola, *Former San Francisco Pride Grand Marshal Who Nominated Bradley Manning Details Board's Capitulation*, Firedoglake http://dissenter.firedoglake.com/2013/04/29/former-san-francisco-pride-grand-marshal-who- nominated-bradley-manning-discusses-boards-capitulation/ (April 29, 2013)

3: Victoria A. Brownworth, "Bradley Manning and Queer Collaboration," *Advocate*, May 1, 2013 (http://www.advocate.com/commentary/2013/05/01/op-ed-bradley-manning-and-queer- collaboration)

4: Gregory B. Lewis, "Lifting the Ban on Gays in the Civil Service: Federal Policy toward Gay and Lesbian Employees since the Cold War," *Public Administration Review* 57:5 (1997), pg 388

5: Ibid

6: Ibid, pg 389

7: Dudely Clendinen, "William Dale Jennings, 82, Writer and Gay Rights Pioneer," *New York Times*, May 22, 2000 (http://www.nytimes.com/2000/05/22/us/william-dale-jennings-82-writer- and-gay-rights-pioneer.html)

8: Athan Theoharis, "Civil Liberties: The Cost of Fighting Terrorism," *Los Angeles Times*, April 30, 1995 (http://articles.latimes.com/1995-04-30/opinion/op-60524_1_fbi-officials)

9: Douglas M. Charles, "From Subversion to Obscenity: The FBI's Investigations of the Early Homophile Movement in the United States, 1953-1958," *Journal of Sexuality* 19:2 (2010), pg 263

10: Charles, pg 264

11: Charles, pg 267

12: Charles, pg 268

13: Lewis, pg 390

14: Ibid

15: Derek J. Burks, "Lesbian, Gay, and Bisexual Victimization in the Military: An Unintended Consequence of 'Don't Ask, Don't Tell?" *American Psychological Association* 66:7 (2011), pg 604

16: Burks, pg 607

17: Ibid

18: Tom Vanden Brook, "Transgender Troops Serve In Silence," *USA Today*, July 23, 2013 (http://www.usatoday.com/story/news/politics/2013/07/23/transsexuals-military-struggle-acceptance/2513153/)

19: Outserve-SLDN, *Transgender People In The Military Service*, http://www.sldn.org/pages/transgender-people-and-military-service

20: Jeff Krehely, *Pvt. Chelsea E. Manning Comes Out, Deserves Respectful Treatment by Media and Officials*, Human Rights Campaign, http://www.hrc.org/blog/entry/pvt.-chelsea-e.-manning- comes-out-deserves-respectful-treatment-by-media-an (August 22, 2013)

21: Christopher Carbone, "Have Gay Rights Groups Abandoned Bradley Manning?," *The Guardian*, July 30, 2013 (http://www.theguardian.com/commentisfree/2013/jul/30/bradley- manning-gay-rights-groups-support)

22: GLAAD, *Support GLAAD: Foundations and Corporate Grants*, http://www.glaad.org/support/grants

23: Robert Lenzner, "AT&T, Verizon, Sprint Are Paid Cash By NSA For Your Private Communications," *Forbes*, September 23, 2013 (http://www.forbes.com/sites/robertlenzner/2013/09/23/attverizonsprint-are-paid-cash-by-nsa- for-your-private-communications/)

24: *The Guardian*, July 30, 2013

25: Jillian T. Weiss, "GL vs. BT: The Archaeology of Biphobia and Transphobia Within the U.S. Gay and Lesbian Community," *Journal of Bisexuality* 3:3 (2004), pg 40

26: *The Guardian*, July 30, 2013

College students and graduates around the nation are buried in debt and trying to succeed in an extremely difficult and competitive economic environment. Many people are graduating only to find out that they are unable to get the jobs they want, whether it be due to the small amount of available jobs or (more usually) the problem of 'experience,' and thus are reduced to having to work menial jobs while paying back exorbitant loans.

So far very little legislation has been passed to aid students in paying back their loans and many are blaming politicians for this. However, the situation goes deeper and in part lies at the feet of a little known institution called the American Bankers Association.

The American Bankers Association, according to their website, is "the voice of the nation's $14 trillion banking industry, which is composed of small, regional and large banks that together employ more than 2 million people, safeguard $11 trillion in deposits and extend nearly $8 trillion in loans" and believes that "Laws and regulations should be tailored to correspond to a bank's charter, business model, geography and risk profile." [1]

While it is quite obvious that the ABA is an organization that works in the interest of the bankers, they have an interesting history with regards to student loans and how they have actively fought against the interest of students.

The ABA's war against students started in the mid-1960s with the rise of the Johnson administration. Johnson ordered the formation of a task force to examine the role of the federal government in higher education, specifically student aid, to be headed by John W. Gardener. In its report, the task forced noted that

 Of the students who did not attend college and who had families who could contribute only $300 or less to their education, about 75 percent of the men and 55 percent of the women indicated that they would have attended college if they had had more money available. [2]

Johnson saw this as a loss of human capital and wanted to remedy this, ultimately signing the Higher Education Opportunity Act of 1965 into law. The law included many suggestions from the Gardner taskforce, such as that the government should aid students monetarily via grants and loans, as well as creating special programs for college-aspiring low-income students.

However, this was a major problem for the ABA. The organization was worried about government encroachment on their business, specifically loans and argued that "the federal government could not replicate the working relationships that locally-owned financial institutions had with state and private non-profit guarantee programs" and "the federal government would end up taking over the industry because there would be little incentive for the state and private non-profit agencies to establish their own programs." [3] In order to placate the bankers, the Johnson administration told them that the government would be the ultimate loan guarantor if no one else was available.

Yet, in the present-day, the ABA is without a doubt waging a quiet war on students by actively combating virtually any legislation that would ease their debt burden. With regards to being able to get rid of student loans in bankruptcy, the ABA stated in 2012 that, if allowed to go into effect, it "would tempt students to rack up big debt that they won't repay [and that] 'The bankruptcy system would be opened to abuse.'" [4] This is rather ironic, accusing that students will engage in irresponsible lending, even though the banks themselves engaged in massive amounts of the exact same activity by giving mortgage loans to people they knew couldn't repay the amount.

The assumption that students would just borrow money and they declare bankruptcy is rather ridiculous as filing bankruptcy has severe negative effects such as "negatively affect your credit and future ability to use money" and can "prevent you from obtaining new lines of credit and may even cause problems when you apply for jobs." [5] Yet, due to the bankers and other groups fighting against being able to get rid of student loans in bankruptcy, the only other option is default, which works quite well for the banks. When a person defaults on their student loans, a number of effects:

**1. Your entire loan balance will be due in full, immediately.**

**2. Collection fees can be added to your outstanding balance.**

**3. Up to 15% of your paychecks can be taken.**

4. Your Social Security, disability income, and state and federal tax refunds can be seized.

5. You will lose eligibility for federal aid, including Pell grants.

6. You will lose deferment or forbearance options.

7. Outstanding fees and unpaid interest can be capitalized (added) onto your principal

balance. [6](emphasis added)

While numbers 1, 2, 3, 4, and 7 are horrible for the borrower, they work quite well for the banks as it allows them to get their money back no matter the cost to you in the immediate aftermath or the future. So your entire economic future has pretty much been destroyed? Well, that's just the cost of doing business.

The ABA has recently fought against efforts to not have the interest rate on student loans double from 3.4% to 6.8%. The bill in question was Senate Bill 2343, also known as the "Stop The Student Loan Interest Rate Hike of 2012."

Democrats wanted to finance the bill by closing a tax loophole in which "wealthy individuals and large corporations [would] often file using 'subchapter S' companies to dodge paying employment taxes." [7] The ABA and other business groups such as the US Chamber of Commerce financing of the bill on the grounds that it "would make tax collection 'less enforceable than current law and will do little to increase compliance.'" [8] Republicans with some Democratic support effectively shut down the bill and thus student loan rates have now doubled.

While many have accused the ABA of having a major sway with Republicans, a report from the organization Campaign For America's future entitled Moneychangers In The Senate noted that "six Democratic senators—Blanche Lincoln, D-Ark.; Mark Warner, D-Va.; Tom Carper, D- Del.; Ben Nelson, D-Neb.; Bill Nelson, D-Fla., and Jim Webb, D-Va.—sent a letter to Senate Majority Leader Harry Reid to make him 'aware of our concern' about reform efforts [to aid students] and urging consideration of 'potential alternative legislative proposals.'" [9] Essentially Democrats who had been bought and paid for by lending companies were urging that Harry Reid abandon legislation that could aid students and instead look for supposed alternatives which would not harm the banks. Yet, what is interesting is that student loan companies all have close ties to each of these senators, such as Blanche Lincoln's former chief of staff working as a lobbyist for the student loan industry and Ben Nelson's former legislative director being a lobbyist for Nelnet, a major student lender.

It must be noted that this campaign against student loan reform has massive amounts of money on the line. From that previously cited report, it was stated that in 2009, Nelnet posted profits of $139 million and that in "In May 2008, the student lenders were bailed out by the Ensuring Continued Access to Student Loans Act (ECASLA), which gave the banks further federal subsidies. The bill allowed lenders like Sallie Mae to sell loans back to the Department o Education through a number of loan-purchase programs." This allows lenders to make even more money. The Congressional Budget Office estimated that the government would save over $68 billion over ten years if they switched over to direct lending, however, now that $68 billion will "subsidize private lenders like Sallie Mae to pay their executives exorbitant salaries and bonuses," such as Sallie Mae chairman Albert Lord who raked in over $225 million during his tenure at Sallie Mae which ended in 2013.

The situation does not end there, however. The Senate has proposed the "Protecting Aid for Students Act for 2014" and its House counterpart is entitled the "Curbing Abusive Marketing Practices with University Student Debit Cards Act," or the CAMPUS Debit Cards Act. Each of these bills is meant to "protect students from unfair banking practices involving campus- sponsored financial products, including debit cards." More specifically, the bills would "remove conflicts of interest and end kickbacks between financial institutions and schools, give students control of their financial aid and banking products, and provide transparency over campus- sponsored financial product." [10]

Yet, this is a problem for the Ken Clayton, Chief Counsel of the ABA. He stated that this legislation "would limit financial choices for students and parents, and raise costs for everybody" and that "Attempts to vilify financial institutions and require free services will limit consumer choice, increase costs for students and universities, and stifle innovation that has helped modernize higher education financing." Apparently eliminating conflicts of interests and kickbacks between colleges and banks as well as giving students control of their finances, is a problem.

While we cannot get rid of the American Bankers Association as an institution, we can actively fight against them by organizing ourselves and demanding that we be treated as human beings, not just an investment. Politicians and colleges will not have our backs, we must do this on our own, we must fight ourselves.


## Endnotes


1: American Bankers Association, *About the American Bankers Association*, http://www.aba.com/About/pages/default.aspx

2: TG Research and Analytical Services, *Opening the Doors to Higher Education: Perspectives on the Higher Education Act 40 Years Later*, http://www.tgslc.org/pdf/hea_history.pdf (November 2005)

3: Ibid

4: Josh Mitchell, "Trying to Shed Student Debt," *Wall Street Journal*, May 3, 2012 (http://www.wsj.com/news/articles/SB10001424052702303978104577364120264435092?mod= WSJ_WSJ_US_News_5&mg=reno64- wsj&url=http%3A%2F%2Fonline.wsj.com%2Farticle%2FSB10001424052702303978104577736 4120264435092.html%3Fmod%3DWSJ_WSJ_US_News_5)

5: Debt.org, *Bankruptcy*, https://www.debt.org/bankruptcy/

6: American Student Assistance, *Consequences of Default-What Happens When You Default On Your Student Loans*, https://web.archive.org/web/20120121024903/http://www.asa.org/in-default/consequences/default.aspx

7: Lee Fang, *Why Are Student Loan Interests Set To Double? Thank These Lobbyists Who Helped Kill The Bill Yesterday*, Republic Report, http://www.republicreport.org/2012/student- loan-interest-rates/ (May 9, 2012)

8: Andrew Joseph, *Business Groups Challenging Student Loan Pay-For*, National Journal, https://web.archive.org/web/20141111020200/http://www.nationaljournal.com/blogs/influenceall ey/2012/05/business-groups-challenging-student-loan-pay-for-03

9: Campaign for The Future, *Money-Changers In The Senate*, https://ourfuture.org/report/money- changers-senate

10: Pymnts.com, *Back To School: Lawmakers Again Targeting 'Abusive' Campus Banking Practices*, http://www.pymnts.com/in-depth/2014/back-to-school-lawmakers-again-targeting- abusive-campus-banking-practices/#.VAC7kGONDaR (June 2, 2014)

Wall Street wrecked the economy in 2007 due to its deals in shady mortgage securities that put the entire global economy on the brink. But do you think the big banks learned their lesson and decided to stop deceiving people with their overly complex financial instruments? The answer is, of course, a resounding No. Not only have the bankers received no human punishment – only fines – for destroying the economy, but they're now involving themselves in the rental arena and may create another financial crisis in the process.

The current crisis began with the Federal Housing Finance Agency's Real-Estate Owned (REO) initiative program in late February 2012. The purpose of the program was to allow "qualified investors to purchase pools of foreclosed properties with the requirement to rent the purchased properties for a specified number of years." The premise of the REO initiative was to "provide relief for local housing markets that continue to be depressed by the volume of foreclosed properties, and provide additional rental options to certain markets." [1]

The initial phase involved allowing companies to purchase large amounts of foreclosed properties from Fannie Mae and Freddie Mac – and in a couple of years the properties could be converted into rental housing. However, an August 2011 information request about the upcoming program had already stated that its more specific goal was to "solicit ideas from market participants that would maximize the economic value that may arise from pooling the single- family REO properties in specified geographic areas." [2]

Granted, this makes sense in that you need information from corporations that can deal in the REO business on a large scale. But it also allows for these same corporations to have influence over what occurs – and to potentially steer the program in a direction that is to their benefit.

## A Swindle Is Born

Once the program opened, companies began snapping up properties quickly, then securitizing them in a process known as REO-to-rental securitization. The first company to do this was Blackstone, which "[packaged] rental income from single-family homes it owns into a pass-through security, similar to a mortgaged-backed security." [3] While some economists argued that this procedure could aid areas hit hardest in the housing crash, others worried that "these new investors could face big challenges managing large portfolios of dispersed rental houses." [4]

Investor companies like Blackstone raced to get into the new business, which had the potential to net returns much higher than investing in Treasury securities or stock dividends. According to Forbes, "while a 10-year Treasury note yields little more than 2%, economists at Goldman Sachs calculate that rental property investments yield more than 6% on average, nationwide." [5]

Even from its earliest beginnings, alarms about the REO initiative were being raised. While Moody's allegedly gave such securitizations a triple-A rating, Fitch Ratings saw a major problem in the "limited performance data for the sector and individual property management firms." [6] Translation: People didn't really know what they were getting into with a new market and a situation actually considered risky. Earlier in 2014, Standard & Poor's went so far as to warn that rental security bonds didn't deserve triple-A status due to their "operational infancy," openly disagreeing with the optimistic forecast touted by Moody's, Krolls, Morningstar and other ratings agencies. [7]

Now, others are coming on board with a similar critique, saying that rent securitization could lead to serious consequences. Daniel Indiviglio, a columnist at *Reuters*, argues that the lack of data on securitization presents a number of challenges, namely that the securities "may require an entirely new infrastructure for appraising how rentable a home is and at what price." [8]

According to Indiviglio, "The faults that the crisis exposed in securitization reinforce how crucial a good crop of historical information is on rental trends," and without any long-term data, investors and rating agencies alike will be forced "to make assumptions on new stats like vacancy rates, tenant turnover costs and property management fees." Additionally, potential bond purchasers will want serious compensation for ponying up the money to buy these vacant houses; there's no assurance that a property is stable unless tenants have lived in it for quite some time or have signed a medium or long-term lease – something quite rare for renters just moving in.

"With foreclosures focused in a few key regions and resulting rentals appealing to specific segments of the population, concentration risk is likely to be magnified," he concluded, raising the serious possibility that rental securitizations may cost more than they are actually worth.

Not only that, but adding to the financial risk for investors is the possibility that rental bonds could possibly be increasing rents. In January 2014, Rep. Mark Takano (D-Calif.) sent a letter to House Financial Services Committee Chairman Jeb Hensarling and Rep. Maxine Waters (D-Calif.) "asking for an investigation into rental-backed securities deals." Rep. Takano saw that rental prices were increasing and that "a surplus of investors in rentals – along with new rental- backed securities deals – could have the effect of artificially raising rental prices, making housing even more costly in parts of California." [9]

To back up his case, Takano cited a 2013 Federal Reserve report stating that in regard to companies buying up houses and renting them out, without proper oversight "investor activity may pose risks to local housing markets if investors have difficulties managing such large stocks of rental properties or fail to adequately maintain their homes." [10]

"Such behavior could lower the quality of the neighborhoods in which investors own rental properties," the report concluded.

**Government Helps Re-Create A Crisis**

One might assume that Congress would weigh the risks and costs and pass – or at least consider – laws to oversee rent securitization before it becomes the going trend. Senate and Congress couldn't just sit idly by and let a similar crisis like the one last decade evolve under the regulatory radar, right? Think again. To date, no legislation whatsoever overseeing rent securitization has occurred. Since Rep. Takano called for Congressional hearings in January, little has happened to address the issue. [11]

But if you think it's a bad situation in Congress, think of the people who inhabit the houses owned by these under-examined corporations. Mindy Culpepper lived on the outskirts of Atlanta in a home inundated with the stench of raw sewage. She had her husband paid $1,225 a month to live in the three-bedroom house even as their landlord, Colony American Homes, ignored their complaints. The Culpeppers have had to live with the stench from the first day they moved in and to date; they see zero sign of any response by Colony to address the problem. [12]

On the subject of houses in Atlanta, on April 15, the organization Occupy Our Homes Atlanta released a report entitled Blackstone: Atlanta's Newest Landlord, which revealed that: (1) Tenants wishing to stay in their homes can face automatic rent increases as much as 20% annually; (2) Survey participants living in homes owned by Invitation Homes pay nearly $300 more in rent than the Metro Atlanta median; (3) 45% of survey participants pay more than 30% of their income on rent, by definition making the rent unaffordable; (4) Tenants face high fees, including a $200 late fee for rental payments; and (5) 78% of the surveyed tenants do not have consistent or reliable access to the landlord or property manager. [13]

Furthermore, a July 2014 report by the same organization noted that while Invitation Homes "claims to have spent $25,000 per home to bring them up to standards, 46 percent of respondents reported plumbing problems, 39 percent found roaches or other insects, and around one in five had issues with air conditioning or mold or leaky roofs." [14] It's safe to say – and at this point should come as no surprise to anyone – that corporations like Invitation Homes only care about making money, not about taking care of tenants.

Conditions like these have a major impact, of course, on working people who already spend more than half their income on rent [15] – but with rent securitization, the economic problems begin even before those people have entered the door. The organization Homes For All released a report focusing on Los Angeles rent securitization programs and found that "a major barrier to rental accessibility, especially for low-income renters, is the required deposit amount." [16]

"In Los Angeles, the average deposit amount equated to 157 percent of respondents' monthly rent amount. The highest deposit required as a percentage of monthly rent was 281 percent, and the lowest was 53 percent," the report stated. With regards to amounts spent on rent, the report found that "67 percent of [the] respondents had unaffordable housing, and 47 percent were severely cost-burdened." [17]

There are other problems as well. In New York City, where private equity firms are buying up apartment buildings that are rent-controlled, companies are pushing long-term residents out of their apartments in order to redo the dwellings and sell them at market prices. These firms are often engaging in illegal tactics such as "mailing fake eviction notices, cutting off the heat or water, and allowing vermin infestations to take hold." [18]

Let's remember that serious money is on the table for these corporations. In 2005, Rockpoint Group "bought a complex of apartment buildings in Harlem known as the Riverton Houses. To justify the whopping $225 million mortgage, the company projected that it would be able to more than triple the rental income from $5.2 million to $23.6 million by forcing out half of the rent-regulated tenants within five years," added the report.

While it has yet to breach the mainstream radar, rent securitization is already a major problem – not only because it mirrors the mortgage crisis that just occurred, but also because of the human impact it is already having. People already living in difficult conditions in rent- controlled apartments are being forced out, and those purchasing these corporate-owned apartments are often living in wretched conditions that rarely get serviced whatsoever. Americans need to say no now to this new scheme, lest we allow the past mortgage crisis to become a current rent fiasco.


**Endnotes**

1: Federal Housing Finance Agency, *Real Estate Owned (REO),* http://www.fhfa.gov/PolicyProgramsResearch/Policy/Pages/Real-Estate-Owned- %28REO%29.aspx

2: Federal Housing Finance Agency, *Request for Information: Enterprise/FHA REO Asset Disposition,* http://www.fhfa.gov/PolicyProgramsResearch/Policy/Documents/RFIFinal081011.pdf (August 10, 2011)

3: Shah Gilali, "Trick or Treat? First-Ever REO to Rental Securitization Deal Looks Spooky," *Forbes,* October 30, 2013 (http://www.forbes.com/sites/shahgilani/2013/10/30/trick-or-treat- first-ever-reo-to-rental-securitization-deal-looks-spooky/)

4: Motoko Rich, "Investors Are Looking to Buy Homes By The Thousands," *New York Times,* April 2, 2012 (http://www.nytimes.com/2012/04/03/business/investors-are-looking-to-buy- homes-by-the-thousands.html?pagewanted=all&_r=1)

5: Morgan Brennan, "Investors Flock To Housing, Looking To Buy Thousands Of Homes In Bulk," *Forbes,* April 3, 2012 (http://www.forbes.com/sites/morganbrennan/2012/04/03/investors-flock-to-housing-aspiring-to- own-thousands-of-homes/)

6: MarketWatch, *Are Rental-Backed Securities The Next Big Thing?* http://www.marketwatch.com/story/are-rental-backed-securities-the-next-big-thing-kkr-bx-ozm- two-2012-08-08 (August 8, 2012)

7: Jacob Gaffney, "S&P: 3 reasons REO-to-rental bonds are not triple-A," *Housingwire,* February 28, 2014 (http://www.housingwire.com/articles/29150-sp-3-reasons-reo-to-rental- bonds-are-not-triple-a)

8: Daniel Indiviglio, "Securitizing rent has more problems than promise," *Reuters*, July 26, 2012 (http://blogs.reuters.com/breakingviews/2012/07/26/securitizing-rent-has-more-problems-than- promise/)

9: Kerri Ann Panchuk, "Are rental bonds driving up rent?" *Housingwire*, January 23, 2014 (http://www.housingwire.com/articles/28708-are-rental-bonds-driving-up-the-rent)

10: Raven Molloy, Rebecca Zarutskie, *Business Investor Activity in Single-Family-Housing Market*, Federal Reserve, http://www.federalreserve.gov/econresdata/notes/feds- notes/2013/business-investor-activity-in-the-single-family-housing-market-20131205.html (December 5, 2013)

11: Nat Rudrakanchana, "Blackstone's Rental-Backed Bonds: Rep. Takano Pushes Oversight," *International Business Times*, January 27, 2014 (http://www.ibtimes.com/blackstones-bx-rental- backed-bonds-rep-takano-pushes-oversight-qa-1548628)

12: Jillian Berman, Ben Hallman, "Here's What Happens When Wall Street Builds A Rental Empire," *Huffington Post*, October 25, 2013 (http://www.huffingtonpost.com/2013/10/25/wall- street-landlords_n_4151345.html)

13: Occupy Our Homes ATL, *Blackstone: Atlanta's Newest Landlord*, https://web.archive.org/web/20140430151537/http://occupyourhomesatl.org/blackstone-atlantas- newest-landlord/ (April 15, 2014)

14: David Dayen, "Slumlord Millionaires," *New Republic*, July 24, 2014 (http://www.newrepublic.com/article/118838/wall-street-slumlords-how-banks-started-buying- rental-units)

15: Constantine Von Hoffman, "More working-class families spend half of income on rent," *CBS Moneywatch*, May 8, 2013 (http://www.cbsnews.com/news/more-working-class-families- spend-half-of-income-on-rent/)

16: Homes For All, *Renting From Wall Street: Blackstone's Invitation Homes in Los Angeles and Riverside*, http://homesforall.org/wp-content/uploads/2014/07/LA-Riverside-Blackstone-   Report-071514.pdf   (July 2014)

17: Ibid

18: Laura Gottesdiener, "How Wall Street Screwed Over Tenants In New York City," *Mother Jones*, April 8, 2014 (http://www.motherjones.com/politics/2014/04/predatory-equity-wall- street-screwed-over-renters-new-york-city)

The debtors' prison is an old, decrepit institution that many thought was abolished in the 19th century, something little more than a relic of the past. This is a problematic view for two reasons. One, debtors' prisons are rarely explored in the classroom or the larger society. And two, these prisons are making a serious comeback in the United States, which is deeply problematic for the poor and working class.

## The History of Debtors' Prisons

The traditional view of debtors' prisons in the U.S. is one of wretched incarceration where debtors were hung out to dry. While this is true, there is also more to the story.

In early colonial America, English law had an influence on colonial law – and laws regarding debt. In 16$^{th}$ century England, creditors had the legal power via the Law of Merchant to regain their money from insolvent debtors. They had this same power in Pennsylvania where, in 1682, the law stated that anyone who was in debt and had been arrested would be kept in prison, or "the debtor [could] satisfy the debt by servitude as the county court shall order, if the creditor desires." [1] While debt servitude was problematic, it provided a way for a debtor to obtain eventual release.

The situation was worse in Massachusetts, which ruled in 1638 that "delinquent taxpayers be jailed, but provided that the Council or any court within Massachusetts could free the prisoner if it found him incapable of paying his taxes." However, as early as the next year, private debtors were being imprisoned as well, and in 1641 the courts ruled that "anyone who failed to pay a private debt could be kept in jail at his own expense until the debt was paid." [2] Laws like these resulted in people dying in prisons when they were unable to pay off their debts.

Debtors were forced to suffer this kind of fate until the end of the 17$^{th}$ century when there was some slight reform. On Valentine's Day, 1729, Pennsylvania officially created debt servitude where debtors had to serve their creditors and, even after being released from prison, "the debt still remained and could be enforced against after-acquired property." [3]

In Massachusetts, much more serious reform came with the Act for the Relief and Release of Poor Prisoners for Debt, which allowed debtors after having been in prison for one month to take an oath swearing that "[they] was unable to pay [their] debts and that [they] had not hidden or transferred title to any property in order to defraud [their] creditors, could apply to be released from jail." [4]

Unfortunately, due to courts rarely adjourning in some counties, debtors often spent months in prison; creditors could keep a debtor in prison for another three months even after they had been ordered to be released by paying the debtors jail fees, and the creditors could also "have a new execution sworn out, under which the debtor could be returned to prison and the whole process started all over again." [5]

Eventually, federal debtors' prisons were abolished in 1833, leaving the power to implement debtors' prisons in the hands of the states, many of which followed Washington's lead. Now, those state debtors' prisons are making a comeback and, just like in the past, are having a disproportionate impact on the poor and working-class.

## The Shackles Return

More and more people around the country are getting sent to debtors' prisons, but exactly how does it happen? According to National Public Radio, companies that people owe money usually sell off the debt to a collection agency, which in turn "files a lawsuit against the debtor requiring a court appearance. A notice to appear in court is supposed to be given to the debtor. If they fail to show up, a warrant is issued for their arrest." [6]

In some cases, judges "don't even know debtors' rights, which could result in the debtor being intimidated into a pay agreement," [7] making an already bad situation worse. News coverage about the rise of debtors' prisons has been picking up steam, especially in regards to judges imprisoning people for their debts.

In 2000, The *New York Times* reported that a small town judge in Arizona was accused in a lawsuit of having "turned the local jail into a debtors' prison, repeatedly jailing poor laborers who were unable to settle debts with local property owners." [8] In 2009, CBS reported that a judge in southern Indiana threatened one Herman Button, who owed $1,800 to a former landlord but had no income beyond Social Security, with contempt and imprisonment if he didn't pay. [9]

The decision to imprison debtors can also come from judges needing money. In this case, judges were pressured to collect on fines and fees lest they find themselves receiving fewer operating funds for their courts. And in 2010, the Times reported that an Alabama circuit judge said openly that his state legislature "was pressuring courts to produce revenue, and that some legislators even believed courts should be financially self-sufficient." [10] In order to have a better chance of extracting the needed money; judges may have threatened people with imprisonment.

However, some of these fees can be problematic. The Brennan Center for Justice completed a study in 2010 which found that 13 states charged the poor "public defenders fees... a practice that encourages indigent defendants to waive their right to counsel." [11] Some of these fees being imposed on the poor can, in fact, force them to give up their rights in order to lessen their payment.

The reinstatement of debtors' prisons has a serious impact on the poor and unemployed who can even be sent to prison for nonpayment of regular bills, due to the fact that "a creditor can petition a court to issue a summons for nonpayment of a bill. If you fail to appear, for one reason or another – and life gets pretty disorganized when you lose your job and possibly your home – then you're in contempt of court. Next stop, jail." [12]

It's rather ridiculous that this is legal if you consider the fact that half of Americans are poor or near poor [13], and 48 million Americans live in poverty. [14] More than a third of U.S. states allow debtors to be jailed. [15]

In conjunction with debtors' prisons, there's also been a rise in collection firms using the courts to force people to pay up on their debts. This has quickly become a problem in some cases where "the debt collection agencies have used threats and lies to get consumers to pay back their debts," and the collectors have "allegedly pressured consumers who didn't owe anything at all." [16] In sum, people who are already having a difficult time paying bills are now being subject to harassment and intimidation from collectors.

And the situation gets even worse when a private probation service (PPS) come on the scene. PPSs work like this: If you get hit with a $200 ticket you can't pay, a private probation company will let you pay it off in installments, for a monthly fee. But there may be additional fees for electronic monitoring, drug testing and classes – many of which are assigned not by a judge, but by the private company itself. [17]

Such PPS harassment can make life extremely difficult for struggling individuals, like in this infamous case of Thomas Barrett. [18] Unemployed and living off food stamps, Barrett was out on probation and ordered to pay a $200 fine for stealing a $2 can of beer from a convenience store. On top of that, Sentinel Offender Services, LLC, the company administering Barrett's probation, charged him $360 per month in supervision and monitoring fees despite the fact that Barrett's only source of income was money he earned selling0 his own blood plasma.

Barrett skipped meals to try to make payments to Sentinel. But he still fell behind and eventually owed the company over $1,000 in fees – five times more than the $200 fine imposed by the court. Seeking to get his money, Sentinel successfully petitioned a court to revoke Barrett's probation, and finally the court jailed him.

Here it must be noted that the 14th Amendment clearly provides that "No state shall make or enforce any law which shall abridge the privileges or immunities of citizens of the United States; nor shall any state deprive any person of life, liberty, or property, without due process of law; nor deny to any person within its jurisdiction the equal protection of the laws." [19] By imprisoning people like Barrett, who are unable to pay their court fees, the state is violating their constitutional right to equal protection under the law. Yet due to the fiscal constraints that many states are in, many are looking the other way while the constitutional violations continue.

And the problems don't end for people once they've paid off their debts and gotten out of prison. The Brennan study found that in all 15 states that were examined – California, Texas, Florida, New York, Georgia, Ohio, Pennsylvania, Michigan, Illinois, Arizona, North Carolina, Louisiana, Virginia, Alabama, and Missouri – "criminal justice debt and related collection practices create a significant barrier for individuals seeking to rebuild their lives after a criminal conviction." For example, in eight of the states, missing debt payments resulted in one's driver's license being suspended – which makes it all the more difficult to get to work, earn money and pay off debts. Seven states even required people to pay off their criminal justice debts In order to regain the right to vote.

This trend should worry us all, as it is not only eroding basic individual rights as established in the U.S. Constitution – but harming the very poorest among us in the process. With the reinstatement of debtors' prisons, we are seeing the most vulnerable people bearing the biggest burden of an unjust legal and economic system. If we knowingly allow this process to proceed, we too are guilty of harming the poor. In the words of Martin Luther King, Jr.: "We shall have to repent in this generation, not so much for the evil deeds of the wicked people, but for the appalling silence of the good people." [20] Let's not remain silent on debtors' prisons any longer.


## Endnotes

1: S. Laurence Shaiman, "The History of Imprisonment for Debt and Insolvency Laws in Pennsylvania as They Evolved from the Common Law," *The American Journal of Legal History* 4:3 (1960), pg 209

2: Robert A. Feer, "Imprisonment for Debt in Massachusetts before 1800," *The Mississippi Valley Historical Review* 48:2 (1961), pg 253

3: Shaiman, pg 211

4: Feer, pg 254

5: Ibid

6: Susie An, "Unpaid Bills Land Some Debtors Behind Bars," *NPR*, December 12, 2011 (http://www.npr.org/2011/12/12/143274773/unpaid-bills-land-some-debtors-behind-bars)

7: Ibid

8: Sam Dillon, "Small-Town Arizona Judge Amasses Fortune, and Indictment," *New York Times*, January 30, 2000 (http://www.nytimes.com/2000/01/30/us/small-town-arizona-judge- amasses-fortune-and-indictment.html)

9: Marlys Harris, "Could Debtors' Prisons Make A Comeback?," *CBS News*, August 10, 2009 (http://www.cbsnews.com/news/could-debtors-prison-make-a-comeback/)

10: Ethan Bronner, "Poor Land In Jail As Companies Add Huge Fees For Probation," *New York Times*, July 2, 2012 (http://www.nytimes.com/2012/07/03/us/probation-fees-multiply-as- companies-profit.html?pagewanted=all&_r=0)

11: Brennan Center For Justice, *The Hidden Costs of Criminal Justice Debt*, http://brennan.3cdn.net/c610802495d901dac3_76m6vqhpy.pdf

12: Harris, August 10, 2009

13: Andre Damon, "Census Report: Half Of Americans Poor Or Near Poor," *World Socialist Web Site*, October 22, 2014 (http://www.wsws.org/en/articles/2014/10/22/pove-o22.html)

14: Anthony Perrucci, "More Than 48,000,000 Americans Impoverished," *WGNO*, October 17, 2014 (http://wgno.com/2014/10/17/more-than-48000000-americans-impoverished/)

15: Jessica Silver-Greenberg, "Debtors Arrests Criticized," *Wall Street Journal*, November 22, 2011 (http://online.wsj.com/news/articles/SB10001424052970203710704577052373900992432)

16: Jillian Berman, "Debtors' Prison Legal In More Than One-Third of US States," *Huffington Post*, November 22, 2011 (http://www.huffingtonpost.com/2011/11/22/debtors-prison-legal-in- more-than-one-third-of-us-states_n_1107524.html)

17: JF, "Private Probation: A Juicy Secret," *The Economist*, April 22, 2014 (http://www.economist.com/blogs/democracyinamerica/2014/04/private-probation)

18: Nusrat Choudhury, *Court-Sanctioned Extortion by Private Probation Companies: Modern Debtors' Prisons*, American Civil Liberties Union, https://www.aclu.org/blog/criminal-law- reform-racial-justice/court-sanctioned-extortion-private-probation-companies (February 6, 2014)

19: Legal Information Institute, *14th Amendment*, http://www.law.cornell.edu/constitution/amendmentxiv

20: Just Quotes, *Evil Quotes*, http://www.just-quotes.com/evil_quotes.html

Currently in the United States, we live in an extremely polarized political sphere. People not only seek out news and op-eds that reinforce their own viewpoints, but also associate mainly with those who align with them politically in order to collectively and viciously demonize 'the other side.' The situation has gotten to the point where people view the policies of the opposing party as a threat to the nation. [1] Globally, it seems that the landscape is even worse with problems arising in the Ukraine; the West once again embroiled in a war in the Middle East, and the knowledge that we've already seen irreversible damage due to climate change [2] and are getting ever-closer to the 2016 deadline [3] where climate change will truly be permanent. These are dark days; however, there is room for optimism. Around the world, we have seen unlikely political alliances that are working to fight for a better future.

**The 'Cowboy-Indian Alliance'**

The 'Cowboy-Indian Alliance' made waves back in April 2014 when they led a five-day 'Reject and Protect' campaign in Washington D.C. against the proposed Keystone XL pipeline. [4] The action was quite prominent, although the origins of the alliance haven't fully been brought to light, nor has the historical importance of such an alliance.

Art Tanderup, a Nebraska farmer who has actively protested against Keystone XL, stated in an April 2014 interview that the alliance formed years ago due to the "common interests between farmers, ranchers and Native Americans in northern Nebraska and southern South Dakota. We've come together as brothers and sisters to fight this Keystone XL pipeline, because of the risk to the Ogallala Aquifer, to the land, to the health of the people." [5]

The pipeline is a common threat to both communities, as the Ogallala Aquifer, a water tablet located beneath the Great Plains, provides water for 2.3 million people. The pipeline also "threatens the Missouri River, which provides drinking water for probably a couple 'nother million," bringing the grand total to about five million people whose clean water supply is under threat due to the proposed construction. In addition, the aquifer also provides water for animals, livestock, and irrigation. All of this means that the pipeline threatens the health and economic stability of the Midwest.

For the Rosebud Sioux Tribe and the Great Sioux Nation, there is historical significance as well. Tanderup stated in the interview that part of the pipeline's route, as well as part of his farm, "is on the Ponca Trail of Tears from back in the 1870s, where Chief Standing Bear and his people were driven from the Niobrara area to Oklahoma."

The extraction processes, such as tar sands mining and the refining and dilution processes, used to obtain the oil are extremely dangerous. Gary Dorr noted in the same interview that, before the oil extraction started, Fort Chip in Canada had "a negligible cancer rate" and now "[has] a cancer rate 400 times the national Canadian per capita average" and that "every single family [in Fort Chip] has cancer in their families."

The alliance, while appearing unlikely on the surface, is rooted in history. It actually isn't new, but is rather "a later incarnation of an alliance that was first formed in 1987 to prevent a Honeywell weapons testing range in the Black Hills, one of the most sacred sites in Lakota cosmology – where, in the 1970s, alliances successfully fended off coal and uranium mining." [6] This current movement is the continuation of a fight for the environment that protects people rather than profits.

This is also affecting Native American-White relations. Take the story of Mekasi Horinek, a member of the Ponca Tribe of Oklahoma who is a Native rights and environmental activist.

When first hearing of the Cowboy-Indian Alliance, he was rather skeptical, saying "I've always been a little bit bitter toward white society" and "I've experienced a lot of racism- growing up on the res, living on the res. When I went to town, I was always treated differently than others." However, with a little convincing from his mother, he eventually joined, realizing the cowboys "have that love and respect for the land the same that we do." [7]

This alliance is having far-reaching effects that go beyond just an environmental coalition. It "is beginning the dialogue not just about broken treaties, but about the long history of colonization, the effects of which are ongoing among some of the United States' poorest populations." [8] This can be shown by the fact that both sides "hope the pipeline, which has caused them both much distress, will be a catalyst for reconciliation," and that they "sense the reconciliation their work is a part of has a historic importance, something healing for both settlers and natives-and both feel that it is, in some way, destined to happen." [9]

Does this mean that everything will be smooth sailing between Native Americans and the descendants of settlers from here on out? Not in the slightest. However, it does offer some hope that a sort of reconciliation and reckoning will take place, changing the views of many so that they will aid the Native Americans in their fight for equal rights, as well as undo the damage done by over a century of mistreatment and cultural destruction.

**Fighting For Peace in Palestine**

The Israeli-Palestinian conflict has been ongoing since 1948, with both groups claiming the same land, and there is currently no end in sight. While the media promotes the narrative that both Palestinians and Israelis hate each other, there has been a large amount of support for the Palestinian cause as of late from Israelis and Jews.

For example, the International Jewish Anti-Zionist Network took an ad out in the *New York Times*, which was "signed by 40 Holocaust survivors and 287 descendants and other relatives" and "[called] for the blockade of Gaza to be lifted and Israel to be boycotted." [10] More specifically, the ad stated that they were "alarmed by the extreme, racist dehumanization of Palestinians in Israeli society, which has reached a fever-pitch. In Israel, politicians and pundits in The Times of Israel and The Jerusalem Post have called openly for genocide of Palestinians and right-wing Israelis are adopting Neo-Nazi insignia." The ad concluded by arguing for collective action, reading: "We must raise our collective voices and use our collective power to bring about an end to all forms of racism, including the ongoing genocide of Palestinian people." [11]

Actions such as these are greatly important as they prove that not all Jewish people support the Israeli war machine and the wanton slaughter of innocent Palestinians.

There were also solidarity actions in Israel itself. However, it seems that it is increasingly dangerous to be anti-war in Israel as there have not only been attacks by right-wing nationalists [12], but the Israeli government itself cracked down on anti-war demonstrations. [13] It even went so far as to attempt to use the IDF to ban anti-war protests, proclaiming that the police must obey IDF Home Front Command orders. These orders "[do] not permit large gatherings in public during times of conflict," [14] which results in people being unable to protest.

There is also increasing support for an end to the conflict in Palestine as well. In June, it was noted that most Palestinians wanted a unity government and a narrow majority favored "peace talks and peaceful coexistence with Israel." [15] An August 2014 poll in Gaza revealed that a majority supported a long-term truce with Israel, even as they opposed the disarmament of the strip. [16]

While the fight for an end to the conflict and the creation of a fully sovereign Palestinian state will continue to be a long and arduous one, it is still good to know that people support peace and are able to reach across lines to form solidarity movements.

**Solidarity of the Suppressed**

Around the world, minority communities are subject to unjust persecution in many societies – persecution which can range from discrimination and a lack or nonexistence of a political voice to outright brutalization and murder by security forces and intense repression. While oppressed groups have fought for their rights individually, rarely have we seen such groups show solidarity with one another and provide support for each other. With help from social media, this seems to be changing.

*Black-Palestinian Solidarity*

An inspiring alliance has formed between Black people in the US and Palestinians in Gaza, each of whom have shown solidarity with one another in their struggles.

To make the situation much more relatable for African-Americans, in May 2014, Kristian Davis Bailey penned the article Why Black People Must Stand With Palestine in which he noted that police brutality faced by Blacks and other minorities is directly related to the violence in Palestine as "Since 2001, thousands of top police officials from cities across the US have gone to Israel for training alongside its military or have participated in joint exercises here." Both communities experience systemic mass incarceration as well: "Forty percent of Palestinian men have been arrested and detained by Israel at some point in their lives. (To put this in perspective, the 2008 figure for Blacks was 1 in 11.) Israel maintains policies of detaining and interrogating Palestinian children that bear resemblance to the stop and frisk policy and disproportionate raids and arrests many of our youth face." [17] The problems of Black people in the US and Palestinians in Gaza are intimately related as the security forces of both countries work together to develop tactics to oppress and brutalize our communities.

In 2012, Jemima Pierre of Black Agenda Report took a historical look of the situation that is still relevant today, noting that many black leaders spoke out in support of the Palestinian cause. Specifically she made mention that

"Palestine was an important issue during the Black Power years as radicals identified with and embraced the anti-colonial struggle against Israel. Huey Newton, even under allegations of anti-Semitism, stated, "...we are not against the Jewish people. We are against that government that will persecute the Palestinian people...The Palestinian people are living in hovels, they don't have any land, they've been stripped and murdered; and we cannot support that for any reason."

Alice Walker made the direct connection of the Palestinian plight to the Black experience: "Going through Israeli checkpoints is like going back in time to the American Civil Rights struggle." By supporting the Palestinian people, Black people today are only continuing the pro-human rights legacy that has been set by many black leaders before them. [18]

Palestinians have reciprocated in the form of supporting the people of Ferguson in their protests against the police. Al Jazeera reported that "Local authorities in Ferguson have begun responding to nightly protests with tear gas and rubber bullets. Palestinians on Twitter could relate, and shared words and images of support with the US protesters." [19]

The Popular Front for the Liberation of Palestine issued a statement of support with Black people, saying that the organization "salutes and stands firmly with the ongoing struggle of Black people and all oppressed communities in the United States" and quoted Khaled Barakat, a Palestinian writer and activist, as saying the fight against US brutality around the world is linked, and that, "When we see the images today in Ferguson, we see another emerging Intifada in the long line of Intifada and struggle that has been carried out by Black people in the US and internationally." [20]

Solidarity between Palestinians and Blacks is important and noteworthy as it shows international solidarity against oppressive social structures and governments as well as forms a space where the two groups can discuss and interact with one another, from promoting awareness about each other's plights to exchanging resistance tactics.

The National Council of Asian Pacific Americans issued a statement of solidarity with Ferguson, saying, in part that, "our own communities' histories in the United States include violence and targeting, often by law enforcement." [21] While a statement may not seem like much, it is rather important as it notes the history of white supremacy and how that ideology is an enemy of all non-whites, no matter their actual skin color.

Soya Jung argued that what is going on in Ferguson mattered to Asian Americans as while Asians "do not move through the world in the crosshairs of a policing system that has its roots in slave patrols, or in a nation that has used me as an 'object of fear' to justify state repression and public disinvestment from the infrastructure on which my community relies," [22] the situation is still important due, firstly, to han.

Jung explains han as a word in Korean culture that "loosely means 'the sorrow and anger that grow from the accumulated experiences of oppression" that has been "expressed in protests against Japanese colonial rule in 1919, in the struggle for self-determination as the Korean war broke out in 1950, during student protests against the oppressive U.S.-backed South Korean government in 1960, and again during the democratic uprising in Kwangju in 1980." This anger against a racist system of oppression and its importance to Jung's identity is partly what connects the histories of Black and Asian America.

She then notes that Black rage "serves as a beacon when faced with the racial quandary that Asian Americans must navigate" with regards to "the invisibility of Asian death and the denial of any form of Asian American identity that doesn't play by the model minority rulebook."

Jaya Sundaresh took a broader view of the subject, in part discussing anti-blackness in the Asian community, writing that South Asian Americans must "work towards change in our own communities so that we do not inadvertently work to reinforce anti-black racism in this country, which is at the root of the police brutality which murdered Michael Brown." She urged others to talk with their "South Asian friends and families about Ferguson, why it is important that we stop perpetuating or staying silent on racist views in our communities, why we should vocally support those in the African-American community who are working towards change, and why we should stop keeping silent when our white friends and colleagues find ways to justify Darren Wilson's murder of Michael Brown." [23]

The solidarity between Blacks and Asians serves as an important avenue to hash out problems and tensions that exist between the communities, with hopes of eliminating those tensions and working together to strike back against racist oppression.

## Conclusion

Do all of these solidarity actions and statements mean that things are now okay? That Native Americans and settlers will get along, that the Israeli-Palestinian conflict will end anytime soon, or that institutionalized and internalized racism will be dismantled? Unfortunately not. However, what these alliances do represent are sparks of hope that suggest we, as people, can put aside superficial differences and come together in an attempt to radically change the situation we currently find ourselves in.

These alliances, whether they are in the form of solidarity statements or marches, articles or tweets, should give people courage and nourishment to continue the fight for freedom and equality.

The world constantly seems like it is going to hell, and many feel that they may give up at any moment, but, to quote Welsh poet Dylan Thomas, "do not go gentle into that good night" instead one must "rage, rage against the dying light." [24]

The light is almost dead and the clock has nearly struck midnight, but this is the chance for everyone to give it their very best. If we are going to go down, let's go down swinging. Let's give 'em hell!

**Endnotes**

1: Pew Research Center, *Political Polarization in the American Public*, http://www.people-press.org/2014/06/12/political-polarization-in-the-american-public/ (June 12, 2014)

2: Alex Morales, "Irreversible Damage Seen From Climate Change in UN Leak," *Bloomberg*, August 27, 2014 (http://www.bloomberg.com/news/articles/2014-08-26/irreversible-damage- seen-from-climate-change-in-un-leak)

3: Fiona Harvey, "World headed for irreversible climate change in five years IAEA warns," *The Guardian*, November 9, 2011 (http://www.theguardian.com/environment/2011/nov/09/fossil- fuel-infrastructure-climate-change)

4: 350.org, *Thousands March with Cowboy and Indian Alliance at 'Reject and Protect' to Protest Keystone XL Pipeline*, http://350.org/thousands-march-with-cowboy-and-indian-alliance- at-reject-and-protect-to-protest-keystone-xl-pipeline/ (August 26, 2014)

5: Democracy Now, *Cowboy Indian Alliance Protests Keystone XL Pipeline in D.C. After Latest Obama Admin Delay*, http://www.democracynow.org/2014/4/28/cowboy_indian_alliance_protests_keystone_xl (April 28, 2014)

6: Kristin Moe, *When Cowboys and Indians Unite- Inside the unlikely alliance that is remaking the climate movement*, Waging Nonviolence, http://wagingnonviolence.org/feature/cowboys- indians-unite-inside-unlikely-alliance-foretells-victory-climate-movement/ (May 2, 2014)

7: Mary Anne Andrei, *Cowboy and Indian Alliance Plants Sacred Ponka Red Corn in the Park of KXL*, Bold Nebraska, http://boldnebraska.org/cowboy-and-indian-alliance-plants-sacred- ponka-red-corn-in-the-path-of-kxl/ (June 22, 2014)

8: http://wagingnonviolence.org/feature/cowboys-indians-unite-inside-unlikely-alliance-foretells- victory-climate-movement/

9: Kristin Moe, "Brought Together by Keystone Pipeline Fight, 'Cowboys and Indians' Heal Old Wounds," *Yes Magazine*, April 24, 2014 (http://www.yesmagazine.org/peace-justice/brought- together-by-pipeline-fight-cowboys-and-indians-heal-old-wounds)

10: BBC, *Holocaust families criticize Israel over Gaza*, http://www.bbc.com/news/world- middle-east-28916761 (August 24, 2014)

11: International Jewish Anti-Zionist Network, *More than 350 Survivors and Descendants of Survivors and Victims of Nazi Genocide Condemn Israel's Assault on Gaza*, http://ijsn.net/nafa/survivors-and-descendants-letter/

12: Omer Raz, "'Unprecedented' violence stalks anti-war demos in Israel," *+972 Magazine*, July 29, 2014 (http://972mag.com/unprecedented-violence-stalks-anti-war-demos-across- israel/94530/)

13: Mya Guarnieri, "Israel cracks down on anti-war protesters," *Al Jazeera*, August 5, 2014 (http://www.aljazeera.com/news/middleeast/2014/08/israel-palestinians-anti-war-protesters- gaza-2014839155862548.html)

14: Lahav Harkov, "Tel Aviv anti-war rally held despite police order," *Jerusalem Post*, August 9, 2014 (http://www.jpost.com/Operation-Protective-Edge/Tel-Aviv-anti-war-protest-canceled- by-police-due-to-public-safety-risk-370569)

15: David Pollock, *Palestinians Want Hamas In, but Want Peace Talks Too*, Washington Institute For Near East Policy, http://www.washingtoninstitute.org/policy- analysis/view/palestinians-want-hamas-in-but-want-peace-talks-too (June 6, 2014)

16: Juan Cole, *Poll: Palestinians of Gaza just like Americans: Want Peace, hate "ISIS," and refuse to give up their guns*, Informed Comment, http://www.juancole.com/2014/08/palestinians- americans-refuse.html (August 25, 2014)

17: Kristian Davis Bailey, "Why Black People Must Stand With Palestine," *Ebony*, May 21, 2014 (http://www.ebony.com/news-views/why-black-people-must-stand-with-palestine-402)

18: Jemima Pierre, "Black Solidarity with Palestine," *Black Agenda Report*, May 16, 2012 (http://www.blackagendareport.com/content/black-solidarity-palestine)

19: Al Jazeera, *Palestinians share tear gas advice with Ferguson protesters*, https://web.archive.org/web/20140816183643/http://stream.aljazeera.com/story/201408141902- 0024060 (August 24, 2014)

20: Popular Front for the Liberation of Palestine, *PFLP salutes the Black struggle in the US: The empire will fall from within*, http://pflp.ps/english/2014/08/19/pflp-salutes-the-black-struggle-in- the-us-the-empire-will-fall-from-within/ (August 19, 2014)

21: NBC News, *Asian American Leaders Stand in Solidarity with Ferguson*, http://www.nbcnews.com/news/asian-america/asian-american-leaders-stand-solidarity-ferguson- n182131 (August 15, 2014)

22: Soya Jung, *Why Ferguson Matters to Asian Americans*, Race Files, http://www.racefiles.com/2014/08/20/why-ferguson-matters-to-asian-americans/ (August 20, 2014)

23: Jaya Sundaresh, *South Asians and Ferguson: #StartTheConversation*, The Aerogram, http://theaerogram.com/south-asians-ferguson-showing-solidarity/ (August 27, 2014)

24: Dylan Thomas, *Do not go gentle into that good night*, Academy of American Poets, http://www.poets.org/poetsorg/poem/do-not-go-gentle-good-night

*"I think that we've got to see that a riot is the language of the unheard. And, what is it that America has failed to hear? It has failed to hear that the economic plight of the Negro poor has worsened over the last few years."- Martin Luther King Jr., Interview with Mike Wallace, September 27, 1966*

*"Now, let's get to what the white press has been calling riots. In the first place don't get confused with the words they use like 'anti-white,' 'hate,' 'militant' and all that nonsense like 'radical' and 'riots.' What's happening is rebellions not riots [.]"- Stokley Carmichael, "Black Power" speech, July 28, 1966*

Many people are telling the people of Ferguson that they should not riot, that it is only hurting their community and they should instead engage in peaceful protests. However, this is deeply problematic as it ignores a number of issues.

People's main concern regarding the riots in Ferguson comes from a concern about private property. One could say that people are more concerned about the theft and destruction of private property than human life, but this needs to be made much clearer. People are more worried about the smashing and theft of inanimate objects than they are about human life. But it isn't specifically human life, its black human life that many of these people could care less about.

On a deeper level, this is where capitalism and racism intersect. One of capitalism's main tenets is the dominance of private property and how it must be protected. We can see that this has been transcribed in law, such as with the Stand Your Ground laws. Yet, also within the larger society there is a lack of caring for black life. In any situation, the media and general public regularly engage in victim blaming and look for anything, anything at all to assassinate the character of those who died at the hand of the police. This can be seen even today, when the media brings up Akai Gurley's criminal record when discussing his death at the hands of a police officer. These two ideas have come together in Ferguson, creating a situation where people are more concerned about private property destruction than they are about the death of Michael Brown.

Many argue that the people of Ferguson are destroying their own community. Yet this is false. To quote Tyler Reinhard: "we don't own neighborhoods. Black businesses exist, it's true. But the emancipation of impoverished communities is not measured in corner-store revenue. It's not measured in minimum-wage jobs. And no, it's especially not measured in how many blackpeople are allowed to become police officers." [1] The neighborhoods like Ferguson were not created by black people; they were created due to racist housing policies that black people had no control over. [2] It should also be noted that Ferguson is 60% black, but has an almost entirely white police force [3] and that the city government and school board are also almost completely white. [4] So while they may live there, the black residents of Ferguson have little representation in the local community and are essentially living under a group of people that isn't responsive to their concerns.

With regards to the riots themselves, the larger society is asking why don't the protesters remain peaceful? The answer is two-part: peace has been tried and we are going to be condemned no matter what.

Society asks why aren't the protesters peaceful, however we have to ask this: Why would you think that people would remain peaceful in the face of constant violence? Why would a people remain peaceful when their young people are being killed on an seemingly weekly basis by the very people who are supposed to protect them?

Black people have tried peace before. We were peaceful in the 1960s when we were peacefully protesting for our civil rights and were met with racist mobs, fire hoses, and dogs, we had crosses burnt on our lawns, lynchings, and a bomb put in a church. During all of that time we remained peaceful even as society enacted massive violence and repression against us. Yet, violence against the black community continues today, the only difference is that it isn't so blatant. Martin Luther King Jr. was nonviolent and died at the hands of an assassin, a violent act. Look at the Occupy protests, which were entirely nonviolent, the protesters were still met with violence, most notably in the form of a pre-dawn raid on Zuccotti Park [5], so even when protesters are nonviolent, they can still be met with violence.

The situation is currently such where if a black person is killed by the police, people immediately come out and find any way in which they can besmirch or blame the victim, such as with the aforementioned example involving Akai Gurley. So they are already looking for ways to take the blame off of the authorities from day one. The situation changes, though, when oppressed people fight back. Not only is the violence denounced, but then it is used as an excuse to use massive amounts of violence against the oppressed, as we saw by the militarized police that have been used in Ferguson.

When people lash out against one incident, one may be inclined to call that violence, but when violence against your community has been going on for decades and people lash out, that's no longer violence on the part of the oppressed, that's called resistance.

When the question is raised of why aren't there peaceful protests, it is also extremely hypocritical. Many have spoken out in person and on social media condemning the riots, but at the same time they are silent on the constant police brutality that the black community deals with and they are silent on the economic violence done against black communities, pushing them into ghettos where not only is there economic poverty but also a poverty of expectations. On a larger scale, they are also silent when other groups riot, such as when white people rioted over pumpkins. [6] It is extremely hypocritical to speak out against rioters, but not have a thing to say about police brutality or to ignore others who riot.

At the heart of this is how society condones state violence, but condemns violence by individuals. This mindset is a serious problem as it only gives more power to the state and consistently puts state forces in the right, with the victims of state violence being forced to prove their innocence, a situation made all the harder due to people already assuming that the victim is in the wrong.

Many have pushed for peace, but peace and safety are not something the black people in America receive, whether we are just looking for help after a car accident, as was the case with Renisha McBride, or we are carrying a toy gun around, as was the case with John Crawford.

This is not the time to ask for peace. This is the time to say "No justice, no peace."


## Endnotes

1: Tyler Reinhard, Hey, *Step Back with the Riot Shaming*, Mask Magazine, http://www.maskmagazine.com/the-substance-issue/struggle/step-back-with-the-riot-shaming

2: Ta-Nehisi Coates, "The Racist Housing Policies That Built Ferguson," *The Atlantic*, October 17, 2014 (http://www.theatlantic.com/business/archive/2014/10/the-racist-housing-policies-that- built-ferguson/381595/)

3: Hannah Levintova, Tasneem Raja, Ivylise Simons, AJ Vicens, "Ferguson Is 60 Percent Black. Virtually All Its Cops Are White," *Mother Jones*, August 13, 2014 (http://www.motherjones.com/politics/2014/08/10-insane-numbers-ferguson-killing)

4: Zachary Roth, "Ferguson's diversity problem goes way beyond its cops," *MSNBC*, August 14, 2014 (http://www.msnbc.com/msnbc/ferguson-lack-diversity-goes-way-beyond-its-cops)

5: Verena Dobnick, Colleen Long, "Zuccotti Park Occupiers get evicted in pre-dawn raid, court order allows them back but city still bars them," *The Register Citizen*, November 15, 2011 (http://www.registercitizen.com/general-news/20111115/zuccotti-park-occupiers-get-evicted-in- predawn-raid-court-order-allows-them-back-in-but-city-still-bars-them)

6: Ed Payne, "New Hampshire Pumpkin Festival crowd sets fires, throws bottles," *CNN*, October 19, 2014 (http://www.cnn.com/2014/10/19/us/new-hampshire-pumpkin-festival-riot/)

Despite what the talking heads are saying, the economy isn't doing so well. With this most recent jobs report, the two main sectors of growth were fast food and retail [1], accounting for a total of about 32.2% of jobs created in October. In part, due to low-paying jobs, many are using payday loans to get by and unfortunately when it comes time to pay up, many are paying much more than what they borrowed due to extremely high interest rates. While this has been bought up in the mainstream every now and then, rarely has anyone taken a look how payday loans came into existence and the type of havoc they wreak on people, mainly the poor. We need to realize that payday loans only harm us and explore alternatives.

According to the Journal of Economic Perspectives, the practice of getting credit against one's next payment goes back to the Great Depression; however, "as the spread of direct deposit and electronic funds transfer technologies slowed the growth in the demand for check cashing services" and payday loans were more of a side job to check cashing businesses. Yet, the situation changed in 1978 that would facilitate the rise of payday lenders.

The beginnings of payday loans can be found in the 1978 Supreme Court case Marquette National Bank v. First of Omaha Service Corp which stated that "national banks were entitled to charge interest rates based on the laws of states where they were physically located, rather than the laws of states where their borrowers lived." [2] This allowed banks to offer credit cards to anyone they deemed qualified. A further empowerment came from the Depository Institutions Deregulation and Monetary Control Act of 1980 which allowed for banks and financial institutions to decide interest rates based on the market. This laid the foundation for payday loans as one could now set up a payday loan company and charge high interest rates, saying they were based on the market which would allow them to make a profit and due to the court case, payday lenders could offer loans to literally anyone they wanted, even those with bad credit.

Payday lenders are able to profit off of the loans they provide by charging interest, which can get out of control. For example, "For a loan of $300, a typical borrower pays on average $775, with $475 going to pay interest and fees over an average borrowing cycle." [3] It was noted by the Federal Reserve Bank of Cleveland in 1999 that the loans have "annualized interest rates often ranging from 213 percent to 913 percent" [4] or 4.4%-19% a week! Thus, while the interest rates might not seem ridiculous at first glance, they can easily grow out of control.

Now, while it's known that mainly working-class people and the poor are the main users of payday loans, that's also a rather broad brush. More specificity was attained in 2012, when Pew Research reported that the majority of payday loan borrowers are 25-44 year old white women, though "there are five groups that have higher odds of having used a payday loan: those without a four-year college degree; home renters; African Americans; those earning below $40,000 annually; and those who are separated or divorced." Furthermore, the Journal of Economic Perspectives found that "three times the percentage of payday loan customers are seriously debt burdened and have been denied credit or not given as much credit as they applied for in the last five years." [5]

So the victims of payday loans are part of groups and communities that are already having economic troubles, even more so due to the current economic climate. In terms of why people utilized payday loans, it was found that "most borrowers use payday loans to cover ordinary living expenses over the course of months, not unexpected emergencies over the course of weeks," which really just speaks to the problem of wages and how people aren't being paid enough.

The situation becomes all the more tragic when one finds that not only are the bottom lines of payday lenders "significantly enhanced by the successful conversion of more and more occasional users into chronic borrowers," but also that "the federal government has found that one of the country's biggest payday lenders provides financial incentives to its staff to encourage chronic borrowing by individual patrons," (emphasis added) as was reported in a 2003 issue of Economic Development Quarterly. So the vulnerable are then put into a cycle of poverty which is extremely difficult to get out of.

There has been an attempt by state governments to regulate payday loans. [6] Some states ban outright, whereas others limit interest rates. The lenders are getting smart and attempting to avoid regulation by "making surface changes to their businesses that don't alter their core products: high-cost, small-dollar loans for people who aren't able to pay them back." [7]

It should be noted that payday lenders are not small chumps in the financial world. For a while major banks were involved in payday lending, such as "Wells Fargo, Bank of America, US Bank, JP Morgan Bank, and National City (PNC Financial Services Group)" [8] and were able to finance 38% of the entire payday lending industry and that is a rather conservative estimate. These banks bowed out of the industry in January 2014 after being warned by federal regulators that they were going to look to see if the loans violated consumer protection laws. [9] But the problem doesn't end there.

There are also middlemen involved that operate on behalf of the payday companies. It was reported in April 2014 that a lawsuit was being filed against Money Mutual which claimed that "[claimed] the company [was] operating as an unlicensed lender by arranging loans that violate a [Illinois] state law that restricts borrower fees." Money Mutual is itself not a lender, but rather "a lead generator that sells sensitive customer information, like bank-account numbers and email addresses, to payday lenders, and federal and state officials increasingly are cracking down on these businesses." [10] Middlemen like Money Mutual can be paid $50-$150 per lead, even if the person doesn't take out a loan. This can quickly add up. In 2012 Bloomberg News found that "lead generators in financial services take in $100 million a year, with the market growing by more than 16 percent annually." [11]

Yet, this is just with storefront lenders, all new problems arise when one delves into the world of online payday lending. It has been reported that many online payday lenders "attempt to skirt the rules and charge exorbitant fees, amongst other affronts to regulations that leave many a consumer seeking payday loan legal help" and that the Pew Research Center "found that about 30 percent of Internet payday loan borrowers claim they have received at least one threat from the lender," [12] whether it be for arrest or that the debtor's employer would be contacted.

One of the worst problems with online payday lenders is theft; just take the story of Jeannie Morris of Kansas City. She entered personal information on websites that offered to match her up with payday lenders, however the situation took a turn for the worse when, "without asking her approval, two unrelated online lenders based in Kansas City had plopped $300 each into her bank account. Together, they began withdrawing $360 a month in interest payments" and after her account was wiped clean, Jeannie was hounded by collection companies. Jeannie is not alone as "many consumers reported that loans they'd never authorized had been dropped into their bank accounts. Then those accounts often evaporated as the lenders snatched out money for interest payments while never applying any of the money to the loan principal." [13] So now online payday lenders can just lend people money without asking them and then clean out people's bank accounts, effectively stealing from families.

The situation may seem hopeless, but there are alternatives to payday loans. One way is with credit union loans where members are allowed to borrow up to $500 each month and each loan is "connected to a SALO cash account, which automatically deducts 5 percent of the loan and places it in a savings account to create a 'rainy day fund' for the borrower." [14] Small consumer loans are another option. They are a lot less expensive than payday loans, for example, "a person can borrow $1,000 from a finance company for a year and pay less than a $200-$300 payday loan over the same period." [15] If possible, someone could also get a cash advance on their credit card. [16] In the long term, credit counseling can help a person to create a debt repayment plan and find a way to balance a budget. [17]

Payday lenders are a major problem and prey on the desperate in order to make money. We need to organize and fight for the economic freedom of everyone. Consumer watchdog groups and payday borrowers and victims of payday theft need to come together to end this practice that creates a cycle of debt. To quote the rallying cry of IWW songwriter Joe Hill: "Don't mourn, organize!"

**Endnotes**

1: Bureau of Labor Statistics, *Employment Situation Summary*, http://www.bls.gov/news.release/archives/empsit_11072014.htm (November 7, 2014)

2: Miron Lulic, *History of Payday Loans*, Loan Now, https://www.loannow.com/history-payday- loans/ (October 13, 2014)

3: National People's Action, *How the Major Banks Finance Payday Lending Companies*, http://npa-us.org/research/payday-lending

4: Julian Neiser, "Check cashing outlets take a big bite," *Pittsburgh Business Times*, October 13, 1997 (http://www.bizjournals.com/pittsburgh/stories/1997/10/13/focus2.html)

5: The Pew Charitable Trusts, *Payday Lending in America: Who Borrows, Where They Borrow, and Why*, http://www.pewtrusts.org/en/research-and-analysis/reports/2012/07/19/who-borrows-    where-they-borrow-and-why (July 19, 2012)

6: Payday Loan Consumer Information, *Legal Status of Payday Loans by State*, http://www.paydayloaninfo.org/state-information

7: Kai Wright, "Bad Credit: How Payday Lenders Evade Regulation," *The Nation*, April 6, 2011 (http://www.thenation.com/article/159750/bad-credit-how-payday-lenders-evade-regulation)

8: http://npa-us.org/research/payday-lending

9: Blake Ellis, "Big banks to stop offering payday-like loans," *CNN*, January 21, 2014 (http://money.cnn.com/2014/01/21/pf/bank-payday-loans/)

10: Center for Responsible Lending, *Middlemen for Payday Lenders Under Fire*, http://www.responsiblelending.org/tools-resources/headlines/middlemen-for-payday-lenders- under-fire.html (April 8, 2014)

11: Carter Dougherty, "Data From Payday Online Applicants Sold in Online Auctions," *Bloomberg*, June 8, 2012 (http://www.bloomberg.com/news/2012-06-08/data-from-payday-loan- applicants-sold-in-online-auctions.html)

12: Gordon Gibb, *Respected Non-Profit Reports Problems With Internet Payday Loans: Survey, Lawyers and Settlements*, http://www.lawyersandsettlements.com/articles/internet-payday- loans/payday-loan-lawsuit-legal-help-5-20179.html#.VFxMmBYXflE (October 18, 2014)

13: Mark Morris, "Kansas City-based payday lenders' practices leave borrowers scrambling," *The Kansas City    Star*,    October    19,    2014    (http://www.kansascity.com/news/business/personal-finance/article3078385.html)

14: Nancy Mann Jackson, *4 Alternatives to Payday Lending*, Bankrate, https://web.archive.org/web/20120327063908/http://www.bankrate.com/finance/personal- finance/4-alternatives-to-payday-lending-1.aspx

15: http://www.responsiblelending.org/payday-lending/tools-resources/alternatives-to-payday- loans.html

16: Pine Tree Legal Assistance, *Alternatives to Payday Loans*, http://www.ptla.org/alternatives- payday-loans

17: Ibid

*Unmasking The Black Bloc: Who They Are, What They Do, How They Work*

*Published on: December 18, 2014*

*"The Black Bloc always defend the demonstrations when the police come here." - Ariane Santos, 26-year-old Brazilian student*

*"The Black Bloc anarchists, who have been active on the streets in Oakland and other cities, are the cancer of the Occupy movement." - Chris Hedges*

The Black Bloc: some love it, others hate it. Many condemn Black Blockers for engaging in property destruction and lack of central organization, yet others appreciate them and see their divisive actions as a positive, arguing for a diversity of tactics. However, what many are lacking is an understanding of the Black Bloc, its history, the types of people who are in it, and the problems within.

While this is a brief exploration of the Black Bloc, those who are interested further should read *Who's Afraid of the Black Blocs? Anarchy In Action Around the World* by Francis Dupuis-Déri (translated by Lazer Lederhendler), which not only provided the research for this article, but also explores on a deeper level what the black block is, the tactics and beliefs of black blockers, and criticism of the Black Bloc.

To begin to discuss black blocs, there must first be an understanding of what a black bloc is. Black blocs are "ad hoc assemblages of individuals or affinity groups that last for the duration of a march or rally" in which members retain their anonymity via head-to-toe black clothing. While there may be uses of force, "more often than not they are content to protest peacefully" with the main objective being to "embody within a demonstration a radical critique of the economic and political system." A black bloc can be one person or thousands. It should be noted the black bloc isn't a group, but rather a tactic to allow for radicals to engage in direct action without fear of arrest; while many black blockers are anarchist, not all of them are.

**Origins**

Black blocs came out of the autonomous movement in Germany in the 1980s, specifically West Germany where "radical feminists had a profound effect on the Automen, injecting the movement with a more anarchist spirit than was the case elsewhere in Western Europe." The Automen expressed their politics via "rent strikes and re-appropriating hundreds of buildings which were turned into squats" that doubled as spaces for political activity.

There is no definitive moment when the term black bloc came into usage, although there are different stories. The first major arrival of a black bloc was in 1986 when a massive black bloc was formed to defend the Hafenstrasse squat where 1,500 black blockers and 10,000 other demonstrators confronted the police and saved the squat.

Black bloc ideas and tactics soon spread to North America via fanzines, personal contacts and punk music groups, but there is also a more interesting reason as to how black bloc tactics spread. Sociologists Charles Tilly, Doug McAdam and Dieter Rucht, all of whom specialize in social movements, have shown that "for different periods and places there exist repertoires of collective action deemed effective and legitimate for the defense and promotion of a cause. These repertories are transformed and disseminated over time and across borders from one social movement to another, in accordance with the experiences of militants and the changes in the political sphere."

Essentially, tactics and ideas spread over time from one social movement to another depending on their effectiveness and how the tactics will work within the context of each movement. Two modern day examples of this could be the physical encampment of spaces from the Occupy movement and the "Hands Up, Don't Shoot" gesture from the anti-police brutality movement that has recently sprung up surrounding the death of Michael Brown in Ferguson.

The first time the black bloc made a major move in North America was during a January 1991 rally against the Persian Gulf War where the World Bank building was targeted. Black bloc tactics were also used by the militant anti-racist group Anti-Racist Action, which focuses on directly confronting neo-Nazis and white supremacists.

**Who They Are, How They are Organized**

While the black bloc may be made up of militants, they are consistently categorized as hooligans, thugs and youths who take joy in private property destruction. Thus, there needs to be further exploration of the types of people under the masks.

It should be noted the black blocs, at least in the U.S. and Europe, are generally overwhelmingly white and male. However, there is some diversity. In a communiqué published days after the demonstrations against the 2001 G8 Summit in Genoa, Mary Black (a pseudonym for a protester who took part in the protests) noted that most of the people she knew who used black bloc tactics "have day jobs working for nonprofits. Some are schoolteachers, labor organizers, or students. Some don't have full-time jobs, but instead spend most of their time working for change in their communities.[...] These are thinking and caring folks who, if they did not have radical political and social agendas, would be compared with nuns, monks, and others who live their lives in service."

Dupuis-Déri himself stated that in interviews he has had with black blockers, many had been involved in the social sciences and that "in a number of cases, their research projects dealt with the political significance and consequences of demonstrations and direct actions," suggesting "that their political involvement was grounded in serious political thinking."

Thus, those who involve themselves in black bloc tactics are not necessarily people who are at protests solely to break things, although such types of people do come in and cause problems.

Before discussing the issue of property destruction, it would be pertinent to know how black blocs are organized. Black bloc groups attempt to function in a horizontal manner, with each person having equal say in deliberating issues and where the goal is consensus rather than voting. In order to do this, black blockers form affinity groups, which are groups "generally composed of between a half-dozen and several dozen individuals whose affinity results from ties that bind them, such as belonging to the same school, workplace, or political organization." By having previous ties to one another, members in affinity groups are able to coordinate much easier.

**The Issue of Property Destruction**

Not all black blockers engage in property destruction. While one may use black bloc tactics, there are different roles one can play. Groups take into account things such as a person's immigration status, health problems, previous arrest record and the like, and at-risk individuals can engage in low-risk tasks such as being "in charge of legal support in the event of arrests, or responsible for transportation, lodging, water and food supplies, media contacts, psychological support" and whatnot.

Black blocs meet to plan and organize before hand, but also during protests as well. One black blocker who took part in the protests against the G8 Summit in 2003 noted in her reflection of the events:

"I found it extraordinary that we could hold delegates' meetings right in the middle of the blocking action. There were barricades, fires had been lit, the police were slinging a lot of tear gas. And still, a meeting was called with someone yelling, 'meeting in ten minutes near the road sign.' The meeting took place barely a few hundred meters from where the police stood, and it allowed us to decide on our course of action. [...] The police officers see you as a crowd and assume you're going to act like a crowd. The affinity group model disrupts that dynamic: you don't act like a crowd anymore but like a rational being."

With regards to property damage, for black blockers, the target is the message. Targets are often chosen for their symbolic value. "On principle, Black Blocs do not strike community centers, public libraries, the offices of women's committees or even small independent businesses." While this may be true generally, the use of property destruction by some black blockers can cause problems, such as can be seen in the recent Berkeley protests, where people were protesting the death of Eric Garner and individuals came and broke the windows of a number of banks. This is deeply problematic as it took the attention off the death of Eric Garner and the larger issues surrounding police brutality against the black community, and put the attention on banks. Actions such as these can potentially create a space for the police to justify a crackdown on all protesters.

The fetishization of property destruction is a problem with the black bloc, as in some cases "violent direct action becomes a means for a would-be militant to affirm [their] political identity in the eyes of other militants. This makes it very tempting for that person to look down on and exclude those who do not equate radicalism with violence." Yet, not all black blockers engage in this fetishization and are aware of the dangers, such as with a participant of the Quebec city black blocs who stated: "I have no patience for dogmatic pacifism, but there is also dogmatic violence, which sees violence as the only and only means to wage the struggle." The protester Sofiane noted that "We don't advocate violence; it's not a program... Because you can easily acquire a taste for violence, you get used to it... But when it comes to doing militant work, not many people show up."

**Diversity of Tactics**

However, there are solutions to the problem of those wanting to engage in direct action and others who want to peacefully protest that should be quoted at some length. Around 2000, there were a few mobilizations in which it was proposed that certain areas of a city be identified by colors in order to allow different types of protests simultaneously:

> "This was done at the Reclaim the Street rally in London on June 18, 1999; at the first Global Day of Action called by the People's Global Action, an anti-capitalist network founded in Geneva in 1998 and close to the Zapatista rebels. [...] Color coding made it possible to distinguish among three separate marches: blue for the Black Bloc, accompanied by the Infernal Noise Brigade band; yellow for the Tute Bianche [a militant Italian social movement]; pink for the Pink and Silver Bloc."

The organization Convergence of Anti-Capitalist Struggles used a similar tactic at demonstrations in which there were three zones: green, yellow, and red. "The green zone was a sanctuary where demonstrators were, theoretically, in no danger of being arrested. The yellow zone was for those undertaking nonviolent civil disobedience and involved a minor risk of being arrested. The red zone was for protesters who were ready for more aggressive tactics, including skirmishes with the police."

This allowed for the concept of a diversity of tactics to be respected, as well as for protesters to have spaces where more or less militant tactics were accepted, all while maintaining the safety of peaceful protesters.

Though the debate surrounding property violence is the largest and loudest of all, there are other problems within black blocs such as sexism and accusations of alienating the working class.

With regards to sexism, many critics of black blocs argue that militant direct action "partakes of a macho mystique and does not encourage women to join in" and that expressing one's anger through destruction "simply [confirms] and [amplifies] aggressive masculinity." Furthermore, the sexual division of labor is often reproduced, with a woman who took part in a number of black blocs in the 2012 Quebec student strike saying that it was women who often did the shopping "when fabric was needed to make flags and banners."

Dupuis-Déri noted that the situation hadn't changed, writing that "more than a decade earlier, during a meeting to prepare a black bloc in Montreal, the men ended up in the backyard of an apartment honing their slingshot skills while the women were in the kitchen making Molotov cocktails." Thus, masculinity is not only reproduced in many black bloc circles, but also creates a space that rejects the participation of women and devalues their labor and thus their importance to the movement.

Some argue that black blocs alienate the working-class "with their clothing and lifestyle choices, which are associated with the anarchist counterculture." While some may argue that there are those in the working-class who support and take part in black blocs, it should be noted that these are not fully representative of the working-class; there is a lack of people of color and women and so the black blocs are more representative of the young, white working-class.

Black blocs tactics are divisive and create a large amount of tension, even within far-left circles. Many condemn black blockers as being nothing but hooligans who want to break things. But by unmasking who they are, one can better understand them and their tactics and ideas, even if one disagrees.

Civil forfeiture is a major issue that's recently gotten into the news, notably due to Attorney General Eric Holder's change to the controversial police action of seizing people's property. [1] Unfortunately, Holder's actions, while laudable, won't stop the massive damage that has already been done – and may very well continue the problem. Because although the media has finally begun to talk about the issue, we still haven't been presented with a full scope of civil forfeiture: what it is and what it means.

To understand forfeiture, one must go back to colonial America. The idea of civil forfeiture comes directly from the British; early forfeiture law "refers to the power of a court over an item of real or personal property." [2] This could include land, in which the court would decide who owned a piece of land, or marriage, where the courts would have the authority to terminate a marriage. [3]

Originally, in rem jurisdiction was "incorporated into American customs and admiralty laws governing the seizure of ships for crimes of piracy, treason and smuggling in the early days of the Republic, and during the American Civil War." It was later formalized in 1966 "in the Supplemental Rules for Certain Admiralty and Maritime Claims which apply to our civil forfeiture cases." So the United States has always had some type of civil forfeiture law.

The situation changed, however, when President Nixon announced the War on Drugs and began to use civil forfeiture as an instrument of law enforcement. Author Montgomery Sibley notes that, as part of the Comprehensive Drug Abuse Prevention and Control Act of 1970, Congress strengthened civil forfeiture as a means of confiscating illegal substances and the means by which they are manufactured and distributed. [4] In 1978, Congress amended the law to authorize the seizure and forfeiture of the proceeds of illegal drug transactions as well.

Under Nixon, the Continuing Criminal Enterprise statute was also enacted, targeting repeat offenders of lucrative drug trafficking. Meanwhile, an important side effect of the Control Act was that it not only allowed police to seize private property being used in a crime – it also made clear that the owner of said property had to prove the property in question was not being used as part of a crime.

In other words, when it comes to proving that someone's property isn't being used for criminal purposes, the burden of proof is on the owner, not the police. This creates a situation where the police can essentially confiscate someone's belongings, allege that the items are being used to further a crime, and the owner must somehow prove that the allegation is false – something that can be extremely difficult to do.

In 1984, under President Ronald Reagan, further changes were made under the Comprehensive Crime Control Act with regards to funds attained from civil forfeiture. Two new forfeiture funds were federally created, "one at the U.S. Department of Justice, which gets revenue from forfeitures done by agencies like the Drug Enforcement Agency and the Federal Bureau of Investigation, and another now run by the U.S. Treasury, which gets revenue from agencies like Customs and the Coast Guard." [5]

As PBS reported, "these funds could now be used for forfeiture-related expenses, payments to informants, prison building, equipment purchase, and other general law enforcement purposes."

However, there was a major change in that local law enforcement this time would also get to have their share of the pie. "Within the 1984 Act was a provision for so-called 'equitable sharing,' which allows local law enforcement agencies to receive a portion of the net proceeds of forfeitures they help make under federal law."

As soon as this occurred, America saw a massive increase in the amount of civil forfeitures carried out by federal agents between 1989 and 1999, when the value of civil forfeiture recoveries nearly doubled from $285,000,039 to $535,767,852 – a 187% increase in only 10 years. [6] And the numbers only grew as time went on. [7]

In 2012, $4.6 billion was acquired via civil forfeiture, compared to a decade earlier, in 2002, when the amount seized was just $322,246,408. The increase of over 1,400% reveals a major cash cow for law enforcement.

There was an attempt to reform civil forfeiture through the Civil Asset Forfeiture Reform Act of 2000. This included several changes most notably in regards to poor or impoverished defendants, where the new law ordered courts to issue the defendant a lawyer "when the property in question is a primary residence," [8] as well as to pay the lawyer regardless of the outcome of the case, whereas before, defendants had to essentially defend themselves.

In addition, the issue of burden of proof changed as the government now had to "establish, by a preponderance of the evidence, that the property [was] subject to forfeiture," where previously the government could seize property solely on probable cause. Put simply, in order to seize property, the government now had not just to present evidence, but to present evidence "based on the more convincing evidence and its probable truth or accuracy, and not on the amount of evidence." [9]

With that reform, it was no longer enough to say there was a possibility that the evidence could have been used in a crime. However, the law didn't deal with the problem that the burden of proof was on the property owner, nor did it deal with the conflict of interest in which the government could seize property and sell it – using the money to fund its own operations. Because the pressing question still remains: how exactly do police use the funds they've gained from civil forfeitures?

In 2013, Vice reported that a district attorney in Georgia used the funds to "to buy football tickets and home furnishings," whereas "officers in Bal Harbor, Florida, took trips to LA and Vegas and rented luxury cars, and other DAs and police chiefs have bought everything from tanning salons to booze for parties." [10]

The *Washington Post* also reported that police are using the funds to militarize themselves, buying an array of items such as "Humvees, automatic weapons, gas grenades, night-vision scopes and sniper gear. Many departments acquired electronic surveillance equipment, including automated license-plate readers and systems that track cell phones." [11] And this spending is on top of the military surplus gear police receive from the Pentagon. [12]

While there is a federal force to ensure that funds are used appropriately, it's wildly understaffed; the Justice Department has about 15 employees assigned to oversee compliance, with some five employees responsible for reviewing thousands of annual reports. Essentially, then, police are free to spend the money they gain from civil forfeitures on anything they want, without fear of punishment.

Besides the previously noted conflict of interest and burden of proof issues, there are also other major problems with civil forfeiture – notably, the disproportionate racial impact and harm it causes to innocent people.

In 2012, Vanita Gupta, the ACLU deputy legal director, was involved in a settlement of several civil forfeiture cases in Texas in which mainly black and Latino drivers were pulled over, many times without justification, and had their assets seized by police. Gupta noted that civil forfeiture laws "invite racial profiling" and "incentivize police agencies to engage in unconstitutional behavior in order to fund themselves off the backs of low-income motorists, most of whom lack the means to fight back, without any hard evidence of criminal activity. It is no way to run our justice system." [13]

Furthermore, in 2014, the Meiklejohn Civil Liberties Institute reported reported that civil forfeiture laws "routinely amount to de facto racial discrimination, as law enforcement officials routinely target low-income people of color, seizing their assets." It quoted the ACLU as saying that "asset forfeiture practices often go hand-in-hand with racial profiling and disproportionally impact low-income African-American or Hispanic people who the police decide look suspicious and for whom the arcane process of trying to get one's property back is an expensive challenge." [14] Thus, like many aspects of the criminal justice system, civil forfeiture disproportionately impacts minorities.

Great harm is also committed against innocent people who are not actually engaging in any crime. Gothamist reported that in March of 2012, the NYPD confiscated $4,800 belonging to Gerald Bryan, and took Bryan "into custody on suspected felony drug distribution, as the police continued their warrantless search." Bryan's case was later dropped, but when he went to reclaim his money "he was told it was too late: the money had been deposited into the NYPD's pension fund." [15]

The NYPD's civil forfeiture was declared unconstitutional twice. [16] However, the process still continues, reflecting a failure to protect the basic rights of citizens – and a breakdown in the rule of law. The very people who are supposed to enforce the law are the ones who profit from ignoring it – something that was proven in a recent study by the Institute for Justice, which found that "civil forfeiture encourages choices by law enforcement officers that leave the public worse off." [17]

"Under civil forfeiture," said the report, "when participants could gain financially by taking property from others, that is overwhelmingly what they did."

While many might argue that the civil forfeiture game has changed due to recent actions taken by AG Holder, unfortunately very little actually has. As Vox reported in January: "Holder's order only curtails 'adoptions' that are requested through the federal program by a local or state police department working on its own. It still allows local and state police to seize and keep assets when working with federal authorities on an investigation, and when the property is linked to public safety concerns — such as illegal firearms, ammunition, and explosives." [18]

Thus, civil forfeitures continue unabated for the most part. This data analysis revealed that "only about a quarter—25.6 percent—of properties seized under equitable sharing were federal 'adoptions' of properties seized by state or local law enforcement, the kind of seizures the new policy targets" and that "of the nearly $6.8 billion in cash and property seized under equitable sharing from 2008 to 2013, adoptions accounted for just 8.7 percent." [19] Put simply: local and state law enforcement can still engage in civil forfeiture and make large amounts of money off it.

To make things worse, incoming Attorney General Loretta Lynch appears undisturbed by the current state of civil forfeiture, since she "has used civil asset forfeiture in more than 120 cases, raking in some $113 million for federal and local coffers," [20] and even calling it a "wonderful tool." [21]

There have been attempts at reform. But both of them – the Civil Asset Forfeiture Reform Act of 2014, and the Fifth Amendment Integrity Restoration Act, which "would protect the rights of citizens and restore the Fifth Amendment's role in seizing property without due process of law," [22] died in Congress. In the meantime, it seems that cops and the government will continue to cash in on the property of U.S. citizens.


**Endnotes**

1: Sari Horwitz, Robert O'Harrow Jr., Steven Rich, "Holder limits seized-asset sharing process that split billions with local, state police," *Washington Post*, January 16, 2015 (http://www.washingtonpost.com/investigations/holder-ends-seized-asset-sharing-process-that- split-billions-with-local-state-police/2015/01/16/0e7ca058-99d4-11e4-bcfb- 059ec7a93ddc_story.html)

2: Legal Information Institute, Cornell University Law School, *In Rem*, https://www.law.cornell.edu/wex/in_rem

3: Jean B. Weld, *Forfeiture Laws and Procedures in the United States of America*, United Nations Asia and Far East Institute for the Prevention of Crime and the Treatment of Offenders, http://www.unafei.or.jp/english/pdf/RS_No83/No83_06VE_Weld1.pdf

4: Montgomery Sibley, *Why Just Her: The Judicial Lynching of the D.C. Madam*, Deborah Jeane Palfrey, (Full Court Press, 2009), pg 9

5: Kyla Dunn, *Reining in Forfeiture: Common Sense Reform in the War on Drugs*, PBS, http://www.pbs.org/wgbh/pages/frontline/shows/drugs/special/forfeiture.html

6: Drug War Facts, *Asset Forfeiture*, http://www.drugwarfacts.org/cms/forfeiture#sthash.iaTBCSxd.dpbs

7: Christopher Ingraham, "Civil asset forfeitures more than double under Obama," *Washington Post*, September 8, 2014 (http://www.washingtonpost.com/blogs/wonkblog/wp/2014/09/08/civil- asset-forfeitures-more-than-double-under-obama/)

8: Barclay Thomas Johnson, *Restoring Civil Liberty-The Civil Asset Forfeiture Reform Act of 2000: Baby Steps Towards A More Civilized Civil Forfeiture System*, https://journals.iupui.edu/index.php/inlawrev/article/viewFile/3549/3493

9: Legal Dictionary, *Preponderance of Evidence*, http://dictionary.law.com/Default.aspx?selected=1586

10: Lucy Steigerwald, "Asset Forfeiture, the Cash Cow of the Drug War," *Vice,* July 15, 2013 (http://www.vice.com/read/bad-cop-blotter-asset-forfeiture-the-cash-cow-of-the-drug-war)

11: Robert O'Harrow Jr., Ted Mellnik, Shelly Tan, "Asset seizures fuel police spending," *Washington Post*, October 11, 2014 (http://www.washingtonpost.com/sf/investigative/2014/10/11/cash-seizures-fuel-police-spending/)

12: Paulina Firozi, "Police forces pick up surplus military supplies," *USA Today*, June 17, 2014 (http://www.usatoday.com/story/news/nation/2014/06/15/local-law-enforcement-agencies- surplus-military-equipment/10286485/)

13: American Civil Liberties Union, *ACLU Announces Settlement in "Highway Robbery" Cases In Texas*, https://www.aclu.org/news/aclu-announces-settlement-highway-robbery-cases- texas?redirect=criminal-law-reform/aclu-announces-settlement-highway-robbery-cases-texas (August 3, 2012)

14: Meiklejohn Civil Liberties Institute, *ICERD Shadow Report: De Facto Racial Discrimination Resulting from Civil Asset Forfeiture Laws*, https://web.archive.org/web/20150318175917/http://mcli.org/wp-content/uploads/2012/05/David_Nelson_ICERD.pdf

15: Max Rivlin-Nader, "How The NYPD's Use of Civil Forfeiture Robs Innocent New Yorkers," *Gothamist*, January 14, 2014 (http://gothamist.com/2014/01/14/nypd_civil_forfeiture.php)

16: Matt Essert, "In Bold New Retirement Strategy, NYPD Takes Innocent People's Money," *Policy Mic*, January 16, 2014 (http://mic.com/articles/79229/in-bold-new-retirement-strategy- nypd-takes-innocent-people-s-money)

17: Michael Preciado, Bart J. Wilson, *Bad Apples or Bad Laws? Testing the Incentives of Civil Forfeiture*, Institute for Justice, http://ij.org/images/pdf_folder/private_property/bad-apples-bad- laws.pdf (September 2014)

18: German Lopez, "Why Eric Holder's civil forfeiture reforms can't keep police from taking your stuff," *Vox*, January 20, 2015 (http://www.vox.com/2015/1/20/7860363/equitable-sharing- police)

19: End Civil Forfeiture, *New Data Analysis Shows Revised Department of Justice Forfeiture Policy Would Stop Only a Fraction of Seizures*, http://endforfeiture.com/new-data-analysis- shows-revised-department-of-justice-forfeiture-policy-would-stop-only-a-fraction-of-seizures-2/ (February 12, 2015)

20: George Leef, "Loretta Lynch Has No Problem With Civil Asset Forfeiture-And That's A Problem," *Forbes*, November 25, 2014 (http://www.forbes.com/sites/georgeleef/2014/11/25/loretta-lynch-has-no-problem-with-civil- asset-forfeiture-and-thats-a-problem/)

21: Robert Everett Johnson, "Loretta Lynch: On civil forfeiture, actions speak louder than words," *The Washington Times*, February 6, 2015 (http://www.washingtontimes.com/news/2015/feb/6/robert-everett-johnson-loretta-lynch-civil- forfeit/)

22: GovTrack, *S. 2644 (113th): FAIR Act*, https://www.govtrack.us/congress/bills/113/s2644

# Interviews

*Libya, Syria, and the West: An Interview with Andrew Gavin Marshall*

*Originally Published on: September 9, 2011*

This is the transcript of an interview I had with Andrew Gavin Marshall, an independent researcher and writer. In the following interview, we discuss the US-NATO "intervention" in Libya and its effects on the African continent, as well as whether or not a Western intervention of Syria is possible. For more information on Libya, read Mr. Marshall's article entitled Lies, War, and Empire: NATO's "Humanitarian Imperialism" in Libya on AndrewGavinMarshall.com.

**1. Seeing as how the rebels are split into factions, do you think this will come back to haunt the US and NATO in the formation of the new Libyan government?**

Mr. Marshall: The fact that the rebels are split into factions is not a surprise to the West. From the beginning of the TNC (Transitional National Council), the organization was factionalized, and with the recent assassination of one of the military commanders (several weeks prior to the storming of Tripoli), these factions were known to be in competition. Thus, it is likely that this potential was taken into consideration by Western strategists. Whoever may become supreme within the TNC in a power struggle, it would be likely that the country could descend into a more chaotic system or civil war. If the al-Qaeda rebel factions (those with the most military training and experience) were to get a strong foothold in the country, this could even provide the West with a pretext for an occupation of Libya in order to "secure" the "transition" of the country into a liberal democratic structure.

It seems unlikely that the West would support a new dictatorship in Libya. In 2005, the Council on Foreign Relations (the premier strategic policy planning institution in the United States - the "imperial brain trust" as some theorists have referred to them) produced a document, "In Support of Arab Democracy" [1]. One of its chief authors was Madeleine Albright, a protégé of the most influential strategic thinker in the American Empire, Zbigniew Brzezinski. The ultimate conclusion laid out in the report was that the United States needed to undertake a strategy of "democracy promotion" in the Arab world, replacing once-pliant dictatorships with more stable, secure liberal democratic states. The report stated quite emphatically, that democracy should be promoted through "Evolution, not revolution." However, it also emphasized the need to employ different strategies in different countries, and not resort to a "one-size fits all" strategy. With the 'Arab Spring', the democracy promotion agenda was forced to the forefront and had to act, pre-empt, and co-opt at a rate in which it was perhaps not prepared. Thus, we have seen the co-optation (or attempted co-optation, since these events have not yet subsided) of the uprisings in Tunisia and Egypt.

A true revolution is a threat to Western domination of the region, its resources and population. Thus, evolution into liberal democratic states is preferable to a true people's revolution. True democracy, however, is not desired by Western strategists. True democracy (where the people would rule) is anathema to American imperial interests for a very clear reason: the public opinion of the Arab world.

In 2010, a major Western polling agency conducted a survey of popular opinion in the Arab world. Among the findings were that a vast majority felt that Iran had a right to a nuclear program (as high as 97% agreed with that in Egypt), that a majority felt Iran obtaining nuclear weapons would be good for the stability of the Middle East, and that the two countries which were perceived as the "biggest threat" to the Middle East were Israel and the United States, respectively (with 88% and 77%) while Iran was perceived as a major threat by only 10%, China by 3%, and Syria by 1%. [2]

Thus, we must see the current upheavals in the Arab world as part of a larger, global strategy. Following the collapse of the USSR, Western liberal capitalist democracy was promoted as the "winner" of the Cold War, and the only system worthy of upholding. Thus, Yugoslavia, a socialist state, had to be dismantled so that no "alternatives" to the Western dominated system may persevere. The Latin American dictatorships, so strongly supported for decades (and indeed much longer), were no longer sustainable. The neoliberal reforms of the age of 'structural adjustment' (promoted and implemented by the IMF and World Bank from the 1980s onward) had thoroughly discredited the states that implemented them, both in Latin America and sub-Saharan Africa.

As poverty spread, and social destruction accelerated, we saw the proliferation of NGOs as modern missionaries, seeking to treat the symptoms of our system of 'global apartheid' (seeking to relieve poverty, address health care, education, etc), while refusing to challenge the system that created these conditions. It was also in this context that we saw the emergence of the "democratization" agenda of Western powers. The "failure" of the 'structural adjustment programs' was framed as being the responsibility of the governments that implemented them, largely dictatorships, and thus, it was perceived as a "governance" issue, not a failure of the economic conditions imposed upon those nations. Thus, democracy promotion became part of future "adjustment" programs. Yet, this version of democracy is very specific, not populist: build a liberal democratic state with multi-party elections, civil society, and a constitution.

The aim and result, however, was to create factions of elites which would compete for power in elections (often taking the form of ethno-centric parties, further dividing subject populations among ethnic lines); civil society would seek to promote and implement the contours of a liberal democratic Western-oriented capitalist state, institutionalizing this Western ideology into the construction of the state system, promoting "human rights", accountability, poverty- reduction, etc., all which while often providing some minimal relief and constructive support to people in need, ultimately provide the hegemonic system (imperial in nature) with an aspect of consent. Hegemony, as defined by Antonio Gramsci, is of a dual nature: coercion and consent.

While the coercive apparatus of the state (police, military, etc) is essential in creating and maintaining hegemony (as the dozens of IMF riots where people rose up and protested against 'structural adjustment' in the 80s and 90s were often violently repressed by the state). However, consent to the system creates a more stable, lasting hegemony.

Consent is engineered largely through civil society, which seeks to make 'reforms' to the system, which lessen the symptoms of imperialist oppression and domination, but thereby enhance the stability of that very system by acting as a pressure valve against revolution. This system was promoted in Asia, Africa and Latin America.

Thus, dictatorships were slowly replaced with liberal democratic states, which were not only more effective in terms of securing consent to the global apartheid system, but were also more subservient to Western domination, as instead of having to deal with entrenched local dictatorships, which could (and have often) challenged Western domination over their country (Saddam Hussein is a good example), they would simply be able to "promote democracy" through funding opposition parties, and just as in the United States itself, you change the parties, but the system remains the same, the same interests are served, and the people are divided into "party politics" instead of united against their true challenge: empire. In Latin America, this system became largely discredited, and thus we saw the emergence of populist democracies, with Jean-Bertrande Aristide in Haiti (who was twice overthrown by the West), and Chavez in Venezuela, Morales in Bolivia, et. al. These populist leaders have challenged (to various degrees) Western domination over their nations and peoples.

In Sub-Saharan Africa, the wave of populist democracies has yet to emerge, if at all. Yet, the liberal democratic states have already been largely discredited in the eyes of the majority of people. The Arab world, long dominated by pliant Western dictatorships (and a few anti-Western dictatorships), is now experiencing its wave of "democratization." The true question then, is whether we will see the emergence of pliant liberal democratic capitalist states (as is preferred by the West in order to maintain hegemony over the region, an absolute imperial necessity), or if we will see the development of populist democracies. It should be noted that populist revolutions and democracies would be ardently opposed by the Western nations. So, just as in Libya, Egypt, Tunisia, Syria, and elsewhere, we will see different strategies and methods all seeking to achieve roughly similar goals: "democratization" of the state in order to secure Western regional hegemony.

As we have seen with Libya, one strategy that will not be shied away from is war (or "humanitarian intervention"). We must also not rule out the possibility of an occupation, presumably under the auspices of securing the "transition to democracy", which I think is a very likely scenario in Libya. Support for radical, militant elements in the Libyan rebels (specifically those linked to al-Qaeda) was a specific strategy which achieved its objective: change of government. This strategy may be employed elsewhere, such as in Syria, Yemen, et. al. However, from an imperial-strategic standpoint, it is not favorable to have a radical Islamist government in power, as the threat of popular revolution would remain. We may see some form of radicalized dictatorships being established for short periods of time, but these would ultimately be harder to control; thus, the ultimate objective is totally dependent, and pliant regimes.

In such a situation, I believe the West will prefer to see the faction in which the leader of the TNC, Jabril, takes control of the country, as he has made it quite clear that he favors neoliberal reforms and Western "investment" in Libya. Documents released by Wikileaks revealed in a 2009 diplomatic cable from the US Ambassador to Libya referring to Jabril as someone who "gets the US perspective" on investment, and suggested supporting him further. Just as has been done from the very origins of al-Qaeda, the United States has covertly supported the organization in order to achieve strategic objectives, largely in terms of overthrowing or waging war against unfavorable regimes. However, another popular strategic aim of supporting al-Qaeda affiliated organizations lies in using them as a pretext to invade and occupy particular countries. We have seen the former strategy already used in Libya, the question is: will we see the latter?


**2. How will other nations react now that the West has a foothold in Africa? Do you think that they will obey the West for fear of "humanitarian intervention?"**

Mr. Marshall: The reactions from other nations will vary. Following the US invasion of Iraq in 2003, many nations were scared into cooperating with the West, including Gaddafi and Libya itself. It was in 2004 that the sanctions were ended and economic cooperation and investment began. The United States and NATO, having displayed their willingness to use force in achieving objectives in Africa, will likely create a more compliant atmosphere among several states in the Arab and African world. However, the populations would likely be more opposed to Western domination over their own nations, so the political leaders will have to play a dangerous game of attempting to secure their own position vis a vis, meeting the demands of the West while placating the demands of their own people.

In the current 'Age of Awakening' (the Arab Spring), domestic leaders are increasingly fearful of their own populations, and must take popular opinion into account more than they previously have. An occupation of Libya would also give the West the opportunity to enhance its military presence on the continent, establish military bases, and possibly even establish a continental headquarters for the Pentagon's newest strategic command, AFRICOM (which is currently based out of Germany, due to no African nations being willing to host it). This would be a strong indication of maintaining a military presence on the continent and thus, resembles a geopolitical threat to all other nations.

**3. Would you say that the African Union truly stood up to the US and NATO? Do you think they could have done more?**

Mr. Marshall: No, the African Union did not truly stand up to NATO. Certainly, their rhetoric of opposition revealed that the only ones who were not buying the line of "humanitarian intervention" in Africa were Africans themselves. This was the most important aspect of the AU's opposition to such an operation. However, ultimately, South Africa was pressured into releasing its frozen Libyan assets for the new government, and the AU is falling into line. In terms of whether or not they could have "done more," their abilities are highly limited. They did, early on, attempt to land in Libya (prior to the intervention, but immediately following the no-fly zone) in order to attempt to negotiate a seize fire and come to a peaceful solution. Yet, as a result of the no-fly zone, the dominant Western powers (in particular, the US, France, and UK) refused to allow the AU's plane to land in Libya and pursue a peaceful resolution. Ultimately, the AU, like the Palestinian Authority in the occupied territories, is not a separate power from that of the greater institution. It is an organization whose power is derived from that which is given to it. The PA is able to employ the authority which it is given to it by Israel. The AU is able to use the authority which is granted to it by the UN, US and the "international community."

The AU takes part in "peacekeeping operations" which are rhetorical covers for occupations, such as in Sudan and Somalia and elsewhere. In such cases, the more Western- complaint nations (such as Uganda and Rwanda in Central Africa) send in their military forces (heavily trained, armed, and subsidized by American "aid") to nations such as Somalia (whose government the US overthrew in 2007) as "AU peacekeepers", thus creating a sense of legitimacy, as it is Africans policing Africans, not white Westerners. In short, the AU is not able to be an effective counter to Western domination because it has been allowed to be built up only so much as it can be integrated into a system of global domination (or "global governance").

A new part for the AU which could potentially challenge Western domination would be to pursue a more overt non-aligned movement type of institution, anti-imperialist and pro- African, bringing Africa together not to allow for more effective co-optation of the continent, but to allow for more effective opposition to Western domination. My hopes for such an organization to achieve that objective are minimal however; I have little to no faith in the 'nation- state' or supra-national institutions in countering the system of domination, as they are institutionally and ideologically a product and part of that very system.

**4. How likely is it that the West will intervene in Syria? If the West does intervene, do you think that the intervention will be in the style of Egypt, with the co-opting of the protest movement or will they decide to militarily intervene, as in the situation with Libya?**

Mr. Marshall: I think a Western intervention in Syria is very likely. This is a dictator who has not been a stalwart puppet of the Western nations. This, in what we refer to as "international politics" is among the greatest sins a nation can commit. Any and all means could be undertaken in order to replace this regime. As the situation is already one mired in violence, it would appear likely that a violent "solution" would be undertaken. Thus far, in the Arab Spring, we have seen very different strategies taking place in very different countries: civil society co-optation in Tunisia, support for the military in creating a new government in Egypt, violent and brutal repression in Bahrain, war and "intervention" in Libya, etc. I think it is premature to declare which strategy will be used in Syria, as I think it will ultimately become the "Syria strategy."

The imperialist powers are not analyzing and implementing strategies in a cookie-cutter one-size-fits-all method, so outside analysts and observers should not view the situation as such.

In order to understand imperialism and contemplate imperial strategies, one must allow themselves to think like an imperialist. What is the aim in Syria? Put simply: a change of government. What are external forces which could likely step into an internal conflict in Syria? Iran, for one; but also Israel. Israel will simply not tolerate a radical and populist government coming to power in Syria. Iran does not want to lose a regional ally. Thus, the costs and consequences of a foreign intervention in Syria are far different from those of Libya.

A foreign military intervention in the country (which I think is a likely possibility), has an enormous potential to result in a rapid and exponentially accelerated descent into chaos for the entire region.

One must not rule out the possibility of a major regional war and destabilization campaign being on the table of imperial strategists. If all else fails, plunge a region into absolute war, and you will, in time, be able to re-shape its political structures through violence and destruction, and "reconstruction". It was, after all, World War One that brought an end to the Ottoman Empire, where at the Paris Peace talks of 1919, the nations of the Middle East were drawn up by French and British imperialists who implanted pliant leaders and consuls. War is a highly effective strategic tool for the aim of total reorganization. For decades now, there have been discussions in various strategic circles about the "re-making of the Middle East", re-drawing the borders, etc. To undertake such a task, if that is the current desired strategy, destabilization and war is the most effective means.


**5. If the West does intervene in Syria, what will be the consequences for Iran and the great Middle East region? How do you think Iran and its allies will react?**

Mr. Marshall: I think Iran would attempt to counter an intervention in Syria through support to counter-revolutionary forces in Syria, supporting such organizations like Hezbollah or Hamas as they do in Palestine and Lebanon. Iran must be careful of being drawn into a more direct conflict by the West, (which could be a strategic aim of a Syrian intervention), as it could likely incur a Western reaction directly against Iran.

If Iran becomes involved, militarily, in Syria, it is unlikely that Israel would remain uninvolved. This would lead to a rapid acceleration of conflict: Israel and Iran would likely go to war, and the entire region would become engulfed in conflict.

We must remember that Israel has upwards of 200 nuclear weapons, the only regional nuclear superpower. Israel, also, would not hesitate to use those weapons. In such a situation, I think it would be likely that we could begin using the term, "World War Three" to describe the global context of such a conflict, which would surely draw in Russia, China, India, and Pakistan, all of which are also nuclear powers.


**Endnotes**

1: Council on Foreign Relations, *In Support of Arab Democracy*, http://www.cfr.org/democratization/support-arab-democracy/p8166 (June 2005)

2: Shibley Telhami, *2010 Arab Public Opinion Poll: Results of Arab Opinion Survey Conducted June 29-July 20, 2010*, Brookings Institution, http://www.brookings.edu/research/reports/2010/08/05-arab-opinion-poll-telhami (August 5, 2010)

This is a transcript of an email interview I had with Andrew Gavin Marshall, Project Manager of The People's Book Project [http://www.thepeoplesbookproject.com]. In it we discuss anarchism, trace its beginnings, delve into some of its history in both the United States and around the world, and conclude by discussing anarchism's effect on today's Occupy movement.

## 1. Could you provide a working definition of anarchism?

Mr. Marshall: Anarchism is difficult to define simply because it is such a diverse political philosophy, with so many different variants. So the definition tends to alter as the particular brand of anarchism differs. However, at its core, anarchism – in its original Greek wording – means simply to be "without a leader." Running in opposition to traditional Liberal thought, such as that articulated by Hobbes' notion of anarchy as a "state of nature" mired in war and conflict, and thus the State was necessary to maintain order, one of the original anarchist thinkers, Pierre- Joseph Proudhon countered, "Anarchy is Order." Despite the connotation of the word "anarchy" to that of "chaos" and "disorder," anarchism and anarchist societies are highly organized and 'ordered.' The central difference between an anarchist conception of order and others is that anarchy removes the structures of authority, so that society is organized through free association and non-hierarchical organization. It promotes both the individual and the collective, simultaneously.

This is opposed to Liberal thought, which promotes the individual above all else, or socialist thought, which promotes the collective above all else. As one of the most influential anarchist thinkers, Mikhail Bakunin, described anarchist thought when he stated, "We are convinced that liberty without socialism is privilege, injustice; and that socialism without liberty is slavery and brutality." This has often led anarchism to be synonymous with what is referred to as "Libertarian Socialism," which is where the root of Libertarianism lies, but has strayed quite far from. Ultimately, what underlies all anarchist thought is a heightened and radical critique and questioning of power and authority: if a source of authority cannot legitimize its existence, it should not exist.

## 2. Who and where was anarchism first thought of? What was the societal context that anarchist thought originated from?

Mr. Marshall: Anarchism is not like Marxism or Liberalism or other firm and concrete ideas, where the originators can be properly identified and understood. Just as it espouses a philosophy of being "without a leader" so too does a great deal of its historical development take place "without a leader." Anarchist thought developed – to various degrees – throughout much of human history, in different times and place, often without any contact between the various civilizations themselves. It is, in this sense, an organic idea that can originate within any context. The first evolution of anarchist ideas has been identified as originating in ancient China, among the Taoists. Peter Marshall wrote in his quintessential, Demanding the Impossible: A History of Anarchism, that, "Throughout recorded history, the anarchist spirit can be seen emerging in the clan, tribe, village community, independent city, guild and union." It emerged in various strains of thought in ancient Greece, and later during the Christian era, most especially with the peasant revolts of the Middle Ages. This all took place, however, before anarchism came to be defined as an ideology or philosophy in and of itself.

This process took place after the end of feudalism, with the rise of Capitalism, and largely brought about by both the Renaissance and the Enlightenment. The Renaissance brought forth the ideas of the individual, and the Enlightenment conceptualized of social progress. It thus arose as a more coherent and distinct philosophy in reaction to the development of centralized States, nationalism, industrialization and capitalism in the late 18th century. Peter Marshall wrote, "Anarchism thus took up the dual challenge of overthrowing both Capital and the State." William Godwin is largely considered the "father of anarchism" as having first articulated the desire for an end to the state, the German philosopher Max Stirner closely followed, but it was Pierre-Joseph Proudhon in France who was the first to call himself an "anarchist." Proudhon articulated a number of anarchist ideas and slogans which still have resonance today, such as the concept that, "Just as man seeks justice in equality, society seeks order in anarchy," and the popular sayings, "Anarchy is Order" and "Property is Theft."

Next followed the Russian revolutionary Mikhail Bakunin, the father of "Libertarian Socialism," and the man who became the principle ideological opponent to Karl Marx. Another Russian, Peter Kropotkin, was one of the most influential anarchist philosophers in history, developing it into a more systematic social philosophy. In the United States, Benjamin Tucker was among the first anarchist thinkers, adding a particularly individualistic character to it. Other prominent anarchist thinkers include Leo Tolstoy, who brought in a religious element, and Emma Goldman, who developed a feminist strand of thought in anarchism. All of these thinkers collectively shaped the development of anarchist thought and practice in the 19th century and paved the way for its evolution over the 20th.


## 3. What form did anarchism first take? How did the state and the populace at large react to it?

Mr. Marshall: Anarchism took different forms in different places and times. Throughout its modern history, regardless of location, the State always reacted defensively and often violently. Since one of the main tenets of anarchism is the abolition of the State, the state has in turn sought (with arguably more success) the abolition of anarchism. Anarchists have been demonized, infiltrated, spied on, deported, killed, or had entire movements violently destroyed. Anarchism was arguably most represented in labor and immigrant movements and activism in the 19th and early 20th centuries, particularly among unions and Jewish emigrants out of Eastern Europe. Poor Jewish emigrants who had to flee Eastern Europe and Russia following the pogroms of the late 19th century took with them an ideology which found a deep grounding in a people without a state, a philosophy which reflected a stateless vision of global solidarity. Many of the Jews who fled were also socialists and Marxists, and radicals of all types, but the most prevalent force was with anarchism. These radical emigrants helped spread the ideas of anarchism into Western Europe, to London, France, Spain, to the United States, and even helping facilitate a massive anarchist movement in Argentina, much larger than the local communist movement.

Radical Jewish emigrants who were articulating anarchist philosophies generally incurred two reactions from their new countries of residence: the poor and working class people and immigrants welcomed these radicals, who struggled for the rights of all, and who were often at the forefront of movements for social justice, labor rights, anti-war, and empowerment; and, on the other hand, the State and media would promote the idea of dangerous "foreigners" and often promoted conceptions of anti-Semitism in order to push this idea. Thus, the reaction from among the general (at least poor and working class) populations was to undermine anti-Semitism and promote cross-ethnic solidarity, while the State and established powers further promoted anti- Semitism, anti-immigration laws, and enhanced police responses. This in turn facilitated police cooperation and coordination between various states, from Western Europe, to the United States and Argentina.


## 4. How did anarchism evolve over time and spread?

Mr. Marshall: As previously mentioned, a great deal of the spread of anarchism was facilitated by the mass emigration of radical Jews out of Eastern Europe and Russia in the late 19th and 20th centuries. The modern history of anarchism is intrinsically linked to modern Jewish history, to a recent history of anti-Semitism, and even to the history of Zionism. This had both negative and positive effects, and promoted two major stereotypes for Jews. On the one hand, it promoted the stereotype of the radical Jewish immigrant, which received a good deal of favor among oppressed populations, but also a great deal of anxiety, xenophobia, anti-Semitism and racism among the ruling classes. On the other hand, Jews were subjected to the stereotype of the rapacious Capitalist, mostly by making reference to the Rothschild banking family.

Many of these stereotypes exist to this very day, but they lack their proper historical context. For example, the Rothschilds in London were very concerned about the radical Jewish emigrants who were entering England and other West European countries from Eastern Europe. These Jews were holding demonstrations and organizing strikes in London and other Western cities, threatening the very interests that the Rothschilds were invested in. The first impulse was to impose immigration restrictions, though this would be perceived as very similar to the expulsions from Eastern Europe, so a new strategy was needed. It was around this time that the Rothschilds became interested in Zionism. Zionism itself had several different brands of thought, and evolved over time. It was originally very radical, and even socialistic. The ideas of Peter Kropotkin and Leo Tolstoy were very influential among many Jewish emigrants in Palestine in the early 20th century, who established the kibbutz movement, a libertarian socialist collective community in Palestine, based originally on agriculture, rejecting the idea of a Jewish nation state and instead promoted Arab-Jewish solidarity.

The Rothschilds had for many years refused to support – whether ideologically or financially – the Zionist movement, and for a number of reasons: it's radical socialist ideas were opposed to the very nature of how the Rothschilds became the Rothschilds, and perhaps more importantly, because the Rothschilds feared that if they promoted the idea of a Jewish nation, they would be forced to leave Western Europe and go to that very nation. As circumstances changed, however, the Rothschilds promoted a non-radical vision of Zionism, not socialistic or anarchistic, but distinctly Western and capitalistic. It became an opportunity to push the spread of Jewish radicalism into a more controllable ideology, and instead of deporting radical Jews, to support immigration to a new location (the Rothschilds were among the main financiers in personally providing for the means to transport Jews to Palestine).

There were, of course, other representations of anarchism. In Russia, the anarchist movement had a great strength and powerful base of support. During the Russian Revolution, there were three main factions fighting: the Reds (the Communists), the Whites (supported by the West as liberal democrats), and often forgotten from history, the anarchists. Both the Reds and Whites would attack and seek to destroy the anarchist movement during the Russian Revolution and civil war. Trotsky himself led armies against anarchist factions in Russia. The Whites and Reds were fighting for control of the State, while the anarchists were struggling for a society without the state. Ultimately, they were of course destroyed in this battle.

By far the most impressive representation of anarchism in modern history was in Spain. As Peter Marshall wrote, "To date, Spain is the only country in the modern era where anarchism can credibly be said to have developed into a major social movement and to have seriously threatened the State." Spain was in part specially suited to this because of its long history dating back to the Middle Ages of having many independent communes with their own particular local laws. Anarchism in Spain became popular among the rural poor in the late 19th century, often inciting local insurrections. In time, the philosophy made its way into mining communities and working communities in Barcelona and Madrid. It became popular among young and radical intellectuals, and reportedly even attracted the likes of a young Pablo Picasso. Spanish anarchism was a struggle primarily against both the Church and the State. Just as in France in the 1890s, Spanish anarchism often had violent expressions in bombings and assassinations, met with brutal government repression.

In time, however, the inability of terrorism to overthrow the State became clear, and instead of violence, propaganda became the primary tactic, of spreading the philosophy among workers and peasants. In 1907, in the midst of industrial unrest, libertarian unions in Catalunya, Spain, formed the syndicalist organization, Solidaridad Obrera (Workers' Unity), and in 1909 it called a general strike. Street battles broke out in which roughly 200 workers were killed, and after which the unions decided to form a stronger and larger organization, the Confederacion Nacional del Trabajo (CNT), which by 1919 had a membership of one million. Between 1917 and 1923 it organized revolutionary strikes all across Spain. In 1919, the CNT adopted the principles of communismo libertario is its main ideology, uniting many unions and workers in opposition to authoritarian socialism.

The highly decentralized structure of the CNT made it resilient to repression, just as several anarchist groups in Russia during the Revolution and Civil War. In the late 1920s and early 1930s, the moderates and reformers were pushed out of the CNT, and the more radical Federacion Anarquista Iberica (FAI) took centre stage. Anarchist workers and peasants attempted to form insurrectional communes across Spain in the early 1930s, often leading to violent state repression. More strikes and insurrections were attempted, one of which included an uprising of 70,000 miners in 1934 which was violently crushed (with the help of Moroccan troops), with hundreds killed. In the following two years, Spain was drifting toward civil war. In 1936, a vision of a new society was outlined at the national congress of the CNT, representing half a million workers by this time, promoting libertarian communism in a society of communes, based on free association syndicalism, linked through regional and national federations, void of social hierarchy.

The individual and collective were simultaneously promoted, so that one was not sacrificed for the other, but rather, both were strengthened in support of one another. Diversity was accepted and promoted, understanding that communes would take on different forms and represent different ideological strands. Education was to be concerned with literacy so that people may think for themselves, and there was no distinction between intellectuals and workers. Courts and prisons were without purpose. These resolutions adopted at the 1936 congress were not to be a blueprint, but rather, "the point of departure for Humanity towards its integral liberation." Between the time of the congress and the end of the year, the membership of the CNT had grown from 500,000 to 1.5 million. Franco rebelled against the Spanish Republic in July of 1936, was his forces were quickly disarmed by popular militias.

Franco still managed to take control of half the country, though the anarcho-syndicalists were running Barcelona, and Catalunya was essentially an independent republic. Ultimately, however, the concept of the social revolution was being sacrificed in order to fight against Franco and his fascist faction. Still, workers and peasants were being organized to manage their own affairs, and Libertarian Communism seemed not only possible, but actual. Anarchists and other groups formed militias to fight against Franco. George Orwell, who was in Spain fighting against Franco, was also correcting the perceptions given about the anarchists, explaining the incredible achievements of Spanish anarchism.

By 1937, roughly 3 million people were living in collective rural communities. Many villages were established, where money was abolished, collectivizing the land, eradicating illiteracy, and the popular assemblies often included woman and children, responsible for electing an administrative committee which would be accountable to the assemblies. There were also some communities which were 'individualist', where people would work their own individual plots of land, while Barcelona became the centre of "urban collectivization." Public services and industries were run remarkably well in a large and diverse city. Between July and October 1936, "virtually all production and distribution were under workers' control." However, the social revolution was undermined by the war against Franco, and the increasing struggle with other factions, such as the Communists.

Some anarchist leaders were being co-opted into government, and the CNT became increasingly ineffective. As the other factions were receiving foreign support, with the Communists getting support from the Soviet Union, Franco getting support from Hitler and Mussolini, and other factions getting support from Western liberal states, the CNT felt that it would have to incorporate with the state in order to get aid in order to win the war. Thus, by the middle of 1937, wrote Peter Marshall, "the greatest anarchist experiment in history was virtually over; it has lasted barely a year." The communists had begin to replace the anarchists due to their foreign aid from the Soviet Union, who also organized a secret police which began a reign of terror, largely against anarchist groups, and ultimately the government itself crushed anarchist resistance and imposed censorship of the CNT.

The conflict between the Communists and Anarchists was perhaps the central reason why the Republicans lost the war against Franco, who ultimately conquered Spain in 1939, establishing a fascist dictatorship which lasted until 1976, and which had caused half a million radical Spaniards to flee into exile. Thus, Spain represented both the greatest achievement and failure of anarchism in the 20th century.

Though the movement itself was largely debased during the Cold War, the ideas continued to evolve, and new strands emerged, such as ecological anarchism and even anarcho- Capitalism, which came to be a driving force behind the modern American libertarian movement.


**4. What role did anarchism play in the 19th century labor movement? How was anarchism received in the general labor movement and the regular populace?**

Mr. Marshall: In the 19th century United States, labor struggles were a consistent historical development. As anarchism became an articulated idea and philosophy, along with Marxism and Socialism, these radical philosophies became increasingly associated with labor movements, especially in the formation and operation of unions. In the 1860s, two anarchist federations were formed in the United States, the New England Labor Reform League and the American Labor Reform League, which, according to William Reichert, "were the source of radical vitality in America for several decades." Arguably the most influential American anarchist of his time, Benjamin Tucker, translated the works of Proudhon in 1875, and started his own anarchist publications and journals.

From the 1880s onward, many immigrants to the United States, such as Emma Goldman, helped facilitate the growing popularity of anarchism. Anarchist ideas had some grounding in the revolutionary labor movement in Chicago in the period of the 1870s to the 1880s, noted especially in the Haymarket Affair in 1886, which was connected with the struggle for the eight- hour workday. Across the country on May 1, 1886, roughly half a million workers demonstrated in support of this idea, with the most extreme cases in Chicago, with the largest strikes and demonstrations. Three days later, on May 4, a bomb was thrown at a protest rally in Chicago's Haymarket Square, killing several police officers and leading to the shooting deaths and injuries of an unknown amount of protesting workers by the police.

The bombing, though its origins remain a mystery, led to the Chicago elite leading a crusade against revolutionary workers movements, with over 200 members of the International Working People's Association (IWPA) arrested and several tried, with the state prosecutor proclaiming, "Anarchy is on trial." Following the Haymarket Affair, working class organizations and unions became increasingly radical, many of them adopting distinctly anarchist principles of organization and ideology, and in turn, state repression became more violent and pronounced. The reason why radical unions did not survive the following decades was not due to some intrinsically American spirit of "rugged individualism," and the national mythology dictates, but rather due to the violent and consistent state repression. Thereafter, and until this very day, May 1 has been celebrated internationally (though ironically not in the United States or Canada) as International Workers' Day (or May Day).

This radical movement that had emerged out of Chicago in this era has often been referred to as a blending of Marxism and Anarchism, as "anarcho-syndicalist," "revolutionary socialist," or even "communistic-anarchist." It did indeed have a profound impact upon all labor struggles in the following era, upon the agitation and strikes, and upon union organization and ideology. However, as it evolved into the 20th century, unions became increasingly crushed, co- opted, and dismembered, so that instead of united and international federations, they became industry and even company-specific, they became reformist, not revolutionary, and they became even corporatist, in which they sought to work with big business and government instead of against.

This is most emblematic today in the organization and ideology of the largest union federation in the U.S., the AFL-CIO, whose leaders are members of the Trilateral Commission, regularly speak at the Council on Foreign Relations, and are involved in foreign imperial policy for the United States, going with U.S. financial backing to poor nations to organize workers along corporatist lines, drawing them away from radical and revolutionary organization and ideology.


## 5. How has anarchist philosophy been distorted over time?

Mr. Marshall: This is a very important question. Anarchism is often considered synonymous with violence and chaos, when in truth; it has far more to do with peace and order. Anarchism has been very easy to dismiss and discredit simply because of its vast diversity. It has had no consistent and rigid structure of thought or action. Yes, there have been violent anarchists and violent agitation, terrorism, and assassinations, and this has done a great deal to discredit an entire and incredibly diverse realm of philosophical thought, but there is much more to anarchist ideas and actions. Anarchist history is often written out of official histories, such as with the Russian and Spanish revolutions, such as with Argentina and the spread of Jewish emigrants. Even today, many in the "alternative" media demonize anarchists.

Anarchist groups were among the first documented cases of having police infiltrators in London in the late 19th century. Infiltration of anarchist groups often still takes place, or more common, is that infiltrators in protests or other demonstrations simply aim to appear like "anarchists", who are often associated with the Black Bloc, wearing black and with faces covered by masks or bandanas. Many in the alternative press blame police infiltrators for all the violence at protests, which is a misrepresentation, and simultaneously they often portray anarchist groups such as the Black Bloc as entirely consisting of police infiltrators, which is also a misrepresentation. In turn, the state and media portray these same anarchistic groups as violent thugs and criminals, and justify state repression against protesters.

Now, while infiltration of such groups has been documented, we cannot conclude therefore that the entire group or its membership is. This is especially true for anarchist organizations, which reject hierarchical organization, and are therefore more challenging to co- opt or control through traditional means. While certain infiltrators may be present, it does not imply that the entire grouping is being led by such individuals, and the groups are often so loosely-knit that they do not even have a traditional organization as we typically understand it. However, such groups are subject to propaganda from all sides, and this has done a great deal to demonize anarchism as a whole.

In Montreal, for example, anarchists have often been blamed for most of the violence and vandalism, when in fact it is the police (in official uniforms) who have been the most violent and destructive against the burgeoning students movement which began back in February. If you look at the "anarchist" violence, it typically consists of vandalism against bank property, such as smashing bank windows, or throwing rocks at police. Some others among the protesters have also participated in these actions, which are almost always reactions against the police brutality that has been taking place. Reading statements of student protesters who were present on the May 4 protest in Victoriaville, Quebec, where several students were shot in the face with rubber bullets by the police and nearly killed, we see another side to the so-called Black Bloc.

Students described being tear gassed and falling to the ground as the riot police approached. Then it was members of the "Black Bloc" (or at least identified as looking like members, since there is hardly a membership roster), with their faces covered and goggles on, who would assist these fallen students, bringing them away from the riot police, treating their eyes, getting them to a medic, kicking the tear gas canisters back to the police. In many protests, when the police violence takes place, it is these individuals who appear to be on the "front lines." And while their specific actions may not be condoned, they do reflect a popular anger among a rather large segment of the students. So in terms of the demonization of anarchists, or very specific anarchist actions of violence, there is a difference between condoning the act, and condemning the anger.

Simply because the act itself may not be helpful in terms of gaining popular support for a cause, or because it "justifies" police repression in turn, does not mean – as many in the alternative press articulate – that the anarchists are "working for the State," are all agent provocateurs or infiltrators. Though this is the case at times, it is misleading to portray it as exclusive, and it simplifies rather complex situations, circumstances, and reactions. When a police truck was driven into a group of students at Victoriaville on May 4, it was a small group of average student protesters who picked up rocks to throw at the truck.

The vast majority of students were peaceful in the face of police violence and repression, but the fact that some will react violently is not a reason to dismiss, but an important point of understanding: it informs us that the situation is more extreme, that the reaction is more intense, that the circumstances are more dire. In the same way that when you corner an animal it becomes both its most vulnerable and most vicious, we are seeing this emerge in various protest movements and demonstrations around the world. Simply blaming "anarchists" does little to quell the violence and unrest, and does a great deal of harm to properly understanding these situations and how best to resolve them. Ironically, as anarchists in Montreal have been blamed for most of the violence at protests here over the past 15 weeks, the most organized and openly admitted anarchist event was in holding a large book fair.

Anarchism is still an intellectual pursuit, and because of its refusal to become a rigid ideology, and because of its acceptance of diversity, there will always be more radical and even violent elements and tactics, but ultimately, it is a philosophy built around the concept of solidarity and cooperation, of free association, liberty, and peace. The most common argument against anarchism, from those who typically do not understand what anarchy is, is that without some form of "authority," the world would be chaos, people would be killing each other, and we would have disorder and destruction.

The simplest answer to this, is to ask the person what we have in the world today: we live in a world of extreme authority, of more globalized authority in every sector of human action and interaction than ever before in human history, yet so much of the world is in chaos, disorder, destruction, war, starvation, decimation, division, segregation, exploitation, and domination. It is not a lack of order and authority that has brought this to be, but rather the exercise of authority in the name of order. People see anarchy as a paradox without acknowledging the paradox of the ideology versus reality of the world we currently live in. This has been the greatest success in distorting the philosophy of anarchism.


**6. How has anarchism been used in other parts of the world as a means of resistance?**

Mr. Marshall: Anarchism historically spread to London, France, Spain, Italy, the United States, and especially Argentina in Latin America, as some of its most obvious examples. As it was largely destroyed as a powerful movement following the two World Wars, it had a re-emergence during the rise of the New Left in the 1960s. The New Left was pivotal in the political agitation and protest movements in Europe and the United States in the late 1960s and early 1970s. It helped to re-invigorate an anti-Capitalist ideology and thinking, and in some cases, spawned an anarcho-Capitalist ideology itself. As the environmental movement emerged, so too did an anarchistic brand of environmentalism. Thus, as new movements and social agitation emerged and erupted, new brands and ideas of anarchism would adapt and evolve to the changed circumstances, just as it has through a great deal of human history.

**7. What is your opinion on modern-day anarchism, specifically anarchists who are a part of Occupy?**

Mr. Marshall: Modern anarchists are simply too diverse to hold a single opinion. It comes down, as it always has, to recognizing the diversity, and forming diverse opinions on different groups and tactics. As I referenced earlier, I may not condone the act, but I cannot condemn the anger. There was a time when I too would portray all violence as destructive and mindless and would even point as those who committed it as mere infiltrators and agents provocateurs. However, after having been witness to and caught in the midst of the student rebellion erupting in the Canadian province of Québec over the past 15 weeks, after having seen the national propaganda campaign against the students and the violent state repression enacted on a daily basis, it does not surprise me to see some people turning to acts of violence in their resistance. It ultimately is not helpful for the student movement as a whole, as it demonizes them and reduces popular support. But what I have come to understand is that it is a symptom of a large and growing anger, frustration, and discontent.

Violence and terror are reactions of the desperate, so instead of demonizing the act itself, we must come to understand the desperation. For if we truly want peace, and peaceful protests, we must understand the origins of violent reactions. Anarchist groups and ideas are re-emerging around the world to a larger and quicker degree than perhaps thought possible. We see anarchists as part of protest movements in Britain, Spain, Greece, Quebec, the United States, in the Occupy Movement, in Iceland and Italy. The tactics and specifics vary from place to place and person to person, of course. For example, in Italy, there was a recent case in which an anarchist group took responsibility for kneecapping an Italian nuclear company executive, and threatened more shootings. I think it is likely we will see a type of historical parallel to what took place in the 1880s in many places around the world, where we see acts of violence and terror which are attributed to or undertaken by individual or specific anarchist groups, and that as these tactics are presented as unhelpful, as counter-productive and problematic, there may be an increased tendency to renounce all forms of violence and to focus on education and "propaganda," which the vast majority of anarchists focus on already.

Just as a contrast, while it may be the case that an anarchist group has shot at industry executives in Italy, an anarchist intellectual – Noam Chomsky – has for decades been speaking softly and eloquently, writing and reading and agitating not with fists but words. Ultimately, Chomsky has done more to advance anarchism and anarchist ideas than any act of violence has or could. This is the direction that should be most pursued, and along the lines of anarchistic organization. If you simply look at the Occupy Movement itself, there are many cases of anarchistic structure: the lack of hierarchy, the general assemblies, the public libraries, etc. The libraries are a fascinating case, especially in this time of "economic austerity" in which libraries are increasingly coming under the harsh gaze of the State to have their funding cut.

What the Occupy groups have shown is that if the State takes away the libraries, people can simply organize their own. In Greece, the State demanded that a hospital close down due to budget cuts. Workers at the hospital occupied it and began to run it themselves. There are also reports that some communities in Greece are attempting to form their own currency or trading system. Around the world we increasingly see workers occupying factories and taking over the management collectively, demonstrating the lack of need for professional "managers" (who take all the profits), and the amazing ability of workers to be both decision-makers and producers. These cases are not discussed often or reported frequently, simply because they represent the problem of a good idea: other people might notice. In this sense, if we understand but don't emphasize the violent actions of a few, and instead if we come to examine and understand anarchism for the vast diversity of philosophy and tactics it truly represents, we are able to see a great degree of hope and progress coming from this movement in the future.

Where the State and corporations and banks work against the people (which is everywhere), where they close factories, foreclose on homes, cut education and health care spending, demand increased costs for people, while decreasing taxes for the rich, there are anarchistic answers and possibilities. In regards to where I currently live in Quebec, with a massive student movement sparked by a 75% increase in tuition, we are suffering under an old paradigm of education, of a political, social, and economic system that benefits the few at the expense of the many. While the first response is to 'defend' the educational system as it currently exists, the long-term solution is to radically reorient our conception and organization of education itself. For example, when the university system originated in the Middle Ages, there were two initial brands of university education: the Paris model, and the Bologna model.

In Paris, the school was run by administrations and cultural-regional elites. Over time, as the nation-state and capitalism evolved, these became the patrons and administrators of universities. In Bologna, Italy, the school was run by the students and staff. For obvious reasons, the Paris model won out, but it would seem that in the face of our current global social, political, and economic crises, it is time for the Bologna model to win the historical battle in a resurgence. The notion of students and staff running schools is distinctly anarchistic, in the same way that workers running factories is. As Proudhon declared, "Anarchy is Order," and in a world of so much chaos and destruction and authority, perhaps it is time for a little anarchy and order.

This is a transcript of an email interview I had with James Corbett of Corbett Report [www.corbettreport.com]. In it, we discuss the ongoing crisis in Syria, the role of the alternative media, and how people can break free from the current system of oppression.

## 1. What is your opinion of the ongoing crisis in Syria?

Mr. Corbett: The crisis in Syria can only be understood through the lens of what the mainstream Western media is leaving out of their reporting, namely the ongoing, on-the-record support of outside actors in arming, equipping, and training the so-called "opposition" that is currently waging a ground war against the Syrian government.

This help is coming in the form of equipment and tactical involvement from the US State Department and the CIA, arms and supplies from Saudi Arabia and Qatar, logistical support and operational bases in Turkey, and armed militants associated with Al Qaeda and other Wahabbi Sunni terror organizations from Libya, Iraq, and elsewhere. In this context, the constant demands of Clinton and other Western representatives for Russia to "stop arming Assad" can be seen as the hypocritical and deeply dishonest position that it is.

In fact, the entire conflict can only be understood when it is seen not as the spontaneous outgrowth of a popular internal resistance, as portrayed by the West, but as a foreign-funded and armed terrorist insurgency whose open terror campaign of car bombings, ethnic cleansings and other war crimes are consistently praised as heroic by the new "humanitarian interventionists" of the neoliberal imperialist set. Given what has taken place in Libya in recent days, those gung-ho interventionists who are currently praising the "Syrian freedom fighters" would be well-served to contemplate who it is they are helping to bring to power in Damascus.

## 2. Many in the alternative media are focusing on the actions of the rebels, while, some would say, ignoring the actions of the Assad regime. This usually results in one being accused of being a regime supporter. Why do you think that the focus is so much on the rebels rather than on the regime and how would you respond to such accusations as being a regime supporter?

Mr. Corbett: Selling war to the public has always involved portraying the issue as a clear-cut case of black and white, good and evil. Once the issue is framed in that way, anyone who opposes the war can be portrayed as a supporter of evil. In every instance, the case for peace is effectively taken off the table by arguing that "if you're not for the war, you're supporting X," where X is the boogeyman du jour.

This has transitioned easily from the Bush era "axis of evil" and "war on terror" to the Obama era of "humanitarian intervention." The rhetoric and reasoning are virtually identical, but they have been transposed into a liberal-friendly context. This thinking necessarily begs the question of who gets to decide who to "help" and what groups will take over in the aftermath. I do not support Assad any more than I supported Gaddafi or Assad. But neither do I support Mugabe, or the Al Khalifa dynasty in Bahrain, or the House of Saud, or Netanyahu, or any of the other leaders of repressive regimes. Why is one leader demonized and the other feted? The answer is obvious.

So the question is whether refusing to support the bombing and military invasion of a foreign country is morally equivalent to supporting that government's leader. This comes down to the question of moral responsibility. As a Canadian citizen in Japan I have absolutely no control over what happens in Syria. I do have a say over what the Canadian government does, what actions it takes, and what its military does. When it lends its support to the bombardment of Libya, I become implicated in the deaths of those civilians who were killed in those strikes. So it is up to us to stop the violence, bloodshed and power grabs made by our leaders under the guise of "humanitarian intervention" as it is up to the people of Syria to deal with the Assad government however they can. This is the nature of moral responsibility.

**3. In the alternative media, we have read and heard time again that the situation is Syria could lead to "a World War 3 scenario," do you actually think that this is possible?**

Mr. Corbett: If NATO were to roll into Damascus tomorrow with guns blazing, there would be military repercussions. Russia has face to save in the Syria situation as well as strategic interests to protect in the country, so it would not sit idly by while the country is taken over by a foreign military. This is precisely why there has been no direct military intervention by any outside military, nor is there likely to be barring some international outrage like a false flag event.

More worrying, perhaps, is the relentless, years-long campaign by Israel to drum up support for a military strike on Iran. Such an event is very much on the table, very much a possibility, and would almost inevitably draw Russia, China, and other military powers into armed conflict with the NATO powers, which very well could lead to a third world war scenario.

**4. Switching gears now, how would you define alternative media and what do you think its purpose is?**

Mr. Corbett: There are two types of alternative media. There is the establishment alternative media and the real alternative media. The establishment alternative media is usually funded (at least partially) by the big name foundations and NGOs with ties back to the usual cast of behind- the-scenes oligarchs. They will present differing views from the mainstream media, and often offer more balanced, thoughtful and contextual reports to their audience. When it comes to key paradigmatic issues like the necessity of R2P or the responsibility of Al Qaeda for 9/11, however, they will circle the wagons and defend the system.

The real alternative media is independent and grassroots, and is not funded by the NGOs or foundations. As a citizen journalist movement, it cannot be defined by any particular ideology or viewpoint; it is a representative of the population at large. Given this media landscape, it is tempting to portray the mainstream and establishment alternative media as inherently bad and the real alternative media as inherently good, but this is too simplistic.

The establishment media occasionally does good work and often reports true facts (with heavy amounts of spin and lies by omission). The establishment alternative media contains some of the best critiques of the prevailing mainstream opinion, even if those critiques are careful never to cross certain lines.

The real alternative media is completely unmuzzled, but it is also unfiltered. There will be brilliant examples of truly independent reporting and analysis, and there will be dreadful examples of unreasoned speculation. No one medium is inherently good, and it is up to all of us to do the (sometimes laborious) work of piecing together the truth from a myriad of sources, each with their own strengths and weaknesses, good points and blind spots.

**5. What role would you say the Corbett Report plays in the overall alternative media scene?**

Mr. Corbett: The Corbett Report is nothing more nor less than my own attempt to fill in the context that is being left out of much of the so-called debate in the mainstream and establishment alternative media. Initially spurred on by the dreadful lack of contextualization of the events of 9/11 in the media, I have branched out my own investigation into economic, social, geopolitical, scientific and philosophical matters. Through my tendency to link back all of my factual statements to source documents; I hope to be in the process of creating a resource that will be valuable for those who are seeking to come to a better understanding of the world at large.

## 6. Why do you think more and more people seem to be turning to the alternative media?

Mr. Corbett: The internet has surpassed newspapers and is the process of eclipsing television as the main source for news and information for most people. This means necessarily that more people are turning to the types of alternative media outlets that can only be found on the web to keep them informed about the world. There are a number of technological and social factors that are playing into this transformation, but the number one issue has to be the public's growing awareness of the information controls that exist in the traditional media. With the internet, people are suddenly able to become their own editors, deciding what stories are important, what sources are reliable, and what pieces of information are worth pursuing.

Why would anyone relinquish the power that comes from this very liberating experience of the world of information back into the hands of a few corporations run by the same few rich, well-connected men who have a vested interest in keeping the current order the way it is? And now that social media and blogging are making the tools for creating media platforms accessible by nearly everyone on the planet, the very idea that "news" is something that is organized by some centralized company in New York or London or Tokyo is being overthrown. The end of the old media paradigm is already here, the newspaper, magazine and TV companies just don't know it yet.

## 7. In your podcasts and radio shows, you have used the term "global enslavement grid" or variations of it. What exactly do you mean by that term?

Mr. Corbett: The global enslavement grid is an interlocking system of economic, social, political and psychological controls that have been put in place to direct society toward a planned future global government structure. Although it has existed in some form or other for centuries (and, presumably, millennia), its modern form can be traced back to the British eugenicists of the late 19th century and the Fabian socialists of the early 20th century. One can trace a line stretching from Francis Galton to Paul Ehrlich, going through such figures as H.G. Wells, Julian Huxley, Walter Lippmann, B.F. Skinner and Bertrand Russell, amongst others, who were all obsessed with the problem of how to create a well-ordered society through scientific methods. To one extent or another, they all wrestled with the question of society and how it is to be governed, as well as the possibility of using scientific methods to control the lower strata of society for the benefit of a ruling elite.

We see this coming to fruition in the creation of the modern surveillance society, where the centuries-old idea of the panopticon is being implemented at a societal level, and in the modern environmental movement, which has produced in many the conviction that humanity itself is a cancer and that the control (and eventual eradication) of humans is in itself a good thing. The history of the development of this enslavement grid and the ways that it operates is too large to encapsulate in short form like this, and it's difficult to do justice to an idea this expansive in so few words. Articulating the enslavement grid has been one of the primary goals of my website, which has so far produced thousands of hours of media and will hopefully be able to produce many thousands more, exploring this idea and its development, as well as fruitful forms of resistance for those who are opposed to this agenda.

**8. How do you think people can unplug from this matrix that has been created by the elites and is fed to us on a daily basis?**

Mr. Corbett: The most important thing people can do (and what I have come to believe is the only thing that people can do) is to realize that the power to change society truly rests with you. We tend to shunt off the big questions about "how to change the world" to the political arena, where we can support this or that political movement or put our hopes in this or that political candidate. This is part of the global enslavement grid itself. By constantly focusing on what is outside of us and waiting for a savior to come and put society back in order, we are ceding our power over our own lives to the very corporate-military-banking-governmental superstructure that is creating the global dictatorship that we are seeking to resist. Worse yet, we continue to support that very structure in the most straightforward way possible: by buying their products, shopping at their stores, banking at their banks, and voting for their politicians. How can we possibly presume to have any effect on changing the current course of society when we are still supporting the very corporations, businesses, governments and institutions that are behind it with our time, money, and energy on a day to day basis?

The only solution is to begin to create the alternative society that we want to live in. That means beginning the long, hard process of decoupling ourselves from the corporate/retail/banking system that we are born into and transitioning into a local, independent economy that bypasses that corporate structure altogether. There are thousands of ways to do this: growing your own food, buying what you need at local markets and independent retailers, participating in local alternative currency systems, supporting independent alternative media and detaching ourselves from the technology that is increasingly embedding us in this matrix. It is not an easy process, and in all likelihood it is a generational project. But it will not begin unless we take those first steps.

The following is the transcript of a recent email interview I did with Michael Edwards, the co-founder of ActivistPost.com. In the interview we discuss alternative media, its influence on the mainstream, and how people can get involved.

## 1. Tell us about yourself.

Mr. Edwards: My name is Michael Edwards; I am the co-founder of ActivistPost.com. My background is in editing technical manuals, magazines, non-fiction books and websites. I'm in my early 40s, married with one child.

## 2. How would you define alternative media?

Mr. Edwards: I would primarily define alternative media as independent journalism, free of corporate or government sponsorship and direction. In terms of ideology, alternative media has a wide range of political views, but tends to be less focused on the traditional left-right political paradigm present in corporate media. I would also say that alternative media tends to promote individual activism as a core principle; learning new information is not enough in our view, it is essential to DO something with that knowledge.

## 3. How did you get involved with alt media generally and specifically with Activist Post?

Mr. Edwards: I have been questioning the official version of events for 15 years, but 4 years ago I really wanted to contribute my own point of view to the various topics. I started a small blog and began submitting my work to the larger outlets at the time. Most of my articles were reposted, so I gained confidence that I could increase the amount of time that I devoted to writing. I met Eric Blair and he had a vision for how to widen our presence. We agreed upon the name of Activist Post and formally launched our site in June, 2010.

## 4. Do you think that the alt media has had an impact on MSM narratives in the past several years?

Mr. Edwards: Yes, in one key way: forcing them to respond to our information. As the strength of our information populates the Internet, more people are questioning what they hear in traditional outlets. The stage of ignoring the information has passed. While the MSM narrative is always going to be one that spins information to their corporate directives, this has caused a couple of significant developments: 1) An increased desperation to shut down debate through labels like "conspiracy theorist" and/or attempted control of the internet. 2) A shift of political message toward the center (independent) by the traditionally left and right wing media.

Both reactions only make matters worse for them as it begins to more blatantly reveal very scripted agendas that are beginning to sound more uniform every day. As a result, we have seen strong mainstream media figures like Ben Swann and Amber Lyon, just to name a couple, who have entered independent alt media with their own unique voices.

## 5. Where do you think you personally and Activist Post fit within the general alt media scene?

Mr. Edwards: From the beginning we wanted to provide a platform for not only the aggregating of information and analysis, but also a platform for debate. We often post articles with opinions that we are either unsure of, or even disagree with, specifically so that all of us together can develop better critical thinking skills. Having an open mind is essential. The topics that alt media covers are extremely serious and complex. While we do have our own strong opinions, we felt it was critical not to become a flipped version of mainstream media with blind followers who just take our word for things as the gospel truth. We heavily source our articles and ask as many questions as possible that encourage people to do their own research. Only when someone searches and finds facts for themselves are they going to be compelled to take action. Another aspect of what we have introduced is a semi-anonymous format.

We felt that it would be interesting not to have a "personality" attached to Activist Post, as we have observed that very often information is overlooked or ignored simply because a certain person is saying it. The information should be put out front for examination, not specific individuals. The power of the Internet affords everyone an equal path to the truth. Finally, we continue to promote solutions.

As we were studying alt media, both Eric and I noticed that alt media is generally criticized for being doom and gloom, only complaining, and never solving anything. Our personalities are optimistic and we wanted that to come through even as we address negative developments in the world. There is nothing wrong with highlighting problems – that is reality – but we have a choice how we react. We want to highlight the power of the individual, the power of positivity, and the power of working toward peaceful ends as core solutions to violence and injustice.

## 6. How can people themselves get involved in alt media?

Mr. Edwards: First it is important to decide what your skills are and what you like to do. Some people love the radio and TV; others prefer the written word to communicate their message, as we do. Secondly, it is important to decide if you are happy to contribute to other sites, or do you want to start a presence of your own? We always welcome new voices, so beginning in alt media is as easy as sending us, or any other site, an e-mail with your work.

I'm firmly convinced that good work will always find a publisher; alt media is far easier to access than traditional media. Also, if radio or video is your thing, technology is so good and so inexpensive now that with a short learning curve anyone can start a YouTube channel or create a podcast to start. Now, if someone is looking to make this a full-time career, we would have to recommend finding 1 or 2 other people who share your passion and can help contribute the massive amount of time that it takes to operate a full-time presence. For example, we essentially have 4 people working 10-15 hour days on our site.

We have been very fortunate to have built a loyal base that continues to grow, but it certainly was not easy. Luckily, we enjoy what we do, which keeps us from ever considering this to be actual work, but people do need to be aware of the time it takes. Above all, we would stress that anyone can contribute something.

Journalism today has, in many cases, become nothing but a joke. Many so-called journalists are essentially stenographers for the government and don't bother to truly look into a story, instead choosing to 'toe the government line' in order to maintain access to officials. It is this problem that has led me to interview independent journalist James Corbett regarding the duty and responsibility of journalists, how people can insert themselves into this ongoing conversation, and why independent journalism is important.

## 1. What do you define as a journalist? How does this conflict with what the mainstream media defines as a journalist?

Mr. Corbett: The term "journalist" is not a job description and it does not define a fixed set of skills, duties and responsibilities the way "auto mechanic" or "accountant" does. Instead, it's a term used to describe a role that is determined by prevailing social relations in a given cultural context. The popular conception of a "journalist" in China is different from that in Qatar and different again from that in Montreal. Also, what we think of today as a "journalist" is different from what was thought of as a journalist 100 years ago or 200 years ago. Going back more than 500 years, it is difficult to say that anything we would define as "journalism" even existed. So in order to understand what we mean today by journalism we have to understand our own cultural context and expectations.

The primary factor underlying these relations today is the technological platform for the delivery of information. Just as the invention of the movable type printing press made something like a newspaper possible, so, too, is the internet making new forms of journalism possible. We are still living through this transformation and the new media of journalism (video reports filed by eyewitnesses via cell phone cameras, podcasts, live blogging of events on social media, etc.) are still in their infancy, so it would be fair to say that we still don't know what a "journalist" in our current era looks like, only that it looks quite different from a "journalist" of 50 (or even 20) years ago.

This concept of course differs markedly from the mainstream definition of journalist, which means something akin to "one who reports for a mainstream media outlet." This concept is tied in with an institutional structure that includes a post-secondary education at an accredited institution that gives recognized qualifications and feeds into traditional print and broadcast media through well-recognized outlets. This was the primary concept of "journalism" in North America in the 20th century, and for whatever good it may have done on various stories it is widely acknowledged that by the end of the century media consolidation had left the industry in the hands of a handful of corporations, leading to the unanimous and unquestioning reporting of government-approved information we saw in the run-up to the Iraq War, in addition to other notable failures of reportage.

The current deconstruction of this concept of "journalism" by the internet and associated technologies is having the effect of broadening our idea of what constitutes "journalism" and who can be a "journalist," leading perhaps to the most radical conclusion: in our current media paradigm, anyone with access to the requisite technologies (even just a smartphone with internet access) can become a journalist.

## 2. What would you say are the responsibility of journalists? Would you say that any journalistic integrity still exists?

Mr. Corbett: The obvious answer is that journalists should be faithful to the material they are reporting, meaning that what is reported should be factual and evidence-based. But it is not enough to say this. There is also the question of context, meaning that a fact presented in isolation might give a certain impression of a subject, but presented in a greater context might give a wholly different (perhaps even contradictory) impression.

The problem of contextualization is not a minor one, because it is almost infinitely scalable. The problem is not merely providing context, but what context to provide and how far that context should be explored. The problem also extends to the nature of "news" itself, what is reported on and what is not reported on. There is no objective viewpoint from which these answers are ultimately decidable, meaning the outdated concept of "journalistic objectivity" has to be seen as nothing more than a ploy to make one editor's (or a group of editors') editorial decisions seem like they are unbiased. But why report on this piece of legislation and not that one? Why interview this person about the subject and not that person? Why include this quote from this government official and not this quote from this government detractor?

Instead of the old concept of "objectivity" in reporting, we are moving toward an era of intense subjectivity. "News" is more and more being sourced from (or at least filtered by) unabashedly biased organizations and individuals. If you follow the US State Department's Twitter feed you know exactly what to expect from them, just as you do when you follow the RSS feed of an organization like the Centre for Research on Globalization. Although this trend is lamented by those caught up in the outdated paradigm of journalistic "objectivity," this era at least potentially empowers the individual to arrive at a more thorough understanding of world events by seeing the various arguments presented directly by their sources (and exploring the source documents online), allowing for the creation of a type of "intersubjectivity" that is more honest than the supposed "objectivity" of old.

In this new paradigm, journalistic integrity involves not only being faithful to the facts, but also up front with the audience about biases and issues of context and viewpoint. Journalists who pretend not to have a position on various issues are decreasingly trusted by the public, and those who come from a clearly defined point of view are viewed as being honest. This is a profound transformation in expectations.


**3. Would you say that independent journalism is in danger with the rise of the federal Shield Law and the death of net neutrality?**

Mr. Corbett: Independent journalism, especially online journalism, represents a profound threat to a status quo that has been bolstered by a highly regulated and highly censored corporate news system. As a result, it is no surprise at all that there are several different vectors from which independent online journalism is under attack. The so-called "Shield Law" being debated in the U.S. is dangerous if for no other reason than that it would set the precedent for the federal government to define specifically what type of journalists would or would not be covered by various legal protections, thus potentially limiting the scope of First Amendment protections to those journalists thus described. This opens the door to accreditation or employment being considered a necessary prerequisite for a "journalist" and thus threatens to return us to a 20th century paradigm wherein the major newspapers, TV and radio stations (and, in our current era, their affiliated websites) would have no effective competition.

Similarly, the elimination of net neutrality threatens to create a system whereby those who cannot afford to pay for top-tier bandwidth (i.e. non-corporate, non-foundation funded entities) would be relegated to a slower, less accessible tier of the internet, thus necessarily reducing their potential audience. This would again create a de facto mirror of the former media paradigm whereby prohibitive publication costs (the cost of a printing press or TV or radio station in former times, the cost of upgraded internet service in modern times) would create an uneven playing field between corporate/foundation/government media and their independent competitors.

**4. Due to there being so many different views on current and past events (eg People supporting Putin because he is against the West) as well as polarizing figures and pseudo- alternative media outlets, do you think it's still possible for the alternative media to make a major impact?**

Mr. Corbett: It is possible for alternative media to have an impact, of course. However, there is the possibility of genuinely important and unique information and perspectives being drowned out in the flood of noise being generated from all corners of the internet. It is a question of whether or not one has faith in the ability of the crowd to filter out the noise and promote the content worth promoting through the concept of "spontaneous order." For those who do not believe this to be possible, they will yearn for a system whereby the flood of noise is filtered out through some type of system (government-approved journalism, cost barriers for top-tier internet service, etc.). For those who do believe in the "wisdom of the crowd," the fact that so many people are participating in the grand conversation that is happening online is not something to be lamented, but celebrated. From this perspective, the more viewpoints that exist for us to consider and choose from, the better.

I am of the latter variety, in that I believe in the principle of spontaneous order, and do trust that the genuinely newsworthy and important information will rise to the top when everyone is allowed to participate freely and evenly in the process of news gathering and interpretation. This is not a popular point of view.


**5. What are some of the reasons you think independent journalism is important? What do you think of credentials and the role they play in shaping the media?**

Mr. Corbett: Independence in journalism is vital in a society where there are so few people with such large megaphones for disseminating their point of view on any subject. Rupert Murdoch owns newspapers, film production companies, television news outlets and publishing imprints that literally span the globe in terms of reach and influence. Michael Bloomberg, Sumner Redstone, Jeff Bezos, Pierre Omidyar and other billionaire media owners are now involved in bringing people "all the news that's fit to print" via established media outlets from CBS News to the *Washington Post* to supposedly "adversarial" online entities like First Look Media. It is a simple truism that these outlets will never report anything from a perspective that is fundamentally damaging to the business interests of their owners.

Now, thanks to the rise of internet technologies, we have for perhaps the first time in human history a relatively level playing field between these media monarchs and the average person blogging from their living room in Hoboken, New Jersey or Ho Chi Minh City, Vietnam. The phenomenal nature of this revolution is only now beginning to be realized, and the power of *The Independent* media is being glimpsed in raising levels of awareness on issues (like "false flag terrorism") that have previously been verboten in the status quo media. We, as a species, are on the cusp of a monumental moment in our history; either we will seize this opportunity to overthrow the previous paradigm wherein the rich and well-connected had a stranglehold over what information we receive on a daily basis, or we push this revolution to its end and eliminate the gatekeepers altogether. As with many such struggles, the choice is ultimately ours to make, but if we don't recognize the importance of this decision it will be made for us by the very rich and well-connected who stand to gain the most from the preservation of the old status quo.

Below is a transcript of a recent email interview I conducted with independent journalist, activist and filmmaker Harry Fear [www.harryfear.co.uk]. Mr. Fear has made a number of documentaries regarding the Gaza Strip and has done reporting directly from the area.

**1. What made you become interested in journalism and specifically the Israel-Palestine conflict?**

Mr. Fear: I believe strongly in the power of documentary and news video to expand people's perceptions and move people. Video can powerfully portray situations of human suffering to audiences, and Westerners so often are in desperate need of being woken to acknowledge international injustices.

The Israel–Palestine conflict, as a prime and long-lasting international injustice, has been both personally and intellectually important to me, since I was at high school. The geopolitical dynamics of the conflict continue to steal my attention and journalistic intrigue. The liberal, advocacy journalist inside of me refuses to remain neutral in the face of war crimes and terrorism, which feeds into my work ethic and agenda. It's a deeply impassioning conflict and as my work on the ground has continued my personal connection to the conflict and its suffering has deepened too.

**2. When you first went to Palestine, what was the ongoing situation and how were you greeted? How did you go about conducting work and how does that compare to now when you go to Palestine?**

Mr. Fear: I first visited Israel, Jerusalem and the West Bank in early 2010, arriving as a photojournalist and working as an internet marketing volunteer for an Israeli NGO. Two years later and I visited Gaza, entering via Egypt. Within a few hours of arriving in Gaza, militants had been killed in targeted drone strikes, of course injuring civilians too. Back then in summer 2012, escalations of violence regularly afflicted Gaza, and the Israeli and Egyptian siege continued to hold back the economy and people's morale. I worked to produce a handful of independent video reports, to try to redress the lack of video news emanating from Gaza, with young Palestinian translators.

Producing news from the Strip presents unique challenges, and over the months I developed an appropriate operating method that works well, to overcome the technical, linguistic, cultural and logistical constraints, of working in a very social conservative environment, with for example only a few hours of electricity per day.

Since I first visited Gaza, the situation has generally improved, in as much as cross- border violence is now at a near-zero level. However, on the other hand, the blockade has actually worsened dramatically, inasmuch as there is now no Palestinian civilian entry or exit into Egypt or Israel. The 1.9m Palestinians in Gaza are literally imprisoned in a tiny strip of land, essentially as punishment for voting for Hamas in their 2006 legislative elections.

When I first visited Gaza, it was easy for internationals to travel between Gaza and Egypt via the infamous Rafah border crossing. Since Egypt's President Morsi was ousted last summer, the border has been permanently closed and only opened a few times for small trickles of Palestinian pilgrims and emergency humanitarian cases to cross. Now, ordinary internationals like myself (who aren't working for a registered international aid agency) can't easily access Gaza at all. Although, in the coming weeks we're hoping to see dramatic improvements, with the hopeful reopening of the Egyptian border, now that both Egyptian and Palestinian politics are stabilizing. Egypt has just elected former military chief Abdelfattah Al-Sisi. Palestinian factions have just formed an interim 'reconciliation government', before instigating desperately-needed elections.

Despite my being of a different country, background, race and language, my passion and love for Gaza and for the Palestinians' just cause is evident in the way I engage with people in the Strip. I've always enjoyed getting along well with Palestinians I've met and worked with. My experience has been that almost all those I've met are extremely keen to tell their personal and national stories and have them transmitted as loudly and as far as possible. Generally, I've been treated incredibly kindly, with open arms and hearts by ordinary Palestinians. Some people have been suspicious and cynical – others even abusive of my work – but they're in a tiny minority. Never have I seen such human hospitality as in Gaza.

**3. The US media consistently generalizes that all Palestinians support attacks on Israel and hate Israel. Since you have been there, what have you seen to be the reality of the situation with regards to people's support for attacks on Israel and feelings regarding Israel?**

Mr. Fear: Western media is guilty of shallow generalizations that steal from their viewers a chance at understanding the basic Palestinian narrative.

Certainly in Gaza, there's no denying that there is hatred for Israel, because of its decades of ethnic cleansing and violent land theft policies towards Palestinians. So Gazans usually refer to Israel as simply 'the occupation', to deny legitimacy to the state that was established on the remains of Palestinian villages that were cleansed in the late 1940's.

There is no doubt that during times of war with Israel and during flash points, ordinary people appear to be overwhelmingly in favor of the attacking Israel in ways that constitute terrorism under the laws of war.

Back in November 2012, after Israel launched its most recent full-scale operation on Gaza, once the ceasefire was agreed, Palestinians celebrated, arguing that their militant groups had hit back and successfully hurt Israel, making Israeli society feel some cost for attacking Gaza. The logic here is that if Israel is made to pay a price when it strikes Gaza, it will deter further attacks. Recent history shows that there is at least some discernible cohesion to that military argument.

Having said all of that, if you ask what Palestinians ultimately desire, it's clear that people generally seem to desperately want a just resolution that simply offers a peaceful and prosperous human existence.

**4. Do you think that independent journalists like yourself are having an impact on the way the Israel-Palestine conflict is viewed?**

Mr. Fear: There is a positive impact being made, especially in making available new insights and hidden facts to increasingly broad audiences.

Social media technology and the latest internet platforms do allow for fairer chances for smaller outlets (and even one man bands like myself) to reach the public in numbers that facilitate sustainable and professional work. Meanwhile, the traditional news networks are increasingly relying on independent stringers and activists in this age of social media reporting, and this helps indie-journos with exposure.

There is a very long way to go, and the dominant channels are fighting strong in this new age in which news is gathered and consumed in ever-changing ways. But I see the trend as positive, exciting, and good for the development and broadening of journalism and democracy.

**5. With this conflict it seems that there are only two options, Israel or Palestine. Are there any other ways in which people can push for peace without siding with either country?**

Mr. Fear: It's true that the conflict can be very polarizing, but you can find positions of genuine neutrality, and there are ways of straddling the two sides.

One way is to stand by international law, which strikes down on both sides, both positively and negatively. Israel's precious 'right to exist' is preserved in the law, as is the novelty of Palestine's right to exist. Two people, two states. Neither Israel nor the Palestinians are permitted to act terroristically during wartime. Both peoples should live in peace and security with full rights and dignities. This is the simplest expression of where international law stands. Organizations like aid charity Oxfam UK follow the line of international law when it comes to positioning themselves on the conflict.

Another approach of neutrality would be to say that the Holy Land is sacred and should be preserved for the world's Christians, Muslims and Jews (who constitute most of the people on this planet). Further, that all religions and people should be free to access a peaceful, not war- torn Holy Land, and that religious sites and religious freedoms should be absolutely protected in the Land. I think this is the neutral position that we see the Pope taking, with both his recent visit to the West Bank and Israel, and his holding of the peace prayer meeting with the Palestinian and Israeli premieres.


**6. Why do you think that the argument regarding the right to self-determination is acknowledged and bought up when it comes to Israel, but always ignored when it comes to Palestine?**

Mr. Fear: Israel continues to successfully maintain a dominant narrative in the West, and there are various reasons for that, including Israel's developed PR and media outreach, as well as innate pro-Israel biases in the West's dominant media because of prejudices like Islamophobia. While it is normal to hear about the importance of 'Israel's right to exist', it seems rude, ridiculous or radical for us to ask, 'what about Palestine's right to exist?!', even though it's an elementary and fair question.

However, Israel's grip on the narrative (and therefore on foreign governments' policy) is slipping, throughout the world, including, importantly in Europe, and even also to an extent in the USA. Israel's control over European and US positions is declining, on issues like settlements, the besiegement of Gaza, racist laws in Israel, economic cooperation between the PA and Israel, and the international recognition of Palestine.


**7. What are your thoughts on the current unity government between the Gaza Strip and the West Bank? Were you surprised that the US is willing to work with this new unity government?**

Mr. Fear: For years, I've been preaching that a necessary condition for progress for the Palestinians is to have internal reconciliation and, most importantly, to have elections. It's a massive relief and immensely hope-inducing to see the interim reconciliation government in power and in place by the agreed deadline. It remains to be seen if the government will hold, whether elections will come in time, what its policies will be, and what practical improvements this will all yield on the ground (including for Gaza's borders crossings, for instance).

Since the reconciliation government has been in place, we are already starting to see more hardball statements emanating from Palestinian leaders — threats to take Israel to international courts, threats to draw international consensus against Israel on key issues like settlements, and threats to escalate international bodies' recognition for Palestine as a state. For those that want to see Israel's power reduced, and therefore a balancing of the power dynamic with the Palestinians, this is good news.

I am hopeful that the interim government will indeed hold and that elections will be held successfully in the next 10 months.

What would be ideal would be for Palestinian factions to hold free elections soon, to install a new democratically-mandated government and leadership (without the tragic violent infighting that we saw in Gaza in 2007), to clearly galvanize popular international sympathy, and to clearly harness international legal avenues. I think this would put the Palestinians in a dramatically strengthened position, in comparison to where they've been at over the last few years.

I was pleasantly surprised to see Washington, Brussels, Moscow, Beijing, et al. tacitly accept the reconciliation and its product, an interim government. If the 'international community' (i.e. the US and whoever it can get to agree with it) is serious about its 'two states for two peoples' proposal for solving the conflict, then having a united and mandated Palestinian leadership to agree to the proposal is a simple prerequisite. Until now, the Palestinian leadership has recently been operating with a hairline mandate from elections back in 2006. So in a sense it was natural for the US to tacitly approve of the reconciliation, because they need the Palestinian leadership to have domestic legitimacy. The contradiction of course is that the internal Palestinian reconciliation has involved the coming together of one essentially US-accepted Palestinian movement (Fatah) and one US-deemed terrorist organization (Hamas).


**8. How do you think, among all the extreme media bias, that people can get information and come to their own conclusions regarding the ongoing struggles in the conflict?**

Mr. Fear: The most important endeavor is to educate oneself about the conflict's present dynamics and histories. The simple rules apply: get as much information as possible, from as many different sources as possible. I follow the conflict in the Palestinian, Israeli, UK, US and Russian news. Only when you look at the events and developments from disparate and even contradictory sources, do you see the real underlying dynamics of what's happening.

The following is the transcript of a recent interview I had with the administrators of the Facebook page ' Anarchist Memes.' In the interview we discuss the creation of the Anarchist Memes page, anarchism as it relates to social media, and how people can learn about anarchist thought.

## 1. How did the Anarchist Memes page come to be?

[Ao]: Anarchist Memes was originally the brainchild of an Australian Wobbly who was experimenting with using social media, and image macros in particular, to spread anarchist ideology. When the page began to draw a lot of attention, he assembled a small team of wobblies and other anarchists he knew online from around the globe to begin keeping up with the demand for images and moderation, as well as to begin giving the page a more serious edge by more regularly posting news and information. The page grew more quickly than anyone had imagined and soon a couple admins became a team of over 30 moderators.

[E]: It should probably be noted here that the current admin collective is actually a "second founding" of sorts. Many of the current admins were added around the same time, in response to a rather controversial situation including a former admin who was removed from the page.

[Ao]: Indeed, this is when we became a 'collective' rather than a loose team and restructured our decision making processes to reflect that democratic and horizontal character. Many of us have been around for a variety of time spans, ranging from 2.5 years to a couple of months depending on the individual admin. This isn't to suggest the page was originally an authoritarian creation, simply that it was small enough for ideological agreement not to be much of an issue. We now represent a much larger section of anarchist thought than we did in the earliest days of the page. This has its benefits and downfalls, but as someone who has been around since the very early days of the page, I'm happy to see us finally functioning as cohesive group with formal processes and a range of ideas (though we have some mandatory principles of agreement), rather than a small team who always seemed to agree on everything. Constant consensus can be a curse when it kills discussion.

## 2. What kind of activities does the page engage in to promote anarchist thought and discussion amongst its members?

[k]: Well, we certainly try to share news articles, opinion pieces, literature, and of course, image macros (we are Anarchist MEMES after all) but that's really surface level stuff. Posting these things in itself tends to instigate conversation amongst fans of the page that we tend to moderate and occasionally join. What I think really works is when admins engage in the conversation and suggest class struggle organizations or any other radical organization to join after briefly getting to know the participants. Whether it's an IWW local or a branch of an anarchist federation or a nearby chapter of the Torch Network, our crowd is the type that wants to get involved and, to borrow a bit of a liberal line, "create real change." Discussion is all fine and dandy, but if we're limited to that we're just another group of assholes standing around a burning building talking about the best way to put it out. Getting people actually involved and active, that's the bee's knees.

[E]: We take quite a bit of care to very specifically and decisively critique reactionary norms within anarchist spaces, too. As many have probably noticed, we take a very strong stance against transphobia, ableism and anti-feminism. Complete internal condemnation of such attitudes has to start somewhere, and we're not swayed by the (oft-repeated) argument that such things 'create division' within 'the movement'. Racism creates division, sexism creates division, transphobia creates division. If someone thinks themselves an anarchist but are not ready to face these facts and change their praxis accordingly, them feeling alienated is not a loss, it's a win.

The main goal is always to have people self-criticize and understand how their own reactionary actions and modes of operation can hurt the ability of revolutionaries to organize among the oppressed sections of society. We've been rather successful in this capacity, and we do get quite a few people sending us messages thanking us for being so hardline about stuff like this. Either because they come from a background where they feel marginalized by many self- termed 'anarchist' spaces (the ones we are critiquing) or because they used to not see the problems inherent in, for example, anti-feminism, and do now because we refused to shut up and had them look up theory to try and argue against it. Stubbornness is sometimes a virtue it seems.

## 3. Why do you think that a social media platform for anarchism is needed as compared to a physical platform?

[E]: I've always disliked the assertion that there is some sort of great divide between 'the real world' and 'the internet', like you have to sacrifice a goat and cast some sort of incantation to cross over into the digital world. It's a very silly assertion that the two are entirely separate, and don't impact each other in any way whatsoever, and yet a lot of people are acting like that is the case. I've seen a lot of people post stuff like "don't take it so seriously, it's just the internet" and I'm like, why? How does the fact that something is on the internet make it any less a part of 'the real world'?

For me, this understanding that what is said and done on the internet is still said and done in 'the real world' makes it very obvious that we need a presence on social media as well if we want our outreach and propaganda to be effective. Quite a few people have taken to shaming, for example, introverts because they 'limit their social life' to 'the internet' rather than 'the real world', which I think is a laughable position. If we actually look at the way things are today, a lot of our social interactions take place online, and we're at a point where this trend exists for almost all groups in industrialized society. Just turning away from that is a waste of potential.

Those people who, back in 1900, would stand on a soapbox on the streets and spread political radicalism, those people have started using social media. Those people did not do that because the streets were 'more real'; it was just the most effective way to spread their views. Don't limit yourself to 'old' platforms, go where the people are, use whatever platform is most efficient. Since so many people are on Facebook and so many of our social interactions take place on Facebook, it only makes sense to create a platform for anarchist outreach and propaganda on Facebook. It helps that Facebook is comparatively easy to use, free, and despite all its flaws, it still manages to get the word out better than shouting at people on the streets or selling physical newspapers would.

[Ao]: Social Media is extremely powerful in current times, especially for youth. As centers for meeting and information sharing have begun to fade from the real world, creating online community is essential to spreading and perpetuating a living ideology. Social media is cost free and is not labor intensive, yet it is a primary way many people find information and events and therefore is essential for spreading ideas and awareness. Many still see anarchists as angry bomb throwing kids without real ideas or organizing, as years of government and corporate propaganda has portrayed us. If we wish to dismantle these ideas and show others that anarchists are serious revolutionaries whose ideas are grounded in a 250+ year theoretical tradition, we must go to where the people are.

Marx once said something along the lines of 'the capitalist will sell us the rope with which we will hang him', and I believe this is essential advice. The government, the corporate media, the right wing, and other agents of disinformation and propaganda utilize social media, so we must do an even better job if we wish for our ideas to be heard. We must not be afraid that facebook is a 'capitalist device'.

We live in capitalism, we must use what it offers us to tear it down and build something new. The beautiful thing about social media, as opposed to mainstream media or books, is that it is user driven, and that we do not need to bring a profit to producers or anyone else to exist. As long as people visit our page and share our posts, our ideas will be seen. Additionally, social media is free and easy to use. That means we can reach those who are curious about anarchist ideas, but who are not yet ready to, for example, buy a book on anarchism, or attend a lecture they may not yet know how to find.

This is, of course, not to say that an online platform is more important than a physical platform. We should be striving to create as many physical anarchists spaces as possible. Nothing is as good as physical organizing. That doesn't mean we shouldn't utilize everything we can to spread our ideas- we should. That's why, although sometimes I find myself more focused on my organizing here in my community, I still think Anarchist Memes has an essential role to play in spreading anarchist thought and inspiring others to become involved in their own communities.

[k]: Same reason we thought newspapers and leaflets were the way to go in the late 1800's and through the 1950's and zines were important from the 60's to today. Gotta put information out where the people have interest in seeing it. Over 750 million people use Facebook every day. 500 million tweets are sent each day. Through any number of the 170+ million Tumblr blogs, every day there are about 100 million unique posts. That kind of potential can't be ignored. It's high time to evolve.

[OM]: In addition to what was said by my fellow admins, organization and propaganda via the internet has two added major benefits:

1. It transcends regional and national boundaries rather easily compared to other forms of organization and propaganda. Looking at globalized capitalism, the importance of international organization cannot be over-estimated for Anarchism. Contemporary Anarchism, at least in my country (Germany) often lacks international orientation, and usage of the internet is often hindered by technophobia and IT illiteracy.

2. For people with disabilities and those who live away from active Anarchist circles, participating online is often the best (or even the only way) of participating. As an example: due to a neurological condition, I am impaired in my auditory processing, which can make face-to- face interaction difficult for me, while online communication is comparatively easy.


**4. What are some of the problems from both Facebook and other users that you all have to deal with? Do you have plans to deal with Facebook if it again represses the page?**

[k]: With the 750+ million daily users on Facebook, you're gonna get some shitty people. We field everything from racism, sexism, transphobia, ableism, and all that shitty verbal stuff to porn, gore, abuse of women, abuse of children, and sometimes combinations of the above. We've dealt with nazis, MRAs, Rothbardian capitalists, TERFs, you know, assholes. It's a daily thing. We've earned ourselves the nickname "Banarchist memes" amongst a lot of these groups because we take a "no platform" stance to this type of asshattery and remove these elements as quickly as possible. Even with a relatively large admin staff, we don't always have enough eyes to catch all of it, so even with the "Banarchist Memes" nickname floating around, there's a contingent that thinks we don't care enough to rid our space of the filth. It's a lose-lose sometimes, but we try, and for the most part I feel we do pretty well.

[D]: We even have our own "Shit Anarchist Memes says," courtesy of the groups [k] mentioned above. There are infamous familiar faces that appear outside of AM, on other anarchist pages, which can be a bit disheartening when we make that effort to keep the reactionaries out. It's a bit like, "First I had to read your horrible stuff as an admin, now you're going to spout it here, too?" Outside of Facebook, or the internet, if you exclude someone problematic from the group, then you're much less likely to see them again shy of something that warrants a restraining order.

[OM]: We have already been taken down once by facebook and the page has only been restored after a major outcry. As precautions, we have spread to other internet platforms, including twitter and our own internet forum at anarchistmemes.org.

And as my fellow admins have stated, the complaints about our safer space policy can get really annoying and removing the people violating definitely is a stressful and repetitive task.

[E]: We've still got the most output on our Facebook page, though, by far. At the high point of our 'seeking out other platforms' phase (don't know if that's the correct word to use, but bear with me) right after our initial takedown we even had a Team Fortress 2 and a Minecraft server for a while. Go where the people are, and all that. In the end, we reach by far the majority of our subscribers on Facebook, and as such we primarily focus on Facebook.


## 5. How do you think that social media can actively combat the stereotypes about anarchist thought?

[k]: Well, first we have to establish a real foothold. I mean the left needs pages that contend with things like "I Fucking Love Science" or George Takei's fan page. We get a great following, but it's a lot of preaching to the choir, pissing off the jerks, and not enough of bringing in new blood. We get people saying we were their gateway to the ethos, but it'll never be enough people. The last "anarchist" tidbit that really went viral was a local news video of some kids bloc'd up during May Day 2014. They all screamed their "fuck you"s to the local reporter

"We're out here to combat the bourgeois liberal notion of a market state and we think your media organization plays into that idea. We're here to combat capitalism in all its forms, which is why most of the people here are not willing to talk to you. This International Workers Day contingent is hell bent on exemplifying the ethos that rule of law is another shackle to break free from, and only horizontal government - truly by the people - is best for the worker. You don't need your boss, you don't need your congressperson, you don't need your president, they all need YOU."

That's what pages on the left need to be instilling in these people taking to the streets. Educating people on how to speak about anarchism to non-anarchists (even though I'd consider that bloc non-anarchist, that's another story) is paramount. With silly kids running around spray painting circle-As on things and screaming obscenities at their local reporters, our message is entirely lost. That's where the stereotypes come from, and that's the type of people social media can reach.

[E]: Yeah, whether we like it or not, the media will be watching. Having some media awareness is key in situations where you will have media attention. We need to get better at "PR", to put it another way.


## 6. Does Anarchist Memes work with other pages and in what fashion?

[E]: We do have a relationship with quite a few pages, such as Lesbians And Feminists Against Transphobia, Fuckin' A, Green Anarchist Agency, Still Laughing At "Anarcho"-Capitalism and so on. Most of the time it's not really all that organized, it's very informal, and I don't want anyone to get the idea that it's like, an iron-bound alliance or anything, because that's about as far from the truth as it can get. We like their work, we share some of their stuff, sometimes they share some of our stuff, sometimes we post on each others pages as our pages, and so on.

[Ao]: Many of us also have personal relationships with admins on other pages and network with them directly, sharing the news and information which each of us deem most important to spread. Again, this is rather informal, but it helps to spread the most essential and time sensitive information quickly and effectively.

[OM]: In addition, quite a few of us also admin other pages like those mentioned by [E].

**7. How do you encourage people to get into the streets or organize/advocate in their own communities?**

[Ao]: Anarchist Memes has always been dedicated to bridging the gap between the online and physical world by inspiring others to learn about and discuss anarchism online was well as to organize in their real lives. Admins regularly post organizing guides, different ideas of ways to get involved, and opportunities to join activists online and in person. Admins also regularly reach out to followers of the page for their organizing questions, tips, and ideas to keep the page as participatory and relevant as possible. Many admins even choose to update followers of the page on their own organizing efforts to inspire them to do the same, as well as to receive support and advice. Above all, we regularly remind our followers that while we appreciate their likes and comments, online activism is never enough on its own, and that they must be even more involved offline as they are online if they wish to make a difference.

[E]: With that said, there are people who can't organize physically in a dedicated organization, for one reason or another (be it health issues, lack of opportunity, lack of time, or something else) and are pretty much limited to either online organizing or day-to-day awareness building and propaganda. We try to have something for that portion of our subscribers as well.


**8. What is the best way for people to learn more about anarchism as a political philosophy?**

[Ao]: There is no one best way to learn about anarchism. While we believe our organizing must always be grounded in theory, we also believe theory will remain stagnant if we do not learn from our real life organizing efforts. Those new to anarchism may want to start off by reading some basic theoretical texts, but the best way to learn is often from those more experienced than us, so we encourage even the newest of anarchists to find their local anarchist organizations, get involved, and to ask questions. We don't learn from pretending to know all the answers, we learn from admitting what we don't yet understand. That being said, revolutionary discipline is essential. There is no excuse not to read, not to understand the ideology which you are seeking to organize towards. I only wish to make it clear that sitting in your bed and reading about organizing will not teach you how to be an effective organizer. For that, you have to get your hands dirty.

[E]: As for specific places to find theoretical texts and explanations of anarchist ideology and theory. If that is what you happen to be looking for, I find that 'An Anarchist FAQ' and its reading list is a great place to start out. I would advise anyone with even the slightest interest to check it out. The struggle, to an extent, is also an intellectual struggle.

*This is a transcript of a recent interview I had with Dana Busgang, who is currently working in Palestine.*

## 1. Tell us about yourself.

Ms. Busgang: My name is Dana Busgang, I am 21 years old, and originally from South Orange, NJ. I am going into my senior year at Goucher College in Baltimore, MD, where I major in Political Science with an International Relations minor.

## 2. What made you want to go to Palestine?

Ms. Busgang: There are a number of factors that influenced my decision to spend my summer in Palestine. Perhaps the largest and most salient reason is that I grew up in a very pro-Israel area and was raised to believe that I should defend Israel and support it no matter what. I was raised to believe that Israel could do no wrong.

Somewhere along the way, I started questioning whether the so called Israeli Defense Forces are really for defense. As I started learning more and more about the atrocities committed against Palestinians daily, continuing my studies as a Political Science student, one sentence repeated itself over and over in my head; not in my name.

I consider it my duty to make sure that the Palestinians receive justice for the injustices that the state of Israel has committed against them in the name of Jews everywhere. The other reason stems from American perceptions of Arabs in general. The way that the Middle East is treated in the mainstream media, the portrayal of Arabs in pop culture, media and in general as "terrorists," "animals," or "uncivilized," always struck me as wrong. A whole civilization of people could not possible be the demonized version we hear of in America.

After spending a semester in Jordan, I knew I had to come back as soon as possible. I want to be able to go home, and tell people what it's really like in Palestine, that not all Arabs, not all Palestinians are terrorists who value death and blood, that these are wonderful people, living in terrible conditions.

## 3. What were your views on the Israel-Palestine conflict before traveling? How have your views changed since?

Ms. Busgang: I have definitely been pushed way farther to the left than I ever imagined due to my stay here and used to consider myself very neutral, very central, but I've definitely begun to start thinking far more along pro-Palestinian lines.

It's hard to keep a level head when surrounded by oppression, death, and pain. I never really believed in a two state solution, and I still don't. While I think it's important for Palestinians to have self determination, I also have come to learn of rampant corruption inside the Palestinian Authority, and the distrust that the Palestinian people have in their "government." Therefore, I believe a new Palestinian state would be ripe for takeover by even more radical parties (such as ISIS), or would fall into a violent struggle for power and control.

As far as how my views have changed, I understand now just how powerless the Palestinians are in the current situation. I understand why they resort to violence to resist, I understand that there are many different ways of resistance, and I understand the necessity of resistance. I also didn't realize until coming here how important and salient the idea of the right of return still is.

**4. Many people would argue that one should have a neutral stance on this issue. Do you think that such a stance is acceptable in anyway, especially given the Desmond Tutu quote, "If you are neutral in situations of injustice, you have chosen the side of the oppressor?"**

Ms. Busgang: I have struggled a lot with the question of what my role and the role of the international community in general is in this conflict. One the one hand, the posts and arguments I witness over Facebook are disgusting, disturbing and ridiculous considering most of them occur between people who are not here on the ground experiencing what is happening.

Even then, the dissemination of trustworthy, non-biased information here is nearly non- existent, with both sides spreading lies and propaganda. I have given up trying to urge people not to make judgments about a situation that they know nothing about, and do my best to inform my friends and family based on the reality that I witness on the ground.

While I do believe it is important, especially for Americans as our government supplies most of the weapons and arms being used against the Palestinians, to not take a neutral stance, I think that the role of ordinary Americans is to pressure our own government to recognize the injustice occurring in Palestine and stop supporting Israel militarily. In this globalized and hyper connected world, it's nearly impossible not to take a stance on an issue like this, and it also makes the international community that much more important.

However, posting on Facebook, sharing articles with like minded friends, or getting into pointless arguments on FB posts is not helping anything. If you want to change something—go to a protest, call your representative, or even sit down and have a face to face, rational discussion with someone without resorting to name calling or shouting.


**5. Tell us about your first couple of days in Palestine.**

Ms. Busgang: Oh goodness, that was a while ago. Lately, I have been feeling and thinking so much, that I cannot find the words to summarize what I have been experiencing. So it may be a little difficult to summarize, but I'll try.

The most shocking thing for me originally upon coming to Palestine was the physical travel itself. In order to get to Nablus from Tel Aviv, I hitched a ride to Jerusalem with my cousin, snagged down a bus to Ramallah and then from there took a private taxi to Nablus instead of dealing with a another bus and my giant suitcase. The road from Ramallah to Nablus has a US state department warning placed on it, due to the amount of settlements and Palestinian villages.

If you drive in a Palestinian taxi, you risk settler attacks. If you go by Israeli car or bus, you risk Palestinian stone throwers-- there's no winning. This road, unlike many others in the West Bank, was nicely paved and had many signs pointing out nearby towns-- but wait; they weren't for towns, just for settlements. The signs that pointed to Palestinian villages were red and angry, warning that they were about to enter a "dangerous" Palestinian village. I laughed to myself, thinking-- what danger do I face from Palestinians? Getting overfed? Too much tea and coffee? After driving through this stretch of settlements, we hit the village of Huwara, which is about 10 minutes away from Nablus.

There were army jeeps and soldiers milling about, dressed like they were at war while just standing near groups of Palestinian youths. Finally we arrived to the Balata refugee camp, where we would be working for the rest of the summer and staying in for a week. Two foreign girls, with giant suitcases looking slightly lost and confused in a refugee camp was definitely not a sight that people are used to. Eventually we found our accommodation, and got settled. Later, we went into the city to meet our co-worker/boss/friend Omar (name has been changed) to have dinner and drink tea in a nice park.

The next day we were taken on a tour of the old city, where we got to see the only Nablusi soap factory still in working order, eat some delicious Knafeh (a traditional Arab sweet that Nablus is famous for), and see Omar's grandparents home that has a beautiful view of the old city. Even until this day, when walking around this city, I hear "Welcome to Palestine," (Ahla wa sahla in Arabic) and it always warms my heart.

The next few days were spent meeting with the kids that we would be working with for the summer, and getting to know the city better. Nablus is unique, in my perspective, because it's very isolated. The Palestinian authority has a visible presence here, and you could spend months staying within the borders of the city and not seeing Israeli soldiers or settlers.

This gives you the feel that you are in Palestine, the country, not Palestine, the occupied territory. The most visible reminder is the Israeli military base that sits atop Mount Gerzim, with its radio towers casting an eerie red glow into the night.


## 6. What has been the most uplifting experience you've had while in the area?

Ms. Busgang: My time here has been marred by violence, and death. When trying to think of one specific moment that helps me see some light in this situation is difficult. Things like seeing the kids I work with get excited and passionate about creating a summer camp program for their friends in the camp, seeing the city come alive at night during the last few days of Ramadan and for Eid al- Fitr (the holiday right after Ramadan), being invited into so many people's homes for tea, coffee, or a meal, being told "Welcome to Palestine," by a group of slightly threatening looking young men whom I was suspicious of beforehand, being able to communicate with a taxi driver or a young child with my broken Arabic-- these are the moments that lift my spirits.

Living in this place is hard, but the people here are so tough and resilient. They find ways to smile, joke and laugh every day, and are generally some of the most well humored people I have ever met. It's truly incredible and inspiring.

*This is the transcript of a recent interview I had with the admin of the Facebook page Son of Baldwin. In it, we discuss the origins of the Facebook page, online social justice activism, and problems in the LGBT community.*

## 1. Why have you named the page Son of Baldwin? What kind of impact has James Baldwin had on you personally?

Son of Baldwin: James Baldwin was the first black gay male intellectual I had ever encountered. His work was really the first time I had seen myself, my identity (as a black gay male), and my point of view represented in art and public discourse in a way that was not meant to be mocked, dismissed, minimized, or dehumanized. His was the first work that started me on the path to thinking critically about myself, the world around me, and my place in it. In tribute to that consciousness raising (which may have come much later, if at all, had it not been for him) and in an effort to answer his final call to dig through the wreckage and use what he left behind to continue the work of trying to make the world a more just, livable, peaceful place, I named the blog "Son of Baldwin." I have been told by friends of Baldwin's family that the family is quite pleased by the work being done and they believe that I am indeed honoring his legacy. That is overwhelming and I am overjoyed.

## 2. What made you want to make a Facebook page in the first place?

Son of Baldwin: Son of Baldwin originally started out as a blog via BlogSpot. But that space wasn't really conducive to conversation. Facebook allows for a kind of direct and extended interaction and dialogue that many other sites, including other social media, don't. And for me, the conversation is the most important part. Despite how I may sometimes come across, this isn't about me. This isn't about being able to proselytize from on high and have everyone applaud the pronouncement. This is about starting conversations and engaging other people in various communities about these causes and concerns in the effort of finding solutions to some of our most pressing social justice issues.

## 3. You talk about a number of topics, from LGBTQ rights to racism, through a critical progressive lens. How did you come to this political awakening of sorts?

Son of Baldwin: I think this awakening started in my childhood. I grew up during the 70s, 80s, and 90s—a child of both Black Southern Baptist and Nation of Islam traditions—in a section of Brooklyn called Bensonhurst (infamous for the racist attack against and murder of Yousef Hawkins in 1989).

Bensonhurst, at least at that time I grew up there, was a neighborhood of primarily Italian and Irish first- and second-generation immigrants. In this neighborhood, I lived in a housing project of mostly black and Latin@ peoples right in the middle of things. We were thus surrounded, if you will, in hostile enemy territory. This made everything tenuous.

As a child and a teen, I had to plot routes home from school that would help me avoid running into the mobs of white children, teens, and adults who--with bats in hand, violence in heart, and death in mind-- made a regular ritual of chasing kids of color back to the projects.

What was different for me when I got back to the projects, having often but not always escaped the battering from racists, is that the battle didn't end there. I had to then contend with the other black and Latin@ peoples who wanted to pound on my head because they perceived me as gay.

When you are not safe in any of the worlds you inhabit, you sort of don't have a choice but to become politicized. You kind of don't have a choice but to "wake up" because if you don't, you'll be murdered. Reading the works of authors like Baldwin, Toni Morrison, Alice Walker, Ralph Ellison, Zora Neale Hurston, Richard Wright, Octavia Butler, Audre Lorde, and others helped to direct these concerns and grievances, and made me feel less alone and more empowered to do something about my circumstances.

**4. Something that I have noticed about you is that you actively allow yourself to be called out by others and acknowledge when you messed up and allow yourself to be corrected. Why do you think that this does not exist in larger political circles, especially liberal or progressive spheres?**

Son of Baldwin: My opinion is that this willingness to be wrong and be corrected doesn't happen in larger political circles and spheres because many of the people working within those areas actually think this work is about them. They believe that in order to be trusted and effective, they have to feign perfection and position themselves as above reproach. Can you imagine?

Many people doing this work think that in order to be trusted they have to lie. The truly sad thing about this contradiction of a strategy is how often it works, and how often complicit audiences are willing to believe the lie if it confirms their system of reality. I guess what I'm saying is that many people doing this work are politicians in the most cynical sense of the word, and that occupation is not something I have any interest in whatsoever. I'm a writer by purpose, training, and profession, and I've never pretended to be anything other than that.

In short, I think ego is at the center of this unwillingness to be incorrect.

**5. You recently made it a requirement that people who post photos on the page to provide a written description. What prompted this?**

Son of Baldwin: This comes from a desire to ensure that as many people as possible are able to participate, as fully as they can, in the conversations and discourses happening in the space. Blind and Deaf/Hard of Hearing people are active members of the Son of Baldwin community and this policy makes it possible for them to be even more vibrant participants in discussions. This is one of the ways I'm trying to address my own collusion in institutionalized ableism/disableism.

**6. What are your thoughts on online social justice work? Do you think that it can make a serious difference in people's lives and on a larger scale? (I often hear people saying that tweeting or writing doesn't really do anything.)**

Son of Baldwin: For starters, I think online social justice work has been a blessing in the sense that it has given a voice to many peoples and communities whose voices were often missing, excluded, or silenced in sociopolitical discussions. Additionally, the Internet has made it possible for many more people to have access to these debates and discussions, such as disabled people/people with disabilities who are often unable to access on-the-ground events because many organizers are unwilling to make accommodations, or poor peoples who simply cannot afford to travel to these events.

There are many absolutely amazing and brilliant online social justice activists doing work that honestly, truly matters, and are, despite narratives to the contrary, affecting the discourse and changing minds.

But like everything else, there is a deeply disturbing dark side to online social justice work. One of the things I deeply dislike about much of the social justice activism and social justice spaces I've encountered is how intentionally vicious they are. And I'm not talking about viciousness between social justice activists and trolls. I'm talking about the viciousness between peoples with the same goals, but who might have different strategies for obtaining those goals.

I've seen some really hateful, ugly, deeply dishonest and self-serving stuff happening in conversations in these spaces—including my own. I'm not talking about disagreements or even heated disagreements. I'm talking about full-on attempts at destroying each other—from credibility to personhood. I'm talking about people who truly get off on making others feel as small as possible so they can feel big.

I'm talking about intentionally committing violence against and silencing other people. I'm talking about people lying and slandering others with the intent of spiritually murdering them as though they were opposing a concept rather than a person. The Internet often helps with the depersonalization of people.

When you think you're arguing with, and trying to obliterate, digitized images and typed words instead of a living being, it's easier to be joyfully inhumane, spiritually toxic, and intellectually genocidal, then reward yourself by calling it "social justice." It's easy to be gleeful about shitting on an opponent (an opponent that you, yourself, manufactured for your own dubious purposes, by the way) and high-five each other about the havoc you wreaked when you can treat the carnage as a concept rather than reality.

I'm talking about people who wear the cloak of victimhood like a Trojan horse in order to sneak into the village, get close to you and- surprise- become the victimizers you never expected. There are people who use their marginalized identities and communities not for the purposes of liberation, but as a hustle, as masturbation, as a way to elevate themselves to a place where they are above reproach. I'm talking about the people who have the audacity to use "trigger" not as a real expression and sign post of lived trauma, but as a strategic pretense to silence any opinions they don't like.

It's like they play this game where the more marginalized identity boxes they can check off, the more they can't be criticized for any behavior they engage in, no matter how abusive and counterrevolutionary. Therefore, the goal is to check off as many marginalized identity boxes as they can—even if they have to invent them or pretend to belong to them. Whoever has the most, wins.

To me, that's the original pimp strategy and I guess what I'm saying is that I don't like pimps. But I have discovered that there are so many of them in this arena. Some folks are out here big pimpin' and calling it "radical" of all things.

I don't know why, but that shocked me. I did some research to determine whether this was a new phenomenon brought on by the anonymity of the Internet. What I discovered is this behavior pre-dates the Internet. Shirley Chisholm, for example, was the target of disgusting attacks by people who should have been in solidarity with her. Richard Wright and Ralph Ellison said such despicable things about James Baldwin that it would make your skin crawl. Much to my dismay, I learned this in-fighting and hostility isn't novel in any respect.

Sometimes, I've been accused of being egotistical, which, okay, fine if that's your opinion. But the truth of the matter is that I'm not trying to be a pimp at this stuff. Part of why I don't do public speaking gigs, etc. is because I'm not trying to become some kind of object of celebrity or fame. I'm not trying to become some kind of some kind of commercial figure or commodity.

I'm not trying to be that person who maneuvers themselves closer to the president in group photo opportunities because they are trying to climb some political ladder. Those people want to be "The One." Not me, though. I'm not trying to be the "go-to" expert. I'm not trying to be in the spotlight. I'm not trying to be anyone's leader. I'm not trying to make money off of this work. I'm not trying to play like I'm perfect and have all the answers. I'm learning right alongside everyone else. I'm not here to be worshiped like some god-thing, but regarded as a human being who is growing and evolving, falling down and getting back up again with increased knowledge. I'm a participant in this conversation.

But increasingly, these aren't conversations anymore. Increasingly, these are encounters with people with not-always-legit agendas trying to push those agendas as liberation strategies. These people are about switching places with the oppressor and will use whichever of the "master's tools" (as Audre Lorde called them) is necessary to do so. However, I'm not interested in being chained and I'm not interested in chaining anyone else. That, for me, is the politics of inertia and I'm interested in progress. I want everyone to be liberated.

Part of the genius of this violence-strategy that some people who call themselves marginalized employ is that it's difficult for the victim of the violence to discern whether the violence is legitimate or illegitimate. Because many of the people in this work are so committed to justice, they err on the side of it being legitimate even when it isn't. So they endure the emotional, psychic, psychological, spiritual, and sometimes even physical abuse because they're afraid if they don't, they will be labeled as a part of the problem. Speaking for myself, I've allowed people to abuse me, even flat-out lie about me on an ongoing basis, just so I wouldn't be perceived as an oppressor and anti-justice (because of the ways in which my identities intersect, in and out, with privilege and oppression and marginalization). To save my "reputation" among the social justice crowd, I've been a masochist. It's so incredibly complicated. And I do not have the answers for it. But I do have the bruises.

So, I'm no longer engaging the brutality. I'm moving away, not from the difficult and needed conversations, but from the egotistical violence. If your concept of social justice is about amassing power at the expense of other victims of hegemonic abuse, I cannot be down for your cause. And if that makes me "bad" at doing this social justice stuff, then so be it. If you need me to be the villain so you can feel like the hero in your own story, play on playa. But you'll be playing sans me. I won't give you the attention you're seeking. I will absolutely refuse to see you no matter what tricks you employ. I've got other work to do.


**7. You are quite critical of the race and class politics of the mainstream LGBT community. Due to this split on multiple levels, from racism to ignoring transgender people, would you say that there is even a real LGBT community? How can people work towards having more inclusive spaces for marginalized LGBT members?**

Son of Baldwin: I would say, currently, that there may be LGTBQIA communities, plural. But the singular community that is commonly addressed in media and conversations is one that is actually serving the needs of one particular subset of the communities—namely, white, middle- to-upper class, cisgender, non-disabled, gender conforming men.

James Baldwin said back in 1984 that the gay movement was really about white people who lost their white privilege struggling and petitioning to get it back. I see no lies in that statement if the national platforms and conversations, if the faces of the movement are any indication.

I witness tons of conversations about why "black people are so homophobic" (which we can actually trace, ironically, to white colonial intervention) but relatively few to none about "why white gay people are so racist." The answer, as Baldwin surmised, was because white gay people are still, at heart, white and Whiteness, which is inextricably linked to the idea of racial superiority, is at the root of most of our problems.

To get to a more inclusive space, people (of all races and creeds) have to give up their addiction to Whiteness and white supremacy. People (or all genders and sexualities) have to give up their addiction to patriarchy and narrow-minded views of masculinity, femininity, gender identity, and sexuality. People of all physical realities have to give up capitalism and incessant materialism, which are commodifications of humanity, and stop treating human bodies as machines that are valuable only for what they can produce for the State—a deeply ableist point of view.

The problem is convincing people to give up the things that define their current comforts. We have to get people to be willing to be uncomfortable, at least for a while, until we can figure all of this out. This may be a continuous journey, rather than a destination.

**8. At the end of the day, what do you want people to get out of your Facebook page?**

Son of Baldwin: My dream for Son of Baldwin is that it serves as a place where we can have uncomfortable conversations about social justice issues without dehumanizing one another. We might occasionally yell at one another. We might occasionally have to be corrected for our errors and apologize for them. But I hope out of the consternation come viable solutions and a greater respect for each other's humanity.

*Below is the transcript of a recent email interview I did with independent journalist James Corbett of the Corbett Report. We discuss the origins of ISIS, the current situation in the Middle East regarding Syria, the possibility of Turkish intervention, and what the West's endgame is.*

## 1. What are the origins of ISIS? They seem to have popped up from nowhere?

Mr. Corbett: ISIS can trace its roots back to a group that was founded as "Jamāʿat al-Tawḥīd wa-al-Jihād" ("The Organization of Monotheism and Jihad") in Jordan in 1999 by a Sunni militant named Abu Musab Al-Zarqawi. Originally founded with the intention of overthrowing the Kingdom of Jordan and replacing it with a religious government, the group was transplanted to Iraq in the wake of the US invasion in 2003. In 2004 Zarqawi pledged allegiance to Bin Laden and the group became "Al Qaeda in Iraq" (Tanzim Qaidat al-Jihad fi Bilad al-Rafidayn or "AQI").

Since that time, the group has undergone so many name changes that one would be forgiven for losing track of its connection to the current "Islamic State," including: al-Qa'ida Group of Jihad in Iraq; al-Qa'ida Group of Jihad in the Land of the Two Rivers; al-Qa'ida in Mesopotamia; al-Qa'ida in the Land of the Two Rivers; al-Qa'ida of Jihad in Iraq; al-Qa'ida of Jihad Organization in the Land of The Two Rivers; al-Qa'ida of the Jihad in the Land of the Two Rivers; al-Tawhid; Jam'at al-Tawhid Wa'al-Jihad; Tanzeem Qa'idat al Jihad/Bilad al Raafidaini; Tanzim Qa'idat al-Jihad fi Bilad al-Rafidayn; The Monotheism and Jihad Group; The Organization Base of Jihad/Country of the Two Rivers; The Organization Base of Jihad/Mesopotamia; The Organization of al-Jihad's Base in Iraq; The Organization of al-Jihad's Base in the Land of the Two Rivers; The Organization of al-Jihad's Base of Operations in Iraq; The Organization of al-Jihad's Base of Operations in the Land of the Two Rivers; The Organization of Jihad's Base in the Country of the Two Rivers; al-Zarqawi Network.

Reporting on the group has always been unreliable at best, with both Zarqawi and his successor (Abu Omar al-Baghdadi) having been reported as dead and/or captured on multiple occasions. Amazingly, a *Washington Post* report in 2006 published leaked documents revealing that the Pentagon was engaged in an admitted PSYOP campaign to make Zarqawi and AQI seem more important to the Iraqi insurgency than they really were. Even more amazingly, a 2007 *Reuters* report confirmed that the US military believed that Abu Omar al-Baghdadi was in fact a fictional character. The group is currently led by "Caliph Ibrahim," about whose history and background almost nothing whatsoever is known.

The issue of where the group has gotten its support in recent years is not even controversial. Aside from all of the weapons, aid, money and other assistance they have taken from other Syrian "opposition" groups (supplied, of course, by the Gulf states, the US and Turkey, primarily), but they have also received and are still receiving direct support and cooperation from various foreign governments. It has also been revealed that some of ISIS' fighters were trained at a secret military base in Jordan that was being used by the CIA and affiliated groups from various countries as a base for training the Syrian "opposition." The latest story about the foreign funding of ISIS comes from a recent report that NGOs and humanitarian groups, including USAID and its associated allied agencies, are paying bribes to ISIS in return for entrance into Islamic State territories, and that ISIS members are even on the payroll of some of these organizations.

## 2. What do you think the purpose of attacks on ISIS is? I have two theories on the issue. 1) The US wants ISIS contained to Syria as to make hell for Assad or 2) The US actively wanted ISIS to go into Iraq as to provide an excuse for renewed US involvement.

Mr. Corbett: The purpose of the attacks on ISIS is manifold. The US has been eager to have an excuse for becoming more militarily involved in Syria since the foreign insurgency began destabilizing the country in 2011. Last year's false flag chemical weapons attack in Ghouta failed to unite the American (or British) public around air strikes, but ISIS seems to be the convenient excuse.

At least part of the motivation for these attacks seems to be the disruption of the so-called "Islamic Pipeline" seeking to feed Iran's South Pars gas reserves to Europe's energy-hungry markets via Iraq and Syria. The memorandum of understanding for the deal was signed in July 2011, precisely as the wave of foreign-funded "protests" in Syria began to boil over into all-out war. The pipeline would have cut out Turkey and other NATO members completely as middle- men for supplying Gulf gas to Europe.

The Gulf States have been heavily involved in supplying, funding and training the Syrian insurgency since its inception as well, motivated by traditional Sunni/Shia rivalries as well as more nuanced geopolitical motives. Syria has been a key ally of Iran without whom Tehran's ability to wield regional power is greatly diminished. The Saudis and even the Qataris see a potential to step into the power vacuum created by a destabilization of Iran/Iraq/Syria, and thus are happy to help with the current air strike campaign.

Israel, meanwhile, is dedicated to a strategy first formally proposed as the "Oded Yinon plan" in 1982 that called for, amongst other things, splitting Iraq and Syria up along sectarian lines: "Lebanon's total dissolution into five provinces serves as a precedent for the entire Arab world including Egypt, Syria, Iraq and the Arabian Peninsula and is already following that track." This strategy is furthered by exacerbating the conflict and further inflaming tensions, an inevitable result of the current round of air strikes.


### 3. What are the larger regional effects that ISIS has had?

Mr. Corbett: The fundamental effect that ISIS has had on the region is to further inflame Sunni/Shia tensions, further radicalize and polarize religious elements in the region, undermine attempts at secular/inclusive governance (both in Syria and Iraq), and to destabilize a key section of the so-called "Shia crescent." It is interesting to note that the area claimed by the Islamic State overlaps completely with a significant portion of that Shia crescent, which was the primary motivation for a lot of the private monetary support that ISIS (and other jihadis in Syria) have received from the Gulf states via Kuwait.

The Kurds of the region have also been deeply affected by both ISIS and the response to it, with the majority of the fighting taking place in Kurdish areas. This could play into Turkey's hands and explain its enthusiasm for supporting ISIS (i.e. hoping that ISIS will wipe out the Kurds and thus take a political problem off of Ankara's hands), but could backfire if the response to the threat brings these geographically and politically distinct Kurdish groups like the Turkish Kurdistan Workers' Party (PKK) and the Syrian Kurdish Democratic Union (PYD) and the Iraqi Kurds together. Recent developments in Kobane reveal that this may in fact be starting to happen, which in the long run may give hope to the Kurdish nationalist movement.


### 4. There have been reports that Iran and Syria are somewhat working with the US to eliminate ISIS. What do you make of these?

Mr. Corbett: It should be no surprise that Iran and Syria, recognizing the ISIS threat as a dagger pointed at their own hearts, are looking to cooperate in any way with the military response to that group. It is surprising that these groups would be willing to talk to or even support a US-backed military coalition in Syria and Iraq, but only if we consider this situation apart from the current crisis. The cooperation that is taking place at the moment is obviously only an alliance of convenience, and presumably as soon as the US starts living up to its threats to bomb both ISIS and Syrian government forces the cooperation with Assad will be over.

---

**5. Increasingly, Turkey's Prime Minister Erdogan has been making mentions of a Turkish intervention in Syria. Do you think one will occur and if so, will it grow to a much larger intervention by the West?**

Mr. Corbett: Thanks to leaked recordings that emerged earlier this year, we know that high- ranking Turkish government and military figures have been conspiring for years on plans to stage false flag events in order to justify a Turkish incursion into Syria. There are Turkish targets in Syria that could plausibly incite a military response from Ankara if attacked, and the recordings show that powerful people in the Turkish government are not above staging an attack on these targets themselves in order to provoke that response.

We also know that the Turkish border is becoming porous in those areas under bombardment. Turkey has just agreed to allow the Iraqi Kurds to cross into Kobane to help participate in the defense against ISIS that is currently being staged there. It is unclear what Turkey may receive in return for this action, but the idea that Turkey would watch as a town on its border fell to ISIS is unlikely at best.

The danger of Turkish involvement in the situation is that any attack on Turkish forces can be interpreted, via the articles of the Washington Treaty, as an attack on a NATO member requiring a NATO response under the terms of the "self-defense clause." This could greatly raise the stakes and be the type of event that could turn this from a bombing and supply campaign into a full, boots-on-the-ground military endeavor.

**6. What are some of the economic effects that this whole ISIS attack has had?**

Mr. Corbett: The rise of ISIS and the other jihadi groups in Syria over the past few years have obviously decimated that countries' economy. The fighting in Syria has decimated the infrastructure in large parts of the country and set it back decades. It has also, as discussed above, frustrated the countries' efforts to use its northern territories as a gateway for Gulf gas to Europe, an idea that would have greatly enlarged Syria's economy.

In Iraq, similarly, the fighting that is now taking place has largely undermined the already-fragile government in Baghdad and sent the northern areas of the country into turmoil. It has also specifically undermined recent efforts by the Iraqi Kurds to carve out their own economy independent of Baghdad. In recent months the Iraqi Kurds have begun selling oil via their own independent oil pipeline network that connects with Turkey, but that has been disrupted by the fact that several key oil fields and pumping stations have been taken over by ISIS fighters.

**7. Do you think that this re-engagement in the Middle East will have a negative effect on the US' Asian pivot, as some have argued?**

Mr. Corbett: Although events in Iraq and Syria have certainly grabbed the attention of the US military, it might not be accurate to look at the Pentagon's reach as a zero sum game. Just because more resources are being pumped into the fight against (and covert support of) ISIS does not mean that resources are being taken out of the Asia-Pacific region. Happily for the American military-industrial complex, Washington has never backed away from increasing military and operational budgets as new threats arise, rather than reducing or pulling back operations in other theaters in order to "maintain a budget." Also happily for the US military, the Asia-Pacific pivot relies largely on naval power, which is less involved in the current campaign against ISIS.

Also, it should be noted that there has been a campaign in recent months to suggest ISIS is setting up branches or franchises in the Southeast Asia region. This threat of increased Islamic militant activity in that region could always be seized upon by the US to re-balance their attention on the Asia-Pacific region when and if it becomes convenient to do so.

## 8. Talk about the myth of 'moderate' rebels.

Mr. Corbett: The idea that there is a magic dividing line between the so-called "moderate" rebels in Syria and the more extreme groups like Al-Nusra or ISIS has always been a myth. It is a convenient myth for the US and its partners in the invasion of Syria to sell that invasion to the public, but after years of failed coalitions, partnerships and alliances claiming to speak for the Syrian opposition, and after years of opposition aid ending up in the hands of the most extreme groups, even large sections of the public are now aware that the idea that "moderate" rebels are differentiable from their extremist counterparts is nothing but fantasy.

## 9. Do you think that the Assad government will fall and if so, what will happen?

Mr. Corbett: It is rather remarkable that the Assad government has lasted this long, a testament to his enduring popularity with vast swathes of the Syrian public (despite what we are being told in the Western media) and the continuing strength of the Syrian military (despite the "waves of defections" that we were being told was going to topple Syria from within). All things being equal, there is no doubt that Assad could (and indeed almost did) defeat the "opposition" forces entirely. All things are obviously not equal, however, and given the very fluid nature of the current situation it is entirely plausible that the current air bombardment campaign will morph into attacks on Syrian government forces.

This is still a dangerous political situation, however. Even though the US and its allies certainly could take on the Syrian military (although not without significant losses due to the countries' significant anti-air defense capabilities), such a direct conflict still brings with it the specter of Russian military involvement in defense of its ally. It would also further incite and inflame tensions with Iran. In short, there is almost no question that a forceful toppling of Assad by outside military intervention would threaten to ignite a much wider regional or even global conflict.

The alternative--the idea that ISIS or other "opposition" groups could finally succeed in overthrowing the Syrian government--brings with it its own problems. The destabilization of another secular government in the region and replacement by some form of Islamic theocratic government would further divide the region and further inflame religious sectarian strife. It would have knock-on effects in Iraq, struggling with its own deeply divided Sunni and Shia population, and threaten Iran, with whom Syria is a key regional partner.

## 10. What do you think is the end game with all of this?

Mr. Corbett: The end game, as described in point (2) above, is different for the different players at the table. But it is important to note that for some of the players (notably the US, Israel, and the NATO allies), the idea of a deeply divided region, with neighbors pitted against neighbors and no clear regional power able to rise above the sectarian fray, plays directly into long-held plans to exert greater power over the region through divide-and-conquer tactics. For those players, simply keeping the chaos in the region going may be the end game, and sadly that is a remarkably easy thing to do, especially when they are funding, arming, supplying and training both sides of the conflict.

*Below is the transcript of a recent email interview I had with the UK-based organization Disabled People against Cuts (DPAC) [www.dpac.uk.net] discussing the history of the group, its activism, and ways in which disabled people can advocate for themselves.*

## 1. Tell us about DPAC.

Disabled People against Cuts (DPAC) are led by disabled people. We welcome all disabled people and non disabled allies to join us. We have an outreach of over 50,000 supporters. We work with lots of other groups, these can be grass root anti-cut groups, identity groups, trade unions-the main aim is equality and human rights for disabled people. But any form of inequality or injustice for any group is wrong and should always be challenged. Since 2010 in the UK we have seen inequality and injustice increase to outrageous levels. This has contributed to an estimated 32 deaths of disabled people per week due to a reorganization of welfare. The Government calls it welfare reform and 'savings', but what we are seeing are cuts that remove even the basic support from people leaving them without food, heat or dignity. This costs lives. We started with a slogan: 'Cuts Kill'. It is heartbreaking to find 4 years down the line that that slogan has become an everyday reality for disabled people.

DPAC are mainly known for their direct actions and occupations. DPAC block major roads, occupy Government buildings and areas to draw attention to what is happening to disabled people in the UK. We are seeing a wholesale attack on disabled people's equality, support, independence and lives that is unprecedented-we have to fight it! As well as direct actions, we do targeted social media campaigns; we support legal challenges, instigate legal challenges, conduct critical research, and are in demand as speakers at events. We have an international outreach working with groups in Europe, Canada, New Zealand, Australia etc. Many internationally are seeing welfare and democratic justice reorganized on the basis of the model used by our Government. The UK was once recognized as an example of good disability policies and progress towards the equality of disabled people- it is now an example of how fast that progress can be decimated and removed. In the UK all improvements that disabled people have fought for decades are being reversed.

Disabled People against Cuts (DPAC) was set up in 2010 by disabled people. We were originally a small group called Disabled People's Protest. We came together initially to lead the march in Birmingham, England outside the Conservative party conference with trade unions and anti-cuts groups in October. One of the leading co-founders Linda Burnip was instrumental in getting disabled people a place at the front of the protest march. We could already see that the Conservative led coalition would attack disabled peoples living standards, and remove social and financial support. We were told we were scaremongering and frightening people by some of the traditional disability organizations and some disabled people, but part of the action was also because we saw that the traditional disability organizations were doing nothing, and not speaking out on the policies of the new Government led by the Conservatives. We needed a new grass roots group that wasn't afraid to speak out and show the UK exactly what was happening to people who had committed no crime, who had done no wrong, but just happened to be disabled. We needed that connection with people on the ground, to open new dialogues and actions that weren't framed by what funds we could get or lose from central or local Government, or from charity that existed to keep us dependent.

We had around a hundred people on that first march. It poured with rain the whole day. We were initially just going to do the march, but lots of people told us to keep going. We changed our name to Disabled People against Cuts after the march. Though maybe we'd carry on for a few months, but 4 years later we're still here. From the early beginnings we now have an outreach of over 50,000 supporters who see the top-down hierarchies of the past as outmoded models that do not deliver. Disabled people must speak for themselves based on their experiences, not via some pre-framed narrative that satisfies funders.

**2. How would you define activism? Why do you think that so many people only associate activism with protesting?**

Activism is any political act that aims to make a change or draws attention to an issue-it is a form of protest. Lots of people seem to equate activism only with physical on the street protest. This may be because it offers an image that is instantly recognizable, it's easy. We have also seen the rise of physical protest on the streets with Occupy, the 99%, and internationally against fascist dictators and worldwide corruption. If it's reported by the mainstream media at all, it's what forms most people's idea of activism. Yet, there are many different kinds of activism and protest through art, film, discussion, writing, research, exposures of oppressive structures; they, and more, come together to form a composite of activism. Activism is more creative than the mainstream media would have us believe.

Consider the Black civil rights movement – is sitting on a bus or going into a wash room activism? History tells us it is. It is a historically diverse expression of anger, rebellion and the recognition of the need to push for change in particular social and cultural contexts. Yet all is driven by the insatiable appetite of capitalism to drive and perpetuate structured inequalities where a few benefit at the expense of the mass of ordinary people, where divisions are set up between differences of visible characteristics of the body, wealth, and perceived power. We all have power and must recognize that we can use it to shape discourse or shape change in a number of different ways. If we don't believe that, then we render ourselves powerless, and allow things to remain the same through inaction.

**3. What are some ways that handicapped individuals protest and involve themselves in activism?**

First, lets us say that in the UK the term handicap is no longer used. It signifies an individual problem, a lack, a dependence on the charity and good will of others. It is a term that dehumanizes.

In the UK we use the social model; quite simply we see that we are disabled by social and cultural constructions, by perceptions of difference and imposed societal divisions. These create socially constructed barriers, the barriers can be others attitudes, environmental barriers and physical barriers. They can all be changed if there is a political will to do so.

The question itself implies that because of a perceived lack of function we will develop ways that may be uniquely different or strange. DPAC campaigns against the cuts, but also for independent living for all disabled people. A concept began in the U.S. led by Ed Roberts and others as students at Berkeley University who demanded access and not segregation, who demanded personal assistants. We now have an international independent living movement led by disabled people. However, independent living doesn't mean being isolated and doing everything alone as the Western liberal individualization myth attempts to dictate- it means achieving the independence to make our own choices on our own lives. We all recognize that everyone is interdependent; everyone relies on and are a part of a range of social connections- and everyone has the right to make choices on their own lives.

Now we might, and often have, chained wheelchairs together in the middle of the road, which we guess is different from what a non-disabled peoples' protest would entail. At a recent occupation camp in the grounds of Westminster Abbey (London) we needed to plan access. We needed to make sure that tents we had were accessible, that we had hoists available, that we had ramps and that people could negotiate grassy areas if they were wheelchair users or if they used walking aids. This was not because of our lack, but because the environment in general doesn't consider the access needs of disabled people so we need to adapt environments so that they do. The occupy camp had around 65 disabled people. It also had around 300 police who were sent in very quickly to guard the area, to prevent the tents being put up and generally make it as difficult as possible. It was this that was extreme. It's a new kind of extreme policing we're seeing more and more of for all protest groups whether they are disabled or not.

The DPAC occupy camp was very successful and hit social media and the news partly because of the excessive police presence. We were protesting against the closure of a central fund called *The Independent* Living Fund. A fund that supports those with the highest support needs to employ personal assistants. A fund that helps disabled people negotiate the barriers they face and which assists them to lead independent lives. The level of policing and the cost of it could have been spent on the fund itself. But we had to endure the power of the state in more oppressive ways.

DPAC, like other grass root groups uses social media (twitter and Facebook mainly), to good effect for campaigns and protests. If we have a physical on street protest we usually match that with a social media presence. It serves to raise the issues of the protest and publicize it, while allowing a wider participation through social media. We also use live -streaming of protests, conferences and events Live streaming is another area where the internet has helped spread political messages and allowed an alternative active critique of mainstream media messages. Social media has also allowed a new participation and collectivism that was missing previously. One survey DPAC carried out said that activism and links between disabled people were better than previously because of DPAC and social media. People felt better informed and more included, as well as benefiting from peer support. DPAC also runs specific 'stand alone' twitter campaigns on particular issues. These can be used to flood conferences about us, but often without any disabled person representing us. Our absence is usually because the high delegate fee excludes all those but highly paid state officials and charity CEOs.


## 4. Why do you think that problems of disabled people in the mainstream are ignored?

It's not clear that they are anymore. DPAC have forced the issue of disability and what is happening to disabled people. This along with the focus of Government on reducing support and removing the welfare state has combined to force the issues into the mainstream. However, the mainstream narrative is not one we would agree with a lot of the time. We don't accept the Government propaganda that support must be slashed. We don't accept the rhetoric or political framing set-up by the bureaucrats and ministers that set out to suggest that many disabled people were fraudulently claiming disability support. This was set -up as a precursor to slashing disability financial support. Yet, we have countered this with the real Government figures on the level of fraud which is just 0.05% and includes departmental error. In the UK a new tougher test to qualify for disability support was introduced. It was a computer based points system developed by Unum previously Unum Provident insurance. Many may recognize this as the same company banned in a large number of States in the US. The test was called the Work Capability Assessment (WCA) it was administered by a company called Atos.

The 2012 Olympics here was sponsored by Atos and other dubious multinational corporations. DPAC held a seven day protest against Atos across the UK. DPAC raised the issues of the bogus and damaging WCAs carried out by Atos. Mainstream news coverage on Atos known principally as an IT company, rocketed. Coverage increased from barely anything to the front pages of national newspapers. Atos became known as a toxic brand, the media coverage never abated to previous levels, but continued leading to dedicated television coverage, a host of whistle-blowers exposing the practices of the company and the harm and unfairness they perpetuated.

Also exposed was the amount of public money paid to the company. There were pickets outside their local centers, pickets of their job recruitment fares by students, and they had major problems recruiting staff. Company shares plummeted and Atos pulled out of the contract early because of the continuing negative press. We need to recognize this as a snowball effect because we were not helped by traditional disability organizations or charities, but DPACs actions meant that even they could no longer stay silent and retain any credibility.

**5. It seems that people want to somewhat help those who are physically disabled, but there is an intense stigma around those who are mentally challenged or labeled mentally ill. Why do you think this flip-flop of a sort occurs?**

The fact is as we age we are all likely to become disabled in some way. We lose hearing, sight, mobility, and memory is less strong. Disability is not a minority experience it's a constant historical fact that affects a large proportion of any population. If we add the effect of wars, environmental damage, dumping of harmful toxic waste, chemical manipulation of food, accidents and so on-we see a picture that despite advances in healthcare shows growing symptoms of the stresses and dangers of contemporary life. Add in family traumas, abuse, mental shut downs, depression, growing anxieties and feelings of inadequacy-none of us escape some levels of damage. Physical, sensory and mental impairments are widespread, with mental health issues increasing to an alarming degree in our 24/7 societies. A further constant of contemporary life is an unending stream of information overload coupled with constant media messages that we are each far from an unattainable ideal of mental and physical perfection. We live in a consumer society that sets unattainable images of perfection- and then attempts to sell perfection to us.

Of these terrors of life it is physical impairment that people shun, but also relate better to too- like the image of the street protest , people can identify more easily with a missing leg, they're more likely to try and understand deafness or visual impairments- how many people wear glasses? Along with this there are a host of cultural stereotypes in books, films etc that present extremes and place them in the public consciousness. The stereotypes of mental health become perpetuated, wrongly, as dangerous, unstable, and unknown. While we celebrate perceived genius as a great thing, we never see it as a different cognitive process nor as a mental health issue. The negative stigma around mental health becomes self-perpetuating; it's based on ignorance and misplaced fear. It's something that should be tackled through greater public knowledge projects and awareness raising, but these should be run by people who have experienced mental health issues themselves. In short disability reminds everyone of their own mortality and vulnerability regardless of the fact that it's widespread. All forms of disability can still be treated as a guilty secret, a personal failing- this is more so with mental health issues or learning difficulties, it is something we must challenge and change.

Finally we need to add that DPAC as a group does not just consist of physically disabled people, but is cross disability. This means that we work with all groups. In addition we have people with a range of different impairment types on the elected steering group.

**6. What are some ways in which disabled people advocate for themselves?**

Non violent DPAC direct actions and civil disobedience, attending and crashing meetings, occupying buildings, social media campaigns, research, writing for media, contributing to the DPAC web site with stories and experiences, taking and supporting legal actions through the courts, questioning MPs, developing peer support to share experiences through our 24 local DPAC groups and social media. Linking up to form alliances of the more active and more political formal disability organizations, engaging with the United Nations, working with the European Parliament through our European links, sharing legal and welfare advice, working with other groups on key policy issues at local and national levels.

## 7. What are some of the differences and similarities between government support and oppression of the disabled in the US and the UK?

A key difference would be that the Americans with Disabilities Act (ADA) was passed sooner than our Disability Discrimination Act (DDA) which was passed five years later in 1995 and was implemented in 1996. Yet in 2010 this was overtaken by the Equality Act which included all equality groups i.e disabled people, gender, age, race, GLBT groupings and faith and belief groups. The Equality Act is considered a watered down version of the DDA, also while apparently based on the ideas of 'mainstreaming', it is seen as a problem in that disability is often at the bottom of the pile when it comes to equality issues. Disabled people fought for a Civil Rights Act for disabled people prior to the DDA but it was defeated, mainly by the disability Charities who were said to have 'sold out' disabled people. Those same people got some of the top jobs at the newly formed Disability Rights Commission which was set up to implement the DDA. The Disability Rights Commission itself is now gone with the 'mainstreaming of disability and all other equality group issues being overseen by the Equality and Human Rights Commission (EHRC). The EHRC has seen funds decimated over the past four years damaging any effectiveness it had.

Many of the punitive 'reforms' we are experiencing in the UK have been imported from the US. For example workfare: A work program imposed on unemployed and disabled people through contracts to private companies where individuals are forced to work without pay or face sanctions- incredibly although non-disabled people have an imposed time limit for this , disabled people do not -meaning they could spend forever working for free. We have previously mentioned Unum insurance who was brought in to increase the private insurance market and aid the dismantling of the UK welfare state. So we see that, despite the fact that people who have paid national insurance most of their life to cover them for illness, disability, unemployment when these things happen -they are subject to a range of punitive tests and assessments which can deny them any support at all via state social insurance frameworks.

The push is to move us to a US private insurance culture in particular for disabled people. We know disabled people in the US who work principally to be able to pay their insurance, but what happens to those who cannot work?

We are also seeing the dismantling of our National Health Service (NHS). This was built on the principle that health care should be free to all at the point of delivery based on need. The NHS is being taken over by private companies who look for the most profitable aspects of the service, take contracts and are paid with public funds. The end result of this is that health care will be provided, if at all, on ability to pay not on need.

So there are now many similarities between the US and UK where previously there were few. We didn't have a perfect system, but the support that was available has now been decimated. We are also seeing an increase in hate crimes against disabled people due to the rhetoric of Government against disabled people. This can be summed up best through the words of Anne Rea a veteran advocate for disabled peoples' rights.

Over a period of 40-odd years, disabled people have worked together, nationally, as a body, to achieve parity in this society we live in.

We concluded that disabling barriers to our full inclusion is society were =inaccessible housing, inaccessible environments, inaccessible public buildings, inaccessible public transport, inaccessible mainstream education, inaccessible workplaces, the widespread institutionalization of disabled people requiring 24 hour personal support, inaccessible housing, and abject poverty.

We also had to address the contorted, subversive cultural contributory factors resulting in overt prejudice and discrimination. To cut to the chase, through blood, sweat and, yes, tears, we overcame all these barriers to a larger rather than lesser, extent. And we became strong, self confident people who understood very clearly that we had the right to be accepted as equal citizens in our own society. This Government has systematically, and quite deliberately, attacked all these gains, and in a way so pernicious as to be despicable, has ruthlessly demonized us as a feckless, work-shy group of people, more or less solely responsible for every financial deficit, justify swinging cuts in benefits, the imposition of the Bedroom Tax, and the dreadful, dreadful threat of the reinstutionalization of disabled people with high personal support needs.

It's this that DPAC fights against, and it's this that drives us to carry on without funds to right the wrongs that have been imposed on us over the past four years.

*The following is the transcript of a recent email interview I had with Frank, the founder and author of AmericaWakieWakie.com in which we discuss political identity, justice, the mid-term elections, and how people can start to build up alternatives to the system.*

## 1. Tell us a little bit about yourself?

Frank: Every time I see a question like this I am hesitant as to how I should begin. This is a limitation of language. We cannot entirely capture "Who we are" in words. Lately I have been thinking a lot about who I am though and a Whitman quote keeps resurfacing: "Do I contradict myself? Very well, then I contradict myself, I am large, I contain multitudes."

I am a first generation Honduran American. I am biracial. I am constantly caught between the struggle of realizing my whiteness and understanding my Otheredness. I am my body and my face, where the turmoil of a childhood lived between the margins rests, a reality where I could never be the sum of all my parts nor an authentic part of my sum. I grew up poor in the backwoods of the Mississippi South where I came to learn the nuances of prejudice and racism.

I am a writer. I am a comrade. I am an educator. I am a student. I am a revolutionary.

*I contain multitudes.*

## 2. What, if anything, do you identify as politically? What are some of the things that led to your political awareness, especially with regards to your intersectionality?

Frank: Nowadays I prefer to call myself an Anarchist Communist, something of the Peter Kropotkin sort. I certainly haven't always identified as that. My political progression has looked something like this:

Anti-Poverty -> Liberal -> Progressive -> Democratic Socialist -> Green -> Anarchist Communist

This is important though for those reading this interview. I cannot express enough how if you continue to challenge your presuppositions, you will evolve. Eventually you will look back on yourself and see your progression as both amazing and silly because some things you will know in your heart to be true, and others you'll be befuddled at how you could have ever been so wrong.

Malcolm X once said, "Don't be in a hurry to condemn because he doesn't do what you do or think as you think or as fast. There was a time when you didn't know what you know today." I try to practice that. My execution is not perfect, but when I remember that I once could get teary-eyed over a flag that represents more genocide and hatred than nearly any other in the world, I humble myself. We all have work to do. We are better equipped for it coming from a place of our imperfections.

As for my intersectionality, again, we all have work to do but I have tried hard to cope with my own contradictions and to be better for them. A principle contradiction for me is the fact that I am half white and if I choose, though not always, I can often pass. This has given me unbridled access to spaces excluded to people of color, and while I could have built a life where I capitalized off that, I have tried to instead use it in a way that amplifies the voices of PoC.

But my contradictions run deep into my own lived experiences. I remember living in a predominantly black area of Mississippi where I was perceived as white. I came to know what prejudice was because I was the only "white" student in the school, except for my brother. Then, as a child, I had no idea what made me so different. It wasn't until my father's alcoholism got my brother and I stripped from him, where we then moved to a predominately white area, that I experienced full on racism from white people that I better understood the circumstances of anti- blackness and white supremacy.

Reflecting on those experiences for a decade makes you question a lot growing up in the South. It is a place of immense contradictions, and I think it is true what Faulkner said, that to understand the world you must first understand a place like Mississippi. I am what I am because of it.

**3. Why do you call yourself and what made you choose the username "AmericaWakieWakie?" Do you think that Americans will ever wake up to the situation that they are in?**

Frank: I chose the name America Wakie Wakie because I just think the majority of the United States needs to wake the fuck up. Admittedly I was a bit more patriotic 4 years ago, so I might have named it something different if I had started the blog today. The "Wakie Wakie" part though comes from a scene I once saw on a television show called Titus. It wasn't a good show, but I was a teenager and I watched it for some reason. In the show the main character was this custom car shop owner who had a REALLY dysfunctional — aka, probably a white supremacist hetero-patriarchal capitalist — family. To highlight this dysfunction the show would feature the main character, Titus, in flashbacks as a teenager where he would look exactly the same as in the present but with a mullet wig. In one flashback he was lying in bed when his father tells him to get up, which he doesn't. The father then throws a big bowl of spaghetti on Titus' face and taunts him with the words "Waaakkie Wakkkie". I don't know why, that's just always stuck with me.

I don't believe we will have mass movements toward liberation with gently nudges to wake up. I feel confident that it is going to be a pretty rude experience that galvanizes large-scale joint resistance. Ferguson is a good example: Black and brown communities are fed up and there is nothing gentle about the police sponsored murder of our youth in the streets. A ton of work has been happening for a long time against the prison industrial complex, the school to prison pipeline, and anti-police brutality, but there has always been a need for a catalyst to really gain (inter)national traction.

"Wakie Wakie" represents that need for a catalyst.

**4. You say on your website that "the waves of change are ever persistent and not even time can withstand the ebbing past." It seems a lot like MLK's statement that the arc of the universe is long and that it bends toward justice.**

**However, I have to ask, with so much injustice around the world and a constant persistence of that injustice, the question becomes, do we truly ever get change? Do we truly ever get justice? What would you say to that? Do you think it is possible that we can truly get justice?**

Frank: You are right, the sentiments are similar, but I was inspired by Chief Seattle's words as they appeared in the Seattle Sunday Star on Oct. 29, 1887, in a column by Dr. Henry A. Smith.

Yes, we will get change, and we will get it exactly when we start to understand that justice is not a thing to have, it is a process that we must go through. Justice is a concept I have been thinking about for quite some time now. I will write more deeply about this in the future, but I have started to understand this much about it:

Justice is not a concrete system, it is fluid. It is always different because it is situational — it must be re-contextualized each time we seek it. This is why it is not a thing to possess but a series of processes which balance human emotions, restoration, community, and accountability. Justice is not for one person to have either. This is tyranny and retribution. Justice, however, takes time, love, patience, and, when necessary, rectification.

Our idea of justice as represented by the current legal system, a system created as a function of capitalism, and more broadly as a symptom of positivist thinking, is as far divorced from justice as seemingly conceivable. Justice cannot be born of an adversarial relationship between absolutes. To say that it can be is to be more obsessed with resolutely assigning the values of right and wrong, of winner and loser, to truly debilitating circumstances. If one poor person is dying of hunger and steals from another, what justice is to be had in punishing hungry mouths?

How we got here to the system we live in now is traceable. This is work my comrades and I have only begun to do, but global change will indeed come. With the blood, sweat, and tears splattered across this Earth with each generation that fights for it, it has already begun.


**5. What are your thoughts on the recent midterm elections? Many are saying that it was the country rejecting Obama and the Democrats.**

Frank: I don't like Republicans but I am direly sick of the "lesser of two evils" garbage pseudo- leftists and progressives trot out every election cycle. Look, if you want to vote, go for it, but electoral politics cannot and will never bring about the liberation of the People. Never. I used to think of Democrats/liberals as the closest thing a radical had to an ally in comparison to Republicans. Reality, it would seem, is not without a sense of irony. In truth Democrats/liberals are the closest thing Republicans have to an ally in comparison to radicals. History is resolute in demonstrating that when it comes to the consolidation of power, the two major U.S. parties will act in coalition to eradicate any radical threat. Read Agents of Repression by Ward Churchill and A People's History of the United States by Howard Zinn, or for starters read my essay Democrats & Republicans: A Political Cartel, for some essential history lessons.[1]

That being said, I still see value in proposition voting.


**6. How do you think that people can start organizing on the ground to create alternatives to the current system?**

*Frank: Respect existence, or expect resistance.*

Organizing has been happening on the ground since oppression was born. For centuries there has been an incredible history of resistance that has never died. From the sabotage on plantations and slave ships to the runaway slaves smuggling their brothers and sisters in bondage to freedom, from the anti-war socialists to the labor union organizers of the '20s, from the Black Panther Party to the American Indian Movement of the late '60s, from Occupy Wall Street to Ferguson, MO, there has been organizing.

There are three basic words folks looking to do work need to know and understand: Educate. Agitate. ORGANIZE. To understand where we are going you need to familiarize yourselves with where we have been. You cannot be afraid of getting your hands dirty either, which means you must be willing to march, protest, and use any means necessary in the pursuit of your education and to develop a praxis of liberation. When you have a foundation for these, you need to find people who will organize with you. Here is a link to a decent write up that is helpful. [2]

Organizing can take on a plethora of forms, so about one thing I want to be clear: There is no one-size-fits-all solution. I keep getting questions in my inbox asking "Well we know the problems, so what is the solution?" There is this implicit assumption that there is ONE solution, but it does not work like that. There is no quick fix. There is no single solution. There are, however, thousands of solutions out there, each unique to their circumstance. And that makes sense too — our solutions ought to be as diverse as the biosphere that sustains this planet and the socioeconomic situations we face.

There is no appointed vanguard to confront all of our problems. Because circumstance ought to necessitate solutions, it would be foolish, as well as impossible, for me to sit here and dictate to all of you how, when, and where we ought to act. Our first obstacle is turning away from the idea that somebody else way out there knows better than we how we ought to live, act, and create in our own communities. An activist's job is to plug into and serve your community. If you are diligent in this, things will happen. You WILL meet people and you will have more work than you know what to do with.

I hope this has been illuminating. Solidarity my friends. Keep fighting.

**Endnotes:**

1: America Wakie Wakie, *Democrats and Republicans: A Political Cartel*, http://americawakiewakie.com/post/89635829268/democrats-republicans-a-political-cartel (June 23, 2014)

2: America Wakie Wakie, *Educate, Agitate, Organize: An Anarchist FAQ*, http://americawakiewakie.com/post/94575144988/educate-agitate-organize-an-anarchist-faq (August 12, 2014)

*Rethinking Anarchism: An Interview with Agency*

*Originally Published On: December 14, 2014*

*Below is the transcript of a recent interview I did with Agency, a new website that looks to promote "contemporary anarchist perspectives and practices through commentary on current events, media relations, and educational campaigns." (http://www.anarchistagency.com/)*

## 1. What made you come up with this idea? What made you come up with the name?

Ryan Only: Separate from one another, Jen Angel and I each had an idea to create "an anarchist PR project." When we came together and started talking about what it could look like, we had a lot of the same ideas and so we came up with the concept and elements for Agency. This felt very organic because both my and Jen's activism and paid work has been around the intersections of media, publicity, and social movements and social justice struggles.

Personally, I'm interested in how the media captivates and compels the public around spectacles and sensationalism. Right after the WTO protests in Seattle, I was involved in organizing many of the mass-actions that followed in DC and other places – and was involved in efforts that tried to give a more honest perspective to the media on anarchists' participation in those actions. There's a history of media bastardizing anarchists, and a history of anarchists either shying away from or outright rejecting the media and also of watering down our politics in fear the media will misrepresent us. I want to explore what it looks like to challenge false perceptions of anarchism, and also to challenge the tactics and approaches anarchists may take out of habit rather than what might actually be best for advancing our ideas and cause.

Jen Angel: During the last few years, especially since Occupy, the mainstream media and public have been more interested in the ideas of anarchism than they have in my lifetime. Like Ryan said, the media often doesn't get it right, or they tend to interview the same anarchists over and over – partially because journalists don't know anything about anarchism and don't know who to interview. We started having these conversations about what would happen if we tried to intervene and give journalists better information – and what if we connected them to other anarchists they could interview?

Anyone who has worked with the media knows that even when you give them good information, it can be manipulated or misrepresented to advance a story or make a sound bite – but what if some of the good information got through? That would be worth it, and that's the kind of thing Ryan and I already do with our media work. With Agency, we are applying those skills to anarchism.

Ryan: I like seeing what happens when anarchists actually talk about what we want and the world we want to live in—and I like talking to people outside of anarchist social scenes. And I think it's uncommonly explored terrain for anarchists – and I think there's a lot that can be done – and moved forward by exploring this terrain.

Agency is also the realization of an inside joke that I've been making with a good friend for the last 10 years. That is, seeing the ways in which PETA are able to take any news story and use it to garner attention for promoting an animal rights perspective. This friend and I have joked for years, what if we had an anarchist PETA? That is, an organization that worked to engage with an anarchist perspective on major news stories – thus promoting radical analysis of how the state and capitalism are at the roots of many social ills, and how a society organized in opposition to these systems can be more healthy and more free – and what if we worked to seize whatever opportunities we could as a platform to promote these ideas?

Jen: The name is a play on words.

Ryan: Yes, the name, Agency, is a play off of the PR industry idea of PR agencies and also in sociology and philosophy, agency is the capacity of a person to act in the world. As anarchists, Agency is what we want: a world where each person has autonomy and self-determination over their lives.

**2. What would you say to those who argue that this is kind of pointless, that anarchists will always get a bad rap in the media?**

Jen: Although we just launched our website in October, we have been working on this project for over a year. Part of that work was reaching out to other anarchists for their input and feedback. I was surprised that very few of the people we talked with said that it was pointless to talk to the media – that was something I heard a lot from people when I first started working in the anarchist community, in the '90s.

Ryan: I think it's wrong to say it is pointless to talk to the media in general. It's really a case by case thing - it can be pointless, sure. But is it always? Or even a majority of the time? No, I would argue that most of the time it is fruitful and effective– and sometimes it can be groundbreaking. Look at the little work that has been done by anarchists in the media. It can be successful, it can reach people and win hearts and minds (look at Seattle and what pictures of anarchists in the black bloc and anarchists on the front lines of human barricades did to bring attention to the horrors of economic globalization), look at the Arab Spring, look at Occupy. Look at the internet and what open source thinking has done to expand humanity's access toi nformation and communication. All of these things are a product of anarchists engaging with the media in some form or another.

Jen: Because of our experience working with media on behalf of other social justice campaigns, we know that it can be one of many effective tools to influencing how the public understanding of issues.

Ryan and I both think that anarchism is a movement – it's not a members-only club. We need more anarchists and people interested in anarchist ways of being in order to make positive change in the world. We want to use every tool that we have to expose others to anarchist ideas and ways of organizing. As I said before, the public and media are talking about anarchism now in an unprecedented way – this is an opportunity for us to use different methods to educate anyone interested in a different way of living.


**4. Do you think that due to the political, economic, and social times that people are more receptive to anarchism?**

Ryan: Absolutely. There has been an "anarchist turn" in the last 20 years at the very least... The anti-globalization movement, the anti-war movement, Occupy, uprisings in the Middle East, the internet – all these things have had an element of anarchist influence or inspiration.

Jen: And the plethora of books and articles on anarchism, especially post-Occupy, is certainly evidence for that.


**5. Is there a diversity of anarchist leanings with regards to contributors? What are some of the differences?**

Ryan: Most importantly, Agency promotes a diversity of anarchist positions that adhere to an anti-state, anti-capitalist, and anti-oppression framework. We acknowledge that there are many different anarchist perspectives and visions, and this project's aim is to make the public aware of a range of anarchist beliefs, in a spirit of solidarity and non-sectarianism.

We are working with anarchists across the spectrum, within that framework. We have already published pieces by anarchists who have historically had tension with each other. My hope is to publish things from everyone from Ashanti Alston to John Zerzan, from Noam Chomsky to Starhawk, from Cindy Milstein to CrimethInc. We are very excited to already be working on or have published contributions from Klee Benally, Natasha Lennard, Mattilda Bernstein Sycamore, Scott Crow, Eric Laursen, Carwil Bjork-James and many others.

We want this project to present a broad spectrum of anarchist ideas. Anarchists often are own worst enemies, and I think that's a sad reality. This is a non-sectarian project, but there's plenty of room for disagreement – we just want our differences to move us forward and not hold us back.

Jen: The goal is to raise awareness of anarchism as a whole, and we are completely prepared to do promote diverse (and contradictory) parts of anarchism as long as the ideas, groups, and individuals we are working with identify publicly as anarchists and share our core beliefs that Ryan mentioned, like opposition to the state and capitalism. We will not, for example, be promoting the work of libertarians or anarcho-capitalists.

This is not an attempt to water down or make palatable the more militant parts of anarchism or of the community. Some anarchists run child-care programs and some anarchists smash windows and engage in sabotage. Sometimes the same individuals do both things.

Helping anarchists is more transparent about what they are doing and why, and with what goals, will make anarchist ideas more accessible in hopes of allowing more folks to understand that a different world is possible.


**6. Do you intend to reach out to other groups online and in the real world to promote anarchism in the media?**

Jen: Yes, we basically want to use our media skills to promote the work of other anarchists. Part of our preparation for the launch of this project was reaching out to comrades around the US for their input and feedback.

There are lots of ways that we work with individual anarchists or groups, such as:

• Soliciting and circulating new or existing commentary on current events from an anarchist perspective, written for non-anarchists

• Creating issue guides for journalists on generally accepted anarchist thinking on specific topics, and connecting journalists to anarchists who work on those topics

• Tracking mentions of anarchists in mainstream media and intervening through Letters to the Editor or building relationships specific reporters


**7. How do you think that Agency will change the dialogue surrounding anarchists and anarchism?**

Ryan: Within anarchist communities – we want to introduce nuance around the idea of engaging with the media. Media engagement by anarchists should be a tactical and strategic question. We need to transcend the knee jerk idea of "corporate media=bad"... and actually have discussions about when and how to engage with the media. As anarchists, we need to write our own narrative instead of letting others tell our story.

I want anarchism – as a world view that promotes freedom, equality, and self- determination – to be a household concept. I want anarchism to be a threat to power structures that rely on and perpetrate inequality and disparity in the world. And we can make anarchism a threat by building understanding among a broader spectrum of people of what anarchism is and how anarchy works.


**8. What are some of the end goals for Agency? What's the endgame?**

Ryan: The endgame is anarchist revolution. The goals of agency are much more modest.

We want to publish and publicize anarchist perspectives on current events and we want them to be heard and read by millions of people.

*Below is a transcript of a recent interview I had with the members of the collective and open access academic journal Abolition: A Journal of Insurgent Politics. (www.abolitionjournal.org)*

## 1. What made you create the journal and what made you go with the name Abolition: A Journal of Insurgent Politics?

Eli Meyerhoff: Academia monopolizes resources for research and study. I see this journal as a tool for siphoning those resources into radical movements. The project started with a few political scientists who organized a mini-conference on abolitionism and decolonization. We wanted to publish the presentations, but it was difficult to find journals of radical politics that were also free and open access. We refused the compromise of submitting them to an existing journal with a pay wall that would be inaccessible to non-academic organizers of radical movements, our ideal audience. So, we started our own journal.

We stuck with our refusal to compromise, turned to the tradition of abolitionists before us, and encoded this principle in our manifesto's first line: "Abolitionist politics is not about what is possible, but about making the impossible a reality." Of course, in our own lives, we are always caught up in compromises—buying commodified goods made through exploited labor, legitimating the settler colonial state through obeying its laws, etc. But why should we let our personal compromises bleed into our radical projects? The title, Abolition: A Journal of Insurgent Politics, also signals this 'no compromises' fanaticism of our approach. We want to distinguish our form of insurgent abolitionism from other approaches that might take on the banner of 'abolition.' Obviously, we oppose its right-wing uses, such as the 'Abolish Human Abortion' campaign. But we also oppose liberal forms of abolitionism that seek mediating, reformist solutions to social problems. To distinguish our approach, we highlight the multiplicity of abolitionist movements—those seeking to end all of the different forms of oppression, exploitation, and domination, from white supremacy, patriarchy, and colonialism to ableism, hetero-and-cis-sexism, and capitalism—while emphasizing the interconnected, co-constitutive character of these institutions.

Trying to hold together these goals for abolitionism—as fanatical, multiplicitous, and intersecting—is really difficult, riddled with complex tensions, and seems almost impossible to do not merely in theory but in practice. As we say in our manifesto: "we seek to understand the specific power dynamics within and between these systems so we can make the impossible possible; so we can bring the entire monstrosity down." Our journal seeks to create forums for grappling collectively with questions about how this can happen—what are our different ways of imagining abolitionism, what are the histories behind our visions, what are the tensions between them, what are the obstacles to realizing them, how can we overcome those obstacles together?

## 2. What kind of political lean does the journal have? It seems to be somewhat anarchistic in nature.

Dylan Rodriguez: I have been encouraged and impressed by the journal collective's decidedly non-sectarian approach to its work. If anything, there is a generally shared commitment to incite a breadth and quality of radical intellectual-cultural work that will both contribute to and potentially disrupt existing academic (and social movement) discourses.

Eli Meyerhoff: The journal's collective members (currently 33) have a variety of political leanings, generally of a far left and/or anarchist persuasion. Yet, the journal's politics are not a mere synthesis of those of its members. Rather, we seek to create a new political position for a radical research and publishing project. The manifesto is an initial attempt at articulating our approach, though we are still working on it and expect to always be working on it, as a living document. We wrote it with the initial six members, and then sent it out as a précis of the project to invite new members. Twenty-seven members have joined since then, including many radical academics from disciplines other than political science as well as twelve non-academic activists, two of whom are currently incarcerated. Given the large size of the collective, we do take on some anarchist practices in how we run the collective, such as embracing the messiness of making decisions amongst many different people, using consensus process, and making it 'leader-full' while avoiding fixed hierarchies of leadership.

Instead of the self-entrepreneurial motivations for doing collaborative intellectual work in academic capitalism, we promote principles of mutual aid and 'from each according to their abilities and passions, to each according to their needs and desires.' These principles play out, for example, in how we recognize that our collective members will have different capacities to contribute at different times, and feeling okay with some members taking on more work without needing to give them some kind of marketable 'credit' for it, such as anointing them with an official position.

With our crew together, we are now putting the engine of the journal to work as a prefigurative project, conducting the process in a way that mirrors the world we desire to live in. The first publication will be an 'Issue Zero' composed of writings by some of the collective members on questions related to the mission of the journal, such as 'what should abolitionism mean today?' So, the journal itself does not have a unified political position in the normal sense, but rather it aims to create a common space for people of various 'abolitionist' stripes to experiment, play, and work together intellectually.

It's an institution of abolition-democracy, creating forums for debating and grappling with the big questions facing abolitionist movements. The collective members bring to the project their understandings of abolitionism out of many different backgrounds and struggles— from decolonization, indigenous resurgence, and 'no borders' work to gender justice, labor organizing, and prison and police abolition. These different experiences lead us to prioritize some questions over others, but we also share a lot of strategic and theoretical questions, due to the intersections of the institutions we are struggling against. This project provides us an opportunity to seek out, explore, and strengthen collaborations between our different movements.

## 3. What do you think that Abolition will bring to the table that many radical journals have not?

Eli Meyerhoff: Many radical journals gesture toward problems with the boundaries between academia and radical activism. We have taken that gesture and made it a core part of our mission. For each of our processes, we ask how academias vs. activism divisions play out and how we could better negotiate them for abolitionist purposes. To guide our grappling with these boundaries, we draw insights from the essay, Accomplices Not Allies: Abolishing the Ally- Industrial Complex: "An accomplice as academic would seek ways to leverage resources and material support and/or betray their institution to further liberation struggles. An intellectual accomplice would strategize with, not for and not be afraid to pick up a hammer."

 Taking on the intertwined ally-and-academic-industrial complexes simultaneously, those of us with institutional positions in academia or other non-profit organizations seek to use our positions for purposes of accompliceship in abolitionist struggles—picking the locks on academia's treasure chests of resources for study.

Conversely, we aim to combat those who try to recuperate struggles for shoring up their institutional positions. Some journals fall into such recuperative roles unwittingly, as academics who publish in them about an abolitionist movement can gain academic capital for their careers without helping the movement (or even hurting the movement by aiding state surveillance of it or exacerbating internal tensions under the guise of 'critique').

## 4. What are some of the overall goals for Abolition?

Andrew Dilts: In one sense, it is difficult to talk about "goals" for this project, in that we think a large part of what we are doing is captured in the doing itself. But at the same time, there are clearly some concrete things that we want to see come of this work, and some specific horizons that we want to bring into the foreground of our lives, first and foremost to make abolition democracy a reality. In the immediate term, we simply want to publish a journal that reflects our manifesto, that is open-access, and that both reflects and reaches people who have been excluded from social and political life by the intersecting oppressions that define our moment. We want to do this in a prefigurative way, that is, to publish a journal whose making is reflective of how we imagine a different world.

## 5. You also state in the manifesto that "academia has more often been an opponent to abolitionist movements," however you do note the exception of people such as W.E.B. Du Bois. Do you think that academia is still a place where the status quo reins? Do you think there are some academics today that actively use the academy as a space of rebellion?

Dylan Rodriguez: Academia--and colleges, universities, and other schooling institutions generally--is no more insulated from the logics of power, domination, and oppressive institutionalized violence than any other hegemonic apparatus. In this sense, it also constitutes a historical site of political-cultural struggle that is tantamount to protracted low-intensity warfare. People who take this site seriously as a place of activist mobilization and radical intellectual innovation have often--usually collectively--played crucial roles in catalyzing, transforming, and/or sustaining liberation/revolutionary movements through their work, from the renaissance of mid-20th century Black freedom struggle to the recent formation of an early-21st century abolitionist politics, theory, and pedagogy.

## 6. How does Abolition operate as a traditional academic journal? In what ways does it veer from tradition?

Eli Meyerhoff: In tension with our struggles against and beyond academia, we recognize the benefits for abolitionist academics to maintain institutional positions within it, for the access to resources that inclusion can offer. The impetus for this project came from academics, particularly some in political science who are fed up with how the tenured ruling class in their discipline use academia's resources to uphold the liberal capitalist status quo. A key role of most academic journals is to act as mechanisms for maintaining a culture of conformity, legitimated with myths of 'political neutrality' and 'meritocracy.' In contrast, we decided to create a new journal that will openly take sides in political struggles—with abolitionist movements. Inspired by previous efforts for radical change in academia, especially the unfinished projects of the campus movements that have created radical new fields like Black Studies, we aim to take on the gate- keepers of the major disciplines—contesting their claims of legitimate control over the resources for studying the phenomena that they frame as 'politics,' 'economics,' 'society,' 'environment,' 'history,' etc.

Rather than taking academics' desires to survive within the academy as eternal necessities, we foresee that the success of abolitionist projects will change the availability of resources for intellectual activity as well as the terms on which we understand what counts as a 'resource.' For such visions, we take inspiration from places where colonial capitalism has relatively less hold, such as the Zapatista communities and the Venezuelan communes, where collective studying infuses everyday life. To help abolitionist academics grapple with the tensions around transgressing academia's boundaries, our journal aims to provide some means for legitimacy within the dominant value practices of academia (e.g., publication requirements for hiring, tenure, and promotion), while simultaneously pushing the limits of those value practices.

One key path toward exploding the limits is to reject the rankings of journals. Following the lead of other radical journals, such as the ACME critical geography journal, we will refuse to submit material for the rankings of the publishing industry. All rankings of journals are biased toward the dominant regime of knowledge production, and submitting to them would catch us in its processes of financialization and dispossession. Our reasoning is not that these particular rankings are 'inaccurate' or 'corrupt,' but rather that the quantification of knowledge production is necessarily bound up with capitalist circuits of value accumulation.

Despite our rejection of the rankings game, we are neither abandoning the institution of peer review nor discounting the value that is associated with it in academia and beyond. Practicing peer review of texts—sharing writing with respected comrades and giving each other feedback for revision before circulation with wider audiences—can be useful for movements to make their intellectual activities better means for building their power. Against academia's control over access to a wealth of resources designated for peer-reviewed knowledge production, our project offers a means for movement actors to contest this control and to expropriate such resources.

Recognizing that the legitimacy and validity of peer review processes are ultimately based on the relationships of trust amongst those who are seen as 'peers,' most academics take for granted the belief that only other academics should be seen as legitimate peers. I question that assumption and wonder why we should view those academics whose work situates them on the opposite side of our struggles as our 'peers.' In doing so, our project takes the lead from the movements, such as the Black Campus Movement, who withdrew their trust from academics in universities bound up with the regimes they sought to abolish. Considering the accumulated capital of the publishing industry—e.g., Thomson *Reuters*'s market capitalization of over 30 billion dollars—I am reminded of a quote from Marx that "capital is dead labor, which, vampire- like, lives only by sucking living labor, and lives the more, the more labor it sucks." With the largest publishing corporation running the key academic rankings system, academia is dead to us. For escaping its vampire fangs, we devote our living labor to building relationships for alternative institutions of peer review.

Our journal's approach to peer review will entail more movement-relevant practices for curating themes of issues, including activist-intellectuals in the peer review process, making the review process more dialogical by allowing reviewers to be involved via open peer review, and promoting a more inclusive and democratic process for evaluating the importance of an article. We are starting this practice in our Issue Zero by having each submission openly reviewed by at least one academic and one non-academic activist. Through such practices, we not only aim to create a means for expropriating academia's resources for abolitionist movements but also to prefigure a mode of collective study beyond academic capitalism.

*Art and Self-Care*

*Originally Published On: February 22, 2015*

*The following is the transcript of a recent email interview I had with Emm Roy, artist and creator of Positive Doodles about art and self-care. She can be found on Facebook (https://www.facebook.com/EMMnotemma?ref=br_tf) as well as on Twitter (https://twitter.com/Emmnotemma).*

## 1. What made you interested in art?

Emm Roy: I'm excited about how we experience and relate to the universe. I want to know, feel and experience as much as possible, and it makes it difficult to focus. I'll see something and I'll think it's the best thing ever, but then five seconds later I'll see something else and I'll fall in love with that too, so it's hard to pay attention.

It made school difficult for me as a kid. Learning was important to me, but I couldn't pay attention in class, so I didn't do well. My dad wanted to help so he researched a few alternate learning methods. We tried several things until we realized that doodling and cartooning worked for me. I can't learn anything just by sitting still and listening to a teacher, but I can learn by creating and interacting with the information I'm receiving.

I spent my childhood drawing because it was the only way I could focus and learn at my maximum potential, and the habit stuck with me into adulthood. To this day, I can't sit still. It's not enough for me to experience life. I also have to create something in response to what I'm experiencing. I get restless when I'm not making art.

## 2. How did you start Positive Doodles and what are some of its goals, if any?

Emm Roy: It was a diary blog that took a positive turn and eventually became a positivity blog. My goal is to share simple positive messages in a cute way. I make all my posts with one specific person in mind (usually myself or one of my friends), but I'm grateful that there are others who enjoy them too. I also have a second goal which is to make art more freely accessible to the general public, but that one is proving to be harder to pull off.

## 3. How did you come to use art as a form of self-care?

Emm Roy: Completely unintentionally. Art helps me cope and express myself, but that's usually not my goal when I sit down to work. It was different when I started as a kid, but now I sit down with the intention to create, and all the other stuff (self-care, self-expression, stories, discussions, etc.) comes after. It's a very fluid and natural process.

## 4. You also keep something of an art diary which is for public viewing. What made you want to keep a personal diary in art form and how do you feel about discussing personal issues on such a public forum?

Emm Roy: My family has a history of mental illness. I have family members who don't talk to each other because of it. Some of my loved ones lost jobs and relationships because of it. Despite all this, it's not something we talk about. It's like a secret shame we carry. This isn't something unique to my family. It's a consequence of living in a culture that fears and stigmatizes mental illness.

If someone had talked to me when I was younger about mental illness and how it runs in my family, I might have understood what was happening when I started suffering from it. I might have been less scared or felt less alone. Most importantly, I could have gotten treatment. Instead, I was in my twenties when I was finally diagnosed.

My childhood self needed someone to talk to her openly about mental illness. That's what I do on my diary blog: I talk openly about all the things I wish someone had talked to me when I was younger. I know I can't go back and help my childhood self, but there are others out there still struggling, and I want to let them know they aren't alone.

I have no problems with discussing things publicly. I ask friends and family for permission before I mention them in anything, but that's about the extent to which I censor my blog.


**5. Why do you think that many people seem not to use art, in any if its forms, as a way to aid in their well-being? Would you say that self-care is something that is heavily rejected in US society?**

Emm Roy: Art itself is a form of self-care. Whether you're making art for fun, to make a statement or to pay the bills, you're working towards fulfilling a need. I don't know why some people prefer not to make art. Maybe they don't enjoy it. Maybe what I get from art, they get from something else like science or sports. Maybe they don't have the time. Maybe it's something else entirely. I imagine every person has their own reason(s) that's personal to them.

I don't think self-care is heavily rejected. I think the problem is that for many, self-care hasn't been offered as a possibility. After working, paying the bills, taking care of personal relationships, taking care of your kids if you have them, dealing with problems and doing everything else you have to do, there often isn't time left. Most mainstream self-care conversations I've seen focus on things like "buy yourself something nice" and "take a long bath", but those things are easier if you have money. A lot of self-care tips are like that; they ignore class differences. Some even ignore health differences. As a result, a lot of people are left out of the self-care movement through no fault of their own.


**6. What advice do you have for people who aspire to use art in a radical fashion? How can we support your work?**

Emm Roy: Here's my advice: make the art you want to make. If nobody likes it or if it doesn't make money, at least you'll have done what you wanted. Don't worry if it's weird or ugly. When it comes to art, those things are good. So are mistakes. Work hard. Don't sell yourself short. It's okay to share your insecurities about your art, but keep in mind that captioning your work with "This sucks. I don't even know why I'm sharing it" doesn't encourage anyone to look at it. If you ever need to take a break, it's okay to take one.

Anyone who wants to support my work should check out my positivity blog: Positivedoodles.tumblr.com.

Information about how to find me elsewhere is on the blog.

*The following is the transcript of a recent email interview I had with several admins of the Anarchist Memes Facebook page discussing racism, sexism, transphobia, and a host of other oppressive behaviors in radical spaces and how to battle those behaviors.*

## 1. How has anarchist thought evolved over time to be more inclusive of marginalized social groups?

[E]: Anarchism is a socialist ideology which had its birth and early infancy (as an actual political movement) within the First Internationale, with the Bakunin/Marx split. Like in socialism more broadly, the question of privilege apart from class privilege has always been a problem in the anarchist movement, with the (white, male, heterosexual, able-bodied) leadership of many anarchist groups refusing to acknowledge other vectors of oppression than the oppression experienced through class struggle, the one avenue of oppression that they themselves feel.

Already early on, though, anarchism experienced some queer theory. Der Eigene (The Unique) was the first gay Journal in the world, published from 1896 to 1932 by Adolf Brand in Berlin. Likewise, influential anarchists like Emma Goldman were far "ahead of their time" in that field, so to say. The politics of marginalized social groups, such as queer liberation and PoC [People of Color] liberation, has always been something that fit perfectly with anarchism because anarchism is opposition to all forms of structural oppression. But, as noted, many anarchist organizations (being dominated in large parts by a white heterosexual proletariat) has had a hard time recognizing this inherent property of anarchism.

Over time, as marginalized groups have gained a voice and prominence due to their own struggle for these things, they have also gained a voice and prominence within the broad anarchist tradition. Something which they should have had from the start, if only all of the early anarchists were as self-consistent as some of them were.

## 2. Why do you think that some on the radical left tend to downplay or outright ignore problems such as sexism and racism? Would you say that it is a major reason why more marginalized groups don't identify/don't become involved with anarchism?

[JA]: I think it is typically, generally, privilege (and white-male anarchists) clouding the analytical and emotional lens of those downplaying/ignoring sexism and racism. Many if not most white western anarchists seem to come to anarchism through a processes of de-conditioning themselves from the values and perceptions imbued in to them from the dominant culture often it's a process, an exponential shedding of negative, bigoted, privileged sensibilities and ideals, which is not to say downplaying racism, sexism or any other oppression is okay/excusable. I'm not suggesting it's incumbent for anyone to have patience with those express or retain bigoted and insensitive views.

To the contrary, I think an environment openly hostile to privilege and bigotry is an effective way of teaching people that there is something very wrong with those sorts of views. And more importantly, I think hostility towards bigotry and privilege rightly creates an environment which preferences the feelings of the oppressed before those who would downplay or deny their oppression. A culture of disdain towards oppressive attitudes and conditions is integral to adjusting attitudes and perceptions in my opinion.

[OM]: One of the main factors in excluding marginalized groups, in my experience especially with German activists, is the massive amount of unchecked privilege. This is especially true for activists who have entered Anarchism not to institute any meaningful social change, but to be part of a scene they consider a cool and edgy place to be in, i.e. they are not into it to build a better society, but to raise their own social status. These people (usually of the white, cishet, male, able-bodied/minded variety) then tend to establish dominance within their groups by all means available, including loads of oppressive behavior, especially shouting down and talking over more marginalized voices. Here in Germany, they have managed to successfully appropriate the concept of privilege, which is now considered a strictly individual property and not a result of structural inequality (e.g., people talk endlessly about the white privilege of individuals, but refuse to acknowledge white supremacy). Some even believe that, if they talk about their privilege a lot and in scene-approved terms, they can unilaterally rid themselves of said privilege, which leads to results to white men shouting down (white) women who raise topics like misogyny with shouts of "Check your white privilege" (white privilege can be interchanged with every other privilege here that is not male privilege).

Another major issue here is in my experience sub-culturalism. The confinement of Anarchism to a very narrow subculture is a major contributor to Anarchism's current state as a white boys club. To participate in most German Anarchist groups, one has to strictly adhere to a host of unwritten rules and to display very specific cultural tastes in the areas of music, clothing, language, leisurely activities and so on. These cultural tastes are often considered more important than a person's political affiliations.

Many of these rules actively exclude marginalized people. For example, everyone who owns a smartphone gets a lot of hate from local Anarchists for "supporting capitalism and consumerism" despite these devices being highly assistive for disabled people (I as an autistic person rely on my smartphone a lot to navigate everyday life, so I get a lot of ableism hurled at me here). Another example would be hostility towards poor/working class people. Since current Anarchist groups in my area are mainly made up of white men from wealthy backgrounds (the stereotypical trust fund kids), antagonism towards people who rely in wage labor (who, in general, tend to be more marginalized than the trust fund kids) for their survival definitely happens. Common critiques of "consumerism" actually go in a similar direction, basically preaching a very protestant-like asceticism and scolding women and working class people for acquiring things that make their lives easier and/or more pleasant (for example TV sets, washing machines, and so on).

A third issue I identify here is an attitude of "we exclude no one," which leads to Anarchist groups actively accepting the presence of racists, sexists and ableists because excluding them would be "authoritarian," while failing to acknowledge that accepting these people automatically excludes PoC, women, queer folx, disabled people and so on.


**3. Do you think that this problem between anarchists who engage in oppressive behavior and those who do their best not to/acknowledge their own privilege; create a major rift in the anarchist movement? That is creates a sort of purity test?**

[JA]: Well, I think this is an issue for socialism broadly - right-wing political philosophies don't have to grapple with people actively not acknowledging their privilege because (and to the degree that) they're ideologies built on privilege.

I think the percentage of abusive, privileged, bigoted people within the ranks of anarchists/marxists/et al are quite low - but that their awful behavior casts a wide shadow. I don't believe there is much disagreement on the importance of safeguarding against and identifying abusers/bigots in our midsts. I think most of the left today, is quite cognizant of the fact that we have to be diligent about allowing patriarchy, white supremacy, and other vectors of oppression to permeate and distort our organizations, praxis, etc.

[OM]: I largely agree with fellow admin [JA] here, but I would like to add that purity tests are already a thing in Anarchist contexts, usually not referring to privilege though (but more to aforementioned cultural tastes and socioeconomic status), and mostly conducted by people with a lot of unchecked privilege.

## 4. What have been some of the problems that you have encountered when bringing up race, sexism, or other oppressive social structures on the AM page?

[JA]: The biggest problems in raising topics concerning racism, sexism, etc (in my opinion) - are non-anarchists flooding the page with their bigoted nonsense. Concomitant with that, are the pacifist-police who ubiquitously argue that any ban or hostile attitude towards racists somehow violates the racist's freedom-of-speech or some tenant of anarchism (which is ludicrous, on multiple levels, as we perpetually explain).

## 5. Why do you think so many anarchists seem to misunderstand anarchism, seemingly in order to continue oppressive behavior?

[JA]: I don't believe the people who misunderstand anarchism, and think that it excuses their oppressive behavior, are actually anarchists. I think they're half-wits who self-apply the label per their misconceptions and intellectual laziness. What they think anarchism is - is not what anarchism is.

Many, many people mistake anarchism for a kind of sociopathic anti-philosophy - a philosophy which eschews order or concern for anyone/anything but the self. Which is, of course, the opposite of what anarchism is.

[E]: From a very cynical power-relations point of view, it makes perfect sense that they are misunderstanding anarchism in order to continue oppressive behavior within self-described "anarchist" spaces. Many of these people don't face the same oppression as members of other marginalized groups do, and as such this experience lies far from their own understanding of the world, which makes empathy with people in those situations extremely hard, especially when your own privilege depends on that relation of power.

## 6. How have racial tensions in the anarchist movement contributed to the rise of so-called nationalist anarchists? What exactly is a nationalist-anarchist?

[JA]: "National-anarchism" didn't come out of anarchism - national anarchists misappropriated "anarchism" in the same way "anarcho-capitalists" have. In the same way American-capitalists misappropriated the term "libertarian" from the left etc. There's really no connection between "national-anarchists" and anarchism, save the title, which they surreptitiously took as their own.

[E]: A nationalist-"anarchist" is either a crypto-fascist seeking to recruit through the use of quasi-anarchist slogans and aesthetics turned towards a fascist mindset (see the "autonome Nationalisten" [Autonomous Nationalists] in Germany for a good example of this, with the Far- Right subverting and using the symbols of the Far-Left), a nationalist who has misunderstood anarchism or a self-proclaimed "anarchist" who has misunderstood anarchism. In all cases, it's an ideology that's built on the sophism of "freedom of association" applying between ethnicities and "peoples." It's a sort of strange mix between völkisch nationalism in the old pre-Nazi conception and all the most surface and hollow thoughts of an early Mikhail Bakunin (who was more interested in pan-Slavism and Slavic nationalism than he would later be, spurning those ideas later in life).

Fascists have also co-opted anarchist thinkers in the past, with the "Cercle Proudhon" being an early Far-Right quasi-fascist organization, and the early Italian fascists had great respect for the syndicalism of Georges Sorel and the conception of political violence that Mikhail Bakunin put forth.

**7. How do you think that people can make their own groups more inclusive of marginalized groups?**

[JA]: I found all these questions originally - and still do - difficult to answer as a cis white male. I can't speak for marginalized communities, and it feels inappropriate to pontificate on their behalf.

[E]: People have to speak up. They have to not accept or be silent in the face of the racist, sexist, transphobic or otherwise reactionary actions taken by their groups. Trying to go for a squeaky- clean image by further silencing the marginalized voices is not the way to go about it, when someone is being a racist asshole you have to confront it, not just ignore it. Otherwise, we're not going to get all that far. In many ways, the reason that Anarchist Memes has evolved in the direction it has is because we refuse to be silent when self-proclaimed anarchists act just like the oppressors they claim they are fighting. Racism, sexism, transphobia, or any other kind of oppression should not be casually accepted in anarchist spaces, and it won't be on Anarchist Memes.

Given that the movie 50 Shades of Grey came out in February 2015, a large amount of media attention has been devoted to not only the movie, but the discussion of Bondage, Dominance, Submission, and Masochism or BDSM. While many condemn 50 Shades of Grey as a film that promotes abuse, rarely, if ever has the media discussed the movie and BDSM more generally with people who are in the BDSM community.

Below is a transcript of an interview I did with three people who identify with and are a part of the BDSM community. In it, we discuss sexuality, how real-life BDSM differs from reality, and the impact 50 Shades of Grey is having on people's ideas of BDSM. They have chosen to remain anonymous and thus will be referred to solely by their initials.

## 1. How would you define your sexuality? How did you come to this realization?

CG: If we're talking about who I'm attracted to, I'd be best defined as a demisexual. While I can tell you whether or not someone is in my opinion sexy, I don't feel any actual urge to engage in any form of sexual activity with them unless I also feel a deep romantic attachment. The people I've felt this way with have all been women. I think that I'd be equally attracted to a male given the right set of circumstances, though I can't say I know what they are. If we're talking about what end of the S&M [Sadism & Masochism] spectrum I'd fall upon, that was something I grappled with. I'm definitely a sadistic dominant. I enjoy being the controlling one in most sexual situations, and I draw a great deal of erotic satisfaction from the pain or humiliation of a willing partner.

It was mostly a question when I was younger and I thought for sure that there couldn't be anyone else who was turned on by the same things I was. As a boy near the onset of puberty, I'd fantasize about the idea of being in pain at the hands of a dominant who controlled me, but I later realized I probably fell on the opposite end of the spectrum in practice once I started to have relationships with other BDSM enthusiasts as a teenager. Still, I think that sexuality and its many facets are quite fluid once you remove the cultural inhibitions and I wouldn't be surprised if I were to change my mind one day.

SW: I think, in all honesty, a person's sexuality is something they spend their whole life discovering. There are always people that vehemently declare that they are as straight as a ruler, but really, there will almost always be an exception. And if not, a straight person can still, usually, appreciate the attractiveness, or lack thereof, of someone of the same gender. For me, love is love. I do not fall in love with someone based on their gender or sexual preference. I fall in love with people based on who they are as a person, on the inside, and physical attraction doesn't hurt.

CR: I'd define my sexuality as pansexual, but my romantic orientation as biromantic. Sexual attraction for me isn't about gender. While the person's gender is important and should be respected, it has no bearing on my ability to feel attracted. However, in a romantic sense I do have preferences in gender.

I came to this conclusion when I was very young (at least on my pansexuality); because despite crushes on boys my first kiss was with a girl. I loved girls (and later gender non- conforming people) just as much as boys.

## 2. How did you find yourself becoming interested in/attracted to BDSM?

CG: When I was about 12 years old, I figured out you could use Google to find pictures of naked women. I'd print them out and pass them around to my friends who didn't have computers. It was mostly out of curiosity and a desire to discuss sexual things with friends who were at a similar stage of development. 'Sex education' always had too much of a dressed up politically correct agenda for my tastes. It was at this point that I first realized there were many other people out there who thought and felt the same way I did about the activities commonly known as BDSM. I found images of men and women bound in different positions, videos of people dominating each other, and everything that came with it. I had always been interested in those sorts of activities, but I could never put a label to it simply because I didn't know of one.

SW: I cannot pinpoint a certain pivotal moment; I think I was always just curious deep down. I have always had interests that deviate from what many people call normal. Speaking of which, the word normal has always translated to boring, in my mind. I pride myself in being simultaneously unique and invisible. I do not like being the center of attention but I like standing out, if that makes any sense at all. It is fascinating to discover the limits of one's body.

CR: To be honest? I'm a multiple abuse victim and rape victim. Certain aspects of my PTSD make it very hard to process, own and deal with that trauma. It is my experience that certain aspects of BDSM can be very helpful in dealing with psychosexual issues. That said, I think it is equally important to criticize, examine and understand why your kinks are your kinks. Sex doesn't exist in a vacuum.


## 3. What are some aspects of BDSM that not many people know about?

CG: I think the most common misconception people have about BDSM is that it's like rape, that it's all about the gratification of the sadist who is an evil person randomly forcing the masochist to endure things for their pleasure. In reality, consent is absolutely everything. Perhaps most emblematic of this is the popular trend of a 'safe word.' Some people use an actual word, others use a system of color coding similar to a traffic light. Whatever your choice, if a safe word is used it means "I am uncomfortable, stop." To continue at that point is the ultimate breach of trust in BDSM, and it can signify the end of a relationship. Since the general conception is that the masochist is the one being used by the dominant, it's supremely ironic that such a powerful tool rests mainly in the hands of the submissive. In fact, I think it's fair to argue that the one with the most control in a BDSM scenario is the submissive. But this control is important, because it makes sure that mutual satisfaction is being achieved.

Some people enjoy inflicting pain in an erotic setting, and some enjoy receiving it. Another thing I'd imagine most people don't know is that healthy BDSM relationships start the same way any other sexual relationship does. Whereas one couple may discuss the fact that they want to save penetrative intercourse for marriage, you might put more emphasis on turn-offs, limits, and a safe word. While people who would fall under the label of BDSM enthusiast may like similar things, it's still a label and not everyone is the same. If one of you doesn't like to perform or receive a certain sex act, or if there's a certain point you don't wish to pass, that's something that should be communicated.

SW: BDSM is not just about ruthlessly flogging people. BDSM is about mutual respect and listening, listening to what your partner likes or when they have had enough. Safe words are key and must be heard and honored. Aftercare is also very important and includes discussion of the experience as well as tending to any more serious injuries sustained.

CR: That is kind of a loaded question. Most people have a very limited idea of what goes into a kink based partnership. Much of BDSM is not inherently sexual in nature. Much of it is, but sometimes you'll have submissives who honestly just want to clean your house. Being submissive fulfills a need for many that isn't always sexual, that they cannot find otherwise.


## 4. Do you think it is up to the BDSM community to make a better image for itself or should society stop being so rigid about the expression of one's sexuality?

CG: That's problematic. On the one hand, I think BDSM participants should be sensitive to non- participants in the same way a person with fiery sexuality should be to an asexual person. Many are simply not into it, and there's nothing wrong with that. It's a matter of respect out of deference. On the other hand, our society is painfully puritanical about even 'vanilla' sex acts and that has to stop. In contrast, the BDSM community is not dissimilar to the larger gay rights movement in that it's big on acceptance, respect, and individual choice. Sure, there are a few yahoos here and there who muddy it up for the rest, but for the most part the mindset is in a good place.

     I like to keep my sex life private (which would be the case even if my preferences were mainstream), but I know there are many others who do not feel the same way and that should be their right. It has to be a give and take. People who don't want anything to do with it should have the right not to be audience to it, and people who do shouldn't be shamed or forced into stifling themselves. I do err more on the side of society needing to abandon a bit of its rigidity, though. The people actively opposing different expressions of human sexuality are the ones with the problem, not the other way around.

SW: I think, at the end of the day, people are going to think what they are going to think. If people want to be close-minded and form baseless, negative opinions, then let them miss out on the fun. You cannot please everyone, nor should you attempt to.

CR: This is a grey issue. Kinksters have a tendency to act like nothing in the scene should be questioned. Vanilla people tend to have a very heteronormative view on what the scene is and can be. The kink community does need to conduct itself better, but society as a whole needs to work through its issues with sex negativity.


## 5. How is/how can the potential for abuse in BDSM be combated?

CG: I think it is sadists practicing with consenting partners who get the brunt of the bad reputation associated with BDSM. Masochism isn't viewed in the same controversial light. As far as combating the assumption of abuse, it's a matter of drawing a distinction between what is abuse and what is consensual. In outdated versions of the DSM, essentially the bible of diagnostics in the field of psychology and psychiatric medicine, sadism and masochism were both classified in a manner not dissimilar to a psychological disorder. Nowadays, they're listed under paraphilia. There are very clear guidelines as to what is defined as disordered sadism, and I happen to agree with them. A person is considered 'disordered' if they experience significant emotional distress to the point of impaired every day function because of their urges. More important is whether or not they practice their urges with an unwilling person. Short of that it can't be abuse because it's consensual, which means that there's no victim.

     Then there's the people who try to hide abuse behind the guise of love. Forgive me if I speak harshly here, but this is a very touchy subject for me. It makes my blood boil that there are people in this world who are so callous as to maliciously abuse another human being and not even own up to it. Worse still, they take the label of what is essentially an oppressed minority and they pervert it for their own temporary protection. And it is temporary. Abusers may not always be punished in the form of legal retribution, but they always get found out and it has an impact on their life. Unfortunately, by that point they've already become a statistic. The vast majority of sex offenders could be classified as disordered sadists. In that respect, I don't know if there's much that can be done. People like to lump things together. It makes it easier for them to process the big world outside their heads with too many things for them to conceptualize at a high level. The only real hope we have is to distinguish between the disordered and those who are just harmlessly kinky. As I keep saying, consent and being informed are everything.

SW: The potential for abuse in BDSM can be combated with aftercare, safe words, compassion, and tenderness. BDSM is not about aggression but about the line between pleasure and pain being crossed and blurred.

CR: Easy. If someone says they have been raped, abused or otherwise harmed by a person, they should not be welcome in the public scene. Vetting should be standard; there should be at least one reference in your profile, or someone willing to vouch for your newness to the scene etc. It really shouldn't be seen as difficult as it is.

**6. If able to, explain how 50 Shades of Grey is problematic and does a disservice to the BDSM community.**

CG: I've personally never read the book, as that would require me giving patronage to the person who wrote it. I have read about a half dozen synopses of it. From what I've seen, it's problematic mainly for the dominant party in BDSM. This is true in three ways. Firstly, it depicts the dominant in an excessively dysfunctional light. Christian Grey goes beyond the bedroom with his 'desires' and invades the personal life of Anastasia in numerous ways such as borderline stalking, and legal coercion. Looming over your lover isn't acceptable in any type of relationship, and a BDSM relationship is no different. As far as legal coercion goes, unless you're Sheldon Cooper you don't need a relationship agreement drafted in the form of a legal document to have a relationship you can feel safe in. This plays into the second problem, his blatant control issues. It's true that BDSM does have some elements involving taking control of or giving control to another party. However, in most cases this takes place behind closed doors.

Christian Grey tries to rig his relationship with Anastasia in such a way that he would have full control over everything that happens regarding their intimacy outside of the bedroom as well. Add this to the whole 'young, aggressive billionaire' thing that he has going on and you're left to wonder what we're not being told about his personality. From another synopsis I've read, I know that we later find out that he has been in therapy because of his urges for over a decade. As I've already mentioned, this is a symptom of disordered sexual sadism. Finally, he seems to be practicing with a non-consenting partner. While Anastasia is somewhat receptive to his advances, from what I've read she never explicitly states that she's okay with what is about to be done to her. Grey seems to be throwing things at a wall and hoping something will stick. This goes against the core of consent and respect within the BDSM community.

CR: Mmmm, see I don't really care as much about the kink community being misrepresented here. Even rudimentary research would show you the glaringly obvious there. I am far more put off by the treatment of Ana. I am concerned about how the popularity of this book will further normalize abusive relationships, possibly leading to even more abuse in the scene.

Below is a transcript of an email interview I did with writers Gregory Smulewicz- Zucker and Michael J. Thompson who co-authored the article "The Treason of Intellectual Radicalism and the Collapse of Leftist Politics" which appeared in the Winter 2015 edition of the academic *journal Logos: A Journal of Modern Society and Culture.*

In the interview, we discuss the problems of current leftist theory, the collapse of the left, and if there is a way to rebuild leftist politics.


**1. You write early in the article that "Today, leftist political theory in the academy has fallen under the spell of ideas so far removed from actual political issues [.]" Do you think that this is a failing that is solely in the academy? It seems that it is a widespread failure by the left as a whole, that they are more focused on the theoretical than anything that is truly concrete.**

We agree that the problem is not solely with the academy. It is important to look at the academy because the kind of work that is done in the academy is, in part, often a reflection of what people think they can achieve on the ground. The main issue seems to be that moral revulsion has supplanted the critique of social mechanisms that produce the problems that outrage people. It is also important to stress that moral revulsion is not a substitute for, nor an equivalent of, political action and political strategy. The key, as we see it, is to understand that politics is about shaping not only the mentality of citizens and the norms of culture, but more crucially about organizing the legitimate power of the state to enforce laws that prevent social injustice and expand the horizon of social justice. This requires understanding the mechanisms of politics, of elections, of the law, of constitutional interpretation, and so on. The contemporary left has abandoned these concerns and has instead decided to view them as attributes of a system that needs to be rejected. This is simply absurd and, in our view, anti-political.

We also think that there is a problem with what theory has become. The only reason that a cleavage has developed between theory and practice is because the function of theory has been abandoned. It is important to recognize that what is now touted as theory is not actually theory. Theory plays a vital role in diagnosing and critiquing concrete political problems. People like Zizek and Badiou do not have theories. Their work is so convoluted and self-referential that there is no link to the concrete. It masquerades as theory. They are able to create their own fan clubs and say whatever they want because they purposefully construct so-called theories that allow them to evade critical evaluation. Esotericism has become a virtue unto itself. From this standpoint, the aversion to theory is understandable. So-called theory has become a world for the initiated. This is a distortion of theory. It is merely the flipside of a society that can dismiss evolution as "only a theory."

**2. You say that social movements are not focused on "unequal distributions of economic and political power which once served as the driving impulse for political, social and cultural transformation." What would you say to those who push back on this idea and argue that there is a deeper analysis than just class?**

There is more to social power and domination than class, it is true. But movements for transforming social and cultural forms of exclusion – for women, minority groups, gay rights, etc. – have all occurred within the confines of the liberal state. Class is the one category that has gotten worse over the past 40 years, not better. Radicals need not only to be able to call into question the backward, provincial views of the racist, the homophobe and the anti-feminist, but also to tie this into a more general theory of what a free, just society ought to be able to achieve and to be able to understand that ending these kinds of exclusion lead us to some radical kind of emancipation, but simply leave us within the liberal-capitalist consensus.

Radicalism must be able to craft a more comprehensive vision of what a free, just society would look like. But it must keep in view the fact that economic power, the power of elite interests, are behind many of the cleavages in race, for instance. That propertied interests have had something invested in preventing blacks from moving to white neighborhoods; that they have been behind the decisions to de-industrialize urban American cities, which has had an enormous destructive effect on contemporary black communities, and so on. The killings of black men that have elicited so much outrage over the past year cannot only be attributed to racism. They occupied a specific class status. Likewise, one of the interesting things about recent writings that have recast sex work as an expression of feminist self-assertion is that they entirely ignore the fact that it is working class women who are compelled to do this work. Racism, homophobia, and sexism are social realities, but we must recognize that the vulnerability to violence and exploitation of these people is exacerbated by their class status.

Identity is simply not a stable enough concept to ground a radical politics. Corporate power can often back culturally liberal causes such as gay rights, or the symbolic issues of the Confederate Battle flag. But what remains after these (liberal) changes in our society and culture is economic power: the power to shape our educational system, to organize social production and consumption, and to chart the values of the society more generally.


**3. Expand upon the statement: "This new radicalism has made itself so irrelevant with respect to real politics that it ends up serving as a kind of cathartic space for the justifiable anxieties wrought by late capitalism further stabilizing its systemic and integrative power rather than disrupting it." What exactly do you mean by this? Also, couldn't some push back and argue that in many ways, this new radicalism is disruptive, as can be seen by the Black Bloc, activists fighting against the Keystone XL pipeline, and those who engage in direct action?**

This was not meant as a critique of those who participate in direct action. Direct action becomes the only means for combating injustices when concrete political programs fade away. What is worrying is the way direct action has supplanted political strategy much in the same way that so-called theory has become fetishized in and of itself. Our critique questions the political salience of these actions as a general political program. Neo-anarchism has become a model for political activity on the left. It has claimed for itself the mantle of engaged politics. We think this is a grave error.

When demonstrations occur, they are more often than not spaces for moral rage, not for political programs. Take the Civil Rights movement. Yes, there were symbolic acts of direct action, but these were integrated into a more general movement that included a political strategy to influence political elites, crafting ideas for legislation to be enacted, as well as a new cultural understanding of civic rights. To isolate ourselves to direct action without a larger movement, without a more radical program for action, for what you want to implement in a positive way through institutions, is simply not radical politics. This is the "cathartic space" we refer to: it grants a moral self-righteousness to the individual who has genuine anger against society. But we should not confuse this with the hard work of political action that has in view the transformation of society through the shaping of law, winning elections, and so on.

Look at modern conservatives as an example. During the 1960s, they were a political, cultural and intellectual minority. Their ideas for destroying public schools (Milton Friedman championed the school voucher idea, considered insane at the time), for constitutional interpretation, for economic liberalization and privatization, and so on were policy non-starters. Now they have reframed American political life. Look at the last two vice presidential Republican candidates. As patently imbecilic as Sarah Palin and Paul Ryan are, the fact that such people are able to run in national elections and advocate political policies evidences how fringe ideas gained some degree of public approval because there is no rational radical left to oppose them. Radicals have no ideas about how to combat these policy imperatives, and this is simply absurd. How can we talk about radical politics that has any efficacy if we oppose the state, taking law, political parties, and so on seriously as mechanisms for change? Not to do so is to suffer from a kind of infantile disorder. This makes Leftists surrender their place in politics to the right.

The dangers are real.

**4. Do you think that class politics have weakened in the post-industrial age due to the fact that there was an illusion that one could move above their current station as well as had more access to credit and high tier goods? [Compared to the industrial age where one knew that they would always be a worker on the factory floor.]**

The transition from a productivist to a consumerist paradigm of economic life is a crucial explanatory variable for the docility of American political consciousness. The basic inequality of our society is just as bad as it was during the gilded age, but the overall size of the economic pie has simply gotten larger. There is just more wealth to be concentrated in the hands of elites. Reconciling individuals to this system has been a long process of legitimating the economic system and the values that underpin it. The weakening of labor class struggles is partly due to economic and sociological shifts. The main thrust is still, we think, ideological: There is no reason why new forms of labor – service, professional, freelance, and so on – should not be protected from the kinds of extractive power that private control over capital requires. The fact is, capitalism has changed some of its contours, but still remains fundamentally the same in the sense that it requires the exploitation of labor for expanded growth and accumulation.

The problem is that the political critique of capital needs to be kept in view. We need to ask again what the purposes and ends of our economy ought to be, to establish a critical discourse on what is necessary and what is merely a means for the opening up of new spaces for profit.

**5. Would you say that the problem with the language that many radicals use is that there is an obsession with using the correct terminology rather than actually engaging in meaningful work? That the language in and of itself is an end?**

**I've also thought that this has made it easier for opponents to infiltrate such groups.**

**What are your thoughts on that?**

Words matter, no question about it. But words without concrete concepts simply create confusion at best and mask imbecility at worst. Language does not create reality, but it can distort it. What the left needs is a coherent connection between the basic values that define its ends and the concepts and ideas it seeks to put out in the world. It needs to see that moral ideas and values require some translation into political reality and this is never going to be perfect or ideal. What makes a rational radicalism salient, what keeps it alive, and what will allow it to breathe new life into the world is its orientation to political reality. The correct terminology is useful if it can explain reality.

If the focus is on language at the expense of establishing a link between language and reality, the issue is not so much that opponents will infiltrate radical movements. On the contrary, opponents will actually be able to draw people out of radical movements. An anti- statist left can be drawn to an anti-statist right, especially when right-wing opponents of the state seem to enjoy actual electoral successes. Even more, it can prevent the formation of a larger, more integrated movement since the fetish of language simply splinters our politics. This is why an objective science of politics is needed by radicals, not language, moral rage, or anything else. An objective vantage point anchored in political principles of social emancipation is what a mature radicalism should seek to achieve.

**6. You bring up the fact that "Liberalism has been highly successful at incorporating many of the social movements that have emerged throughout the twentieth century." However, do you think that liberalism is now failing since we are seeing the rollback of rights for women and minorities, the welfare state, jobs for working-class Americans, and the like?**

It's not evident that rights for women and minorities have been receding. It is, however, demonstrably true that political rights are simply not enough. You need to reshape economic life to grant them any full social meaning. Blacks have been excluded by income just as much as by overt racial exclusion from migrating out of decaying cities to more affluent areas with superior public goods such as education. Civic and cultural rights are expanding, but at the expense of economic rights that give them any kind of real significance and meaning. The civic equality for excluded groups satisfies the narrow demand for recognition, but it does nothing for the richer need for creating a social context for genuine human growth and forms of modern social solidarity.

The emphasis on cultural liberalism as opposed to economic liberalism has also allowed the welfare state to be slowly chiseled away. What is needed is a conception of economic justice that allows for the concrete development of individuals, that grants all equal access not only to "opportunity" but to the means for self-development and for human growth. This is what liberalism cannot provide and what radicalism must insist upon.

**7. Would you argue that liberalism has effectively defanged a number of previously radical movements and essentially acted as a co-optation of these movements on an ideological and strategic/tactical level?**

Liberalism has historically been able to reconcile every major social movement into a more general legitimacy. But it has done this not only because of its basic principles, but also because it is good for business. It is good for Wal-Mart to get women out of patriarchal structures of domestic life because it gives it a cheap labor force to exploit. The same can be said about ending homophobia in the workplace. Liberalism allows for the erasure of pre-liberal forms of inequality, but protects the class inequalities of bourgeois life. It has had more success in allowing women, minority groups of all kinds inclusion into our political and cultural life. But radicalism must push beyond liberalism: it must question the generic values and norms that pervade our reality not simply because they exist, but interrogate them on the basis of their ability to expand or to contract the realm of human development.

None of this means that liberal values are irrelevant, quite the opposite. Radicals need to be vigilant against pre-liberal norms and practices: against racism, homophobia, gender discrimination, and the like. But it must insist that these categories be tied to a concept of the public good, that they are not simply interests of minority groups, but part of a general public good to live in a society of self-development, expression, difference and non-exploitation. The main issue is that economic forms of domination and exploitation are more universal and more damaging in modern societies. The destruction of the planet, the amount of human waste (both as refuse and as "wasted" forms of life), the cultural realities of alienation, the withering of artistic and cultural life – all of it is tied to the increased, wasteful commodification and consumerism of late-capitalism. Radicalism needs a more unified theory of all of this, and it needs to see the stakes clearly.

**8. Please expand upon the collapse of Marxism within a US/Western context and how that has created both a political and intellectual vacuum which the liberal left has come to fill. It seems that there has been a massive collapse not only due to the triumph of global capitalism and the corporate state, but also inner conflicts and, most importantly, the attack on the Marxist left by the state itself.**

Of course the decline of Marxism is a complex, highly debated narrative. There was good reason for members of the New Left in the 1960s to move away from categories of class since the overt racism of many unions and the labor movement made alliances with them odious. But the reality is, the fall of the Soviet Union, the emergence of neoliberalism as a resurgent form of capitalism, and the new cultural mentalities cultivated by an empty, commodified culture have all come together to create a fertile ground for a post-marxist (postmodern, poststructuralist, and, simply post-rational) intellectual environment. Mediating institutions like unions have been eroded; the suburbanization of several generations of people since the 1950s has atomized consciousness, and a unified culture industry has exerted strong pressures on the values and norms of the population.

Historically, Marxism was a challenge to the liberal state. When it went into decline, it ceased to be a threat. There is no longer need for the state to attack the Marxist left. Right-wing pundits might sound the alarm that President Obama is a socialist, but this is only a rhetorical tactic for trying to oust Democratic politicians from office. As for internal disputes, true believers of different sectarian castes mainly dominate them. Dogmatically invoking Marx or the Marxist theorists of past is not, on its own, sufficient to a revitalized radicalism. Their ideas are resources that can be built upon to confront our contemporary crises. Indeed, this is precisely what the best theorists did.

About all of this, the core values and ideas of Marx still have a lot to say and to explicate. What we tried to call into question in our article was the lack of real political depth to the new radical intellectuals and their ideas about particularist forms of identity, puerile anti-statism, and abstract notions of freedom. What is important is that we see that advanced capitalism has been able to destroy the very foundations and resources needed to advance a coherent, politically viable form of critique and movements for enlightened, rational, progressive political change. Our polemic was aimed at those that do not realize that the conception of leftist politics they endorse are molded from the very stuff that ought to be critiqued.


**9. Do you think that there is any way to reverse this trend of the Left falling further and further into the abyss of political irrelevancy?**

Yes, there is a way. Rediscover what politics actually is. It is not a path to utopia. It should not be a means to only vent frustrations. These are the qualities of a dogmatic and fractured left. Concrete political engagement through social movements directed at concrete aims forges solidarity. Part of why Occupy Wall Street was initially so successful was because it seemed to create solidarity around the issue of economic inequality. It got people out onto the streets. Part of why it failed was because, in its rejection of demands, it did not show how protests could lead to meaningful change. This was not true of the civil rights movement or the labor movement. In the midst of the AIDs crisis, gay rights activists protested to demand government action. Feminist activists mobilized to try to get the Equal Rights Amendment passed. These examples of movements were inspired by liberalism, but they attest to the fact that movements need an object. Recognizing that the state is an institution that can be used to serve the public good and is not some abstract apparatus gives the radical left a concrete object.

A rational radical politics would have the effect of exposing the irrelevance of anti- modern and irrational theories. It would marginalize self-righteous rebelliousness. A left that is concerned with realizing the public good has no use for self-indulgent flights from reality. It was in response to these dangerous and alarmingly prevalent distractions that we wrote our essay. A left that has nothing to say about the real world, material interests, mechanisms of exploitation, political policy, or the function of institutions in serving the public good will fall into the abyss of political irrelevance. But these are tendencies on the left that have come to prominence over the last forty years. It is not an accident that these tendencies occurred in tandem with the revitalization of capitalism. Yet, we believe that the current morass can and should serve as an impetus for making people articulate a rational radical politics, rather than encourage people to retreat into the kinds of theoretical incoherence, chic radicalism and cynicism, and romanticized rebelliousness that simply uphold the status quo.

*This is a transcript of a recent email interview I did with independent journalist James Corbett, where we discuss BRICS, the view that many have of the organization as a resistance force and the truth behind that, and end with on how we can fight back against the powers that be in our own way.*

**1. What are BRICS and the Asian Infrastructure Investment Bank (AAIB) really about? Many people argue that it is these countries challenging the dominate US-based system. How is that true or not true in some respects?**

Mr. Corbett: Who is contending that the AIIB or the BRICS' New Development Bank is in any way competitive with the Bretton Woods institutions (IMF/World Bank)? Certainly not anyone involved with any of these institutions.

In March 2015, IMF chief Christine Lagarde pledged IMF cooperation with the AIIB. [1] In June 2015, World Bank chief Jim Yong Kim issued a statement congratulating the AIIB on its formation and calling it an "important new partner" for the Washington-led development bank. [2]

In July 2015, NDB [New Development Bank] President K.V. Kamath returned the favor, conceding that the NDB and the IMF/World Bank are complementary institutions, not rivals. [3]

Also in July, the AIIB and the World Bank signed an actual cooperation agreement, promising to identify projects for joint financing later this fall. [4]

No, these institutions do not view themselves as competitive. It is only various media pundits who have speculated that these new banks are in fact some sort of challenge to the so- called "Washington consensus." What none of these experts has bothered to report (for obvious reasons) is the remarkable fact that the Vice President of the NDB is also an Executive Board member of the IMF [5], who then went on to pledge cooperation and joint action [6] between the NDB and IMF. Also missing from this narrative is the fact that the NDB's chief, Kundapur Vaman Kamath [7], is a former staffer of the supposed NDB "rival" Asia Development Bank. Or there's Jin Liqun [8], widely tipped to be the head of the AIIB, who also happens to be a former Vice President of the Asia Development Bank and alternative Executive Director of the World Bank.

In fact, the only sign that these Beijing-backed development banks pose any challenge to the existing order whatsoever is that the NDB has already confirmed [9] that their first loan will be denominated in yuan, not dollars, and the AIIB is considering a basket of currencies, including the Yuan. [10]

But even this is not as much of a challenge to the Bretton Woods institutions as it appears on first glance. Although Beijing is obviously seeking to bolster the Yuan as an international settlement currency, this is not being done in an effort to make the Yuan itself a world reserve currency in the same way that the dollar is today. Instead, this is being done in service of a policy goal outlined by People's Bank of China Governor Zhou Xiaochuan in 2009 that is seeking to establish the "Special Drawing Rights" currency basket as the new world reserve currency.

China's goal is to have the Yuan included in the SDR basket along with the dollar, yen, euro and pound. But the SDR itself is issued and administered by the IMF so once again we see that Beijing is not seeking to undermine these US-led hegemonic institutions at all, merely to increase their status and clout within these institutions.

**2. Are there any cracks in BRICS, as in problems and disputes between member nations?**

Mr. Corbett: It would almost be better to ask if there are any points of accord between the BRICS nations other than occasional alignment of bilateral trade or security goals.

The idea that there is any such thing as a shared BRICS economic, military or foreign policy is part of the fundamental fraud of the "BRICS" idea itself. The truth is that the BRICS (formerly "BRIC") are not a coherent or organic grouping of like-minded states at all, but an arbitrary grouping of economies first identified by Goldman Sachs as emerging economies who were all expected to outperform the developed world in the coming decades. It was the BRIC countries that took this Goldman Sachs concept and attempted to make it into a real-world political reality, and the ploy becomes even more obvious when one realizes that the "S" (South Africa) was added not for any rational economic or political reason, but primarily to give the organization a footing in another continent. [11]

China and India were at war in 1962 and have suffered through decades of tense relations. Even as late as 2006 Indian parliamentarians were openly urging a harder line [12] on ongoing border disputes between the two countries and border issues continue to this very day, with a tense military standoff in the disputed border region occurring last year, over a decade after the BRIC's inception. [13]

China and Russia likewise share their traditional rivalries. Ever since the Sino-Soviet split in 1960, the two countries have been famously distrustful of each other. They have competing security and economic interests in places like Central Asia, where Putin is trying to construct his Eurasian Economic Union and Xi is attempting to solidify his New Silk Road. The fact that China, the world's largest energy importer, and Russia, the world's largest natural gas exporter, have only just now completed a pipeline agreement shows the degree to which their warming economic relations are a matter of political expediency, not mutual trust.

Brazil has enjoyed a close trading relationship with China in recent years, but even so Brazil has joined fellow BRICS member India in openly criticizing Beijing for its foot-dragging on Yuan appreciation. [14]

Brazil, India and South Africa have attempted to create closer relations in recent years through mechanisms like the IBSA Dialogue as part of the "South-South Policy," but the very fact that they are seeking to expand cooperation through alternative dialogues and fora show the ineffectiveness of the BRICS to address these issues within the BRICS framework.

The BRICS are an artificial creation of a US investment bank, and the glacial pace at which the organization moves and the constant internal jockeying for status and position (see deliberations over where to locate the NDB for example) show that it is little more than an afterthought in these countries' economic and foreign policies.


### 3. Are there any ways in which the interests of countries like Russia and China aligned with the interests of the US? What do you make of this cooperation on one front, while they disagree and fight on another front?

Mr. Corbett: I think the problem with thinking of international relations this way is that it presupposes that the people in positions of political power and financial influence are interested in vague concepts of "national interest" rather than in the preservation and expansion of their own power and influence and that of their colleagues and associates.

As insiders like David Rothkopf and others have shown in recent years, there is a "Superclass" of several thousand individuals in positions of influence who have the ability to act trans-nationally, and who actively do so in the pursuit of their own international relation and economic policy goals. Seen from within this framework, a billionaire financier from one country with global assets to protect has demonstrably more in common with a billionaire financier from another country with global assets to protect than he does a poor manual laborer from his own country. [15]

Consequently, global political and economic relations are more fruitfully seen as a mish- mash of sometimes rivalrous, sometimes complementary interests of various multinational banks and corporations and the various think tanks and international institutions they control. Although there may be greater points of accord and room for cooperation between elite oligarchs who share a language, history, culture or geographical location, it by no means rules out cooperation with others, even in countries that are nominally suffering through poor relations.

Thus, what does it even mean to ask whether the interests of "Russia" and "China" align with the interests of the "US"? Surely these nation-state entities do not have interests in and of themselves. The people in positions of power in those countries have interests, but we would be better served in narrowing the scope of the question by identifying them in particular. Do the interests of Gazprom and Rosneft align with the interests of BP or Royal Dutch Shell? Sometimes, in certain contexts, yes. In other contexts they would be rivals.

Similarly with JP Morgan and HSBC and the Bank of China, or the various central bankers at the Bank for International Settlements, or the members of the Trilateral Commission. Their deliberations have very little to do with amorphous national interests and everything to do with jockeying for personal position and control of the global economic and political chessboard.

**4. Why do you think that people buy into this narrative that countries like Russia and China are a 'resistance' force?**

Mr. Corbett: We have been conditioned our entire lives to expect that anything that opposes a demonstrably evil entity must itself be good. Whether it be the Star Wars Rebel Alliance fighting the Galactic Empire or the heroic Allies fighting the villanous Axis or even the more nuanced case of a valiant Serpico fighting the corruption within his own NYPD, we are almost invariably given narratives with identifiable "good guys" fighting risible "bad guys."

But when it comes to the machinations of global geopolitics, this is completely the wrong lens through which to understand what is happening. Much more to the point would be the metaphor of rival gangs competing for territory. It is not the case that the Bloods are the "good guys" and the Crips the "bad guys" or vice versa; they are both criminal networks that use brutality and violence to enforce their control over given areas and to terrorize others.

Similarly, if we understand that rivalries between various international organizations (to the extent that they exist at all) are really only battles between gangsters for control over the global turf, we can more clearly understand that it is not a question of choosing sides in the struggle, but opposing the very ideologies of centralized, hierarchical control that make these institutions possible.


**5. Talk about the history of China and the US, specifically with regards to how the build-up of the Chinese economy is due to, at least in part, the involvement of US companies.**

Mr. Corbett: The modern era of Sino-American relations famously began with Henry Kissinger's secret trip to China in 1971 that paved the way for Nixon's own trip and the renormalization of relations between the two countries. But even that narrative is grossly misleading. It neglects, for example, that Kissinger was a protégé of David Rockefeller, whose family had been intimately involved in China since the early part of the 20th century and who "supported" Kissinger's China initiative, which later resulted in his Chase bank becoming the first US correspondent bank of the National Bank of China.

Regardless, Kissinger's efforts blended seamlessly into subsequent National Security Advisor Zbigniew Brzezinski's (also, not coincidentally, a Rockefeller protégé and co-founder with David of the Trilateral Commission), and by the end of the decade the death of Mao and rise of Deng Xiaoping created the condition for the "Red Capitalism" that has led to the rise of modern China. This process was overseen by a small cadre of politically connected individuals (known in Chinese as the "Eight Immortals") whose families still continue to control vast portions of China's "national" wealth. (http://go.bloomberg.com/multimedia/mapping-chinas- red-nobility/)

These "capitalist road" reforms created the conditions for massive foreign investment in the country, which began in the 1980s [16] with the establishment of the Beijing Central Business District and the formation of Chinese subsidiaries of major Fortune 500 companies like HP. This influx of foreign capital increased in the 1990s when direct investment of US-based multinationals in China quadrupled (from $2.6 billion in 1994 to $10.5 billion in 2001). [17]

During this period, China became a cheap labor pool for American corporations looking to outsource manufacturing during an era of easing regulations and even direct incentives to move American jobs offshore. According to the US government's own reports [18], China's open door came with a price: "forced" technology transfers that allowed China to leapfrog many other developing nations to become a player on the international scene in advanced technologies. There have also been numerous military technology transfers from the US to China over the last two decades that have doubtless played a role in the rise of the PLA Navy and Air Force's capabilities. [19]

In short, the rise of China as an economic and military power has been facilitated by a small group of oligarchical families working in close conjunction with businessmen, politicians and financiers representing oligarchical interests in the West, specifically in the US.


## 6. What would you say are our alternatives to trusting in this 'resistance' forces and how do we keep hope alive?

Mr. Corbett: If what we are combating is, as I posit, essentially two (or more) gangs competing for turf, then it is self-evident that we gain nothing from supporting one gang over another other than the vague hope that the other gang will treat us more kindly.

The real solution to centralized, hierarchical international institutions created by and for the interests of the oligarchical elite are decentralized, non-hierarchical relations created by and for the grassroots. One aspect of this decentralized approach is the peer-to-peer economy, i.e. the notion that technology is enabling humanity for the first time to seek out and source answers to their problems instantaneously and internationally without recourse to unwieldy institutions like the World Bank, IMF, BRICS, AIIB, NDB, WTO, etc. [20]

Through open-source collaboration people can construct more detailed (and accurate) reports of ongoing events than can ever come from slanted mainstream media journalists who are beholden to corporate interests. Through complementary currencies, LETS programs, crypto- currencies, barter exchanges, peer-to-peer lending and other means, both high-tech and low-tech, people can carry on economic transactions even when national (or regional) currencies fail. People are finding economic, social and other forms of support through grassroots community organizations that deliver the type of aid that national governments are incapable of providing. Collaborative learning and internet technologies have enabled a flowering of auto-didacticism that is rendering traditional government-sponsored and highly centralized and authoritarian forms of education all but obsolete.

In short, there is a revolution that is happening all around us, even as we speak. It does not require guns or bombs or pitchforks or protests, only participation. And it is threatening to turn the ideology of statism and its associated forms of centralization on its head, and international mafias like the IMF/World Bank and the BRICS along with it. The only question is whether we are discerning enough to perceive it, wise enough to understand it, and brave enough to see it through to its completion.

**Endnotes**

1: Dominique Patton, "IMF Happy To Cooperate With China on AIIB: Largarde," *Reuters*, March 22, 2015 (http://finance.yahoo.com/news/imf-happy-cooperate-china-aiib- 075757066.html)

2: World Bank, *Statement by World Bank President Jim Yong Kim on the Establishment of the AIIB*, http://www.worldbank.org/en/news/press-release/2015/06/28/statement-by-world-bank- group-president-jim-yong-kim-on-the-establishment-of-aiib (June 28, 2015)

3: China Daily, *A New Answer to Global Development Challenges*, http://usa.chinadaily.com.cn/opinion/2015-07/22/content_21374817.htm (July 22, 2015)

4: Chen Jia, "AIIB, World Bank Planning Closer Project Cooperation," *China Daily*, July 17, 2015 (http://www.chinadaily.com.cn/business/2015-07/17/content_21308703.htm)

5: Investment Watch Blog, *Globalist Agenda Watch 2015: Update 51- Guess Who's Running The New BRICS Bank*, http://investmentwatchblog.com/globalist-agenda-watch-2015-update-51- guess-whos-running-the-new-brics-bank/ (July 2, 2015)

6: The BRICS Post, *If BRICS Interests Protected, NDB Could Cooperate With World Bank*, http://thebricspost.com/if-brics-interests-protected-ndb-could-cooperate-with-world-bank/ (June 15, 2015)

7: Wikipedia, *K. V. Kamath*, https://en.wikipedia.org/wiki/K._V._Kamath

8: Wikipedia, *Jin Liqun*, https://en.wikipedia.org/wiki/Jin_Liqun

9: The BRICS Post, *BRICS Bank's 1st Loan To Be Issued in Yuan*, http://thebricspost.com/brics- banks-1st-loan-to-be-issued-in-yuan/ (July 24, 2015)

10: Cary Huang, "China Seeks Role for Yuan in AIIB to Extend Currency's Global Reach," *South China Morning Post*, April 14, 2015 (http://www.scmp.com/news/china/economy/article/1766627/china-seeks-role-yuan-aiib-extend- currencys-global-reach)

11: Jim O'Neill, *Building Better Global Economic BRICS, Goldman Sachs*, http://www.goldmansachs.com/our-thinking/archive/archive-pdfs/build-better-brics.pdf (November 30, 2001)

12: Onkar Singh, *India soft on China's Arunachal Claim*, Rediff India Abroad, http://www.rediff.com/news/2006/nov/20jintao1.htm (November 20, 2006)

13: Gordon Fairclough, "India-China Border Standoff: High in the Mountains, Thousands of Troops go Toe-To-Toe," *Wall Street Journal*, October 30, 2014 (http://www.wsj.com/articles/india-china-border-standoff-high-in-the-mountains-thousands-of- troops-go-toe-to-toe-1414704602)

14: Geoff Dyer, "Brazil and India join renminbi call," *Financial Times*, April 22, 2010 (http://www.ft.com/intl/cms/s/0/29c50e84-4da5-11df-9560-00144feab49a.html?siteedition=intl#axzz1BrF0tuyy)

15: James Corbett, *The Process of Indoctrination*, The Corbett Report, https://www.corbettreport.com/articles/20080714_the_process_of_indoctrination.htm (July 14, 2008)

16: eBeijing, Fortune 500, Important Engine Driving Beijing CBD Economic Development, http://www.ebeijing.gov.cn/feature_2/spirit_of_arrival_2009spring/Discover_Beijing/t1028522.h tm

17: Francisco Moris, *U.S.-China R&D Linkages: Direct Investment and Industrial Alliances in the 1990s*, National Science Foundation, http://www.nsf.gov/statistics/infbrief/nsf04306/ (February 2004)

18: Federation of American Scientists, *U.S. Commercial Technology Transfers to the People's Republic of China*, http://fas.org/nuke/guide/china/doctrine/dmrr_chinatech.htm (January 1999)

19: Shirley A. Kan, *China: Possible Missile Technology Transfers from U.S. Satellite Export Policy-Actions and Chronology*, The Air University, http://www.au.af.mil/au/awc/awcgate/crs/98-485.pdf (January 11, 2002)

20: The Corbett Report, "Episode 303- Solutions: The Peer-To-Peer Economy," March 29, 2015, https://www.corbettreport.com/episode-303-solutions-the-peer-to-peer-economy/

Seeing the bombings, killings, and general injustices committed in the US and around the world is extremely disheartening and discouraging. Hopelessness and a general feeling that nothing can be done can easily over-wash a person. It is even more frustrating if you are in a situation where you are unable to attend protests, rallies, or marches. However, there is something that we can all do: bear witness. By that I mean we keep abreast of what is going on in the world and make a point to discuss important issues and topics with people in our everyday lives, especially those who may not be too interested in politics. To discuss this in more detail, I recently had an email interview with Melissa R. and Geoff W. about "bearing witness."

*Melissa R. is a queer woman living in the southern United States. She works full time in healthcare and encourages self-education.*

*Geoffrey W. is an activist and economics student at Washington State. He is the president of his campus' Queer-Straight Alliance, and enjoys spending his time attempting to overthrow the colonialist, patriarchal, discriminatory powers that be. When asked for comments, one person said Geoff was, "...born in the cesspool of multiculturalist liberal propaganda."*


## 1. How do you define this idea of 'bearing witness?'

Melissa: I think of this in a broader sense so that it includes practices of mine as well as what I imagine would be a more common interpretation. By a more common interpretation I mean those interactions with other people that involve sharing experiences, knowledge, and ideas without the religious missionary aspect. In my broader explanation it's really about developing a wide ranging base of knowledge and ideas without being locked into any so that others are off limits. There is self study and education at the core. I suppose that bearing witness would come in again to personal practices of mine would in conversation, observation, conflict resolution, and then again sharing information and ideas. For me it isn't about changing someone's core ideas or bringing them over to a team but more about giving them an impetus to consideration on their own.

I also take bearing witness to mean putting thoughtful attention to what is going on around me or in the world. One could on a level know that there is a drone program and maybe even know details of it to the extent they are available. Many people do and yet choose to turn off at the junction of seeing the testimony of the families who were fortunate enough to have survived, such as Rafiq ur Rehman and his two children. They came to D.C. to testify about the drone attack on Waziristan in which Rafiq's mother was killed and children injured. Only five "lawmakers" and very few journalists showed. Hearing and spreading these truths be it pretty or harsh is a form of bearing witness that is essential, in my opinion.

Geoff: Christians have the best definition, "to share the good news." Unfortunately, not everything lefties bear witness to can be considered remotely close to "good," so we must adopt our own definition. Let the truth be said, then. At the least, let your truth be said.


## 2. Why do you think that bearing witness is important?

Melissa: So many are in debt to extend their education, didn't complete their high school education, or are engaging in self education because they don't want to add to debt in order to go to college. In addition to these means of education bearing witness can be educational moments as well. Even if this is watching documentaries, listening to programs, talking to people of varying opinions, a new takeaway can be gained. I think there is also something gained for both parties when a compassionate or attentive audience is present for particularly important moments. It doesn't have to lead to a change of mind or an urge to move. It could just give someone perspective or give one person a sense of dignity for being recognized.

Geoff: Bearing witness startles people. I can't speak for humans globally, but in America we tend to segregate ourselves based on personal beliefs. When an individual has the opportunity to say something contrary to their peers' opinions, there is a small moment where people have to decide either to dismiss the new opinion out of hand, or think critically about both options presented. It's that latter action we as activists should hope to prompt.


### 3. How do you go about doing this in your own lives?

Melissa: I feel in addition to having a wide base of knowledge we also need to take in a wide variety of experiences and kinds of life, not necessarily through having them ourselves. We can do this by earnestly communicating them with other people. It's never been easier for this to take place than in this time of instant mass information. One problem that I see is what I call "teaming" which is really just tribalism. The corporate media is only distributing limited information and even within those there are sides to be chosen. Even with so much information available many people still choose to wall themselves off in these reinforcement chambers. What I think we can do in our own lives is just engage with people, read a wider variety of information with a critical eye, but not with the intent of moving from one side to another. This whole notion of "sides" is problematic and exactly what enhances power structures. Be with people and give them compassion. Smile at people who flick you off in traffic.

Geoff: I'm a student and an activist, so an overwhelming number of opportunities to discuss controversial issues are made available to me. They run the gamut, from voicing an opinion in a classroom to directing weekly workshops. My university is in a fairly conservative region, so many people are unfamiliar with concepts of neocolonialism, of queer theory, feminist thought, racism, and most all of the anti-prejudice work radicals in left-leaning areas take for granted. As a queer transgender individual, I find myself most often bearing witness to my own experience, through questions asked by professors and students alike. It's not something I can keep on all the time, eventually any person becomes weary of defending their own existence. This leads into the next question,


### 4. Would you consider bearing witness a form of activism?

Melissa: The label of activism has been contested over the past few years in such a manner that it is constantly changing but that happens with language so I do and I don't. In certain situations, I can see where it could be applicable but I don't seek that label out. There is a real problem with language policing even among more conscientious people so I don't really think too much about if I am being an activist today or not. I do think that the spreading of knowledge and information is an act that is so important that it is activism even if you aren't outside with a microphone, especially when you don't have the means or opportunity to do other things. Arthur Ashe said "Start where you are. Use what you have. Do what you can." It's simple but it says it all.

Geoff: Is bearing witness a form of activism? Yes. Unabashedly, whole-heartedly yes. The first time I realized how important bearing witness is as a form of activism, I was fresh into college. A professor had decided we'd spend the quarter having a variety of conversations around controversial issues, and would let the students work things out between ourselves. For one day of class, affirmative action was the topic at hand. Unsurprisingly, no one in the class supported (or had bother reading up about) affirmative action, except for myself and one woman. The conversation quickly devolved from any constructive discussion of the policy, or even of systemic prejudices, into one peppered with seriously racist commentary.

As a white person, this would have been an opportunity to cash in my privilege card and step back. Instead, I decided it'd be better to "bear witness." The woman and I spent the entire 50 minute class period arguing against 33 other students. It wasn't fun, nor did it feel terribly productive. It was after the class, however, that the significance of what seems to be a small action was explained to me. The woman, whose name I have since forgotten, pulled me aside and thanked me. It turns out, this wasn't the first time she'd had to discuss racism in class, but as a woman of color in a predominantly white campus, she was always forced to be the sole defender of anti-racist, anti-discriminatory policy. She'd gone into the discussion expecting to play the role again, but having a second person there to back her up, and to call out bullshit as I saw fit, meant that the burden of proof was shared.

In a similar vein, every time an issue in classes or conversation comes up that relates to me specifically, I wish desperately that I'll not be the only person defending the politics I align with. Because it's isolating, exhausting, and downright demoralizing to be the only person in a class of 60 who speaks up in defense of transgender people. It puts minority groups on the defense, and perpetuates a campus environment that effectively excludes us. This can be applied to the workplace, social spaces, activist groups, and more.


**5. How would you contrast it with more traditional ideas of protesting such as marches and rallies?**

Melissa: Marches and rallies seek to bring masses together. What I'm talking about is examining everything and not taking a single issue focus, which is one of the things that has bothered me. It should be noted that I do not live in a large city that is noted for even good turnout at protests. The few that I have been to were very disheartening. I do see that among protests taking place when they do happen they are single issue focuses and it appears that nationwide there is a problem with this. Another thing that keeps me from participating with causes I would mostly agree with is their tactics. I'm not going to go and join a PETA protest outside of Barnum and Bailey's Circus even though it is a tortuous affair because I don't see how dousing a naked person in fake blood on a busy street for children to walk by conveys that message. That is just the tip of the disaster that is PETA.

I'm not trying to downplay the work of activists; I am speaking from my perspective as someone who thinks that there should be a broader focus. The handful of Gay Groups receiving millions in funding pushing marriage initiatives are a prime example of single issue focus. They completely leave out the trans community, issues of elder rights, job protections, and have written off Chelsea Manning as if she isn't still serving a prison sentence for telling the truth. This is just my perspective as one queer person.

Geoff: Rallies and marches are effective tools for changing top down policies. Campus administration, corporations, and especially governments are more responsive to a rally and other forms of direct action. I don't know how effective they are at changing the hearts and minds of people. In many instances, just making your opinion known is a radical action. Ideally, traditional forms of activism and bearing witness should go hand in hand.


**6. Some would criticize this as doing nothing and not having any major impact. What would be your response to such an argument?**

Melissa: Doing nothing will have no impact. Like I mentioned before, use what you have and do what you can. I didn't know about Leonard Peltier until a teacher of mine in high school told me his story. I learned about Leonard Peltier, AIM, John Trudell, read Malcolm X's autobiography, and began relearning history. You never know the thing that will be a catalyst for change whether for yourself or someone else. It could be a book, a documentary, being with a person through an experience, living through intense trauma or bullying just to name a few.

Geoff: I would say the people arguing against it need to step back and think critically about their position. There are many people who cannot safely do more than voice their opinions. There are even more people whose opinions are unsafe to voice. In some areas of the country, probably more areas than people in urban areas might believe, bearing witness can and does result in a job loss, isolation, and violence.